The
Emergence
of
Market Economies
in
Eastern Europe

EDITED BY

Christopher Clague and
Gordon C. Rausser

BLACKWELL
Cambridge MA & Oxford UK

Copyright © Basil Blackwell 1992

First published 1992

Blackwell Publishers
Three Cambridge Center
Cambridge, Massachusetts 02142
USA

108 Cowley Road
Oxford OX4 1JF
UK

Library of Congress Cataloging-in-Publication Data
A CIP catalogue record for this book is available
from the Library of Congress

ISBN 1-55786-333-4
       1-55786-334-2 (pbk)

British Library Cataloguing in Publication Data
A CIP catalogue record for this book is available
from the British Library.

Printed in the USA by Maple-Vail, New York

This book is printed on acid-free paper

Contents

Part III   Government Policy Toward the Private Sector: Antitrust Policy and the Safety Net

Part IV   The Privatization Process

Part V   Conclusions

Contributors

CHRISTOPHER CLAGUE: Professor of Economics, University of Maryland; Director of Research, Center for Institutional Reform and the Informal Sector, College Park, Maryland.

ROBERT D. COOTER: Professor of Law, University of California, Berkeley, California.

SEBASTIAN EDWARDS: Professor of Economics, University of California, Los Angeles, California. Research Fellow, Institute for Policy Reform.

STANLEY FISCHER: Professor of Economics, Massachusetts Institute of Technology, Cambridge, Massachusetts. Research Fellow, Institute for Policy Reform.

ARNOLD C. HARBERGER: Professor of Economics, University of California, Los Angeles, California.

ANNE O. KRUEGER: Professor of Economics, Duke University, Durham, North Carolina. Research Fellow, Institute for Policy Reform.

RONALD I. MCKINNON: William Eberle Professor of International Economics, Department of Economics, Stanford University, Stanford, California.

PETER MURRELL: Professor of Economics, University of Maryland, College Park, Maryland. Research Fellow, Center for Institutional Reform and the Informal Sector.

ANDRAS NAGY: Professor, Institute of Economics, Hungarian Academy of Sciences, Budapest.

DAVID M. NEWBERY: Professor and Director, Department of Applied Economics, University of Cambridge, Cambridge, England. Research Fellow, Institute for Policy Reform.

MANCUR OLSON: Distinguished Professor of Economics, University of Maryland; Chair/Principal Investigator, Center for Institutional Reform and the Informal Sector, College Park, Maryland.

GORDON C. RAUSSER: Robert Gordon Sproul Distinguished Professor, Department of Agricultural and Resource Economics, University of California, Berkeley, California. President, Institute for Policy Reform.

LEO K. SIMON: Department of Agricultural and Resource Economics, University of California, Berkeley, California.

JOSEPH E. STIGLITZ: Professor of Economics, Stanford University, Stanford, California. Research Fellow, Institute for Policy Reform.

LAWRENCE SUMMERS: Chief Economist, and Vice-President for Research, The World Bank; Professor of Economics, Harvard University, Cambridge, Massachusetts.

SCOTT THOMAS: Principal Economist for Eastern Europe, Europe and Near East Bureau, Agency for International Development, Washington, D.C.

SIR ALAN WALTERS: Vice Chairman, American International Group, Washington, D.C.

JAN WINIECKI: Professor of Economics, Institute of Production, Aalborg University, Denmark, and President, Adam Smith Research Center, Warsaw.

ROBERT D. WILLIG: Professor of Economics, Woodrow Wilson School of Public and International Affairs, Princeton University, Princeton, New Jersey.

Preface

Almost everyone now agrees that the government domination of economic life in Soviet-type societies largely explains their economic collapse. With the sweeping repudiation of communism — even those who announced the failed Soviet *putsch* of August, 1991, did not use the word — government control over the once-communist societies has diminished. All of the ex-communist countries have introduced some liberalizing measures and the first and largest communist government — the Union of Soviet Socialist Republics — has been literally dissolved. Thus the comprehensive governmental management of the economy that led to the economic failure of the communist societies has been cut back.

Though this scaling down of government control was expected to improve economic performance, the national incomes of most of these societies have, in fact, fallen — drastically in some cases. Why? If too much government control of the economy brought about the failure of the communist economies, why did economic performance not improve as communism was repudiated and government control cut back?

Once the drop in national income after the repudiation of communism was apparent, it became commonplace to suppose that a transition from one set of economic arrangements to another inevitably reduces output. Not so. Major changes in economic institutions and policies are not regularly associated with drops in national income. The economic liberalization that Deng introduced in China not long after the death of Mao promptly generated large increases in production. After the defeat of the right-wing dictatorships of World War II, it was almost universally assumed that the German and Japanese economies would take decades to recover from wartime devastation, changed boundaries, and totalitarian controls, yet they soon enjoyed economic miracles. Even the Soviet-imposed transition **to** communism in East-Central Europe, for all its tragedy and brutality, was not associated with at least any protracted reduction in output.

At a loss to explain the severity of the economic problems after the collapse of communism, many seek refuge in metaphors: "it is easy enough to make fish stew out of an aquarium, but you cannot make an aquarium out of fish stew." But why should a transition from communism to a market economy be more difficult than the transition the other way? The conventional wisdom is that markets do not need to be painstakingly constructed by government — they emerge spontaneously. Indeed, many argue that they work best with *laissez faire*. Certainly the market economy that led to the Industrial Revolution, like the more rudimentary markets that preceded it, was not the result of any government plan to create a market economy. A communist economy, by contrast, has to be centrally planned and implemented — organizing a transition to a planned economy should be the harder task.

Thus the difficulties of the transitions that are now underway in the countries that are emerging from communism suggest that neither the familiar assumptions about the spontaneous emergence of market economies nor the new metaphors will do. The transition from a dictatorial planned economy to a democracy with a market economy is not only as important as any other problem the world faces today, but also a challenge to familiar ideas.

A thriving market economy is not, contrary to what some say, simply the result of "letting capitalism happen" — not something that emerges spontaneously out of thin air. It requires a special set of institutional arrangements that most countries in the world do not have. The most prosperous countries happen to have these institutional arrangements, but they take them for granted. These arrangements are usually overlooked in ideological debate and in scholarly research and their importance is not generally appreciated in either the mature market economies or in the societies in transition.

The importance of these neglected institutions becomes evident when one examines the central word in most discussions of the transition: "privatization". The meaning of this word is clear when it is applied to the developed democracies with market economies, such as Britain in the time when Margaret Thatcher was Prime Minister. These societies have elaborate **public** mechanisms for protecting that which is **private.** When individuals or firms in these societies, in pursuing their private advantage, make legitimate contracts with one another, they are confident that these agreements will be enforced by the government, and that any dispute about a contract can be resolved by judges who have no stake in the dispute and whose jobs do not depend upon the pleasure of the current political leadership. The individuals and the firms in these societies can also be confident that their rights to private property will be protected by public officials who will, if need be, call upon the coercive power of the government to protect those rights. An individual may have possessions, in the sense that a dog possesses a bone, but there is no private property without government.

Indeed, private property in general is not secure unless there is a government of a very special type — one in which no government official (including a dictator) has the power to deprive an individual or firm of property without due process of law (as interpreted by an independent judiciary) and the payment of compensation. Private contracts are similarly not generally secure unless the society's institutions give even opponents of the current political leadership, and those without political influence or citizenship, the right to impartial government enforcement of contracts.

These private rights, like the others that are needed for a sophisticated market economy, scarcely existed under communism, and they are still far from secure in most of the societies in transition. In the absence of institutions that reliably secure a broad range of contract and property rights, unequivocal privatization is impossible. State-owned industry is unproductive in the societies in transition partly because the rights of those involved with it are jumbled and unclear, but privatization by itself does not generate the unambiguous individual rights needed for a successful market economy. These rights will exist only if a society has the right institutions. In the absence of these institutions, communism can be repudiated, and the suffocating government control removed, yet output can at the same time fall.

Thus, even though this volume is the product of many authors with different perspectives, the chapters repeatedly lead the reader to question whether the privatization of the big state enterprises is indeed the first and most important element in the transition to a market economy. Privatized enterprises will work well only after a society has established the institutions that are needed for an efficient private sector. These institutions are, moreover, essential if a society is to reap the full potential of the many new firms that every thriving economy — and especially lately communist economies — must have.

Privatization of state enterprise in a post-communist society entails dividing up most of the tangible capital of the society, and the conflicts of interest that are inherent in this process are politically divisive and resolved only slowly. A society needs to live and to produce as this difficult and protracted process goes on, and it can best do this if it establishes the institutions needed for a dynamic private sector as rapidly as possible. Establishing these institutions will increase the number and productivity of the new firms and create an environment in which unambiguous privatization can occur. Observations of capitalist societies suggest that the old capital stock is often worth less than is usually supposed and that a surprisingly large share of progress comes from new firms and new investments. The investments made by the state-owned firms in the Soviet-type societies were not guided by competitive markets and were therefore particularly likely to have been misdirected. The uncompetitive habits and organizational patterns of the old state enterprises also raise doubts about how productive these enterprises will be. Often the old state enterprises are so unproductive or inappropriate to the new conditions that the main contribution of privatization will be to reduce an enterprise's lobbying power and special access to the power of government and the society's resources. Accordingly, rich and diverse as the perspectives of the authors of this book are, the book as a whole reinforces my conviction that the privatization issue deserves somewhat less — and the institutional requirements of a market economy much more — priority than in the past.

This volume grows out of a conference held in Prague in March, 1991. The conference brought those who contributed chapters to this volume and others into a most constructive dialogue with economics ministers and others responsible for economic policy in countries in transition to a market economy. Though the cost of and responsibility for this volume rests with the Center for Institutional Reform and the Informal Sector (IRIS) of the University of Maryland, the conference was sponsored jointly by the Institute for Policy Reform (IPR) and IRIS. My colleagues at IRIS and I are grateful for this collaboration with the IPR. I especially appreciate my membership on the IPR Advisory Board, the invaluable work of Gordon Rausser, President of the IPR, as co-editor of this volume, and the crucial role of Stanley Johnson, Secretary-Treasurer of the IPR, in the planning for the Prague conference.

The largest part of the work on the Prague conference was done by Charles Cadwell and Christopher Clague of IRIS, to whom I am most thankful. Chris Clague was involved from the start and was a decisive influence on the intellectual design of the conference and on this volume. Though he joined the IRIS enterprise a little later, Chas Cadwell has since his arrival not only made crucial contributions to its intellectual focus, but also managed for me not only the conference out of which this volume grows but also most other activities of the IRIS Center. My colleagues at IRIS and I are thankful, as we know those at the IPR also are, for the support of the US Agency for International Development. Last but not least, I am most thankful for Catherine Gordon of AID for her unfailing cooperation from the very inception of the plan for the Prague conference and for this volume.

Mancur Olson
Chair and Principal Investigator
IRIS

1 The Journey to a Market Economy

Christopher Clague

1 Finding a Roadmap: The Intellectual Challenge

The last few years have witnessed truly extraordinary events in the formerly communist societies. Under newly established conditions of free speech and freedom of organization, communist principles of political and economic control have been widely repudiated, and communist governments have been swept aside, replaced by governments committed to democratic principles and a market economy. While in some countries and parts of countries former communist governments have not been decisively dislodged, in almost all cases communism has lost whatever remaining legitimacy it possessed, and in most of these societies the crucial **economic** issue has suddenly changed from reforming the socialist planning system by the introduction of market-like elements to moving to a market economy with private ownership of most of society's assets. The present volume is oriented toward the problems of this transition in three countries of East-Central Europe, namely Poland, Hungary, and Czechoslovakia, all of which are attempting to make the transition under a democratic, parliamentary form of government. However, the issues discussed in this volume are extremely relevant to the transition problems in other reforming countries, notably Bulgaria, Yugoslavia, Romania, Mongolia, Albania, and the various parts of the Soviet Union.

This chapter has benefitted substantially from discussions with and comments from Charles Cadwell, Mark Goldberg, Steve Knack, George Kopits, Ronald McKinnon, Peter Murrell, and Mancur Olson but responsibility for remaining deficiencies rests with the author. Support from the Center for Institutional Reform and the Informal Sector is gratefully acknowledged.

1

There are several reasons why the task of designing this transition is fascinating, especially to economists. First, the problem is new: no country prior to 1989 had ever abandoned the communist political and economic system. Second, the experience to date indicates that countries attempting transition face a number of common problems and difficulties (Summers, Ch. 2). While there are important differences in the inherited situations and in the choices made by governments of these countries, the similarities in the problems they face and the difficulties they are encountering suggest that there is a logic to the transition process. Third, the absence of any close historical parallels and the limited experience of the economies in transition offer an opportunity and a challenge for the development of normative transition scenarios. These turn out, however, to be extraordinarily difficult to construct. Finally, the problems are not waiting for analysts' solutions; decisions currently being made may lead to an evolution with irreversible consequences. In summary, one may say that the problems are compelling because they are new, because they affect large numbers of people in very major ways, because they are intellectually intriguing, and because intellectual progress may make an important contribution to the quality of decisions.

The development of a transition scenario would seem to require not only a deep understanding of how a market economy works but also an understanding of how the essential elements can be put into place over the course of time. Briefly, what makes the problem so difficult is that economists think that the major benefits of a market economy are not realized unless most of its key features are in place; that is, partial implementation of market-oriented reforms may either produce negative results or results that yield relatively small benefits.[1] On the other hand, governments cannot do everything at once. There are clear limits on the speed with which governments can make decisions and implement those that have been made.

Innovations in economic theory in the last two decades undoubtedly affect the way economists look at the transition problem and have probably made them more pessimistic about the ease with which it can be accomplished. Developments in transaction cost economics, the economics of information, the new institutional economics, and evolutionary approaches to economics have sensitized economists to the vital role that institutions play in economic processes. One way of thinking about a successful market economy is that it is a set of

---

[1] This point will come up repeatedly in this introduction and throughout the book, but two examples will suffice here. First, it would make little sense to reward the managers of state enterprises on the basis of profits if prices do not reflect scarcities. Second, since levels of firm concentration are extremely high in the formerly centrally planned economies, allowing firms freedom to set their own prices runs the risk of severe monopolistic distortions, which cannot be rectified by entry of new firms until factor markets are developed.

convergent **expectations** in the population about how other people will behave; these expectations support an extremely elaborate division of labor, or a high degree of specialization among individuals, organizations, and geographic areas. This specialization increases the profitability of innovative activity and skill acquisition. Recent work on the interaction of expectations and behavior in the development of norms (see Schotter 1981; Sugden 1986) illustrates that the emergence of convergent expectations supporting an elaborate division of labor is not automatic and in the best case is not likely to take place quickly.

In the period from 1930 to about 1970, the key advantages of the market economy were perceived by the majority of economists to lie in its approximation of the rules of allocative efficiency. These rules relate to marginal rates of transformation and substitution across goods, consumers, producers, and time. The emphasis in, for example, Bator (1958), was on allocative decisions with a given technology and set of consumer preferences. The institutional structure was described very simply, and little attention was paid to the implications of costly information. This assumption supported the theoretical framework in which Lange could propose that market socialism could allocate resources efficiently, and while this claim was vigorously disputed by Hayek, von Mises, and others (for reasons that the economics of information makes clear), this framework remained prominent in the minds of economists, and according to Kornai (1986a) strongly influenced those economists in the Eastern bloc who wished to reform central planning.

In recent decades, many economists have returned to the Schumpeterian view that the advantage of the market economy (relative to its alternatives) lies more in its facilitation of innovative activity than in its allocative efficiency. The system of central planning is surely deficient in both respects, but its shortcomings seem to be much greater in the area of innovation than in allocative efficiency (Murrell 1990a). Innovative activity usually carries a high risk of failure, and bureaucracies normally are incapable of providing the high-powered incentives (O. Williamson 1985, Ch. 6) that induce some people to become entrepreneurs in market economies. While innovation normally generates large externalities in any economy, most economists would contend that a well-functioning capital market with clearly defined property rights over organizations and ideas as well as goods and factors has been essential in increasing the returns to innovative activity above what it would be in a society with poorly developed market institutions (Olson, Ch. 4; Cooter, Ch. 5; Stiglitz, Ch. 9).

Another development in economics that has reduced the attractiveness of the Lange conception of market socialism is the increased attention paid to the motivation of government officials, both legislators and bureaucrats. In the 1950s and 1960s, much of economic analysis was focused on market failures and government action to remedy these failures, under the implicit assumption that government officials would follow the rules laid down by the authorities. The analysis of the logic of collective action and the formation of interest groups, the theory of rent-seeking behavior, and the study of the evolution of cooperation and norms have emphasized that government failure as well as market failure must be taken into consideration in designing institutions. Reinforcing these theoretical considerations has been the experience of those socialist economies that have attempted reform through decentralization of decision making under public ownership. Control over resources by central planners has been replaced by an anarchic situation in which loss-making enterprises appeal to bureaucrats for protection and subsidies and to state-owned banks for additional credit; decentralized decision making under a soft budget constraint may lead to worse results than central planning. The transition is even more challenging if market socialism is not a viable intermediate step.

A vivid analogy stated by Vladimir Benachek of Charles University is that the socialist economies are at the top of a small hill (the planned economy), and they want to get to the top of a larger hill (the market economy). But in between the two hills is a valley, which may be both wide and deep. The analogy illustrates the point that the centrally planned economies did have a coherent economic system (i.e. they were at the top of their hill). One might add that the smaller hill was being eroded by the strengthening of special interest groups (Nagy, Ch. 18, Murrell and Olson 1991) and was, perhaps, settling due to the seismic rumblings that shattered the communist authority. The band of travelers must settle their differences, agree on a route, and avoid the pitfalls and chasms along the way.

Perhaps economic analysis can facilitate the journey by designing a bridge between the two hills. Given the absence of close historical parallels and the severe limitations of economic models of society, it is clearly beyond the capacity of social engineers to draw up very precise plans for the bridge. Moreover, the various post-communist societies have inherited different situations from their communist past and are adopting different strategies for the transition. Nevertheless, it does seem essential to try to understand the logic of the transition process and to anticipate some of the ways in which the societies can get onto the wrong track. The goal of this volume is to contribute to this discussion.

The next section describes the nature of the challenge, or the tasks of the transition. Section 3 discusses the start of the transition, or the initial phase of marketization. The difficult problems of macroeconomic balance are taken up in section 4. Incentives for restructuring and government policy toward the private sector are the topics of sections 5 and 6, while privatization is taken up in section 7. The sections of this introduction correspond very roughly to the parts of the book in a manner that is obvious from the titles of the sections and the parts. No attempt is made in this introduction to summarize the individual chapters of the book; instead references to these chapters are provided where the ideas are discussed.

2   The Tasks of the Transition

The list of activities which governments must undertake in countries attempting the transition to a market economy is truly staggering. The list given here is designed to convey to the reader something of the enormity and complexity of the job. First, there is a group of activities related to creating a new set of rules:

1. **Setting up the legal infrastructure for the private sector:** commercial and contract law, antitrust and labor law, environmental and health regulations; rules regarding foreign partnerships and wholly foreign-owned companies; courts to settle disputes and enforce the laws.

2. **Devising a system of taxation of the new private sector:** defining accounting rules for taxation purposes, organizing an Internal Revenue Service to collect taxes from the private sector.

3. **Devising the rules for the new financial sector:** defining accounting rules for reporting business results to banks and investors; setting up a system of bank regulation.

4. **Determining ownership rights to existing real property:** devising laws relating to the transfer of property, and laws affecting landlord-tenant relations; resolving the vexatious issue of restitution of property confiscated by communist governments.

5. **Foreign exchange:** (a) setting the rules under which private firms and individuals may acquire and sell foreign exchange and foreign goods; (b) setting the rules in the same area for the not-yet-privatized enterprises.

Next there are some tasks related to managing the economy:

6. **Reforming prices:** enterprises that have been privatized will presumably be largely free to set their own prices, but early on in the process, the demands of the government budget will require raising prices on many consumer goods that have been provided at prices far below cost.

7. **Creating a safety net:** setting up an emergency unemployment compensation scheme; targeting aid in kind or in cash to those threatened with severe hardship by the reforms.

8. **Stabilizing the macroeconomy:** managing the government budget to avoid an excessive fiscal deficit and managing the total credit provided by the banking system.

Finally there are tasks related to privatization:

9. **Small-scale privatization:** releasing to the private sector trucks and buses, retail shops, restaurants, repair shops, warehouses, and other building space for economic activities; establishing the private right to purchase services from railroads, ports, and other enterprises which may remain in the public sector.

10. **Large-scale privatization:** transferring medium and large-scale enterprises to the private sector; managing the enterprises that have not yet been privatized.

11. **Financial reorganization:** clearing the existing state banks of uncollectible debts and recapitalizing these banks; privatizing these banks; managing these banks before they are privatized, including arrangements for loans to new businesses.

The above list of institutional changes is by no means complete. But in addition to these changes, governments must also deal with another legacy of communist rule: the badly distorted resource allocation resulting from decades of central planning under Soviet tutelage. The Eastern European economies have been heavily oriented toward trade within the Eastern bloc. They exported shoddy manufactured goods to the Soviet Union and to one another and imported under-priced petroleum and other raw materials from the Soviet Union. Their air and water are dangerously polluted as a result of the under-pricing of energy, the absence of private property rights in natural resources, and the neglect of any kind of environmental protection. Telecommunications networks are extremely primitive. In short, there is an enormous task of restructuring, entirely apart from the problem of institutional reform. Related to the restructuring of the economy is the acquisition by the population of an entirely new set of skills. In addition to the institutional reform of the business economy to encourage the formation of human capital, the government needs to revamp parts of the educational system to facilitate the acquisition of the technical, managerial, and professional skills required in a modern market economy. Finally, these countries do not have the luxury of gradual adjustment to the need for restructuring; the Soviet and East German markets are collapsing, and the old trade arrangements among the Eastern European countries have fallen apart.

It is an enormous understatement to say that the governments in East-Central Europe cannot resolve all these problems at once. If nothing else, there is a limit on the number and complexity of issues that political leaders and policy makers can address at one time. Moreover, there is a well-known tendency under democratic governments for contentious issues such as the restitution of property to previous owners to remain unresolved for considerable periods of time. Thus, while some of the tasks listed above, particularly the drawing up of laws, rules, and regulations, could be accomplished rather quickly in a society with consensus on the strategy for the transition or one in which all the decisions were made by a ruling clique, the same speed and decisiveness cannot be expected in the emerging democracies of the region.

The immediate task of the transition is to get the economy and the society started in the right direction. The ultimate goal is to enable the society to develop the respect for property rights and for democratic political practices which form the institutional base for the highly productive Western democracies (Olson, Ch. 4; Cooter, Ch. 5). The first task is the topic of the next section.

3 Starting the Transition: Marketization

In the traditional centrally planned economy more than 90 percent of value added was generated in the state sector (see figures in Fischer, Ch. 13, table 10). Prices bore only a very approximate relation to scarcity values in most of the economy. Consumers did allocate their budgets among the goods and services available, but many of the prices they faced were far below the cost of production.

The production side of the economy was organized through the mechanisms of central planning. Firms were supposed to meet production targets, and they were to receive physical quantities of input supplies. There was a process of bargaining between the enterprise managers and the branch ministry officials about the level of production targets and of input supplies, and managers may have bargained with each other over supplies and outputs in a kind of barter economy (Olson, Ch. 4), but these barter arrangements were surely much less efficient than a regime of secure property rights (Cooter, Ch. 5). Prices of inputs and outputs played very little role in guiding resource allocation. Credit was also passive. Firms were not permitted to use their money balances freely, and investment projects required approval by the central authorities (McKinnon, Ch. 7). Managers did not think in terms of profits. The enterprises and ministries had adapted to this system, and in spite of its many shortcomings in terms of resource allocation and product quality, the system did deliver goods to the economy.

Czechoslovakia had made very few changes in this system prior to the reforms implemented on January 1, 1991. Hungary and Poland had been introducing market elements prior to the events of 1989, in Hungary's case since 1968, in Poland's since the early 1980s. These differences are likely to have an important effect on the transition, as will be discussed below and throughout the volume. Nevertheless, none of the three countries had made the decisive break to a market economy. Hungary was the economy in which the market played the largest role, but still nearly two-thirds of value added was generated by the state sector, and there continued to be extensive bureaucratic regulation of enterprises. In short, profits were only one of the guides to resource allocation in the public sector.

The question to be discussed in this section is how to initiate the transition in a country where communist political authority has been replaced by a new government that wants to move to a market economy with private property. Among the commentators on the transition problem, one can distinguish two broad approaches or perspectives. One approach, represented by Kornai, McKinnon, Murrell, and others, emphasizes that economic systems and the organizations within them cannot change quickly and that, therefore, a degree of gradualism in the transition is imperative; this approach might be called the "organic" or "evolutionary" approach. The other approach stresses the desirability of getting the various elements of a market economy in place quickly, so that the right incentives will be provided; representatives of this second approach, which for lack of a better name might be called the "incentives" approach, include Lipton and Sachs, the WIDER group (Blanchard *et al.*), Fischer, Newbery, and probably a majority of the economists at the World Bank and the IMF. The "incentives" approach assumes that organizations will respond to the right incentives in an appropriate manner, even when dramatically new types of behavior are called for.

The rest of this section will present the author's version of the case for a decisive stroke early in the transition, or for what John Williamson calls the "minimum bang" (J. Williamson 1991). At the same time, some of the concerns of the "organic-evolutionary" approach are also addressed, although probably not to the satisfaction of representatives of that approach. The argument for a decisive stroke early in the transition is perfectly consistent with, and even requires, a prior period of discussion, debate, and consensus formation on the steps that will be taken at the beginning of implementation.

In presenting this case for the "minimum bang," it will be argued that two vital tasks of the transition are the following: the creation of a new private sector (that is, one composed of newly organized firms rather than privatized state enterprises) and the maintenance or restoration of macroeconomic equilibrium. The evolutionary approach, which is pessimistic about the prospects for reforming existing state enterprises, stresses the creation of new organizations and new institutions in the private sector. Emphasis on this sector is also perfectly consistent with the incentives approach. Both approaches insist that macroeconomic balance is extremely important in the transition.

To launch a new private sector, prices in most of the economy must reflect scarcity values to a reasonable extent. In particular, prices in the state sector must not be too far from scarcity values. Otherwise, private sector firms could buy goods from the state firms at below-market prices and make excess profits selling them at market prices. Even if such sales were illegal, the temptation to make them would be strong, and they would be very difficult to prevent. Such transactions would do nothing to improve resource allocation and would run the danger of undermining public support for moving to a market economy.[2] If the state enterprises have to interact with the new private sector through the mechanism of sales and purchases at realistic prices, then there is a good case for making them interact with each other in the same way.

Macroeconomic equilibrium in an economy with a very large state sector requires that the government exercise control over aggregate spending. This

---

[2] The "dual price" system in China's reforming economy is thought to have contributed importantly to popular indignation at middleman profits that led to the demonstrations at Tienanmen Square (Perkins 1991).

control can be achieved in two ways. The government can control directly the spending of enterprises and other spending units, or it can allow enterprises to make their own spending decisions subject to a hard budget constraint, or some combination of the two methods. The idea of a hard budget constraint is that a firm must pay its employees and owners (if any) out of its net income and its borrowing from lenders who realistically expect to be repaid. The firm must not have the power to induce the government to alter the tax regime or the degree of protection against competitors. Clearly, letting firms make their own decisions with respect to paying employees and undertaking investments makes no sense unless the firms are subject to hard budget constraints (and realistic prices).

How then can a transition best be started from a centrally planned to a market economy? Taking account of the inter-connected nature of the elements of a market economy, and at the same time of the limitations on policy implementation, it seems sensible to try to formulate the minimal package of reforms that gets the transition proceeding in the right direction.

Based on the discussion above, a minimal package would consist of (1) setting out the rules for the new private sector (basically items 1 through 5 in the list of tasks in the previous section), (2) reforming prices and creating an emergency safety net (items 6 and 7), (3) maintaining macroeconomic balance (item 8), and (4) "marketizing" the state sector.

The term "marketization" is used here to mean getting the state enterprises to interact with each other and with final consumers through purchases and sales at realistic prices. The term does not imply that enterprises are free to make decisions about wages and investments without central authorization (although the term does not rule it out either), but it does imply that firms are free to select inputs, to change the product mix, to hire and fire workers, and that they are largely free to set their own prices, subject to anti-monopoly regulations. The term "marketized sector" includes all private firms, all state-owned firms that have been "commercialized" and set free to make all their own decisions subject to the discipline of the market, and state-owned firms that remain under government supervision with respect to such matters as wages and investments. Marketized firms calculate profits or losses and their managers are monitored, at least in part, on the basis of these financial results, even though some of the firms that are under government supervision may be receiving subsidies in order to stay afloat. The concept of marketizing the state sector refers not only to the change in mentality and behavior of managers and workers in the enterprises, but also to these changes in government bureaucrats who must allow the firms to act independently.

An important component of marketization that deserves to be mentioned separately is the establishment of the right of the private sector and the independent public sector firms to deal in foreign exchange. The price of foreign exchange is one of the most important prices in small economies, and there is a great need to reorient the trade of East-Central Europe from East to West. Marketization thus includes something close to current account convertibility.[3]

The marketization package has been described in such a way as to take account of the concerns of both the evolutionary and the incentives approaches. The two approaches do lead to considerable differences in emphasis, however. Proponents of the incentives approach hope that getting the prices right in the initial phase will soon be followed by a phase in which enterprises will be acting independently under hard budget constraints. Proponents of the evolutionary approach (Kornai, McKinnon, and Murrell) are skeptical of the ability of the government to impose hard budget constraints on independently acting firms (see the discussion of macroeconomic balance in the next section), and thus they favor continuing government controls on enterprise behavior.

The minimal package sketched above involves some dramatic changes in the lives of managers, who will have to reorient their thinking toward profits and losses, and consumers, who will face drastic increases in the prices of many consumer goods (Newbery, Ch. 11). But the changes described so far do not necessarily equip the economy for rapid resource reallocation. During this first phase, the bulk of resources remain in the state sector, and experience indicates that state-operated enterprises tend to change slowly in all economies. In particular, in the reforming socialist economies mass layoffs tend not to occur even in the face of considerable output declines (for Polish experience during 1990, see Frydman and Welliscz 1990 and Jorgenson *et al.* 1990).

One would expect that this "minimum bang" would generate considerable anxiety in the population as price increases are combined with the threat of loss of employment and drastic changes in a variety of working relationships. In the present situation in East-Central Europe, the anxiety and the threat of disruption are accentuated by the collapse of the Soviet and East German markets and the loss of Middle East markets as a result of the Gulf War. Nevertheless, there seems to be a good case for introducing these changes at one stroke, as recommended by many proponents of the incentives approach. The experience of Poland after January 1990 has been cited to support this case (Lipton and Sachs 1990b): goods appeared on the shelves, shortages were eliminated, hundreds of thousands of new firms were organized, and established firms responded in an appropriate direction by diverting exports from the collapsing Soviet market toward the West. (For a less positive assessment of the Polish big bang, see Murrell, Ch. 3.)

---

[3] See J. Williamson (1991) for a discussion of different concepts of convertibility and for reasons why countries in transition should not introduce capital account convertibility at an early stage. Note also that enterprises whose investment decisions are under central control would not necessarily be permitted to purchase foreign exchange freely in order to buy foreign investment goods.

Earlier in this section, it was mentioned that one of the vital tasks of the transition is the creation and rapid expansion of a new private sector. A strong case can be made that the major technological and organizational innovations in the economy will be made in new enterprises rather than in the transformed enterprises of the centrally planned economy. This idea is developed at some length in Murrell (Ch. 3), and it is emphasized by Fischer (Ch. 13) and Winiecki (Ch. 15). Krueger (Ch. 12) makes the point that in rapidly growing market economies most of the growth in production comes from new capital.

What is required for the rapid expansion of the new private sector? First, the rules of the game need to be appropriate and need to be clear. Among these are rules that permit the new private sector to purchase inputs and services from public sector enterprises. (These rules can be very simple as long as the prices in the public sector reflect scarcity values.) Second, factors of production need to be released to the new private sector. Land and building space should be made available; labor needs to move out of the public sector, and loans should be provided. Since it is unlikely that private banks would provide sufficient capital for the new private sector if it is expanding at an appropriate speed, state banks will probably need to channel capital to new private enterprises. These are points on which the two approaches may agree,[4] and yet, the institutional environment for the new private sector in East-Central Europe leaves a lot to be desired: there are difficulties in buying or leasing land, in obtaining inputs from state firms, and in securing intellectual property rights.

4   Macroeconomic Balance

There is a pronounced tendency for decentralizing socialist economies to encounter inflation. Conceptually, there are two different types or causes of this inflation. The first is related to the fact that under central planning many prices were kept at levels at which there was excess demand. There was a certain logic to this practice for consumer prices, since non-price allocation mechanisms could work more effectively when prices were a relatively small obstacle to the purchase of an item. In addition, of course, relative prices were badly out of line with scarcity values. The move to a market economy thus requires a once-over increase in wages, interest rates, and the prices of energy, many intermediate products, and many basic consumer products. The second type or cause of inflation is the tendency of the government to lose control over its budget and over the volume of credit in the economy. The two types overlap when the government

---

[4] State provision of loans to new enterprises is not unanimously endorsed; McKinnon is skeptical of the practice, especially in his "worst case" scenario of fiscal and macroeconomic imbalance (Ch. 7, section 5).

loses fiscal and monetary control and at the same time continues to control wages and prices, thereby creating a monetary overhang.

Governments with strong central planning have a rather good record of maintaining macroeconomic balance. The problems tend to arise as decision making is transferred from the central authorities to enterprises. An important aspect of the problem, as emphasized by McKinnon (Ch. 7), is that revenue collection under central planning does not require a separate system of personal income taxation or consumer excises. Rather, the government simply expropriates the cash surpluses of enterprises. Prices are not used to guide resource allocation, but they are used to collect revenue (Naughton 1991). As prices are brought into line with scarcity values and as enterprises acquire more control over decisions, the revenues transmitted to the central authorities decline. Other sources of revenue can be developed, but this step requires institutional innovation, in particular the creation of an internal revenue service with accompanying accounting rules for enterprises and other taxpayers.

Another problem encountered by reforming socialist governments concerns the control of the volume of credit extended by the banking system. Under central planning, again as explained by McKinnon, credit was passive; once an enterprise obtained permission to undertake an investment or acquire materials, credit from the banking system was automatic. On the other side, enterprises were not free to use their bank balances without obtaining permission from the central authorities. Enterprises were accustomed to bargaining with the central authorities and with other firms over the acquisition of resources. As decentralization of decision making occurred in some countries, enterprises continued to borrow from banks to cover losses; the relaxation of central planning controls was not always supplanted by financial discipline. The sanctions that banks could impose against delinquent enterprises were weak and the motivation of bank officials to hold enterprises on a tight leash was limited. When the central authorities were able to restrict the total volume of bank credit, the enterprises often effectively increased the money supply by extending credit to each other. This sorry history of a lack of financial discipline is part of what Kornai (1980, 1986) described as the soft budget constraint.[5]

In all three countries of East-Central Europe, the banking system has been converted to a two-tier system with a central bank and a set of commercial banks. However, the commercial banks have inherited the portfolios of the old banking system and many of their assets are of dubious quality, to say the least

---

[5] In Kornai's classic contribution, the soft budget constraint includes various strategies by which a loss-making enterprise can avoid cutting costs to meet the discipline of the market. These include negotiating increases in the prices of outputs or reductions in the prices of inputs, reductions in taxes, subsidies from the government budget, and additional loans.

(Brainard 1990a). It is generally agreed that the banking system and the capital market must play an important role in the transition, in channelling resources to productive uses and in imposing discipline on enterprises. A common suggestion by commentators is to separate out the "bad" loans from the "good" banks, so that the latter can play the role envisaged for them in a market economy (Brainard 1990a; Fischer and Gelb 1990). A key set of issues involves how to organize this separation and how to insure that the banks impose discipline on the enterprises (Stiglitz, Ch. 4; Fischer, Ch. 13).

The three East-Central European countries differed quite sharply in the degree of macroeconomic imbalance they faced at the beginning of their transitions. Poland's retreat from central planning in the 1970s and attempts at reform socialism in the 1980s led to a severe macroeconomic imbalance that resulted in a foreign debt of some $47 billion and an annual inflation rate exceeding 1000 percent in the latter part of 1989. Consequently Poland's "big bang" in January 1990 included a strong stabilization package along with devaluation of the zloty and marketization of most of the economy. Czechoslovakia's economy, on the other hand, was not badly out of balance at the beginning of its marketization phase in January 1991. Its inflation rate had been very modest (less than 3 percent during the 1980s) and its foreign debt was only $7 billion. (The other side of this favorable situation is that Czechoslovakian enterprises had had very little experience with the market.) Hungary was in an intermediate position: its inflation in 1989 and 1990 was running around 30 percent per year, and its foreign debt was quite large at around $20 billion.

As the experience of some Latin American countries illustrates, stabilization in countries with histories of inflation and with high foreign-debt burdens is itself a very difficult task. Edwards (Ch. 8) highlights several key issues in the design and implementation of stabilization programs for economies in transition. The first point is that fiscal balance is critical to a successful stabilization, and for that reason, it is vital to have a tax collection system that is not itself vulnerable to inflation. A second point is that wages should not be fully indexed to past inflation, as this procedure will perpetuate inflation. A third issue concerns the use of the exchange rate as a nominal anchor for the anti-inflation program. Since fixing the exchange rate (as Poland did in January 1990) runs the risk of letting it become overvalued in the event that domestic prices rise more than was anticipated in the program, the use of this tool should be contemplated only if the initial rate is somewhat undervalued.[6]

In the author's scenario in section 3 above, the first goal of marketization is to move the economy toward realistic prices and to establish the conditions

---

[6] In May 1991 Poland, fearing that the zloty was becoming overvalued, devalued the zloty, thereby giving up the use of the exchange rate as a nominal anchor.

under which the new private sector can begin to grow rapidly. Once the decisive step toward marketization is taken, a critical question concerns the degree of independence that should be accorded to state enterprises. One scenario, favored by some proponents of the incentives approach, would be to allow these enterprises to act independently, subject to the discipline of market forces; such a scenario is described in the next section. However, many commentators fear that the established patterns of soft-budget-constraint behavior of enterprises, banks, and bureaucrats will not be broken by mere announcement that the rules of the market are supposed to apply. A strategy proposed by some observers for breaking these patterns of behavior is rapid privatization; this topic is discussed in section 7. On the other hand, commentators favoring the evolutionary approach (Kornai, McKinnon, Murrell) recommend continuing government controls over wages and investments in state-owned enterprises in order to forestall loss of macroeconomic control. In his "worst-case" scenario of the transition, McKinnon (Ch. 7) proposes a tripartite classification of enterprises: (a) traditional firms would remain under tight state control in all aspects of their behavior; (b) liberalized state-owned firms and (c) privatized and newly created firms would not be permitted to borrow **at all** from state banks but would be required to depend on internal finance. Wages would remain under state control in the liberalized state-owned firms but not in the private sector.

5   Incentives for Restructuring

As mentioned in section 2 above, there are enormous tasks of restructuring the economies of East-Central Europe; in particular, production processes need to be reorganized so that they are environmentally sound and they produce goods of sufficient quality to be saleable on Western markets. For these tasks to be accomplished, various individual actors need to be given appropriate **incentives:** managers need to be given incentives to cut costs, to install quality-control systems, to shift resources among product lines, and to meet financial obligations. Workers need to be given incentives to learn new skills, to be willing to take the risks of changing companies, occupations, and places of residence, and to perform well on the job. Perhaps most important of all, potential entrepreneurs must be rewarded for undertaking the highly risky activity of innovation.

How can these incentives be provided? Managers can be given bonuses for successful financial results, workers can be rewarded by substantial wage differentials, and entrepreneurs can be allowed to become very wealthy if they succeed. Conversely, managers and workers in failing companies can be fired and forced to search for new employment. These rewards and penalties are provided in a market economy where the government does a proper job of enforcing contracts, securing property rights, maintaining macroeconomic balance, and supplying necessary infrastructure and services. In the context of the economies in transition, the question arises, why cannot these incentives be put into place very quickly?

Let us consider this question first under the assumption that there are no "political" constraints; that is, let us assume that economic policy is being made and implemented by a competent government bureaucracy that is interested in raising the general standard of living. This "technocratic" approach permits us to deal with the "basic economics" of the matter.

What would such a technocratic government do? A possible scenario is the following. After the decisive marketization step described in section 3, the state enterprises would be quickly commercialized, that is, put in the charge of boards of directors and allowed to act independently. The status of past debts to other enterprises, banks, and the government would be clarified, and enterprises would be allowed to sink or swim in the market environment. (Forcing a few firms into closure would convey a tough message to the others.) The boards would have the power to select (and replace) the top management and to determine its reward structure, and managers would be given the power to reorganize production and lay off workers. There are complex questions regarding the speed of privatization (see section 7), but even in an enterprise in the commercialization phase, strong incentives can be provided to managers and workers to carry out the needed restructuring.

It might be thought that a decisive objection to the implementation of market or market-like incentives is that it would be inequitable to the poor or to other deserving groups. But under technocratic assumptions, it is quite possible to devise compensation schemes that do not seriously impair efficiency. For example, if a factory is so obsolete or environmentally damaging or otherwise inefficient that it should be closed and sold for scrap, the workers can, without loss of efficiency, be compensated with shares in mutual funds of companies being privatized. The recipients of such compensation still have incentives to allocate their labor and effort in socially productive ways. Income transfers do not impair efficiency as long as their receipt is not conditioned on behavior (Olson 1990b), and the resources required for the transfer are not raised by distortionary taxes (as they are not in the case where the state is able to give away its property). Unemployment compensation schemes and other features of the safety net can be devised in such a way that they do not seriously impair incentives (Newbery, Ch. 11). Resource misallocation in centrally planned economies has been so colossal that it is not difficult to devise technocratic incentive schemes that improve equity and efficiency at the same time.

This technocratic scenario is an example of what is proposed by representatives of the incentives approach. But proponents of the evolutionary perspective would not disagree that an efficient set of incentives is highly desirable. The difference between the two approaches lies primarily in judgments about what is **politically** feasible. To some extent the evolutionary approach can be interpreted as a **prediction** (rather than a **prescription**) that institutions and patterns of behavior will not change rapidly and that policies favoring, for example, free competition and foreclosure on unprofitable enterprises will be resisted by groups with the power to do so.

Of course, the assumption of the technocratic scenario, that policy is made by a competent government bureaucracy interested in raising the country's standard of living, is naive. A proper analysis must take into consideration the motivation and incentives of political leaders, government bureaucrats, and interest groups; and there are cogent reasons why interest groups prefer to lobby for government-mandated income transfers that **are** conditioned on behavior and hence **do** interfere with efficient resource allocation (Olson 1990b, pp. 59-62). Still, it is worth keeping in mind the point that dramatic improvements in arrangements are possible, if only they can be negotiated by the interested parties. This perspective enables the analyst to focus on the decisive policy-relevant obstacles to reform; it will inform the subsequent discussion of government policies with respect to the private sector and privatization.

6   Government Policy toward the Private Sector: Trade Policy, Demonopolization, Antitrust Policy, and the Safety Net

Trade policy is vitally important for the three economies of East-Central Europe, as all of them are heavily involved in foreign trade and all three governments want to reorient their trade from East to West. Moreover, opening the economy to foreign trade can be an effective way to import a rational price structure and to limit the monopoly power of domestic firms. Monopoly power is a serious issue in these economies, because part of the legacy of central planning is an extraordinarily high degree of industrial concentration. The information requirements of central planning were probably reduced through the creation of very large, vertically integrated enterprises, many of which were sole domestic suppliers of some of their outputs. Perhaps ideological considerations and interest group pressures contributed to gigantism, but in any case the industrial sectors of these countries contain a disproportionately large number of firms with many thousands of employees and a relative dearth of mid-sized enterprises.

One issue is whether there should be some gradualism in the exposure of domestic industry to the full force of competition from Western suppliers. Some sectors and enterprises may become viable if given a few years to modernize and improve efficiency. As McKinnon (Ch. 7) points out, enterprises have adjusted to low prices of energy and certain materials, and they have been permitted to sell shoddy goods on the Eastern markets. To expose the industrial sector at one stroke to Western goods under free trade might lead to a wholesale collapse. Moreover, governments can conveniently raise a good deal of revenue in the near term from import tariffs. To avoid shifting resources back and forth under trade liberalization, Harberger (Ch. 17) proposes a comprehensive, "radial" approach to tariff reduction in which all the different sectors move toward free trade by a series of parallel steps over (say) a five-year period. On the other hand, some commentators argue for rapid trade liberalization, on efficiency grounds, given the existence of a well-designed safety net (Newbery, Ch. 11), or because of concern about the emergence of vested interests (Krueger, Ch. 12), or specifically to combat monopoly (Newbery 1991).

A case can be made for breaking up the very large enterprises prior to privatization (Newbery 1991). Not only is monopoly power reduced directly, but smaller units would be easier to privatize through sale. A further argument is that experience in Western countries indicates that it is very difficult and time-consuming to break up existing private monopolies. Finally, in this context, the government could be accused of bad faith if the enterprise were sold as a unit and subsequently broken up by government mandate. A counter-argument is that some enterprises may only be viable if they remain intact and that decisions on restructuring enterprises should in general be made by those with a stake in the outcome, i.e. private owners.

It is generally agreed that a market economy needs an antitrust agency to prevent collusion, predatory pricing, and other abusive business practices (Willig, Ch. 10). Of course, there is also a need to regulate natural monopolies such as electric power and telephone companies. A more contentious issue arises during the early phases of marketization. A case can be made for giving the antitrust agency certain powers that would not be necessary in a mature market economy, such as the power to roll back price increases. The argument would be that in the early stages of marketization, the conditions for free entry are not met and, consequently, firms may have very high degrees of market power. There is, however, a powerful consideration on the other side of the argument. Marketization requires that government bureaucrats learn how to operate in a market economy, that is, they must learn to let firms act independently and sink or swim. An antitrust agency that negotiates prices with firms by looking at the firm's costs may become subject to political pressures to prevent the market from exercising its discipline. Pressures for political interference in the setting of prices are likely to arise from many sources, and they may be hard to resist in countries without a tradition of respect for the independence of enterprises (Nagy, Ch. 18).

There is little controversy among commentators about the desirability of establishing a safety net for those who lose their jobs or are otherwise threatened with severe hardship as a result of the transition. A basic economic principle of an efficient but humane market economy is that the safety net should protect individuals from poverty but not enterprises or industries from extinction by market forces (Newbery, Ch. 11; Olson, Ch. 4). The organizational task of developing a set of safety net institutions appropriate for a market economy is especially challenging because as Newbery (Ch. 11) explains, income security under communism was provided in ways that are incompatible with an efficient market economy.

7   Privatization

It is unfortunate that the same term, "privatization", has come to be applied both to the sale of public enterprises to private shareholders in Western economies and to the wholesale transformation of the state enterprise sector in East-Central Europe into private ownership. The former involves changing the ownership of the shares from the public treasury to private hands in an already existing market economy; the latter involves changing the rules of the game for all the actors, or creating the institutions of a market economy. Like the palace coup and the social revolution, the two kinds of privatization describe changes of a different order of magnitude. The terminology is too deeply entrenched to be resisted, but it is well to keep the differences in mind so as not to draw inappropriate lessons from the Western experience.[7]

In the design of the transition process, there is some conflict between efficiency and equity. Efficiency calls for putting enterprises into the hands of capable managers and giving them incentives to act like entrepreneurs. On the other hand, the principles of equity require, first, *ex ante* equity, or that people be given equal opportunity to be gainers or losers, and second, *ex post* equity, or that there not be excessive windfall gains and losses. A privatization scheme that is eminently fair is the free and equal distribution of shares in each enterprise to each citizen. But such a scheme fails the efficiency criterion, because it does not provide a mechanism for effective outside control over the enterprise management. A mechanism that is likely to be rather efficient is the so-called spontaneous privatization, in which the enterprise is sold in a sweetheart deal to the existing management. This management may be able to restructure the firm efficiently, or if it cannot, it at least has the monetary incentive to sell the firm to a management group that can.[8] But spontaneous privatization was seen to be blatantly inequitable in Hungary in 1989, and steps were taken to control it (Fischer, Ch. 13).

In view of the lack of accumulated savings of the population, the desire for a rapid transfer of assets out of state hands, and the unwillingness to allow foreigners

---

[7] The statement is sometimes made that privatization is not certain to lead to increases in efficiency in East-Central Europe because the evidence on the efficiency effects of change in ownership of public corporations in the West is ambiguous. Whatever one thinks about the evidence on privatization in the West or the prospects for economic transformation in the East, it should be clear that the two phenomena bear little relationship to one another. To assess the long-run effects of an economic system, it is appropriate to compare the experience of whole economies, such as the two Germanies, the two Koreas, and the two Chinas.

[8] The statement in the text assumes that property rights are secure enough to allow the original team to resell their ownership rights.

to buy up large amounts of state property, many commentators have come to the conclusion that a substantial portion of the assets needs to be given away. To combine a mechanism of corporate control with the equitable distribution of assets, the use of some kind of financial intermediary has usually been recommended. The shares in the enterprises are somehow divided among the financial intermediaries and the shares in the intermediaries are distributed to the population. Many possibilities exist; the reader is referred to Fischer's excellent survey (Ch. 13) of the issues and to the references cited there. The privatization plans in Poland, Czechoslovakia, and Hungary are described in Thomas (Ch. 16).

The remainder of this section highlights several general issues that need to be addressed in the design and implementation of privatization scenarios. The first concerns the danger that the perception of unfairness associated with privatization may generate resistance to the process. The second concerns the mechanism of corporate control when assets are to be given away. The third deals with the relationship between the speed and the quality of the privatization process and some reasons why a very rapid privatization might not be optimal. The last refers to the decision-making process itself: who should decide on the mechanisms of privatization and on which mechanisms should apply to particular enterprises?

A couple of examples will illustrate the first issue:

1. Mass layoffs may be more socially acceptable if they are mandated by a board of directors that does not have a financial stake in the outcome. This consideration would argue for some restructuring during the commercialization stage, prior to privatization.

2. The financial viability of enterprises is likely to change dramatically as the economy responds to the events of the transition. If enterprises are rapidly privatized in such a way that shareholdings are concentrated rather than dispersed, there will be large windfall gains and losses. Even if the distribution process were *ex ante* equitable, the *ex post* inequity may generate resentment. This consideration argues for not relying on the re-concentration of shareholdings through trading to provide a mechanism of corporate control.

On the second issue, an effective corporate control mechanism requires that there be an ownership group with enough shares to be able to replace the board of directors; control would be enhanced if there were other ownership groups with the potential to take over the company. On the other hand, some dispersion of shares is required to avoid excessive windfall gains and losses. A thoughtful scheme reconciling these two goals is in Lipton and Sachs (1990b). Blocks of shares in an enterprise are allocated to mutual funds, pension funds, and banks. The government retains a block of shares which it attempts eventually to sell to a "stable core" investor whose performance would then be indirectly monitored by the other holders of blocks of shares. To limit the fluctuations in the portfolios of individual members of the population, Lipton and Sachs propose to give each citizen one share in **one** of five mutual funds; each mutual fund would have a highly diversified portfolio, but there would presumably be some difference in the performance of the five funds. (For doubts about the Lipton-Sachs proposal, both with regard to the number of financial intermediaries and the search for a "stable core" of investors, see Fischer, Ch. 13, pp. 239-41.)

On the third issue, that of the speed of privatization or the number of enterprises privatized per year, many commentators seem to assume that the process should take place as rapidly as is administratively feasible. However, there may be a trade-off between the speed of privatization and its quality, where by quality is meant the achievement of the twin goals of effective corporate control and perceived equity. To put it another way, premature privatization is likely to involve either ineffective corporate control or large windfall gains and losses. The passage of time facilitates the process in various ways. The population accumulates savings, managers develop track records, capital markets improve, commodity and factor prices become more predictable, and it becomes easier to find appropriate core investors. Some commentators who caution against premature privatization (e.g. Newbery, Ch. 11, Walters, Ch. 6) implicitly assume that when enterprises are commercialized, a reasonably competent government appoints boards of directors and then forces the enterprises to operate independently in a market environment (perhaps as in the technocratic approach described in section 5). In this case the argument is that privatization should not be rushed because substantial benefits can be achieved without it. A different line of argument against premature privatization comes from the evolutionary approach, which characterizes rapid privatization schemes as unrealistic social engineering experiments (Murrell, Ch. 3).

On the other hand, other commentators argue for rapid privatization because they have little confidence in the integrity and competence of the governments. Speedy privatization has been urged on the grounds first, that this step is necessary to wrest control of the enterprises from the workers and the incumbent management (Lipton and Sachs 1990b), and second, that this is the only way to enforce hard budget constraints on the enterprises; otherwise, governments will interfere in the operation of market forces by coming to the rescue of failing enterprises (Rausser and Simon, Ch. 14; Frydman and Rapaczynski 1990a; but see Stiglitz, Ch. 9 for doubts about this argument).

Finally, the question of who should decide on privatization issues has been raised by Rausser and Simon (Ch. 14). Their argument is presented in the context of a game-theoretic bargaining model with many participants and several stages in the bargaining game. While most of the rest of the literature assumes that the central government should appoint the boards of directors of commercialized enterprises and set the rules under which they manage the enterprises and prepare them for privatization, Rausser and Simon suggest that the privatization process should be more decentralized, with enterprises and local governments being given a menu of privatization procedures; the choices of both personnel and procedures would be left to appropriately designed bargaining groups.

8   Concluding Observations

Like most of the literature on the problems of the transition to a market economy, this book is not mainly based on the experience of the transition itself; the statements instead are based on general theoretical principles, experiences of other countries, or the difficulties of reform socialism under communist leadership. Given the conceptual orientation of this volume, much of the discussion will be relevant to the problems of the transition in all formerly communist countries, not just those in East-Central Europe. Although many of the same problems will arise, they may well appear in somewhat different combinations and degrees of strength. Some conjectures about the transition in other economies are offered here.

For countries attempting the transition, it will be an enormous advantage to have a government with authority; the tasks of drawing up the new laws and regulations for the private sector and of maintaining macro-economic balance are surely much easier if the government has the authority to act, either because it has been democratically elected or for other reasons. The road to be traveled will also be much easier if the trade patterns derived from central planning are not altered abruptly and if the political scene is not dominated by ethnic rivalries and struggles. These problems, while present in East-Central Europe, may be much more salient in the economies emerging out of the Soviet Union (if, as seems likely to the present author, the authority of the center collapses, the ruble succumbs to severe inflation, and trade among the republics suffers from drastic dislocation as local authorities make decisions independently of the center). In this dismal scenario the populations would suffer greatly before the benefits of a market economy can take hold. Ironically, the prospects for building support for market-oriented reforms might be better under a government that takes over **after** trade and the monetary system have been seriously disrupted. In Slovenia, for example, the hardship brought on by inflation, the civil war, and the associated collapse of intra-Yugoslav trade are not attributable in the minds of the population to the transition to a market economy; there is likely to be less resistance to changing the old system when it is no longer functioning.

While the situation in East-Central Europe may not be so dire as in the Soviet Union, there are many grounds for pessimism about the near-term outlook for Hungary, Poland, and Czechoslovakia. The dismantling of the system of central planning is bound to lead to declines in production and consumption and dislocations for many people. The initial widespread enthusiasm, based on hopes of early prosperity, for moving rapidly to a market economy, may well turn to disenchantment as the negative experiences accumulate (Winiecki, Ch. 15). A very real danger would seem to be the emergence or strengthening of rent-seeking special interests within state enterprises and the government bureaucracy (Nagy, Ch. 18).

Intelligent analysis of the ongoing process of the transitions could help people to see that some of the negative experiences are either the inevitable short-run costs of changing the economic system or the avoidable consequences of poor economic policies, rather than deficiencies in the market system itself. The authors of this volume hope that their essays will contribute to the policy debates and to the early emergence of well-functioning market economies in the post-communist societies.

PART I
The Problem of the Transition

2 The Next Decade in Central and Eastern Europe

Lawrence Summers

The initial euphoria that accompanied the political and economic revolutions of Central and Eastern Europe has since been replaced with a much more sober, and sometimes outright pessimistic, assessment of possibilities. The region currently faces a deep economic recession and widespread economic disarray. It has become increasingly obvious that the magnitude of the task ahead — the transformation of East-Central Europe into a market economy — is vast, and progress likely to be slow.

This chapter attempts to provide some empirical context to the debate over prospects for Central and Eastern Europe (CEE), by assessing where the economies of the region stand today, and where they seem to be going. Since the resulting forecast is rather bleak, the chapter also considers what measures can be taken to accelerate the process.

1 Where Do the Historically Planned Economies Stand Right Now?

One approach to computing estimates of living standards, and the one that paints the starkest picture, uses nominal exchange rates to convert income in the previously centrally planned economies into income per capita in dollars. Under this method, GNP per capita in Central and Eastern Europe ranges from $1,500 in Romania to $3,000 in Czechoslovakia and Hungary (see Table 1). To put these figures in perspective, $3,000 is about halfway between Argentina and Korea in 1990. Or, to state things in another and more dramatic way, $3000 is equivalent to per capita income in the United States in the year 1900. Consensus estimates place Czechoslovak real income, which is probably the highest of the CEE economies, at the level of France and Germany in 1950.

Of course, the logic of using nominal exchange rates is questionable. If one applies this methodology to the Soviet Union using generally accepted estimates that at current Soviet prices a convertible ruble would trade at an exchange rate of between 5 and 10 to the dollar, the implied value of Soviet GNP is between $150 and $300 billion, or between $550 and $1100 per capita. This calculation may say more about the ruble than it does about the real income of the Soviet Union. The same doubts can be raised about exchange rate-based comparisons for CEE, and indeed almost anywhere else (see Summers and Heston 1991).

An alternative way of computing income per capita levels is to use purchasing-power parity (PPP) as a basis for comparison. This approach involves pricing comparable goods in different countries and using the resulting price comparisons to deflate nominal incomes. The catch comes in the word "comparable". Take a standard Soviet or Central European dustpan which apparently has no ridge in it for catching dust, so you sweep the dust in and the dust slides out. How do you compare this to the Western version of the product? If you ask Western producers what it costs to produce one of those, they say it

TABLE 1
1990 Output Per Capita:
PPP and Exchange-Rate Measures
(US$ Thousands)

	GNP Per Capita	
	Exchange rate basis	PPP basis
Bulgaria	2,530	5,430
Czechoslovakia	2,978	7,940
Hungary	3,028	5,920
Poland	1,630	3,910
Romania	1,530	2,950
Yugoslavia	2,460	5,140
United States	21,098	—
Germany	21,298	—
France	18,265	—
United Kingdom	14,844	—

Source: World Bank, execpt PPP estimates from PlanEcon.

costs about as much as it costs to produce the kind with the ridge — it's just that the former is not very useful.

PPP estimates are about 2.5 times as great as the exchange-rate estimates just mentioned (table 1). And so, they almost surely represent an upper bound on true value of perhaps $7,500 per capita for the most affluent parts of Central Europe. However, even taking PPP estimates, the richest parts of Central Europe enjoy a standard of living today that is lower than that which the United States enjoyed in the 1920s.

2   Where are the Historically Planned Economies Going?

It is clear that CEE has a long way to go in catching up with the rest of Europe. The disturbing fact is that it is not getting there very fast. Let me highlight four conclusions from a recent unofficial World Bank exercise that tried to forecast Eastern Europe's prospects (see table 2).

First, when 1991 statistics are compiled, average output in Eastern and Central Europe will have fallen nearly 15 percent from its 1989 level for the average country. In the eastern half of Germany, the drop will have been considerably larger: there, output has fallen by approximately 20 percent this year, and is projected to fall by another 20 percent the coming year as full-time equivalent unemployment rates approach 30 percent.

Second, conservative estimates suggest that per capita income in the northern countries of East-Central Europe will not regain its 1989 level until 1996. Similarly, output in Southeastern Europe will not return to the level it had reached in 1989 until the year 2000.

Third, since real output will continue to grow rapidly over this period in Western Europe, the economies of East-Central Europe will not regain their 1989 position in relation to Western Europe until the middle of the first decade of the next century.

Fourth, if the World Bank's unofficial projection for growth in CEE after the transition process — 5 percent a year in the 1990s — is correct, and if output grows at what seems a reasonable estimate of 3 percent in Western Europe, it will take closer to a lifetime than to a generation before output per capita in East-Central Europe approaches the level in Western Europe.

These conclusions are based on some internal work from the Bank. Are these somehow overly pessimistic? Not at all. The Bank estimates are, in fact, broadly consistent with consensus estimates from other places, and if anything, are more optimistic. For example, a recent survey of a large number of forecasting organizations projected 1991/92 growth rates for Poland and Hungary that are below the estimates just cited — 1.5 percent versus 8 percent growth for Poland, and -2.6 percent versus -1.5 percent for Hungary. The OECD projections for 1991 are quite similar to the Bank estimates: they range from a low of -10 percent

TABLE 2
GDP Growth Rates

	Base	1990	1991	1992	1993	1994	1995	1996	1997	1998	1999	2000
Bulgaria	100.0	-0.108	-0.080	-0.002	0.023	0.023	0.024	0.024	0.024	0.024	0.024	0.024
Czechoslovakia	100.0	-0.035	-0.098	-0.048	0.012	0.034	0.040	0.043	0.049	0.049	0.049	0.050
Hungary	100.0	-0.065	-0.030	0.015	0.031	0.035	0.038	0.042	0.044	0.045	0.045	0.045
Poland	100.0	-0.140	0.020	0.060	0.060	0.050	0.050	0.050	0.050	0.050	0.050	0.050
Romania	100.0	-0.102	-0.040	0.019	0.025	0.030	0.030	0.030	0.040	0.040	0.045	0.045
Yugoslavia	100.0	-0.072	-0.035	0.003	0.007	0.011	0.013	0.015	0.018	0.021	0.025	0.029
UNWEIGHTED MEAN:												
ALL COUNTRIES	100.0	-0.087	-0.044	0.008	0.026	0.031	0.033	0.034	0.038	0.038	0.040	0.041
NORTHERN COUNTRIES[1]	100.0	-0.080	-0.036	0.009	0.034	0.040	0.043	0.045	0.048	0.048	0.048	0.048
SOUTHERN COUNTRIES[2]	100.0	-0.094	-0.052	0.007	0.018	0.021	0.022	0.023	0.027	0.028	0.031	0.033

[1]Czechoslovakia, Hungary, Poland
[2]Bulgaria, Romania, Yugoslavia

Source: World Bank

for Bulgaria to a high of zero percent for Poland. The OECD's long-term forecast for the northern countries is slightly more optimistic, calling for a somewhat higher growth path and a quicker bounce-back than the Bank: by the year 2000, the OECD projects a GDP for those countries that is approximately 5 percent higher than the Bank's projection. On the southern tier the OECD estimates are very similar to the Bank's.

There is a related bit of evidence justifying negative forecasts. Experience suggests that revisions to forecasts are positively correlated. Forecasts for central Europe in the last eighteen months have been consistently revised downwards. Furthermore, these forecasts typically assume success, that is, they typically assume the path of reform is pursued more or less consistently and do not factor in the very real possibility of policy reversal. *A priori* it seems unlikely that the forecasts are too pessimistic.

Are the data deceiving us? A number of arguments have been put forward. The growth in the informal sector that has accompanied the decline of the formal sector is almost surely understated in our statistics. Perhaps, the numbers paint a much darker picture than is warranted.

There is no doubt that in formerly socialist countries, private sector output and employment are severely underreported. However, at present, the private sector represents such a small fraction of output and employment that even extremely fast growth in this sector has a negligible impact on aggregate performance. In Czechoslovakia, the private sector accounts for less than 0.5 percent of non-agricultural output. In Poland, it accounts for about 8 percent of output. Even if it were to double and all of the increases were unobserved, informal sector gains would not offset formal sector declines.

Another argument against official data holds that people are better off when they do not have to stand in line, yet this increase in welfare does not show up in the official statistics. Thus, in some sense, the numbers fail to reflect the true improvement in living conditions in CEE. This argument is difficult to quantify especially now when the labor market will have a difficult time absorbing increased labor input. It must also be balanced against terms-of-trade losses that are not reflected in GNP level.

It may be that the projections are simply too pessimistic because we have failed to judge correctly the potential for take-off. Perhaps the existing projections are missing this possibility, just as projections missed the possibility of a take-off in Germany and in Japan after World War II, or in Korea in the late 1950s. However, if one studies development projections, they err on the side of optimism far more frequently than they err on the side of pessimism.

What about the historic examples? These are sobering as well. Take the example of New Zealand, which beginning in 1985 pursued a most comprehensive program of economic reform that liberalized on many fronts. It has experienced no growth during this period. It is true that world agricultural policies have not been favorable to New Zealand, but then again, the breakdown of the

Soviet Union has not been kind to Eastern Europe. Of course, it is also true that New Zealand missed a few points in its reform and that labor markets remain relatively rigid. But it seems unlikely that reform in the average Central European country will prove to be more complete.

Even if one looks at the "miracle" countries, one finds that it took until about 1955 for output in Germany to return to 1939 levels. Similarly, it took until the early 1950s for output in Japan to return to its level prior to World War II. Perhaps the closest Latin American case is Chile, where it took until 1989 for output to return to its 1981 level. There is ample historical precedent for thinking that the current projections will not prove to be overly pessimistic.

Recent studies of cross-country growth experiences have examined the issue of convergence in some detail. The general finding is that there is no very strong tendency for poorer countries to grow faster than richer ones. But if certain characteristics like national investment rates are held constant, there is a strong tendency toward convergence at the relatively slow rate of 2 percent per year. One might hope that convergence in Eastern Europe would be more rapid given its proximity to Western Europe. But the history of regional growth in industrialized countries is discouraging in this regard. In a recent paper, Barro and Sala-i-Martin (1991) examine the experience of the southern US states after the Civil War, that of Southern Italy since WWII, and that of the poorer parts of West Germany. They find that convergence is very slow. In the US case, the gap between rich and poor states was reduced at an average of only 2 percent per year. The same trend was observed for southern Italy and for the poor regions of Germany. Extrapolating these experiences to Eastern Europe suggests it will take a lifetime on average for the nations of Eastern Europe to close three quarters of the gap with Western Europe.

A second possible reaction, besides dismissing these projections as too pessimistic, is to reevaluate the benefits of reform and to argue that reform is so costly that it is simply not worth it. This strategy is wrong.

First, the success or failure of reform should be measured by standards other than just the volume of goods produced. Democracy and economic reform are almost certainly intertwined.

Second, it is easy to lose sight of just how rapidly the old system was collapsing. Consider the following statistic: Between 1970 and 1985, the death rate for middle-aged men in Western Europe declined by 25 percent. During the same period, the death rate for middle-aged men in Central Europe actually rose by 25 percent. That 50 percent spread is greater than the effect of eliminating all forms of cancer. Nobody knows quite why that happened — a combination of slow growth, discouragement, etc. Ultimately, the example of what is happening in the Soviet Union is sufficient to reject the alternative of turning back.

A third response to the pessimistic forecast is to blame the problem on the absence of capital. If only capital could flow in on a substantial scale, Eastern Europe could be rebuilt just as Western Europe was rebuilt after World War II.

What is needed is a new Marshall Plan. If only the governments of the West were willing to produce such a Marshall Plan, much more rapid growth in East-Central Europe could ensue. We have every reason to think that this view is misguided. A few reasons why merit attention.

First, the projections suggest that the problem in East-Central Europe is not the absence of investment but rather a relatively high incremental capital-to-output ratio. Investment shares in East-Central Europe are in the 20 percent range with growth projected in the 3 to 4 percent range after the initial decline. That implies an incremental capital-output ratio in the 5 to 7 range. The comparable incremental capital-output ratio in Germany and Japan after World War II was in the 2 to 3 range, and in the miracle growth countries in Asia, it was around 4. Investment rates in Eastern Europe are nearly twice what investment rates were in Chile. It is simply not correct to say that the problem appears to be a lack of capital. The problem is that given the amount of capital, growth is relatively slow.

Second, some of the strongest rhetoric regarding the need for a Marshall Plan is based on a faulty understanding of what the Marshall Plan actually did. The Marshall Plan provided aid over a four-year period that totalled $12 billion (in the dollars of the late 1940s). That represented 2 percent a year of the GDP of the recipient countries. To replicate what the Marshall Plan did would require only about $5 billion a year in assistance to Eastern Europe, or about $20 billion over four years.

Third, only about 30 percent of the aid from the Marshall Plan went to finance investment. A substantial portion went to support consumption of various kinds. During the period when it was in place, total Marshall Plan aid was equal to about 10 percent of total investment in the recipient countries, while the fraction of Marshall Plan aid going to finance investment accounted for about three percent of total investment. If one is trying to achieve the kind of success that took place in Western Europe following World War II, which albeit did not involve a sizeable transition period, the answer does not appear to be in simply providing more capital. Rather it seems to require raising the rate of return on the capital investment.

Fourth, the current estimates suggest a net flow to Central and Eastern Europe of about $7 billion a year. If that were quadrupled to $28 billion a year, and if all of that capital investment earned a 10 percent rate of return, the effect would be to raise the annual growth rate by only one percentage point. If growth is to be accelerated, one needs to create a more productive institutional environment in which investment is made more profitable, and not simply provide increasing amounts of capital.

The rather pessimistic picture presented at the beginning implicitly assumes that it will take a long time to create the institutions and capabilities that are necessary to assimilate large amounts of capital productively. It is that institutional gap, and not a capital gap, that needs to be solved if Central Europe is to have a chance of taking off.

3 The Reform of the Central and Eastern European Economies: What are the Priorities?

An interesting fact about reform in CEE economies is the broad agreement among economists about what needs to be done. Broadly, the elements of reform can be grouped into four categories:

1. **Macroeconomic stabilization:** tightening fiscal and credit policies, and addressing internal and external imbalances;

2. **Price and market reform:** removing price controls, liberalizing trade, and creating competitive factor markets;

3. **Enterprise reform and restructuring:** private sector development: establishing and clarifying property rights, facilitating entry and exit of firms, restructuring of enterprises;

4. **Institutional reform:** redefining the role of the state: legal and regulatory reform, social safety net, reform of government institutions (tax administration, budget and expenditure control, monetary control).

While there is general consensus over the nature of the reforms to be implemented, the sequencing of those reforms has been intensely debated. Most economists agree that certain components must precede or occur simultaneously with others, but because many reforms will take a long time, problems are likely to emerge. It has become clear that most elements of reform are closely intertwined, and that although some early reforms will produce immediate benefits, serious improvements in economic performance will require more time.

There is broad agreement that macroeconomic stabilization, followed by price and trade reform, should occur at the very beginning of the reform process. Tax reform, the development of a social safety net, and measures to encourage the private sector should follow quickly thereafter. Restructuring, privatization, institutional, regulatory and legal reform can be addressed early in the reform process, but completion of reform in these areas will take more time. Financial liberalization, full convertibility of the capital account and full wage liberalization should come in later in the reform sequence. Figure 1 presents a consensus strategy for long- term systemic reform.

4 Conclusion: The Challenge to the Industrialized Countries

Although much progress has been made in defining and initiating the process of reform in CEE economies, it has become clear that reform will entail high short-term

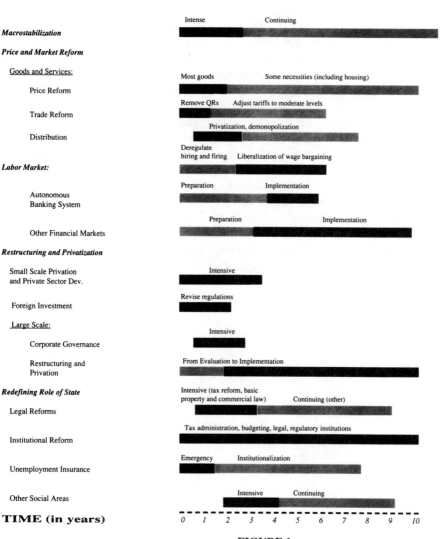

FIGURE 1
Phasing of Reform

costs and that the process of convergence with the economies of Western Europe will take decades. What can be done to accelerate this process?

First of all, industrialized countries can provide **financial assistance.** However, as argued above, if growth is to be accelerated one needs to create an appropriate institutional environment, capable of absorbing large amounts of capital productively, and not simply provide more capital. This strategy calls for accompanying **technical assistance** aimed at developing a more productive institutional framework. Finally, industrialized countries can provide **market access** to support trade and price reforms in the CEE economies.

The last point is crucial. In the long run, open markets will contribute more to increasing the growth rates in the economies of East-Central Europe than will vast capital flows. Yet in an increasingly protectionist world, are Western markets likely to be open? Collins and Rodrik (1991) suggest that CEE's main trading partner will be Western Europe. They estimate that in the long run CEE could account for as much as 27-28 percent of total European Community (EC) trade, as compared to the 4-5 percent it now represents. It seems unlikely that the EC would tolerate such substantial market penetration by CEE producers without some protectionist response, particularly in sensitive areas such as agriculture. On the other hand, the alternative to open markets is likely to be mass migration from East-Central Europe to the West, and a massive labor migration problem for the EC. Western Europe will be serving its own interests by providing open access to its markets.

3 Evolution in Economics and in the Economic Reform of the Centrally Planned Economies

Peter Murrell

The science of constructing a commonwealth, or renovating it, or reforming it, is like every other experimental science, not to be taught *a priori*. Nor is it a short experience that can instruct in that practical science; because the real effects of moral causes are not always immediate....The science of government being therefore so practical in itself, and intended for such practical purposes, a matter which requires experience, and even more experience than any person can gain in his whole life, however sagacious and observing he may be, it is with infinite caution that any man ought to venture upon pulling down an edifice which has answered in any tolerable degree for ages the common purposes of society, or on building it up again, without having models and patterns of approved utility before his eyes.

Edmund Burke, *Reflections on the Revolution in France*, 1789.

1 Introduction

The transformation of the centrally planned economies into market economies is an immensely complicated task for which economic theories can only provide loose metaphors, rather than precise lessons. Economists are not so fortunate as

The author would like to thank the Center for Institutional Reform and the Informal Sector at the University of Maryland for financial support in the writing of this paper. For helpful comments on this paper and related ideas, I would like to thank Josef Brada, Chris Clague, Jacques Cremer, Ed Hewett, Norbert Hornstein, Michael Marrese, Richard Nelson, Mancur Olson, Randi Ryterman, Jan Svejnar and the economists and economic policy makers in Czechoslovakia, Hungary, Poland, Mongolia, and the Soviet Union who freely discussed with me their ideas about their own countries' reforms.

35

engineers assigned to build a bridge, armed with a simple goal and with hard and fast, and tested, scientific principles. Rather, economists must rely upon sets of theoretical propositions known to be true only under highly stylized circumstances and empirical results often connected to the basic theories by tenuous extra assumptions. Thus, in deliberating on economy-wide economic reforms, economists should remind themselves that their theories are incomplete metaphors, rather than precise instruction manuals laying out the path to progress in a clear and definite way.

The purpose of the present chapter is to present the lessons of one such economic metaphor: to examine an evolutionary approach to economic reform. When the word "evolutionary" is used in common parlance, it usually conjures up two images. The first image is of slow and gradual change, rather than a revolutionary leap. Secondly, there is the connotation with the theory of natural systems that is central in biology. This chapter attempts to show that the conjunction of these two images is no simple matter of coincidence. The economic theories that are related to the theory of evolution do, on balance, suggest that the economic reform process should be gradual. Perhaps more importantly, these theories suggest that economists should be wary of emphasizing the benefits of privatization and instead should focus on the postive effects of building a market economy by encouraging the growth of a nascent private sector.

The ideas comprising the "evolutionary paradigm" derive from a number of sources. The early impetus was from Schumpeter (1950). At the simplest level, the theory also draws some insights by analogy with biological evolution. However, as Nelson and Winter (1982) make clear, the underlying basis of the evolutionary paradigm rests securely on a systematic articulation of theories of individual and organizational behavior, particularly focusing on informational problems. This fact implies that there are many links to be made between the evolutionary paradigm and that part of current economic theory focusing on informational processes — for example, investigations of the informational limitations of markets, the role of institutions in informational transmittal, the game theory approach to economic organizations, etc.[1] Of pertinence in the present context, Murrell (1990a) argues that the evolutionary paradigm identifies those systemic features most responsible for the differences in the economic performance of capitalist and centrally planned economies. These are the features of centrally planned economies that must be most urgently changed in the process of reform.

Section 2 of this chapter presents a summary of those elements of evolutionary theory that seem most pertinent when deliberating on the process of economic reform. Section 3 considers the connection between the speed of imposition

---

[1]Stiglitz (1989a) and Murrell (1991), although not addressing this point directly, show connections between some recent theoretical results and evolutionary views.

Evolution in Economics 37

of reform and the level of economic performance in the immediate post-reform phase. Section 4 examines the hopes for privatization and considers whether the process of privatization itself might impede the attainment of other worthwhile objectives of reform. The nature of stabilization programs is considered in section 5, particularly the extent to which those programs should rely solely on market-based measures. Using the view of organizations emanating from the evolutionary paradigm, section 6 considers whether the existing organizations of the pre-reform economy should have any role in the transition process.

2 The Evolutionary Paradigm from the Perspective of Reform

The evolutionary paradigm begins with two premises.[2] First, in order to understand the success of capitalism, one must primarily focus upon mechanisms that produce growth and change, not on equilibrium processes. Second, one must begin one's economic theorizing with a satisfactory description of the behavior of economic agents, especially one that takes full account of problems of decision making and organization in the face of severe limits on information-processing abilities. Then, the description of economic processes must follow directly from this view of the nature of agents.

At the center of the evolutionary emphasis on growth and change is the notion that innovation has been the driving force behind the immense increases in wealth occurring since the industrial revolution. However, one must be careful not to attach too narrow a meaning to the notion of innovation. Progress has come not only from new technologies, but also from organizational and institutional innovation. Thus, the notion of innovation should conjure up not only the invention of the blast furnace or the semiconductor, but also the development of the multi-divisional corporation and fast-food franchising.

In emphasizing growth and change, and thus innovation, the evolutionary perspective implicitly accords relatively less importance to the property of allocative efficiency. According to this perspective, the neoclassical paradigm's primary focus upon allocative efficiency and competition within an equilibrium framework is misleading. Rather, as Schumpeter (1950, pp. 84-85) stated most forcefully, these features are of secondary importance compared to capitalism's mechanisms for change and innovation:

---

[2] Nelson and Winter (1982) provide the most complete modern exposition of evolutionary theory. The present discussion closely follows their treatment, emphasizing elements most critical to reforms.

[I]t is...competition within a rigid pattern of invariant conditions, methods of production and forms of organization in particular, that practically monopolizes attention. But in capitalist reality as distinguished from its textbook picture, it is not that kind of competition that counts but the competition from the new commodity, the new technology, the new source of supply, the new type of organization....This kind of competition is much more effective than the other as a bombardment is in comparison with forcing a door, and so much more important that it becomes a matter of comparative indifference whether competition in the ordinary sense functions more or less promptly.

A direct implication of this quotation — and the evolutionary approach — is the notion that economic reform proposals concentrating on the pursuit of allocative efficiency will not address the main problems of socialist economies (Murrell 1990).

In modelling processes of growth and change, the evolutionary approach begins by acknowledging the effects on behavior of rampant uncertainty and the consequent demands on informational resources.[3] Thus, agents are constrained, not only by financial and physical constraints, but also by limits on information-processing capabilities and by the difficulties of exercising control in complex organizations. The latter constraints have profound consequences for the construction of effective organization.

A complex system organizing the interaction of many individuals must be able to coordinate the actions of those individuals and to process the information that flows between them. The exercise of routine operations is an efficient means of handling such coordination. Through the repetition of tasks varying only over a narrow range, an organization is able to economize on the scarce information-processing resources of each member. Then, each member can clearly interpret the flow of messages that provides the coordination that is the essence of large-scale organization. Hence, organizational efficiency is intimately tied to the exercise of a particular "routine," or narrow range of routines.

With this view of organizations, it is important to realize exactly where information, or technology, resides. That information should not be viewed as held by individuals, but rather as maintained in the continuing interactions between individuals. Information and skills, then, have value largely through interactions taken in the context of the exercise of a particular organizational routine. The productivity of an organization (and the individuals within that organization) depends to no small degree on the ability of that organization to continue its operations within some small neighborhood of its past behavior.

---

[3] The justification for the view of organizational behavior taken in the evolutionary paradigm is provided in detail in Nelson and Winter (1982). Here, I follow these authors in emphasizing the importance of organizational routines. One could reach essentially the same conclusions using the concept of corporate culture, as developed by Cremer (1987).

As well as solving the coordination problem, routines are also an element in the solution to organizational incentive and income distribution. A routine is essentially one equilibrium of the complex non-cooperative game that is at the heart of efficient organizational design. There are usually many equilibria of such games, of widely varying efficiency. Hence, the process of reaching efficient solutions could entail a long search. Thus, the perpetuation of a routine is itself a protection against the creation of conflict that would arise in any attempt to find an alternative solution to the organizational game. During such conflict the efficiency, and indeed the existence, of the organization would be under great threat.

Of course, organizations are not totally inflexible. They do change routines. But the search for alternatives is constrained by an existing stock of information. Since that information is intimately bound to the exercise of an existing routine, search is highly prescribed. Hence, the search for alternatives should be characterized, not as wide-ranging choice over a universe of alternatives, but rather as a history-bound process of discovery within a neighborhood of existing operations. Moreover, when such search occurs, the existing routine is itself threatened, jeopardizing the stability of the organization by calling into question the existing division of organizational income.

Given the reliance on routines and the constraints on search, societies that succeed in a changing world must have a mechanism freeing them from the inertia inherent in the operations of an existing set of organizations. Capitalism provides such a mechanism in several ways. First, there is the automatic way in which markets reallocate the control over resources from inefficient organizations to efficient ones. Second, bankruptcy and, to some extent, takeovers and mergers remove inefficient organizations. Third, there is the process of entry — the creation of a variety of new organizations, some of which will find an effective organizational structure in the new circumstances. Then, in a process that marks the evolutionary approach to economic change, according to Nelson and Winter (1982, p.9): "Patterns of differential survival and growth in a population can produce change in economic aggregates characterizing that population, even if the corresponding characteristics of firms remain constant."

It is now possible to summarize the elements of the evolutionary paradigm that must be kept most firmly in mind when deliberating upon economic reform.

1. The use of routines and the fact that search reflects the historical experience of an organization mean that one should expect much **persistence in organizational behavior.**

2. The evolutionary approach forces one to focus on the concept of the **economic environment** — the set of external influences that affect an organization's performance, including the set of other organizations in society. Given a stable environment for a long enough period, the types of routines and behaviors that are present in any society will be conditioned by the environment in which

society's organizations have survived and adapted.[4] Hence, in an initial period after a change in environment, the types of behaviors observed will be to a large extent a reflection of the past environment.

3. The evolutionary approach emphasizes the importance of selection processes, or **entry and exit,** in accomplishing change. Changes within organizations are de-emphasized in favor of a focus on shifts in economic resources from inefficient (or technologically obsolete) to efficient (technologically progressive) organizations or to new organizations better suited to the new economic environment.

4. To aid in the efficacy of the selection process, there is a need to generate **variety in the types of organizations** that are present in society. This need is especially great when a radical change in environment is considered and society's stock of organizations has been honed in a different environment. Moreover, it must also be emphasized that a variety of organizational forms is characteristic of modern capitalist societies (R. Nelson 1990).

5. The **uncertainty and the limits on information processing** that are emphasized in the evolutionary approach to organizations must also be acknowledged as elements in the policy-making process. Policy makers' knowledge of the behavior of the economy outside a narrow domain close to past experience will be highly inaccurate.

We turn now to a discussion of the importance of these points for understanding the process of reform and for deliberation on the types of policies that should be implemented during reform.

3   Reform, Organizational Response to Adversity, and Economic Performance

Comprehensive economic reform means first and foremost a radical change in the economic environment. However, the existing stock of organizational routines and information is a product of the old environment. In the case of

---

[4]This statement does not, of course, mean that the society will necessarily become progressively more productive over time. Increasing fitness of organizations to the conditions of a social system will be sure to result in improved productivity only when a social system encourages only productive behavior. However, it is assumed in this chapter that socially productive behavior was encouraged to some degree by the old systems, but not to the degree that such behavior is encouraged in market economies, of course. Thus, at the beginning of transition the socialist economies have a stock of enterprises whose productivity, within the old system, is certainly better than that of a random set of organizational arrangements and whose productivity, within a market environment, cannot be assumed to be better than this random set of organizational arrangements.

most Eastern European countries, this past environment is the centralized, bureaucratic system of administrative allocation and control. Given that this system survived for a number of decades in a number of countries, it is reasonable to suppose that organizational routines were selected according to the needs of the unreformed environment and are largely suited to that environment.[5] Moreover, the allocation of personnel to positions has occurred within that bureaucratic system. Thus, the centrally planned systems will have an allocation of human capital and of management styles that matches the dictates of a nonmarket environment.[6]

Because the stock of existing routines, behavioral patterns, and expectations — organizational structure for short — is suited to the existing environment, it is unlikely to be suitable for a new market environment. A radical change in the economic system requires large changes in organizational structure, which will induce much poorer economic performance during the lengthy and difficult process of changing organizational routines and reallocating managerial personnel. This decline in performance is all the more certain when the change in environment produces adversity that removes the possibility of simply continuing past behavior. Organizational efficiency tends to diminish rapidly in the face of adversity when long-stable cooperative agreements are no longer viable and must be replaced with less attractive ones (Nelson and Winter 1982, pp. 121-4). Thus, a precipitate change in the economic system could be equivalent to reducing, at a single blow, the productivity of each enterprise by a substantial amount.[7]

The decline in economic performance that is immediate on the implementation of reform would occur even if the new economic system would be exactly

---

[5]For fear of misinterpretation, the points in the previous footnote must be emphasized. This analysis does not imply that the centrally planned economies became progressively more productive, nor does it mean that the centrally planned system will be an efficient one. All that is necessary for the present argument is that pressures to be socially productive were not totally absent in the old system.

[6]Consider, for example, the following statement about the Hungarian chemical industry (a convertible-currency export-oriented industry in the most reformed Eastern European country): "Managers selected by officials of the ruling party in the past have conformed with communist traditions: loyalism, mediocrity, and inflexibility. The number of western-type entrepreneurial managers remains low..." *Chemical and Engineering News,* November 12, 1990.

[7]It should be emphasized that there are two effects of change that need to be taken into account. The first effect arises from the fact that the features of organization that are productive in one environment are not necessarily productive in another environment. The second effect arises because all organizations are less productive while undergoing the process of change.

the one that would be best in the long run, after things have had time to hammer logic into men.[8] Thus, whereas in the long run a market system might be the most productive economic environment, in the short run, when routines and expectations are still adapted to the bureaucratic environment of central planning, a swift changeover to the market could be very destructive of the capacity of the existing enterprises to produce output.[9]

It is important to emphasize here that these phenomena are general ones, widely observed in market societies, and not simply the product of socialist economic reform.[10] For example, in the United States "...there's an important correlation between change and corporate crises. Most big companies have built in immobility....Consequently, some changes in markets or competition demand a degree of flexibility they simply aren't capable of, and could not reasonably be expected to possess." (Austin-Smith 1966, p. 8) What is unique about the Eastern European situation is of course the number of companies that will be simultaneously subject to the stress of change and therefore the likely feedback between declines in performance in one area and the pressures of adversity elsewhere. Moreover, it seems that there is a highly non-linear relation between adversity and declines in performance. Whereas moderate amounts of adversity might be salutary, inducing productive reactions, extreme adversity appears to produce highly dysfunctional response, enhancing crisis rather than diminishing it (P. Nelson 1981).[11]

The previous point leads directly to the question of whether the present observations are relevant to decisions on the speed of reform. Given a non-linear relation between organizational performance and degree of adversity, and given that declines in performance in one sector due to adversity will produce adversity in others, then it could well be that a slow reform results in a larger sum of discounted national income over the relevant time period than does a fast reform.

The notion that one might want to change only gradually to a better environment (i.e., the market) could at first seem paradoxical. But the element of paradox

---

[8]The last phrase is of course a slight rewording of Schumpeter's (1934, p. 80) dictum on when one can use theories that assume that "conduct is prompt and rational".

[9]Thus, an interpretation is provided here of the causes of the declines in output in Polish industry in early 1990 that is very different from those that rely on macroeconomic imbalances (Frydman and Wellisz 1990 and Coricelli and Calvo 1990).

[10]Abernathy and Clark (1985, p. 18) point out that deregulation of a capitalist industry can create conditions that are similar to those in a new industry. Hence, reform (i.e., deregulation) is essentially equivalent to the creation of a new selection environment.

[11]Large amounts of adversity destroy the existing cooperative agreements that are the basis of organizational performance. Conflicts that had been suppressed will surface and the members of the organization will turn to the struggle over distribution rather than focusing on production.

vanishes as soon as one realizes that there are inherent externalities in the creation, design, and destruction of large organizations. These externalities arise from the non-market elements of coordination intrinsic in organizations and from the public-goods nature of organizational performance that is a consequence of the impossibility of establishing an automatic link between individual performance and individual rewards. In such situations, cooperation unsupported by immediate short-term incentives is essential for organizational performance. If existing cooperative arrangements are rendered non-viable by a large change in the environment, then a long and costly search for new cooperative arrangements is necessitated.[12] During this process, the productivity of each worker will be lower than before, because each worker's productivity is intimately connected to the behavior of other workers. In sum, in the transition to a market economy, there is an inherent market failure arising from the destruction of system-specific organizational capital, which is the solution to the externalities problem that is intrinsic in organization itself.

Given that reform calls for the replacement of a large portion of society's organizational capital, one can view the speed of reform through the lens of optimal capital replacement policy. Decisions on the speed of reform must depend upon the cost of borrowing for consumption smoothing during transition. If such borrowing is not possible to the degree necessary, which seems likely given the present situation of the reforming economies, then the optimal path of reform would be one that conserves some of the existing organizational capital in the early stages of transition. Such conservation would seem all the more necessary if it is important to ensure that living standards are not radically depressed in the early stages of democracy.

4   On the Benefits of Privatization

Quick privatization of existing state enterprises is often viewed as a necessary and sufficient condition for the success of reform. It is assumed that, given a new ownership structure and market competition, there will be large increases in the efficiency and output of the existing stock of enterprises, which will more than repay the rather large political, social, and organizational costs incurred in the privatization process itself. Here, the evolutionary paradigm is used to illuminate the likely benefits from privatization.

The construction of new organizations is costly and difficult. However, it could be even more costly to restructure old organizations that must be transformed

---

[12]It is important to understand that strikes and large amounts of manager-worker hostilities are inherent in this process and not simply a symptom of some type of social and political failure.

because of a change in economic environment.[13]   An existing organizational structure entails the adaptation of behavior and language of communication to existing conditions, the alignment of organization with an existing structure of physical plant, and many commitments to existing members that are costly to negate. Because of the difficulties of changing such organizational features, the reconstruction of existing organizations involves costs that are not present in the construction of new organizations. Hence, there can be no *a priori* assumption that privatization is better than simply shutting down existing enterprises in coordination with the gradual rise of new private enterprise. In the process of privatization and restructuring of state enterprises, more capital might be used than would be required in the process of creating new enterprises, especially if "restructuring grants" (i.e., subsidies) were a part of the whole privatization process.

This argument gains force when one remembers that it is the experience of capitalist societies that large organizations are often quite unresponsive to new circumstances.[14] As Arrow (1974, pp. 56-9) emphasizes, new organizations are often essential for change, because established ones are likely to have an irreversible commitment to existing arrangements. In capitalist societies, in new industries and in existing industries where the technology is new, new firms are of enormous importance for these very reasons (Mansfield *et al.* 1977, p. 16 and R. Nelson 1981, pp. 1051-2). It seems plausible that the situation of a newly privatized enterprise would be every bit as demanding as that of an existing capitalist firm confronted by a new technology.[15]

The difficulties of reorganizing existing enterprises would be especially large if restructuring would require fundamental changes in an enterprise's sectoral specialization, production technology, or market orientation. Yet, there is reason to believe that Eastern European enterprises will have to make changes of all three types during the restructuring process. Judging by comparisons with capitalist countries at an analogous level of development, there are large structural shifts to be made from industry to services and within industry from heavy to light.[16] Changes in production technology will be needed because of the

---

[13]Leszek Balcerowicz recently emphasized that the costs of transition were much higher than expected, resulting in unexpectedly poor economic performance in the early part of 1991. One of the reasons that he cited was the slow pace of changes in management structure. See Foreign Broadcast Information Service (1991).

[14]The reasons for this claim are clear given the arguments of section 2.

[15]Moreover, the factors that give large established firms an advantage in market economies — economies of scale in science-based R&D and the benefits of accumulated learning-by-doing — will not be as relevant to the situation of large established enterprises in reforming economies.

[16]If one compares the size of industry in an average Eastern European economy to that in the poorer European countries, then the over-production of industrial goods is probably between 25 percent and 33 percent.

imposition of more stringent environmental policies, the higher quality standards of new Western markets, and the downsizing of factories that are of inefficient scale for a market economy.[17] Large changes in market orientation follow from the demise of the Council for Mutual Economic Assistance and the desire to become more fully integrated in international markets.

The foregoing argument gains additional force when one acknowledges the strength of entry and exit processes in capitalism. In a normal market economy, there is substantial turnover of firms. If this process were imitated during the next few years in Eastern Europe, a substantial number of enterprises would be expected to close anyway. For example, only 60 percent of large, new, single-plant firms survive their first five years of operation in the United States (Dunne, Roberts, Samuelson 1989, p. 694). Given the status of Eastern European enter-prises — large organizations being cast into a new market environment — one could expect their failure rate after privatization to be of the same order.

The implication of the previous discussion is that perhaps too many hopes have been invested in privatization and rather too much intellectual, social, and political capital is being consumed in the process of privatization. The argument is strengthened when the efforts behind privatization are contrasted to the lack of attention being paid to creating and fostering the development of new private sector firms. In many Eastern European countries, policy toward the private sector can be characterized, at best, as one of benign neglect. In particular, little attention has been paid to the question of how to generate the additional capital to realize investment in the private sector.[18]

In fact, in the early stages of reform, there is a trade-off between efforts to create a new private sector and the speed and scope of privatization. In the cen-trally planned period, the state extracted the surplus from its enterprises and used it to reallocate investment across sectors. During reform, the state could either surrender its claims on such revenues through decentralization and privati-zation or continue to use state-sector surpluses as a means of financing the

---

[17]On the basis of very crude calculations, I estimate that the Eastern European economies would have to shut down half of the manufacturing capacity of large plants (and create a similar amount of capacity in small plants) in order to obtain a distribution of plant sizes that was roughly comparable to that in Western Europe. In individual industries, such as textiles, the figure could be as large as 70 percent.

[18]Other authors (e.g., Svejnar 1990) have consistently emphasized the benefits that can come only from a new private sector, rather than from privatized firms. However, it is my perception of the literature that such emphases are not the major focus of the major-ity of discussions of the transition process. For example, it is common to see the terms "privatization" and "creating a private sector" used synonymously. Conversely, it is quite unusual to find authors who emphasize the costliness of the privatization process and the need to slow down this process in order to channel resources to the new private sector.

growth of the private sector. In that case, there is an inverse relationship between the amount of privatization and the rate of growth of a new private sector.[19] This inverse relationship also occurs because a significant part of the country's entrepreneurial talents and scarce financial infrastructure will be consumed in the process of privatization itself, rather than being freed to participate in the new private sector. Moreover, the desire to privatize ongoing operations, rather than to sell their assets by the piece, leads to a lack of facilities, particularly buildings and land, that are easily available to new entrepreneurs.

In conclusion, one might venture the thought that "privatization" has gained too much prominence as an objective of reform policy. The appropriate goal is "creation of a private sector". Privatization is only one route to that latter goal. Moreover, it might be a very costly route, one whose implementation impedes more effective means of creating a private sector, particularly the encouragement of the development of the nascent private sector.

5   On Market-Based Macroeconomic Stabilization Measures

The evolutionary paradigm emphasizes that there is a strong tendency for organizations to continue behavior that has been successful in the past. If so, there is one particular aspect of pre-reform enterprise behavior that would prove to be very dysfunctional in a swift change to a market-regulated regime. Kornai (1980) has emphasized that excess demand pressures are almost intrinsic in the operations of economies with large state productive sectors, due to enterprise manipulation of soft-budget constraints. When reforms are being implemented, the organizational behavior that led to excess demand in the past is likely to be an important determinant of economic outcomes. Until a process of large-scale restructuring and entry and exit has taken place, it is likely that the Eastern European economies will have a much stronger tendency to generate macroeconomic instability than economies that have had dominant private sectors in their recent past.

This prediction has been borne out in the recent reform experience of Hungary and Poland. Enterprises in those countries have used their previously learned channels of action against adversity in the new environment. Hence, there has been a very large growth of inter-enterprise credit in Poland and Hungary in the past year, after the reforming governments tightened banking system credit. The growth of inter-enterprise credit can be viewed as a simple continuation

---

[19]Exactly this trade-off is appearing in the most dramatic way in Poland. The Huta Katowice steel plant is under consideration for privatization and commercialization, but the government is reluctant to begin the process because of the drop in tax revenues that will result (*Financial Times,* April 19, 1991).

of the passive monetary system of central planning, where credits and debts were built largely to accommodate changes in the real side of the economy and where creditors were largely unconcerned about the risks of non-payment.

The essence of the problem of macroeconomic stability during reform lies in the incompatibility between the new market environment and the enterprise behavior and expectations that are a heritage of the past.[20]   The old systems accommodated themselves to certain features of enterprise behavior, among them the tendency to disregard financial constraints in the face of seemingly more urgent real priorities.   Given the stability of the old system over a number of decades, one might conclude that, within the constraints of that system, such accommodation was successful in controlling or neutralizing those elements of enterprise behavior that had most immediate dysfunctional consequences.[21] Thus, policy and institutions under the old regime were matched to the behaviors and expectations of enterprises.   But with a swift change to market-based stabilization policies and with the destruction of old institutions, deep problems arise when the old expectations are still held and when the old patterns of behavior continue.[22]   Hence, market-based stabilization policies will be much more costly for reforming economies than they are in economies with a tradition of markets and private enterprise.

The main policy conclusion to be derived from the above observations is that during transition there might be a case for direct controls on state enterprises to promote macroeconomic stability, rather than relying upon solely market-based measures.   At the very least, the economist's usual presumption of non-interference in markets can hardly be accepted without question.   Certainly, for the state sector, price and wage controls, direct credit restrictions, and exchange controls must be considered as potential candidates for use by macroeconomic policymakers.

---

[20]An interesting example of this phenomenon has been identified in capitalist economies in the period after deregulation of an industry.   In such cases, it has been observed that firms continue cartelistic behavior, using the very instruments that were legal before the deregulation took place.   See Willig (Ch. 10) for details of the US experience in this respect.

[21]The old centrally planned system was moderately successful in keeping macroeconomic imbalances in check, in the sense that these imbalances did not threaten the short-term stability of the system.   In such a way the system accommodated to the most immediate consequence of state-sector financial indiscipline.   Of course, all the negative effects of macroeconomic imbalance on productivity, work effort, and quality emphasized by Kornai (1980) were not ameliorated.

[22]One Eastern European central banker explained the extending of inter-enterprise credit by saying "If only our managers had just once seen a company not paying its debt, but this is not part of our corporate culture."

The foregoing also contains lessons on the manner in which stabilization programs should be implemented. With the melange of old enterprises and new market institutions, there will be very little knowledge in society of how the new system functions. Hence, the early period of reform will provide valuable information about the characteristics of the new system. Where there is some element of irreversibility to the actions involved in stabilization,[23] there is some value to implementing a stabilization program with caution. The fact of learning through experience implies that there is value to be had from preserving options through the implementation of appropriate policies (Arrow and Fisher 1974).

Moreover, while learning is taking place, it might be unwise to base stabilization too heavily upon schemes that depend upon "nominal anchors". The fixing of such anchors relies upon the necessarily scanty knowledge about the structure and behavior of the newly reformed economy. Hence, such anchors can only be set with large margins of error, thus causing the stabilization program itself to be wide of its target, putting the government under the severe pressure of weakening its very commitment to stabilization. Hence, observers of the Polish economy comment frequently about the overshooting that was the cause of the unexpectedly large macroeconomic adjustments that occurred in the first part of 1990. It is crucial, however, to emphasize that this overshooting must not be viewed as the result of mistakes or poor planning. Rather, it was a normal outcome for a stabilization relying upon the setting of nominal variables in an environment where policymakers are only beginning to understand the structural features of the economy.[24]

The points emphasized in the preceding paragraphs gain extra force when stabilization is considered within the context of the reform process as a whole. In that process, the creation of a viable private sector is the *sine qua non* of success. The essence of market-based stabilization policies is to contain the expansionary impulses of enterprises and firms, usually by imposing very tight money policies and high real interest rates. These policies will, if the state and private sectors are treated symmetrically, greatly constrain the growth of new private sector firms at a time when the economy most needs them.[25]   Hence, one

---

[23]Elements of irreversibility include, for example, decentralization of the enterprise sector and loss of the government's political capital if there is a failure to keep to commitments.

[24]The Polish stabilization policy depended rather crucially on estimates of the appropriate exchange rate and forecasts of the rate of inflation, which helped to establish monetary and credit targets and affected enterprise evaluations of the implications of the tax-based wage control measures.

[25]In the Polish stabilization, the tight credit policy in Poland applied both to the private and state sectors, as did the draconian wage control policies. Thus, despite all the exaggerated claims for the growth of the private sector in Poland in 1990, investment in the private sector went down from 1989 to 1990 (*Rzeczpospolita,* February 2, 1991).

observes again the very important trade-off between the creation of a private sector and the short-run decentralization and marketization of the state sector. That initial decentralization, before privatization, will impede the development of the new private sector in a manner that will ultimately lengthen the transition itself. In deciding whether only market-type stabilization measures are to be used or whether more *dirigiste* policies might be countenanced, one should perhaps consider whether the growth of the private sector might be a more important goal than decentralization of the state sector.

6 Do Existing Institutions Have Any Value?

To some reformers, a market economy is synonymous with the decentralization of decision making. In this view, the destruction of the existing control institutions of central planning is sufficient to lead to a viable market economy.[26] That notion, together with some justifiable resentment of the past impositions of the center, probably contributed in no small degree to the destruction of the old system of planning and control in many countries in the latter half of the 1980s, before any market institutions had been created. In turn, that destruction, together with the accompanying decentralization of decision making, was the proximate cause of the loss of macroeconomic control that was evidenced in a majority of East European countries in the late 1980s.

But this market-as-decentralization view overlooks the role of the many important institutions of control present in modern capitalist systems, each contributing at a microeconomic level to macroeconomic stability. First and foremost, there is the institution of private property, which places responsibility at the individual level, especially the immediate responsibility for obeying budget constraints. Second, there are large sets of institutions ensuring that allocation of responsibility is clear and can be enforced — for example, commercial codes, civil law procedures, collateral, and bankruptcy. Third, there are the institutions that monitor and control the behavior of those who hold the property of others in trust — accounting practices, banking regulators, stock markets, securities regulators, etc. Lastly, there is a whole set of expectations about the way other economic agents will behave, and these expectations apply most importantly to the actions of government itself.[27]

---

[26]This view was shown to me most clearly by one top official of a reforming regime who proudly boasted of the "liquidation" of the central planning apparatus, at a time when no market economy institutions had been created.

[27]In the foregoing, emphasis has been put on the control functions of the institutions of capitalism rather than their incentive properties. There is no implication here that those incentive properties are less important in the long run. Rather, it is the control functions that need to be emphasized in the present discussion of the treatment of state enterprises, before they are privatized.

It is a given that these institutions will take many years to create.[28]   Thus, there is a decision to be made at the beginning of the reform process concerning how society is to exert the necessary degree of control over the actions of economic agents in order to preserve budgetary, financial, and monetary stability during the early stages of reform. The central issue in this decision is whether it is optimal at the earliest stages of reform to rely exclusively upon the disciplining force of the free market. The alternative is, of course, to use some of the existing state institutions on a selective and temporary basis to exert control over the state enterprises in the period before privatization and creation of market institutions can take place.[29]   Although this latter alternative is politically less attractive, there are some economic arguments implying that this option should be put on the agenda for consideration.

The suggestion of using some of the existing structures of the old regime rests upon the thesis that the creation of workable institutions and organizations is a lengthy process requiring much trial and error. The information and skills of existing personnel are attuned to the existing set of institutions and lose much of their value when those institutions are destroyed. In situations of increasing uncertainty, that is, reform, the value of information sources increases (Hess 1982). Therefore, some economic value might lie in existing institutions, even though they are not the best from a long-run point of view and even though there are firm intentions to scrap these institutions during the transition process. This argument is, of course, the obverse of the argument that privatized firms might not be able to change to fit the requirements of the new capitalist market: the old institutions might still be useful for temporarily carrying out the tasks for which they were originally designed.

What possible job could the old institutions do in the early stages of reform? One property of traditional central planing — probably much envied by some reforming regimes — was the ability of the old system to produce some semblance of macroeconomic balance.[30] The traditional central planning systems had a passably good record of budgetary, financial, and monetary stability (of course at a cost in terms of economic efficiency). There is thus a *prima facie* case to suggest that some elements of the traditional central control system could

---

[28]For example, Fischer and Gelb (1990) cite the very revealing fact that it takes five years to train a bank examiner in the United States. Additionally, the privatization process is inherently a slow one.

[29]Here, the important point is that the nascent private sector should not be subject to the same control.

[30]In questioning the veracity of this statement, the reader should keep in mind the exact time periods when traditional central planning was operating. For example, Poland had essentially given up economy-wide macroeconomic balancing in the mid-1970s. See Montias (1982).

be kept in the early stages of reform.[31] This case is strengthened once one realizes that there is virtually no example to which one can point of a decentralized socialist economy that has evidenced macroeconomic balance and stability. (Privatization takes long enough that reforming economies are still dominantly socialist ones in the first few years of reform.) Decentralization and liberalization can occur too early. Old inefficient institutions may be better than ones that are planned, but which do not yet exist.

Beyond these remarks, there are good reasons not to be more precise when talking about reforms in general. Given the differing histories of different countries during the period of central planning and given that each country is now at a different stage of reform, few general points can be made. Analogous institutions will have functioned with varying degrees of effectiveness in different countries. Reform and change might have already irreversibly destroyed many institutions of the old systems. Nevertheless, at the beginning of the reform process policymakers should take stock of the effectiveness of the existing institutions and ask whether there are some that would be useful in the early stages of reform.

This section concludes with a theme that has run through the conclusions to previous sections. This theme is the trade-off between the reform of the old state sector institutions and the creation of new private sector ones. In the context of the present section, this trade-off appears in two ways. First, if old institutions are immediately scrapped, there is an immediate need to create market institutions that help to control state enterprises. Assuming that there is a scarcity of talented personnel, some precious talent will be used in the state sector that might be more advantageously employed in creating the institutions most needed by the new private sector.[32] Second, when the state is not willing to use the old state control mechanisms to constrain the activities of the state enterprises, the effects of their actions are much more likely to impinge on the nascent private sector. For example, monetary policy might need to be more stringent and foreign currency less available for the private sector, if the state eschews all non-market means of controlling its own enterprises. Hence, the growth of the new private sector would be slowed.

---

[31]In particular, it would seem that there is an argument to keep some central control over the state enterprise use of credit, access to foreign exchange, and payment of wages.

[32]For example, the creation of a commercial code is probably more important to the new entrepreneurs who are building new commercial relationships and who do not have the backing of the state, than to the state sector firms with their traditional ties. Hence, the creation of a authoritative commercial code at the outset of reform is essential if the emphasis is on the creation of a new private sector. However, this element of the legal infrastructure will perhaps receive lower priority when the new free markets are dominated by state sector firms than when the government is concentrating on the needs of the new private sector.

7   Conclusion: Conflict Between Reforming the Old and Creating the New?

This chapter has explored the implications of using evolutionary economics to examine the central policy questions that arise during the early stages of the transition from socialism to market capitalism. One concern has consistently recurred in the discussions of the diverse elements of policy — the fact that there is a trade-off between promoting the growth of a new private sector and reforming the old state sector. The centrality of this concern arises from the basic insights of the evolutionary paradigm, especially the existence of rigidities in organizational behavior and the importance of entry and exit processes to the dynamism of capitalism. Hence, restructuring and privatizing the state enterprise system, which is the central hope of most transition plans, is bound to be a long and costly process, using resources that might be more profitably employed in facilitating the growth of the new private sector.

The case for a go-fast policy in the state enterprise sector weakens once one acknowledges the competition for scarce resources between the state enterprise sector and the nascent private sector. Rapid reforms in the state sector might actually impede the vitality of the entry and exit mechanism in the new private sector. Since this mechanism is vital in imparting dynamism to the transition, the overall speed of change in the economy might be inversely related to the effort spent on reforming the state sector.

Although inconsistent with the views of rapid marketizers who are in the majority in the Western academic community, the observations made in this chapter do find reflection in the actual course of reforms. The economic reforms have proceeded at a much slower pace than the rapid marketizers first believed would be the case. Moreover, the need for nonmarket constraints on existing state enterprises is recognized even in the policies of the fastest reforming countries: wages are still subject to very severe controls; full convertibility has still not arrived; and domestic credit is still rationed. The present chapter shows why such constraints are consistent with the desire to create market capitalism as quickly as possible. However, this chapter argues that such policies of state-sector restraint should be set within a consistent program that promotes the growth of the private sector, rather than as epicycles patching up a free-market theory of reform.

There are echoes of the conclusions reached in this chapter in other general analyses of reform that have appeared in the last year. Kornai (1990, p. 62) writes: "Precisely because I am a proponent of liberalization of the economy...I would like to see tight control over the ways in which taxpayers' money is spent. In this respect I classify the manager of a state-owned firm among the state officers." The identification of the possible conflict between liberalization of the economy and liberalization of the state sector, as well as Kornai's emphasis on organic development of the private sector, mark his theories as broadly consistent with an evolutionary approach. Similarly, the phenomena of "negative value added" and the "shoddy product syndrome," identified by McKinnon (1991), can be viewed as examples of the organizational legacies emphasized above. Moreover, the role of these legacies in justifying McKinnon's advocacy of a gradual reduction in tariffs is also consistent with an evolutionary approach to policy during the transition.

A significant omission in the argument of this chapter is the political dimension of reform policy, which is obviously very important given the intertwining of democratic and economic transitions. The particulars of the politics of each country are important in defining the exact implications of the foregoing arguments, for at least two reasons. First, the efficacy of the old institutions during the transition will depend on the extent to which these institutions were dependent on the structures of the old political system. The lesser was this dependence, the more use will the old institutions have during reform. Second, it is possible that some reformers might see a non-economic, political need to destroy the old system. The structure and rhythm of the economic transition must certainly be attuned to the needs of the democratic transition from the old political structures. Indeed, this need is one of the lessons of the evolutionary paradigm, which emphasizes the importance of the legacies of the past, both political and economic.

4 The Hidden Path To A Successful Economy

Mancur Olson

Since an economy in transition from a communist to a market economy contains many of the mechanisms of the old regime as well as new markets, its performance depends both on what is left from the past as well as on the markets that have been introduced. To understand the transition, then, we not only need to understand why markets work as well as they do, but also why central planning and state enterprises produce whatever amounts they produce. Most discussions in both the East and the West now emphasize, appropriately, the obviously unsatisfactory character of Soviet-type arrangements and the superiority of market-oriented democracies.

But we will not understand why the level of output has actually **fallen** in virtually all of the societies undergoing transition to a market economy, nor be able to improve performance during the transition, unless we also understand why the centrally planned economies were ever able to survive and even, at times, to grow. After all, the Soviet Union survived as a totalitarian planned economy for nearly three quarters of a century. It was productive enough to become — or at least appear to be — a superpower. Though even the best available statistics on the Soviet-type economies are not completely convincing, they suggest that during the 1950s and early 1960s these economies grew approximately as rapidly as West European economies at comparable levels of development, and they undoubtedly did then grow significantly. Why did this growth occur? Why did it fail to continue? As it turns out, the answers to these questions will make it clear why the transition to a market economy has been as difficult as it has been.

I am thankful to Christopher Clague, Mark Goldberg, Jac Heckelman, Steve Knack, Christos Kostopoulos, and Peter Murrell for detailed criticisms and to the Center for Institutional Reform and the Informal Sector for support of my research, but I am solely responsible for all shortcomings of this chapter.

Though economists have a relatively well developed theory of why markets work, neither they nor specialists in any other discipline have any satisfactory explanation of why Soviet-type economies worked at all. Economic theory shows that markets can make major contributions to social welfare in a wide variety of situations. Even though the conditions needed for perfect competition or Pareto-efficiency are not achieved in practice, it is easy to show, for example, that there are gains from trade — and thus from markets — in the most diverse circumstances. The same economic theory also explains the conditions in which markets will tend to fail — for example, why *laissez faire* will often generate excessive amounts of pollution. It also explains various pathologies that should be expected in Soviet-type economies, such as long queues.

By contrast, no one, whether using economic theory or any other tool of thought, has been able to explain why the Soviet-type economies were able to produce what they produced and to last as long as they lasted. The closest thing there is to such a theory is the model of a hypothetical socialism that mimics, and tries to improve upon, the markets of capitalism. In addition to other difficulties, this theory does not describe the actual policies that most of the Soviet-type economies followed. Thus the intellectual challenge is not to explain why the market economies outperformed the Soviet-type economies, but to explain why the latter managed to get by as long as they did. One cannot understand the combination of the old and the new that makes up the economy in transition until this challenge is met. This chapter will attempt to offer a theory that meets this challenge and then use this theory to illuminate the choices facing the societies in transition.

1   Encompassing Interests

The Soviet-type societies grew as rapidly as they did in the first two decades after World War II because they were impelled to grow by an "encompassing interest". The concept of an encompassing interest is developed and tested in *The Rise and Decline of Nations* (Olson 1982) and will be only briefly outlined here. If an individual, or an organization with enough coherence and discipline to act with rational self-interest, obtains a substantial portion of any increase in the output of a society and bears a large proportion of any drop in this social output, then that individual or organization has an encompassing interest in that society. This encompassing interest gives the actor in question an incentive to care about the productivity of the society and to attempt to increase it. In other words, the encompassing actor's interests are not only served by obtaining a larger share of the social output, but also by increasing the total output of the society. By contrast, an individual or organization with a "narrow" interest — one that receives only a minuscule share of any increase or decrease in the society's output — will have no incentive to try to increase social output. That

individual or organization has only an incentive to strive to obtain a larger share
of the society's output through distributional struggle, even if this distributional
struggle reduces the national income by much more than the narrow interest
obtains.

Thus lobbying and cartelistic organizations that are small in relation to the
society as a whole work to win special-interest legislation and monopoly advantages even if the society's losses are large in relation to the amount the organization's clients receive. Those organizations, at the same time, make no effort to
increase social output. Similarly, individual members of the US Congress, each
of whom represents only a tiny part of the society, have an incentive to seek
"pork" for their districts and political contributions from special-interest groups
rather than to concentrate on increasing the productivity of the nation. By contrast, the presidents in countries like the United States or France, or disciplined
political parties like the Conservative party in Great Britain or the Social Democratic party in Sweden, represent encompassing constituencies, and accordingly
have an incentive to try to bring about "peace and prosperity" and to limit the
social losses from struggles over how the social pie is sliced.

In the first decades after World War II, the dictators of the communist societies — and especially Stalin — had an exceptionally encompassing and secure
interest in the outputs of their domains (see Murrell and Olson 1991). Stalin
was, in effect, the owner of the Soviet Union. He therefore had an interest in the
productivity of his domain similar to the interest an owner of a firm has in maximizing the value of the firm's output. Stalin and some of his successors could
use a large portion of any increase in Soviet output to increase their military
power, international influence, and personal prestige. Since the claims that communism was the wave of the future and that the capitalist societies were destined
for the dustbin of history were strengthened by a rapid rate of growth, the leaders of the communist societies also had an incentive to use forced savings to
finance exceptionally high levels of investment.

Though the dictators and politburos of the Soviet-type societies were handi-
capped in their efforts to increase output by their aversion to markets, they were
able to use competition among subordinates and information on prices in pre-
revolutionary times to get some of the information needed to draw up coherent
plans. They used punishments as well as rewards to give subordinates an incentive to increase production in accord with the plans. So far as one can tell from
the best available data, such measures, in combination with exceptionally high
levels of saving and investment, gave the Soviet-type societies growth rates in
the early postwar period that were roughly comparable to those of the market
economies of Western Europe, even after allowing for the greater catch-up
potential arising from their low initial levels of income.

As time went on, subordinates in each industry, office, and region gradually
could overcome the difficulties of collective action and tacitly collude to keep
their superior from getting a full knowledge of how much they really could produce

with the resources available. This collusion made production quotas lower and subordinates' lives easier.[1] The aggregation of separate enterprises into super-monopolies also increased the difficulty for the center in using competition among subordinates to elicit information and increases in productivity. The passage of time also made the information from relative prices in pre-communist times less applicable. In fullness of time, the subordinates of subordinates could also collude in their own interest. Ultimately much of the power that had once been concentrated almost exclusively in the dictator was diffused throughout a "new class" of *apparatchiks,* and sometimes even to groups of workers in individual establishments.

Whereas a dictator like Stalin had an exceptionally encompassing interest in the productivity of the society, each coterie of subordinates engaging in tacit collective action in each industry, office, or locality had only a narrow interest. Each coterie would get only a trivial share of any increase in the national income and therefore would not share the dictator's incentive to increase the society's output. Thus over time the single most important incentive to increase output under the central plan in a Soviet-type economy — the encompassing interest of the dictator — became less potent, and the influence of *apparatchiks* without any incentive to be concerned about the output of the society became greater. In short, the Soviet-type societies were subject to a more severe if less blatant form of the "institutional sclerosis" that has been evident in the market democracies (Olson 1982).

As the foregoing theory predicts, the performance of the Soviet societies deteriorated over time. By the late 1960s and 1970s, the centrally planned economies, in spite of the large opportunities for catch-up growth that were still available, suffered slower and slower growth and ultimately began to fall further and further behind the market democracies of the West. This stagnation became even more serious in the 1980s.

For the most part, the reform or democratization that began with Gorbachev in 1985 and accelerated with the communist collapses of 1989 has not generated large and disciplined political parties or strong, democratically elected presidents. It has not, in other words, created encompassing interests that would have an incentive to extract the maximum productivity out of the state-owned industry and planning agencies that remain in the societies in transition. The coteries of managers and planners with their narrow special interests are often still in place and continue to have interests that are largely inconsistent with the advance and reform of the society. In every communist or lately communist society except China — where, because of the cultural revolution, the *apparatchiks*

---

[1]The reasons why collective action is difficult and time consuming, even when it does not have to be covert, are set out in *The Logic of Collective Action* (Olson 1965) and so will not be discussed here.

had been removed or humiliated — the planners have subverted decentralizing reforms and the managers have often excluded competitors (Winiecki 1990c). With the onset of democratization, an even larger number of narrow special interests has usually come to have influence.

This absence of encompassing interests in large part explains why the level of output is even lower in most of the societies in transition than it was under the old regime. The foregoing argument also suggests that the societies in transition should not expect that they will be able to carry out a well-planned sequence of gradual reforms over an extended period.

2 Primitive Trade

The theory that has just been set out should not be pushed too far. Some detailed features of the operation of the centrally planned economies suggest that this theory cannot be the whole of the story. If the encompassing interest of a totalitarian leader was sufficient by itself to explain the relatively good rates of growth of the centrally planned societies in the early post-war years, the planners would have had to go through some procedures that would ensure at least a moderate level of efficiency in the allocation of resources. In other words, they would have had to go through a process of optimization — they would somehow have had to use the information gathered through the process of bureaucratic competition to calculate a plan that was at least a faint approximation of an optimal allocation of resources. They would also have had to work out strong or "high-powered" incentives to encourage managers of enterprises to take the big risks that have to be taken to exploit the potential of new technologies and the advancement of knowledge in general.

It appears that the planners in the centrally planned economies did not do either of these things. In planning, they tended to use iterative procedures and endeavored to make the plans consistent and coherent, but they did not make the calculations necessary to provide any approximation to an optimal allocation of resources. They also did not, with their aversion to anything that closely resembled profit, work out schemes that would give innovators any significant fraction of the gains from risky innovation. The centrally planned economies therefore suffered from the risk-averse cover-your-tail behavior that is characteristically observed in bureaucracies without a profit motive.

Thus, though the communist dictators in the early period of communism had a powerful incentive to make their societies productive and did many things that did in fact increase production (like punish noncompliance and force extraordinarily high rates of saving and investment), they did not succeed in working out the procedures for getting efficient resource allocations or innovative enterprises. To explain the surprising rates of growth of the centrally planned economies in the first two decades after World War II, and even the maintenance or slow growth of output during the 1970s and 1980s, one needs not only to take account of the encompassing interests of the dictators, but also to bring in at least one other factor.

Surprisingly, this further factor making the Soviet-type societies produce as much and last as long as they did is also evident in primitive societies. In one respect that apparently has not been noted before, the Soviet-type societies were like the societies in the beginning of history. Consider the following observation from the ancient world, as described in the following passage from Herodotus's *The History:*

> "The Carthaginians also say that there is a place in Libya, and people living in it, beyond the Pillars of Heracles. When they, the Carthaginians, come there and disembark their cargo, they range it along the seashore and go back again to their boats and light a smoke signal. The natives, as soon as they see the smoke, come down to the shore and then deposit gold to pay for the merchandise and retreat again, away from the goods. The Carthaginians disembark and look; if they think the price deposited is fair for the merchandise, they take it up and go home again. If not, they go back to their boats and sit there. The natives approach and bring more gold in addition to what they have brought there already, until such time as the Carthaginians are persuaded to accept what is offered."

There was, of course, no court system or government in common between the Carthaginians and their trading partners to facilitate trade. But trade nonetheless took place. Indeed, it seems from Herodotus's account that this particular trade had even taken place often enough for signals to be recognized and certain procedures to have become customary. The parties probably expected to gain from similar trades in the future and thus found it in their interest to avoid anything that would prevent future trade. There are many other examples from many different cultures of this "silent trade," or transactions between individuals who have no government or institutions, and perhaps also no religion[2] or language, in common. There are, for example, even accounts of tribes at war that have nonetheless arranged some trades with each other through their women.[3]

One reason that some trade often takes place, even in the most difficult and primitive circumstances, is that the gains from trades are often huge. The gains from specialization and trade in the aggregate are so large that most of the world's population could not survive if none of these gains were realized (Olson 1984). **Some** of these gains can be realized immediately in on-the-spot

---

[2]Some schools of sociology in the West (and especially the school of thought descending from Talcott Parsons) have argued that markets will not exist unless a society has a prior consensus, often coming from a common religion, about basic values. The extensive evidence about trade across cultures, and especially between unrelated and at times even hostile tribes, contradicts this argument.

[3]See Grierson (1903).

transactions. Hence some trade takes place even across primitive societies. A moment's reflection about trades in primitive societies also reveals the cognition that there are many gains from trade that cannot be realized in circumstances such as those described by Herodotus. Surely the Carthaginians and the natives could not have worked out a long-term loan, no matter how much one party would have gained from borrowing even at high interest rates and no matter how much the other would have liked a high return on its capital. If one of the parties had wanted to buy insurance against an adverse contingency, or to buy something made-to-order from the other, he would again probably not have been able to work out the deal. The foregoing types of transactions presumably could not have been realized because the parties had no court and legal system to enforce the necessary contracts.

3   The Parable of Discreet Managers

The practical pertinence of this example from primitive conditions to a planned economy can perhaps best be shown through a parable. Consider a state firm, to be called enterprise One, in a modern planned economy. Suppose that this firm, though it wants more of most inputs, is unknowingly given more of input A by the planners than it really needs. At the same time the planners have not allocated it enough of input B so that it can safely meet its production quota. Enterprise Two, while similarly anxious to get more resources of most kinds, happens to have been given more of input B than it should have been given, but the planners have not understood that it must have more of input A. Each of the enterprise managers will, of course, have an incentive to argue to higher authorities that he has not been given enough of the particular input his enterprise needs most, but he will also have an incentive to argue that his enterprise needs more of almost everything (i.e. that it needs more of what would simply be called a larger budget in a society with an efficient market system). Given that each enterprise manager normally has an incentive to say his enterprise needs more inputs, neither can count on the planners accepting his argument, or being able to give him the needed input in time even when they do. Neither of the enterprise managers has an incentive to reveal to his superiors that he has been given a needlessly large allocation of any input.

In this case, if both managers can do so without being observed by higher authorities, each of them can sell the input that it has in surplus to the other, thereby solving both shortages. This deal will normally make the two managers better off, for each will have control over a more valuable bundle of inputs when he has traded his surplus input for another input which he badly needs. This type of trade will usually also make the planned economy work better, since the trade increases production by correcting a shortcoming in the design or implementation of the plan.

So common have trades of this type become that in the Soviet Union the Russian word *tolkach,* for pusher or expediter, is commonly used for the person who is sent out to barter for the needed resources. Even though illicit trades undercut the ideology, rationale, and laws of a planned economy, they become so obviously indispensable that they are often tacitly countenanced by higher officials.

The foregoing parable of trade by discreet managers and the evidence of trade by primitive peoples tell us that trade takes place in spite of the lack of institutions to facilitate it and often even in environments hostile to trade. Some trades are irrepressible because:

1. the gains from making them are substantial, if not colossal; and
2. some trades, and especially those that can be consummated on the spot, are essentially self-enforcing in that the interests of the parties are by themselves sufficient to make the transactions happen. This means that some trade can take place when there is no legal system to enforce contracts and sometimes even when the trade is illegal.

4   Large Gains from Trade in Bad Markets

The foregoing analysis also explains why markets have been so common in the centrally planned economies, even though these economies were set up on the principle that markets are fundamentally a means of exploitation of labor. The planned economies not only have many illicit, semi-licit, informal, and implicit markets, but also vast numbers of officially arranged markets. The importance of these markets is shown by the colossal number of officially approved prices. Soviet sources long before the Gorbachev era declare "that there are at least 10 million 'state' prices (excluding collective farm prices and prices for consumer cooperative commission sales for collective farms). In the industrial price 'reform' (*reforma*) of 1966-67, 'several million' new prices were established, and new price books totalling about 38,000 pages were published."[4] In addition, there are the prices of custom-made goods and agricultural goods grown on private plots (which are determined approximately the same way they are in the West). There is further evidence of how important fully legal markets have been in the Soviet-type economies in the fact they use money so extensively. If there were no markets, money would have no value and no one would want it.

It might be said that the huge number of markets and the ubiquitous use of money in the centrally planned economies is not significant since the prices in the officially sanctioned markets are normally set by the authorities at arbitrary levels, so that the markets do not perform the functions that they perform in

---

[4]Bornstein (1978, p. 467), quoting from various published Soviet sources. I am grateful to Peter Murrell for this information and reference.

capitalistic societies. In fact, this seemingly plausible objection is wrong. The centrally planned societies have all along been getting many of the benefits from markets that a Western society obtains even though their prices are usually distorted: most of the gains from trade can be realized even with prices that depart considerably from efficient levels.

Suppose that the price of the water were set arbitrarily at $10 a liter, which is obviously a huge multiple of the marginal cost of water. Irrational as such a price would be, most of the gains from the consumption of water would still be obtained. Most people would no longer water their lawns or wash their cars, but almost all would still buy enough water to maintain their health and quench their thirst: the water they would purchase would still yield most of the gains from trade in water.

More generally, suppose that a price in an officially sanctioned market in a centrally planned economy is set at such an irrational level that only half as much is traded as would be traded in an ideal competitive market. Even in such a case, most of the total gains from trade will usually be realized, because it is the most valuable trades — the ones that generate the largest social surplus — that will tend to occur. Since supply curves typically slope upward and demand curves downward, an arbitrary price that prevents half of the mutually advantageous trades from occurring will not normally eliminate anything like half of the gains from trade. The arbitrary price will certainly lead to some losses from queueing, retrading, or similar phenomena, and those losses are another reason why arbitrary prices are undesirable. If, as has usually been the case in Soviet-type societies, the officially fixed price is too low, there will be a waste of time waiting in line, but the buyers with the most urgent needs will usually be the first ones standing in the line or the ones who repurchase the good informally from those who are. The suppliers who can produce the good most cheaply are the ones who will have an incentive to produce and sell the good that is underpriced. Therefore, deplorable as officially fixed prices are, markets with such prices will often still obtain most of the gains from the use of markets.

These examples illustrate the second reason why the Soviet-type societies produced as much as they produced and lasted as long as they lasted. *Paradoxically, they performed as well as and survived as long as they did in part because of the many markets, legal and illegal, explicit and implicit, that they contained.* Just as the instinct for survival of primitive man enabled him to get some of the gains from trade, so the mother wit of the peoples of the planned economies enabled them to obtain huge gains from trade from the networks of contracts, swaps, deals, arrangements, reciprocal relationships, and black markets that they ingeniously (and usually informally) worked out. Though not all of the implicit and illicit transactions were socially desirable, many of them were indispensable for correcting the shortcomings in the state plans and for maintaining production in state enterprises.

5   The Law Makes Many Markets Possible

Great and unappreciated as the contribution of markets to the performance of the centrally planned economies has been, this contribution may be exaggerated, and an important lesson for the transition to a market economy may be missed, if one does not examine another feature of the parable of the discreet managers. Recall that these managers had an incentive to conceal their excess allocations of an input from higher authorities and to trade this excess input for something more valuable to them. Because unsanctioned trade and transactions that contravene the plan have normally been illegal in the centrally planned economies, the managers naturally found it advisable to be discreet about their swap. This meant, in turn, that neither was well placed to get the help of the "government" — the police, the courts, or the higher authorities — if the other did not fulfill his side of the bargain. Neither would have been wise to go the police when doing so would reveal that he had behaved illegally or at least concealed information from his superiors.

The two enterprise managers, knowing of this risk in advance, have an incentive to make only those deals that are self-enforcing. The gains from trade may be realized only when the two inputs can be traded simultaneously or when reputations will be at stake even though the deal is kept quiet. Trades that have to take place over a long period of time, or involve many parties, or are complex, are normally not feasible when there is no reliable and impartial mechanism to enforce the needed contracts.

Obviously, trading in the tacit, informal, grey, and black markets in a planned economy, in general, has the disadvantages described in this parable of trade by discreet managers. Some trades are so advantageous to both parties and so easy to enforce that they take place even when the parties cannot rely on the police or the courts; that is one reason why markets are so important even in planned economies. But many mutually advantageous trades — trades that must take place if a society is to realize its potential — do not take place because there is no reliable outside enforcement of the relevant contracts. In this respect, the markets of a planned economy are incomplete, unreliable, and even analogous to the trade of primitive peoples.

6   The Parable of the Self-Made Entrepreneur

One can get a quick appreciation of the social importance of trades that are not self-enforcing, and of the institutions that are needed to obtain the gains from other kinds of trades, from another parable: that of the "self-made entrepreneur". Suppose that a young man from a low-income family has no capital, but a lot of ambition, energy, and entrepreneurial ability. In the same society there are individuals with wealth, but some of them do not happen to have as much productive ability as our self-made entrepreneur. There are also old people with accumulated savings but not so much energy. Since the poor young man can get more productivity out of capital than his rich and elderly counterparts, he can afford to pay them more out of the income he could generate with their assets than they can earn when they employ these assets themselves. There is, therefore, a potential for mutually advantageous trade under which some of the accumulated resources of the rich and of the elderly are lent to the self-made businessman or invested as equity in a business he creates. Suppose that the best use of the capital is for the able, young man to construct a factory that will last for thirty years.

Such a transaction obviously makes no sense for the rich and the elderly unless they can be confident that the able young man will not just keep the money for himself. The harvest of the investment is earned over thirty years and no one can know that the young man will honor his promises for that long. Given that the transaction in question is not by any means self-enforcing, the young man will have little chance to raise the capital needed for his productive enterprise, unless he can ensure that he will be **required** to keep his promise over the thirty years. The requirement must be sufficient to persuade those with the capital that it is in their interest to invest in his enterprise. If the capital in question is to be put under the control of the young man, he and those with the capital must agree on a contract that each believes is in his interest and expect that this contract will be impartially enforced. Those with the capital may well insist that they hold a mortgage on the factory, or that a joint stock company be created in which they own most of the stock.

Those with capital also may not participate unless they have a secure right to sell the asset they obtain as a result of the transaction, whether it be the asset of the young man's promise to repay or the corporate stock of the company he manages. The elderly, for example, would not rationally lend money to or buy stock in a project that finishes paying off only after they are dead unless they expect that they can advantageously sell the loan or the stock at an earlier time. Thus all the institutions needed for an on-going and widely used capital market may be needed if some productive projects are to be financed.

Given the great risks and obligations the young man in the parable has to take on, it may not make sense for him — or for the lenders and investors — to proceed unless the pattern of institutions and government policies is fairly stable and predictable. Uncertainty about prices and other economic conditions is inevitable. If there is also a lot of institutional uncertainty, projects will proceed only if gigantic returns are expected.

To realize all the gains from trade, then, there has to be a legal system and political order that enforces contracts, protects property rights, carries out mortgage agreements, provides for limited liability corporations, and facilitates a lasting and widely used capital market that makes the investments and loans more liquid than they would otherwise be. These arrangements must also be thought likely to last for some time.

Without such institutions, a society also will not be able to reap the full benefits of a market in insurance, be able efficiently to produce those complex goods that require the cooperation of many people over an extended period of time, or be able to reap the gains from other multi-party or multi-period arrangements. Without the right institutional environment, a country will be restricted to those trades that are self-enforcing.

7   Individual Rights and Lasting Democracy Ensure More Gains from Trade

To realize the gains from complex transactions and those that take place over a long time, the individuals in a society not only need the freedom to trade, but also the right to establish secure title to property and to mortgage property. They must also have guaranteed access to impartial courts that will enforce the contracts they make. They also must have the right to create new forms of extended cooperation and organization, such as the joint-stock corporation.

They must, in short, have a broad and secure set of individual rights and freedoms. Individual rights and freedoms are often regarded as morally desirable but costly to economic performance — as a luxury that the less-developed countries, or countries in especially difficult situations, may need to do without. This error is as tragic as it is commonplace.

In fact, those gains from trade beyond those that primitive societies can obtain are often attainable only in environments where individual rights are both extensive and secure. It is no accident that the developed democracies with the best established individual rights are also the societies with the most sophisticated and extended transactions (such as those in futures markets or at Lloyds of London) for realizing the gains from trade. They are also the societies with the highest levels of per capita income.

The gains from trade in the Soviet-type societies were limited not only by their ideological antagonism to markets, but also by the dictatorial nature of their governments. If a country is totally under the control of a dictator, his subjects have only those rights that the dictator chooses to allow, and then only for so long as the dictator permits. Suppose that the dictator has an understanding of the gains from trade and recognizes that the economy he controls will be more productive, and his tax receipts therefore greater, if there is a market system. The dictator may then decide to respect individual property rights and to make sure that courts enforce contracts impartially. To encourage capital accumulation and economic growth and thereby increase tax collections, the dictator even has an incentive to promise to respect property and contracts at all times.

This promise cannot be fully credible. When the dictator is in an insecure situation or for any other reason has a short time horizon, he will often gain more from going back on his promise. In the short run, he can, for example, gain by refusing to honor his promises to pay back the public debt or by expropriating large holdings of property. Countless monarchs and dictators have done so throughout history. The limited credibility of a dictator's promise to respect contracts and property, and the inevitable uncertainty about succession in dictatorships, keeps some long-run trades that would have been advantageous to his subjects and to the society from taking place. There have, of course, been some dictators who have guarded the contract and property rights of their subjects and presided over rapid economic growth, but no country with a dictatorship has continued to attract capital from abroad the way that democracies like Switzerland, the United States, and the United Kingdom have.

As the failed *putsch* of August, 1991, in the Soviet Union reminds us, it is particularly unlikely that any dictatorship that emerges in the lately communist countries would credibly promise secure property and contract rights to its subjects. Though even those who might seek dictatorial power in the lately communist countries are aware that the centrally planned economies performed much less well than the market economies, their connections with the power centers of the old regimes and their intellectual backgrounds would probably keep them from being advocates of individual rights to property and contract enforcement. Nor are the peoples they would aspire to control be likely to believe any promises they made to respect individual rights.

8   Administrative Discretion

The societies in transition from a centrally planned economy also face another insidious and related problem. The centrally planned societies were not well-ordered, but they were, nonetheless, ordered societies. For all their faults they worked better than anarchies do. Apart from the primitive implicit and explicit markets, the main sources of order were the administrators and political leaders who led the regimes. Since the degree of order that arose from the primitive markets was relatively harder to understand and much less conspicuous than that which came from the hierarchies, it was only natural for many people to take it for granted that administrative and political leadership is the natural or inevitable source of order.

It was, moreover, political and administrative **discretion** that was the conspicuous source of order. Consider the admittedly extreme case of the Stalinist years. The leadership of Soviet-type regimes was not fundamentally constrained by laws or by the interpretations of an independent judiciary, since the judicial system was totally subordinate to the political leadership. Stalin himself was manifestly not controlled by the laws of the Soviet Union; he changed or ignored these laws whenever he liked. There was order under Stalin and his administrators, but not **law** and order.

Since the vast discretion available to the hierarchies of the Soviet-type societies was often used in ways that were not at all in the interest of the peoples in these societies, it is natural to attribute the poor results of these societies to defects of the personalities and ideologies of the political leadership and the *apparatchiks*. The main problem has seemed to be the misuse or abuse of the discretion available to political leader and the *nomenklatura* who manned his administrative hierarchy. By the same token, it seems natural to suppose that better political leaders with better ideas and different bureaucrats will lead to incomparably better results.

There is an element of truth in the suppositions that have just been described. But they are also partly false, as some of the difficulties of the transitions to market democracies demonstrate. One crucial defect of the centrally planned economies was the vast amount of discretion that was available to political leaders and administrators, not simply the misuse or abuse of that discretion.

Although, as Lord Acton said, power corrupts, and absolute power corrupts absolutely, this corruption is **not** the only problem. At least from the point of view of the society in transition to democracy, the more subtle and tenacious problem may be that political and administrative discretion generates needless uncertainty, makes individual planning by ordinary citizens more difficult, leaves individual rights less secure, and reduces the ability of the individuals in a society to reap the gains from the sophisticated transactions that coordinate interaction over many parties or many periods.

The more discretion the administrators have, the harder it is for those beneath them to plan and to realize the gains from the long term or multi-party coordination that complex contracts can permit, and the less efficient the economy may be. How can anyone know whether a given pattern of coordination of different individuals or enterprises, or a long-run deal between two or more parties, will be advantageous when the political leaders and governmental administrators have so much discretion that the rules and the rights of the separate parties are not clear?

9   Inherent Unpredictability

Another problem with the discretion that has been available to officials in Soviet-type societies is that neither the officials with the wide discretion nor anyone else has the foresight needed to make the right decisions about where resources should be invested in an economy. As the old saying goes, prophecy is very difficult, especially with respect to the future. Every investment entails some explicit or implicit prediction. Some people are worse at forecasting than others, often because they are not perceptive enough to know that they do **not** know the future and thereby fail to take into account as many possibilities as others do. But while some are worse at making prophecies than others, there is no one who can regularly make general and reliable forecasts. A modern economy, a wondrously complex system, converges toward a general equilibrium in all markets. Yet it almost always fails to reach equilibrium because it incessantly faces new opportunities and shocks. There is not even enough information to calculate the present situation of an economy with any detail or accuracy, much less its future position. The society as a whole is even more complex than the market economy, and there are the uncertainties of international relations as well.

Because uncertainties are so pervasive and unfathomable, the most dynamic and prosperous societies are those that try many, many different things. They are societies with countless thousands of entrepreneurs who have relatively good access to credit and venture capital, trying this and that and almost everything else. There is no way that a society can predict the future, but if it has a wide enough span of entrepreneurs able to make a broad enough array of mutually advantageous transactions, including those for credit and venture capital, it can cover a lot of the options — more than any single person or agency could ever think of.

At least when a society has the appropriate institutions and government policies, the overwhelming majority of the firms that make huge profits are doing a huge service to the population. In a society with the right institutions and public policies, the prevailing prices will approximate the true values and costs of marginal quantities of the goods and productive inputs. A great excess of revenues over costs means that the enterprise is almost certainly putting more value into the society than it is taking out.

10   The Importance of Luck

Since no one knows the future, a large part of the fortunes made and the losses suffered in a modern economy are explained by luck as much as by the strengths or failings of the entrepreneurs involved. Some of those who correctly celebrate the social importance of the entrepreneur, and emphasize that it is impossible to get the information needed to design a rational plan for an economy, fail to point out that many successful entrepreneurs who are their heroes have been successful at least partly because they have been lucky. By the same token, many of the unsuccessful have been unfortunate. One implication of this reality for the society in transition is that many of the newly established private enterprises, and some of the newly privatized firms, will (if there is a sufficient liberalization of the economy) make fortunes due more to luck than to the virtues or talents of the relevant entrepreneurs or managers. Some of the failures will similarly be due to bad luck.

In part because luck plays such a large role, there is some tendency to treat very high rates of profit as "unconscionable" and exceptional losses as social problems that a humane government should remedy. This thinking, in turn, often leads to subsidies to industries, enterprises, and localities that lose money at the expense of activities that generate a surplus. In the context of the economies in transition, these subsidies are part of what is called a "soft budget constraint".

At the level of **individuals,** covering some of the losses of the unfortunate from the windfalls of the lucky makes moral sense. In the market democracies, the private insurance market and social insurance mechanisms of the modern welfare state redistribute income toward the victims of bad luck. Some transfers of consumption from those who have the most to those who have the least can increase utility (see Olson 1986).

The pertinent point here is that subsidizing those **industries, firms, and localities** that lose money, **even if it is due solely to bad luck,** at the expense of those that make money, **even as a result of pure chance,** is typically disastrous for the efficiency and dynamism of an economy, in a way that transfers to poor individuals need not be. As mentioned above, if there is any rhyme or reason in the prevailing prices, the activities that are making exceptionally high returns are likely to be generating a social surplus, and those that are suffering exceptional losses are likely to be operating at a net loss to the society. Therefore, the value of a society's output will normally be much greater if some resources are shifted from the money-losing to the money-making activities. In a market economy with appropriate institutions, this shift will tend to be brought about automatically by the disparities in the returns. Any society that does not shift resources from the losing activities to those that generate a social surplus is irrational, since it is throwing away useful resources in a way that ruins economic performance without the least assurance that it is helping individuals with low incomes. A rational and humane society, then, will confine its distributional transfers to poor and unfortunate individuals.

It is only a modest exaggeration to say that in this respect the Soviet-type societies have followed exactly the opposite policies from the ones that they should have followed. They have usually not enacted national systems of progressive income taxation nor unemployment insurance nor many other national safety-net programs that the welfare states of the West have had. They have relied in large part on the socialized enterprises for welfare services. They have, on the other hand, transferred huge amounts of resources from profitable activities to those industries, enterprises, and localities whose output was not valuable enough to cover the costs of the resources they utilized. What explains this striking difference between the Soviet-type societies and the market democracies?

countries, there are extensive institutional mechanisms to protect individual rights that normally limit the extent to which governmental discretion can be used to prevent the changes in returns and the resource reallocations needed for an efficient and dynamic economy. If individual rights are sufficiently extensive, political and administrative discretion is inevitably limited to some extent.

Suppose there is a large unexpected increase in demand for the economist's favorite hypothetical product, widgets. Most people in a long-established democracy with markets realize that if Jones happens to be manufacturing widgets when the boom in demand for widgets occurs, then Jones is probably just lucky. But if Jones has acquired his widget factory legally, he will still have a **right** to the factory's extra profits. This right will be recognized by the courts and protected by the police. To the extent that individual rights keep the government from capturing the returns in exceptionally profitable enterprises, they also leave the government with less resources to dissipate on enterprises that are a drain to the society.

The strength of individual rights in long-standing democracies is, therefore, a major explanation of the toleration by these democracies of large variations in short-run rates of return across firms, industries, and localities. This toleration is indispensable for a dynamic and prosperous economy. It provides an incentive for the reallocation of resources from activities where resources produce lower rates of return to where they earn higher rates of return and thereby generates a more nearly rational allocation of society's resources across activities. It also provides the incentive that makes firms and individuals undertake the inherently risky entrepreneurship that is needed for the advance of technology and productivity.

The wide latitude for official discretion and the concomitant lack of individual rights that characterized the Soviet-type societies, and the fact that these rights have not yet been unambiguously established in the societies in transition, also help explain poor economic performance. Individuals do not have secure and unambiguous rights to most of the assets in Soviet-type societies. Even assets that are supposed to be privately owned are by no means always unambiguously and securely owned. The traditionally wide latitude for official discretion, the relatively slight role for law, and the neglect of individual rights under the Soviet-type arrangements has meant that the individuals' rights to ownership of assets are by no means always clear. They are often still unclear in the societies in transition.

The word "privatization," widely used as it may be, is accordingly ambiguous in the recently communist societies: the institutional arrangements that protect and guarantee private rights are in doubt, so privatization does not have the clear meaning that it has in the mature democracies of the West.

It would also now be much too simple to say that the state "owns" most of the assets. In the days of Stalin, it was meaningful in the Soviet Union to say that the state owned the assets of the society because Stalin had relatively complete control over them; in effect, he owned them. But, for the reasons set out at the beginning of this chapter, much of the power over these assets has with the passage of time and collective action by coteries of subordinates shifted away from the center. As time has gone on, the number of people with some claim upon and influence over each "state-owned" asset has become larger and larger. The center, the ministries, and the planning offices still share some authority over state-owned assets, but so does the manager, the workers, the suppliers, the creditors, the principal customers, the other firms in the industry, and the local government in which the enterprise is located. The tradition of using the enterprise as the provider of much of the social insurance that in the West is the responsibility of welfare and unemployment insurance offices has jumbled the rights to enterprises even further. With the arrival of democracy, the number of people with some claim to the ownership of state-owned assets has expanded to the entire population, but the partial ownership of the managers, workers, etc. has not been eliminated.

The lack or the jumbling of individual rights means that it is not clear who has control over assets or the claim to what is produced with them. No one, then, has an incentive to make the most of the assets. In addition, the absence of any clear and socially enforced individual claims to the yield of assets that generate exceptional returns means that these returns are fair game for being divided among all the claimants. In part because it is recognized that chance has played a role in determining which enterprises are making or losing money, the claims of "needy" enterprises, industries, and localities will usually be given greater credence than the claims of those who are already doing well.

The paucity and jumbling of individual rights is, therefore, the main explanation of the "soft budget constraints" in the societies that have had to endure Soviet-type arrangements. The absence and ambiguity of individual rights also helps explain why the Soviet-type societies have had to rely mainly on innovations from abroad. If contract and property rights are not secure and well-defined, how can the entrepreneur be confident he will be rewarded for undertaking the investment and risk needed for innovation?

12   A Recapitulation

This chapter began with the obvious fact that the economy in transition is a mix of the remnants of the old regime and of new markets. It suggests that an understanding of the sources of productivity of both parts of this mix is necessary. While the ways in which markets generate productivity have, in a general way, been understood, the motive forces of a planned economy with state enterprise have not been. The intellectual challenge, then, is to understand why the Soviet-type economies produced as much as they produced and lasted as long as they did.

There are two main sources of growth in Soviet-type economies. The first is the encompassing interest of a totalitarian leader who will be able to use a large part of any increase in the output of his domain to achieve his own objectives. This motive force was important in the early postwar years when the leader could rely on bureaucratic competition for the information and energy needed to increase the output of the economy, but, as time has gone on, collective action by coteries of subordinates reduced the power of the center. Each coterie has only a narrow special interest and does not have an incentive to be concerned about the output of the society as a whole. And, as time has gone on, the economic performance of the Soviet-type economies has therefore deteriorated. Though certain democratic political arrangements can also establish an encompassing interest, the democratic developments in Eastern and Central Europe and the Soviet Union, for the most part, have not succeeded in doing this.

In most cases there is no center of power with a sufficiently encompassing interest to make the system of planning and state enterprise work coherently and efficiently. Planning and state enterprise tend to work even less well under most democratic arrangements than under totalitarian control. This weakening of the encompassing interest of the center in large part explains why output has fallen in most of the societies in transition. From the foregoing, one can conclude that the chance that the democratic governments of the societies in transition will be able to succeed in any protracted and carefully sequenced transition is small.

The second source of productivity in the Soviet-type societies was, paradoxically, the many markets, both explicit and implicit, in these societies. In many cases the gains from trade are large and can be realized with on-the-spot transactions and often even when the trade is illegal. Many of the gains from markets can also be realized with distorted prices. Many of the gains from trade cannot, however, be attained through spot transactions. They require legal and governmental institutions that guarantee, among other things, individual rights to impartial enforcement of contracts and to property. The order in Soviet-type societies came from administration — from official discretion — rather than from the rule of law. These societies have been woefully lacking in individual rights.

In the absence of well-defined individual rights, the incentive to maximize the output of assets is missing, since the control over assets and the rights to the harvests they yield are unclear. Because the future is unknowable, economic progress for a society requires that many different risks be taken. In the short run, luck is an important determinant of the rate of return to activities and individuals. In part because of the importance of luck, there is a natural tendency in societies to redistribute resources from winners to losers. Such transfers to needy individuals can be socially rational, but transfers to socially unprofitable activities or enterprises cannot be. Well-defined individual rights to assets and impartial enforcement of contracts make it less likely that the returns to highly profitable activities will be diffused to socially unprofitable enterprises. Without well-defined individual rights, "privatization" is a somewhat misleading word, since the rights to and the control over that which is allegedly private are unclear.

13   The Hidden Path to A Successful Economy

The argument in this chapter suggests that there is a hidden, or at least not widely recognized, path to a successful economy. It has often been assumed that individual rights, while desirable on moral grounds, are more likely to be a hindrance than a source of economic development; they are a luxury that the most prosperous countries can afford, rather than one of the causes of the prosperity of these countries. This is the opposite of the truth. It is no accident that the most prosperous societies are also those with the institutions that provide the greatest individual rights.

The path to development that emphasizes the institutions needed for individual rights is especially relevant for the societies in transition from Soviet-type arrangements. The citizens of these societies want democracy, and democracy (while it tends to reduce the output of a planned economy) is the only form of government that has been able to preserve individual rights over the very long run. In the communist past, individual rights were almost nonexistent and there is a demand now for these rights that is independent of the contribution they make to development.

While decisions about how government-owned assets should be divided among the citizenry are inherently controversial and divisive, there is no inherent conflict of interest in giving every individual in the society secure individual rights. The dangers of the conflicts of interest inherent in privatization argue that a society will be better off if it can get through this process as quickly as possible. Nonetheless, creating the institutions needed for an effective private sector is not only something that logically precedes privatization, but it may also be something that can be obtained with less social conflict. It should, accordingly, have the top priority.

To take the individual-rights path to development, the societies in transition should begin by making certain that their citizens have clear and secure property rights and the fullest rights to draw up contracts enforceable by an impartial judiciary whose tenure does not depend upon which party is in power. In more general and familiar language, they should establish institutions that give individuals the maximum rights that they can have without infringing on the like rights of others.

The crucial objective of helping low-income people and mitigating extreme inequalities of income should be met through **general** anti-poverty programs and progressive and uniform income or expenditure taxes that take no account of the industry or occupation or locality of those helped or taxed. In other words, the compassion and the desire to mitigate inequality should be served through programs that are as neutral and predictable as possible, not by programs that jumble individual property and contract rights. The use of political and administrative discretion or aid to unprofitable industries or depressed occupations or *ex post facto* changes in the rules of the game should be avoided at all costs because they take away and dissipate some of the gains of those lines of activity that happen for a time to offer especially high returns. The firms that are privatized should be given unambiguous property rights, and the rights of these firms should not be changed because they make high profits or because they go bankrupt.

With well-defined rights, the societies in transition will ensure that every asset is unambiguously controlled by someone with a strong incentive to use that asset as productively as possible. They will also capture the gains from sophisticated as well as primitive trade. Finally, they will reduce the danger that activities that produce a social surplus will be penalized to subsidize and expand those that take more value out of the society than they put back in.

5 Organization as Property: Economic Analysis of Property Law Applied to Privatization

Robert D. Cooter

Most production in capitalist countries occurs in organizations, which come in many forms, such as corporations and partnerships. Private property and capitalism ideally provide a framework for competition among them. The most productive organizations should flourish in a capitalist environment and the less productive forms should disappear. In practice, however, fundamental differences in organization, especially in the way leaders are chosen and dismissed, result from differences in law and public policy. For example, management in public corporations faces the possibility of a hostile take-over in America, but not in Germany or Japan. The difference is a consequence of law, not competition. This observation raises questions about the limits of competition. Are private property and capitalism incomplete until law and policy favor particular forms of business organization? Or can private property and capitalism provide a neutral framework for competition among enterprises with different forms of organization? This chapter seeks to answer these questions in section 1 by explaining the concept of property as developed in the economic analysis of law, and then relating property to markets and organizations concluding that imperfections in markets for corporate control preclude pure neutrality of the law.

In section 2 this conclusion is applied to the privatization process in the post-communist countries. They must develop a legal framework for corporate control by choosing among alternative models such as those offered by America, Germany, and Japan, or developing their own hybrid. This chapter suggests some guidelines for the law. Section 3 discusses the legal process to assess the prospects that privatization will yield good laws.

The author thanks Chris Clague for comments on an earlier draft. Support from the Center for Institutional Reform and the Informal Sector is gratefully acknowledged.

1   A Pure Property Regime

Property is the institution that gives people discretion over scarce resources. Discretion is created by assigning rights to owners and prohibiting others from interfering with their exercise. Rights convey upon owners the legal power to act or forbear without imposing the obligation to do either. The owner is not legally bound to answer to others, whether private persons or public officials, concerning how he exercises his property rights, unless he has voluntarily assumed such obligations by contract. By surrounding the owner with discretion, property creates a zone of privacy within which he can do as he pleases.[1]

The phrase, "a pure property regime," refers to a body of law that creates full and complete rights of ownership and protects them from interference. A conventional list of full and complete property rights includes the right to use, consume, deplete, destroy, improve, develop, transform, sell, donate, bequeath, mortgage, or lease the resource. Full and complete protection from interference by private persons or governments includes prohibitions against trespass, invasion, theft, destruction, nuisance, pollution, flooding, unauthorized use, appropriation, expropriation, takings, and nationalization. Violation of the owner's rights might result in liability for past harm, injunction against future recurrences, or criminal punishment.

1.1   Principle of constrained maximum discretion

How large should the owner's zone of discretion be? An owner enjoys the most discretion justifiable purely within a framework of liberty when he can do anything with his resources that does not harm others. In economic terms, the law maximizes the owner's discretion subject to the constraint that its exercise does not cause harm to anyone. This proposition is called the principle of constrained maximum discretion. As defined in liability law, "harm" encompasses pain, fear, injury, or loss of income or wealth. Causing harm is a necessary condition for legal liability in most circumstances and it is a sufficient condition in some circumstances ("strict liability"). The attribution of causation is problematic because people and nature form a complex ecology of interdependence. In such a world, the definition of "not harming others" is not purely technical and partly normative. Social and legal norms stipulate what counts as causing harm to others.

To illustrate, charging a monopoly price harms buyers and often results in liability under antitrust law. In contrast, bidding down the price of a good harms competing suppliers without ordinarily resulting in liability. The relevant legal norms for ascertaining harm and liability are formalized in the law of property,

---

[1]The relationship between property and liberty is an old theme in political philosophy. A thorough bibliography and critical discussion is in Underkuffler (1990).

torts, contracts, crimes, and other bodies of law, such as antitrust and regulation. Property is thus imbedded in a larger normative framework.

1.2 Efficiency of a pure property regime

Property serves a variety of purposes. First, it constitutes a significant aspect of liberty. As an aspect of liberty, property is important for its own sake, independent of its effect. Second, property helps to preserve liberty by decentralizing power and resisting tyranny. One of its effects is the preservation of all the other forms of liberty. Third, property promotes efficiency. The latter is within the focus of this chapter. The law pertaining to property ideally internalizes the effects of using resources. To achieve internalization, property law assigns to the owner the immediate benefits and costs from using a resource. Sometimes the use of a resource causes spillovers such as pollution of air, reduction of light, or contamination of water. Nuisance law assigns liability for spillovers to the owner of the resource that causes them. Similarly, risks are sometimes imposed upon others by, say, driving cars, blasting rocks, serving food that can spoil, or selling potentially defective products. When these risks materialize, the law of torts may assign liability for the resulting harm to the owner of the resource that caused it.[2] Property law thus satisfies the principle of rectification by making people bear the cost of the harm that they do to others.

The law of nuisance and torts can be viewed as a mechanism for internalizing costs. When internalization is perfect, all the costs and benefits from using property enter the decision calculus of a self-interested owner. Assigning the net benefits of resource use to its owner gives him an incentive to maximize them. Maximizing the net benefits from resource use requires enterprise and innovation. Internalization is thus both efficient and fair.

Besides internalization, property law promotes efficiency by channelling transactions into voluntary exchange. Much of microeconomic theory since Adam Smith is built upon the insight that trade usually benefits everyone who engages in it, and competitive markets maximize the total surplus from trade. Property law promotes trade, first, by providing clear and secure definition of ownership rights. To illustrate, a public registry of deeds assures the purchasers of real estate that their title is clear. Conversely, obscure or insecure ownership rights burden exchange with high information costs and heavy risk discounting.

Similarly, contract law promotes trade by reducing coordination costs. Coordination becomes problematic when exchange of value is not simultaneous. The party who delivers value first runs the risk that the other party will not reciprocate

---

[2]Causing harm is almost always necessary for liability (vicarious liability is the exception). If causing harm is sufficient for liability, the rule of law is said to be "strict liability". In contrast, liability under a negligence rule requires the injurer to cause the harm and also to be at fault.

as promised. In the event of a breach of contract, the standard legal remedy is either to make the promisor perform as promised ("specific performance"), or to make the promisor pay compensation at a level that leaves the promisee just as well off as if the promise had been kept ("expectation damages"). Contract law, thus, overcomes the reluctance of the promisee to advance value by guaranteeing that he will enjoy the expected benefit of the bargain. The preceding remarks about trade and law are succinctly summarized in the technical language of economics. Economists lump together information costs, risk discounting, and coordination costs into the general category of "transaction costs". Thus, it can be said that the law pertaining to property ideally promotes trade by minimizing the transaction costs of exchange.

1.3   Mixed property regimes

The pure property regime sketched above has never been realized historically. In some respects, the closest approximation was achieved in the second half of the nineteenth century in Britain and America when politics was dominated by the philosophy of liberalism. In this period, voters rejected most forms of regulation of the market, so interference was minimal. Nevertheless, law in the period fell short of the ideal of a pure property regime in two respects.

First, many social costs were externalized, including pollution, hazards from defective consumer products, and spillovers from real estate development without town planning. In America and Britain, manufacturers were shielded from consumer suits by the legal doctrine that the consumers' contract was with the retailer ("privity of contract"), not the manufacturer. Polluters and others who harmed many people a little and no one a lot ("public bads") were shielded from liability by the absence of class action suits or regulations. Town planning in the rapidly expanding cities required a regulatory framework that was absent in nineteenth century America and Britain and still seems inadequate today, especially in America. Second, the public in this period had little recourse against exploitation by private monopolies, including monopolies in financial markets. Judges did not fill the gaps in legislation by extending common law doctrines or interpreting existing statutes sufficiently to protect against monopoly. Antitrust laws were not enacted in America until the end of the nineteenth century. These defects in the nineteenth century liberal state came under increasing criticism in the late nineteenth and early twentieth centuries from progressives, populists, and socialists. The more modest reformers wanted zoning and public health ordinances, safety in the work place, job security, worker's benefits, and recognition of labor unions, while extremists wanted a social revolution ending in socialism or communism. In America, the nineteenth century liberal state was brought to a decisive end in the 1930s when Roosevelt's New Deal introduced extensive regulations and restrictions on property owners. The story of how law changed is worth re-telling because it illuminates the connection between property and constitutions.

American courts have arrogated to themselves the power to review federal and state statutes to determine whether or not they conform to the constitution. An amendment to the US Constitution states that the government cannot take property from its owner except for a public purpose and with full compensation. In addition, American courts have found in the constitution the right of citizens to contract freely with each other. These constitutional rights protect the owners of property from expropriation by majority vote of the citizens.

Whether these rights are interpreted broadly or narrowly by courts determines the extent to which legislatures can regulate property without violating the constitution. In the early years of this century, the US Supreme Court vigorously protected property rights by striking down as unconstitutional those statutes that limited freedom of contract. The symbol of this approach is the 1905 case of Lochner v. New York (198 US 45, 1905), where the Supreme Court struck down a New York statute prohibiting employers from requiring or permitting bakers to work for more than sixty hours a week. In a similar decision in 1923, the Supreme Court invalidated a minimum wage statute for women and children (Adkins v. Childrens Hospital: 261 US 525, 1923).

In the Lochner era, the courts "constitutionalized contracts," meaning that regulations passed by the majority in legislatures to control the terms of contracts were often judged to violate the individual's constitutional rights. The rejection of this tradition marks a turning point in American constitutional history. By 1937 the Supreme Court repudiated Lochner by upholding a minimum wage law for women (West Coast Hotel v. Parrish: 300 US 379, 1937). Subsequently the court reversed its previous rulings and upheld many new regulations of contracts favored by President Roosevelt, thus ending the Lochner era.

The American constitution guarantees both human rights and property rights. Before the New Deal, the courts vigorously protected property rights but neglected human rights as currently conceived. In the years after the second world war, the Supreme Court reversed itself. Human rights were aggressively protected, especially in such areas as racial discrimination, freedom of speech, freedom of religion, and "due process" (the right not to be harmed by government actions which are illegal). In this same period, the court permitted a wide interference by government with property rights in the form of zoning laws, regulation of industry and contracts, and redistributive taxation. Especially relevant to this chapter are regulations enacted in the field of finance. After Roosevelt's New Deal, commercial banks could not own industrial companies, and the ability of other financial institutions to do so was curtailed. Thus commercial banking was separated from investment banking.

Beginning in the 1930s, regulation of property in America and Britain went far beyond cost internalization or control of monopolies. Instead of a pure property regime, the capitalist democracies have a mixed regime of regulated property. Some laws imposed burdensome regulations that redistributed wealth to politically favored groups. Other laws addressed real market failures, like environmental pollution and urban sprawl, but employed clumsy policies that raised the cost of public goods, like clean air and town planning, so that people demanded too little of them.

A general critique of the mixed economy, however, is not this chapter's aim. Instead, the focus is on industrial organization and corporate leadership. The stock market is often called capitalism's heart but is more accurately called its brains, because it directs the allocation of resources among alternative uses.

In every country this market is regulated by law. Section 2 explains why regulation of capital and corporate control is an inevitable part of contemporary capitalism. Understanding this fact is essential to guiding the process of privatization in the formerly communist countries. However, regulation of capital markets tends to go far beyond what is inevitable or necessary. Inappropriate and burdensome regulations tend to proliferate in capital markets, as in so many other markets. For example, regulations ostensibly protecting executives from hostile takeovers have proliferated in America just as much as laws ostensibly protecting workers.

2   Organization as Property

Property law promotes economic efficiency in two ways, specifically by internalizing net benefits of resource use and minimizing the transaction costs of trade. These two efficiency mechanisms apply, not just to natural resources, but also to the organization of enterprises. The relationship of property law to organization is subtle and confusing, so detailed explanation is needed. Any organization can own property, as when a corporation owns real estate. In addition, some organizations can **be** property, as when J. Paul Getty owns the Getty Oil Company. Sole proprietorships, partnerships, and closely-held corporations are pure property. Property in this sense is a **form** of organization. To be property, an organization must have a form that gives someone discretion over it. Discretion is conveyed by a full and complete set of rights as listed above including the right to use, improve, develop, transform, reorganize, deplete, destroy, sell, donate, bequeath, mortgage, or lease the organization. Owning an organization as pure property is much the same as owning a toothbrush, a farm, a song, a patent, or an oil well, because a pure property regime allows owners full discretion to do what they want with their property.

Organizations that cannot be property can own it. Thus a cooperative or government can own property such as real estate and machinery, which form the material base of production, or it can own patents, trademarks, and copyrights, which form the information base for production and marketing. Furthermore, a cooperative or government can make contracts with sellers, buyers, and employees. The property of a cooperative or government can be sold and the contractual rights can be assigned. But an organization is not its assets, just as a person is not the property that he owns. Cooperatives and governments cannot be sold because they are not themselves property.

To understand why some organizations can be property and others cannot, the general idea of an organization — its definition and terms — must be explained. From a sociological viewpoint, an organization is a structure of offices and roles capable of corporate action. An office is a job with legal powers and obligations explicitly attached to it. The fundamental offices in a business organization are usually defined and powers are allocated to them in a constitutional document such as a corporate charter. The organization's constitution also stipulates how to make operating rules.

Much of the activity of the organization follows informal practices, not formal rules laid down in its constitution or operating rules. The informal practices are organized around roles formed by shared expectations about the division of labor. To illustrate, the accountant's role includes keeping the books, and the secretary's role includes transcribing reports. The people who perform roles often have employment contracts, but the contracts do not explicitly state in detail what the employees' powers and duties are.

Offices and roles can be structured to direct peoples' efforts toward common goals, whose pursuit constitutes corporate action. To facilitate corporate action in a business organization, offices and roles are usually arranged hierarchically. Information flows up the hierarchy, and orders flow down it. Hierarchical structure gives the organization the capacity to act quickly and decisively. Some businesses have departed from the traditional hierarchical model and formed decentralized networks. Such a network remains a single organization so long as it retains the capacity for corporate action. If this capacity is lost, the network is best described as a relationship among different organizations.

Inside an organization, people have offices and roles that coordinate their behavior. Outside the organization, goods are exchanged in markets, and behavior is coordinated by prices. Thus, the boundary of an organization is formed by the markets in which it operates. To illustrate, the Ford Motor Company needs tires for its automobiles. Ford could go outside its organization and buy tires on the market from another manufacturer. Alternatively, Ford could establish a subsidiary to manufacture tires. Production in a subsidiary keeps the activity within the same organization.

When an organization is pure property, the owner has the legal right to choose its goals. In addition, the owner can restructure its offices and roles to suit his own ends. Thus the owner can transform, dissolve, merge, or sell the organization in whole or part. In a corporation or partnership, these ownership rights are conveyed by the organization's constitutional document and by applicable law. In a cooperative or government, which is not property, ownership rights are suppressed by the organization's constitution and applicable laws, which limit any individual's discretionary power over the organization.

As explained, property conveys discretion on the owner to do as he pleases with it. An alternative is to vest power in a group of people acting collectively. To illustrate, the members of a cooperative usually determine how to use its assets by majority vote. When several parties must participate in a decision, a problem of governance exists. Thus, the alternative to property in organizations is politics. Property is a form of individual choice, while non-property control of resources is usually a form of collective choice.

The economic advantage of an organization having an owner is the same as for any other resource. Specifically, ownership aligns incentives for effort and risk-taking by internalizing benefits and costs of resource use. The same person — the owner — determines the organization's structure and also enjoys the resulting profits or suffers the resulting losses. In addition, only organizations that are property can be bought and sold. Trade in organizations, like trade in toothbrushes or coal mines, usually creates a surplus. Empirical research on the stock market indicates a substantial surplus from buying companies.[3] The surplus often arises from replacing inferior management, cutting unprofitable product lines, and re-arranging industrial structure to take advantage of complementarities and synergies. The sale of an organization redeploys its resources very quickly enabling rapid adjustment to changes in technology and demand.

There are also disadvantages of organizational property. Concentrating benefits and costs in an individual focuses risk, while risk spreading may be more efficient. In addition, the owner's discretion over the organization may undermine the loyalty of its members, as will be explained later. An advantage of governance over property concerns norms. An old tradition in Western thought, called contractarianism, holds that law's authority comes from the consent of the people to whom it applies. Consent is more likely to result in voluntary or enthusiastic compliance rather than evasion or grudging compliance. A system of governance in an organization generates consent and creates effective norms better than a system of ownership. So property and non-property forms of organization each have their advantages and disadvantages.

2.1 Property as framework for competition

Organizations compete for money and members. Ideally, organizations should flourish that are judged best by the people who decide where to invest and what to join. The law should be neutral in this competition. To achieve neutrality, the law declares that organizations are "legal persons" and formulates property law in terms of the rights and obligations of people. An owner ideally has the same property rights over material resources whether it is an individual, family,

---

[3]The acquiring firm usually pays a premium, and the higher stock price persists after the acquisition while the acquiring firm's stock price remains largely unchanged. See Jensen and Ruback (1989).

clan, tribe, partner, stockholder, cooperative, corporation, collective, foundation, pension fund, bank, or government. Thus, a pure property regime takes no interest in the identity of owners.

Indifference of law over owners' identity helps create a neutral legal framework. To understand why, contrast property that is actively traded, such as toothbrushes and trucks, with property that seldom changes owners, such as Rembrandt's paintings. If the market for organizations is active, they change owners from time to time becoming the subsidiary first of one company and then another. In inactive markets, organizations persist for long periods of time as the property of the same legal person, such as a large holding company.

Active markets are needed for competition. An important question of public policy toward any market concerns the legal framework needed to sustain competition. In the most favorable circumstances, law sustains competition merely by defining and enforcing property rights. An industry is naturally competitive when the efficient scale of production is small relative to demand for the industry's product. In the absence of collusion, a naturally competitive industry is very active, and it has too many buyers and sellers for any one of them to influence prices. Alternatively, a natural monopoly exists when competition extinguishes itself, because economies of scale are large relative to demand, so that the largest producer always has the lowest costs.[4]

Unfortunately, a market for large organizations inevitably has at least two elements of natural monopoly. First, potential buyers may hesitate to purchase an organization unless they possess the technical knowledge required to manage it. To illustrate, primary candidates to acquire a failing airline are other airlines, and there are few airlines in many markets. Second, potential buyers of large organizations are limited to those who can assemble sufficient capital, and capital markets are notoriously imperfect. Lending necessarily involves asymmetrical information and moral hazard, which are inconsistent with perfect competition.

Policy makers often face a trade-off between monopoly power in markets for products and organizations. To illustrate, if the antitrust authorities allow one airline to acquire another, competition decreases in the market for airline travel. If the antitrust authorities forbid one airline from acquiring another, competition decreases in the market for airline companies. Similarly, if the antitrust authorities allow small banks to merge or collaborate to finance the purchase of large companies, competition may decrease in the market for financial services. Conversely, if the banking industry is fragmented by law as in the United States, few buyers exist for large organizations.

---

[4]Borrowers usually know more about their credit-worthiness than lenders (asymmetrical information), and borrowers may take excessive risk with the creditor's money (moral hazard).

2.2   Biased frameworks

The element of natural monopoly partly accounts for inactivity in markets for organizations, but contract and law are also important. To see why, recall that a pure property regime allows the owner to do anything with the resource that does not harm others. The constraint of not harming others becomes problematical when the property is an organization staffed by people. People in an organization, unlike a toothbrush or coal mine, have legal and moral rights, and their interests and welfare are matters of public concern.

Restructuring an organization and re-targeting its goals directly affect the welfare of its members. People care about the offices and roles assigned to them. They want good, secure jobs. To achieve job security, the current holders of jobs seek to limit the rights of the owners to restructure the organization. Ownership rights over organizations are typically circumscribed and regulated rather than full and complete.

The limits most familiar to the public concern the protection of workers. Less familiar, but no less important to productivity, are the protections for directors and managers. While the variety of executive protections from one country to another is vast, a few examples merit mention. A vivid American example is the so-called "golden parachute". This phrase refers to generous severance pay guaranteed to executives if they lose their jobs in a hostile takeover of the company. The severance pay can be large enough to deter corporate raiders.

In Germany, corporate charters of large firms often contain a "5 percent" rule, which stipulates that no single stockholder can have more than 5 percent of the votes, even if he owns more than 5 percent of the stock. As a consequence of this rule, German banks enjoy secure control over many German companies. Control is secured by virtue of the fact that owners leave stocks on deposit at the banks, and the banks have the right to vote them. Thus, the banks, unlike other large investors, have more than 5 percent of the votes in the companies (Baums 1990). German banks almost never relinquish control over their client-corporations.

In Japan, job security is more a matter of role than contract. The corporate culture favors employment for life including managers. The main bank and the network of suppliers, who together own a controlling share of the corporation's stock, may shunt unsuccessful management aside in the corporate hierarchy but will not fire them. Selling an organization is perceived as disloyal to its members (Sheshido 1991).

In these three examples, limits on dismissing executives are imposed by contract or custom. These private agreements reduce the level of activity and competition in the market for organizations by increasing the cost and difficulty of restructuring and selling them. In addition to private agreements, limits on the market for organizations are usually imposed by law. To illustrate by an American example, the Williams Act requires someone who purchases 5 percent of the stock of a company to announce that fact publicly and to delay further purchases for a specified period of time.

Adam Smith observed that, monopoly being more profitable than competition, businessmen can seldom talk together without conspiring against the public. Are the agreements and laws protecting executives conspiracies against the public? This question has no simple answer. To illustrate, a "golden parachute" can be legitimate severance pay that enables a company to hire the most able managers, or it can be an insidious device for protecting inferior managers from competition. In spite of this complexity, a simple fact provides some guidance to law and policy. Executives are not a class of people who need the state's paternalistic protection. They have the knowledge and power to negotiate protection for themselves by private agreement. A strong argument, therefore, exists against any laws or regulations ostensibly protecting executives or otherwise impeding the market for organizations on behalf of executives. Executive protection should arise from private agreement, never from law.

A more difficult question concerns whether law should refuse to enforce, or actively suppress, private agreements to protect executives. Should such agreements be suppressed by antitrust law on the grounds that they are conspiracies to restrain trade? The question is complicated because private constraints in markets for organizations can promote efficiency. Efficiency is promoted when security induces loyalty and effort as the next section suggests.

2.3 Separation of profits and power

When an organization is pure property, someone ideally possesses full discretion over it and also internalizes the net benefits of its use. To illustrate, power and responsibility are joined in a family business where the sole proprietor makes the decisions and absorbs the profits or losses. In modern capitalism, however, it is uneconomic for the owners of flourishing businesses to finance expansion internally. Funds must shift rapidly from one large organization to another in response to the market's creative destruction. To acquire funds quickly, corporations must sell bonds or stocks. A corporation that sells stock to the public is not wholly the property of the people who run it. In public corporations, sale of stock to the general public fragments and distributes the bundle of rights constituting ownership.

To understand fragmentation, consider the public corporation's governance. The stockholders are usually entitled to one vote per stock on matters of central importance to the corporation including the choice of its directors. The directors, in turn, appoint management and approve policies. In closely held companies, a single person or small group of associates owns enough stock to control the election of directors. Secure control of small companies requires owning 51 percent of the shares. Control may be achieved in large companies by owning a much smaller percent.

Collective choice theorists sometimes define the "power" of a vote as the probability that it will be decisive. To illustrate, each vote is powerful in a close election between two candidates, and each vote has little power in a landslide victory by one candidate. The power of a vote belonging to the controlling block of a company is high while the power of a vote by a minority shareholder is nil. Controlling shareholders hold power and enjoy part of the profits. Minority shareholders enjoy part of the profits and hold no power.

In reality, the managers of a corporation often control it even though they own a small percent of its stock. Thus, power and responsibility are imperfectly conjoined in a public corporation. The resulting separation of profits and power, which is called the "separation of ownership from control," has been studied intensively, most recently by game theorists (see Holmstrom and Tirole 1989, or Tirole 1988). In the standard formulation, the stockholders are described as the "principal" and management is described as an "agent". The principal-agent problem is to design an incentive scheme so that the agent's best interest is served by doing what benefits the principal the most. A perfect solution to the principal-agent problem is an incentive scheme such that the agent maximizes his own utility or income when his actions maximize the principal's utility or income.

Solutions to the principal-agent problem depend upon the constraints built into the model. Typically, a perfect solution requires the principal's information about the agent's behavior to be perfect. If the principal's information is imperfect, the agent usually has incentives to do some acts that benefit him at the principal's expense. In practice, the monitoring of managers by stockholders is costly, so information is asymmetrical. Thus, the principal-agent problem raised by the modern corporation does not have a perfect solution. Instead of perfection, the aim must be a constrained optimum.

To achieve a constrained optimum, a variety of means are employed by contract and law to elicit effort and appropriate risk-taking from managers. Contractual solutions include stock options to increase management's share of ownership, and bonuses or performance pay to reward effort and results. Legal solutions include civil and criminal liability, especially for breach of fiduciary duty. Fiduciary law is noteworthy for its clean solution to the problem of asymmetrical information. Stockholders seldom obtain sufficient evidence of manager's wrongdoing to satisfy the standards of proof ordinarily demanded by courts. Consequently, fiduciary law replaces the usual standards of proof and presumes wrongdoing from its appearance. For example, a manager who appropriates a corporate opportunity is presumed by law to have damaged the stockholders, and he must disgorge the profits to the corporation even if damage to the stockholders cannot be proved (Cooter and Freedman, forthcoming).

A familiar fact of business life is that people are more inclined toward sharp practices or cheating in short run relationships than in long run relationships. The corresponding technical proposition is that many inefficiencies in one-shot games disappear in repeated games.[5] Consequently, lengthening the time horizon helps solve the principal-agent problem. The time horizon is lengthened by contracts and practices that create job security and loyalty among executives. The optimal solutions to the principal-agent problem often rely upon contracts and practices that sustain long run relationships.

Creating monopoly power for members of an organization builds loyalty to it. Who would quit a job that pays monopoly wages to take a job that pays competitive wages? Lawmakers and regulators, thus, face a difficult problem of trying to sort out optimal solutions to the principal-agent problem and private agreements to create monopoly profits for executives. No general solution for this problem is readily apparent. It has no general solution, because the relevant markets are naturally too thin to be perfectly competitive.

Scholars sometimes say that only four numbers should matter to antitrust policy: one, two, three, and four-or-more. These cryptic remarks mean that a market with four or more suppliers behaves much like a perfectly competitive market, whereas each reduction in suppliers below four increases the likelihood of monopolistic practices. Although not strictly true, this rule of thumb provides a focal point for discussing markets for organizations.

For purposes of discussion, ignore complexities like import competition, contestable markets, and barriers to entry. Assume that when the market for organizations has, say, four or more active participants, it is naturally large enough for effective competition. To illustrate, assume that more than four airlines compete against each other. Furthermore, assume that they actively search for airline companies to acquire and that no airlines companies have created obstacles to hostile takeovers. By assumption, the market for airline organizations is naturally competitive. Now suppose that a contract between an airline and its executives creates obstacles to a takeover, such as "golden parachutes". By assumption, the "golden parachutes" remove this company from the market for hostile takeovers.

The antitrust authorities must decide whether to allow its removal. The preceding rule of thumb suggests an answer. If at least four companies remain in the market, then the rule of thumb suggests that the market will remain competitive. Consequently, the antitrust authorities should allow the restrictive contract.

As a rule, private restrictions that inhibit competition for owning organizations are not troublesome if they effectively remove one company from a market with more than four competitors. Under such conditions of workable competition, the law can provide a neutral framework for competition among organizations and, thus, realize the ideal of a pure property regime. Competition will subsequently determine whether the restrictive contract is inferior or superior to unrestricted contracts.

---

[5]In general, see Fudenberg and Maskin (1986). For application to the law of contracts, see Hadfield (1990).

To illustrate, suppose the law permitted organizations to make contracts with executives that interfere with takeovers or restructuring. Some manufacturers might form tight links with banks, as in Germany. Other manufacturers might form networks with a main bank and suppliers, as in Japan. Other manufacturers might maintain distance from banks and networks, as in America. If enough companies of different types exist, competition among them would decide in time which form of organization is more efficient.

This scenario assumes a large market for corporate control, so that diverse types of organizations can co-exist. To consider the opposite possibility, return to the example of the airline company that wants to preclude hostile takeovers. However, change the assumptions and assume that less than four companies remain in the market for corporate control after one company adopts restrictive practices to preclude a hostile takeover. The rule of thumb for antitrust law suggests that the market will become uncompetitive. Here the authorities face a much tougher decision. Allowing the contract will undermine competition. Prohibiting the contract may undermine loyalty to firms that is needed to solve the principal-agent problem. This dilemma has no general policy solution. When the market for organizations is thin, a neutral framework is impossible. Instead, the law must adopt a policy of enforcing or suppressing the relevant contracts and practices.

Unfortunately, neither theory nor empirical research provides clear guidance to lawmakers. The differences between the American, German, and Japanese systems have been inadequately analyzed and researched in spite of intensive policy debate. At this point, scholars can only guess about the best policy. One can argue cogently that companies should be private or public depending upon their stage in the industry's history. Failing companies that must be restructured need the decisiveness and agility of private owners in contrast to companies that are flourishing and expanding which need access to public funds. So one can conclude that the best legal framework would permit transitions from public to private organization and back again. However, these remarks only hint at the issues involved in a complex subject.[6]

3   Property Theory Applied to the Post-Communist Countries

The communist revolutions in Europe went beyond regulating private property and attempted to abolish it. Not all forms of private property were abolished, but private property as a form of organization in large enterprises was eliminated in all communist countries. Property theory offers an interpretation of the

---

[6]For example, leveraged buy-outs by which management takes a failing company private are commended, yet these transactions have been called the "ultimate insider trading".

consequences. The aim of state socialism under Stalin was for the dictator to have complete discretion over economic life including organizational structure, offices, roles, personnel, and material resources. If ownership is equated with discretion over resources, then Stalin owned everything. His control was exercised through centralized planning, which proceeds by issuing commands backed by threats. The economic theory of deterrence offers an insight into the rationality of central planning under Stalin. A perfectly rational, self-interested person will disobey a command when the benefit of disobedience exceeds the expected sanction.[7] The expected sanction equals the magnitude of punishment times its probability. Raising the probability of punishing wrongdoing requires more police, courts, prosecutors, and so forth, which is costly. The cost is especially high for economic crimes where catching offenders is difficult. In contrast, a bullet in the head is cheap. Similarly, the state can actually make a profit by enslaving the wrongdoer. Thus the efficient deterrence of many economic crimes calls for extremely harsh punishments, like shooting or enslaving people, applied with low probability and little discernment (Becker 1968). Deterrence theory implies that terror minimizes the costs of enforcing central planning. Stalin apparently enforced the central plan at moderate cost to government and appalling human costs.

The Stalinist model of central planning enforced by terror was implemented in varying degrees by sector and country. His death created room for contending factions and more humane policies. Property theory explains how the growth of factions and the decline of terror may have contributed to falling economic growth rates in eastern Europe in the 1970s, which turned to stagnation in the 1980s.

As explained, terror is the rational way to enforce central planning. Once terror was abandoned, central planning became too costly to enforce, and the central plan lost its effectiveness. When the single dictator gave way to contending factions, no one had discretion over the entire economy. It was not owned by anyone; instead, property rights were diffuse. In socially owned enterprises, no one person or small group of people joined power and profit. Politics replaced discretion, collective choice replaced individual choice, and governance replaced commands.

Socially owned enterprises had various types of governance that varied by time and place according to political currents (Olson, Ch. 4). A Hungarian scholar has argued that political ends were served by keeping ownership rights vague and uncertain in Hungarian enterprises. They were, in his view, owned by no one (Sajo 1990). His findings are reminiscent of a saying in Croatia: "We know what social ownership isn't, but not what it is."

When property rights are diffuse and uncertain, people devote their energies to trying to secure wealth, rather than to produce it. In general, game theory

---

[7]This statement assumes that the agent is risk neutral.

shows that uncertainty over entitlements diverts energies from production to redistribution. This result can be explained by analogy. When oil wells were first drilled in America, the party who pumped oil to the surface was entitled to keep it by law. In other words, oil in the ground was unowned, and oil raised to the surface was owned by the party who possessed it. As a consequence, oil companies raced each other to extract as much oil from the ground as quickly as possible. Oil in the ground is analogous to social property in the sense that no one clearly owns it. Consequently, people in post-communist countries are engaged in a wasteful race to remove property from social ownership and obtain private possession of it.

The race to appropriate social property is one cause of the spontaneous disintegration of socialist enterprises. After 1989, however, disintegration accelerated into a collapse in many countries. Game theory suggests why. When the legal framework for contract law is underdeveloped, so that promises are difficult to enforce, long run relationships will replace contracts as a device for coordinating behavior (Cooter and Landa 1984; Cooter 1989). Exchange in long run relationships takes the form of reciprocal favors that follow the principle of "tit-for-tat" or "I'll scratch your back if you scratch mine". To illustrate, a mechanic repairs a truck for the driver as a "favor," but the mechanic later receives a crate of oranges off the truck as a "gift". Economic agents engage in barter and keep implicit accounts to make sure that they receive as much as they get.

State socialism, in this way, replaced market exchange with less efficient long term reciprocal and political relationships. A problem arises with a system of reciprocity when the parties see it coming to an end. As the end draws near, economic agents begin to doubt that they will ever be paid back for the favors that they do. Consequently, they are no longer willing to do favors. A loss of faith in the future of social ownership, thus, undermines the reciprocal relationships that made it work. In technical terms, games have cooperative solutions when they are repeated indefinitely while cooperation collapses when the game approaches its end (the "endgame problem").

3.1   Property law and the problems of privatization

Leaders in the post-communist countries perceive privatization as the only way out of their current dilemma. The theory of organizational property offers a framework for a few observations about privatization, based on the US experience. The last few years have seen a massive failure of American banks that specialize in real estate investments. (Technically, they are called "savings and loan institutions," not "banks," but they are banks.) When these banks fail, the money is lost that is needed to repay depositors, and the US government is legally obligated to reimburse them. The US government often becomes the temporary owner of a failed bank that it must subsequently reorganize and sell. Thus, the US banking authorities are effectively engaged in nationalizing, reorganizing, and privatizing banks.

Ideally, government agencies in the US and post-communist countries would privatize each enterprise quickly and thoroughly. In reality, the agencies do not have enough personnel or resources for this task. The US banking authorities respond by dealing quickly with small banks that are easy to dispose of and then focusing their energies on those banks that are losing the most money. The philosophy is "stop the hemorrhaging". Perhaps, the post-communist countries will react similarly.

Privatizing assets involves the difficult problem of valuing them. The value of an enterprise is the market price of a controlling interest in it, which is established by entrepreneurs, not accountants. Economists recommend various auctions and similar devices to dispose of companies. Auctions are ideal, but in reality auctions for failed banks do not usually succeed in the US because there are not enough bidders. If the US banking authorities cannot organize an effective auction for, say, a small bank in Arizona, how likely is it for Czechoslovakia to organize an effective auction for a large steel mill?

Instead of auctions, the US authorities typically negotiate with several possible buyers. These practices suggest some strategies that might be useful in post-communist countries. Valuation is relatively easy for standardized assets that are regularly bought and sold in markets, such as a truck, a desk, or a piece of real estate. Valuation is relatively difficult for unique assets that are seldom bought and sold, such as an art work or an historic villa. Another unique asset is the enterprise as an organization. Entrepreneurs are sure to disagree over the value of the enterprise as a going concern especially when markets for organizations tend to be thin in the sense of not having enough participants for effective competition. In the post-communist countries, uncertainty will make these markets even thinner.

Given the magnitude of the problem, it is probably best to let small privatizing enterprises have the organization's value for free in post-communist countries. However, the government might appropriately recoup a share of the value of the material assets of small enterprises. Thus, the valuation problem for small enterprises concerns material assets not organizations.

As explained, the valuation of small, privatizing enterprises focuses upon their wealth, not their income. With respect to large enterprises, the opposite should be the case. One can argue that the primary concern of the government should not be the valuation of the current assets of large enterprises, but their future economic performance. How many new workers will be employed? How much will production increase? How much will be exported? How soon can subsidies, artificial prices, and tariff protection end?

The valuation of large enterprises must take place as an aspect of the negotiating process by which the government's privatization agencies bargain with investors including foreigners, who seek to acquire the enterprises. The "best deal" is the transfer of the assets to private owners who provide the best terms as measured in future employment and production.

3.2   Which capitalism?

Many people in the post-communist countries observed that social ownership caused irresponsible management. They mistakenly concluded that a stock market will automatically cure the problem. The mistake arises from the failure to distinguish between buying stock and buying a company. As explained, the managers of capitalist corporations have devices for insulating themselves from outside pressures so that they can pursue ineffective or irresponsible policies. When a company has an owner with a controlling interest, that person or organization can force managers to be responsible, whereas dispersed stockholders cannot. Germany, Japan, and the US offer different models for overseeing managers. As explained, the controlling stockholders in Germany are banks; in Japan, the controlling stockholders are the company's main bank and suppliers; in the US, most financial institutions like commercial banks are not allowed to own a controlling share of stocks. Instead, the US has developed hostile takeovers, so the market oversees the managers. The post-communist countries thus face the question, "which capitalism"?

There can be no neutral framework for competition to decide this question. Instead, it must be answered by law and policy. A neutral framework is impossible because the potential market for corporate control is not large enough for the full range of alternative forms of finance and control to compete with each other. When privatizing, the roles must be delineated for commercial banks, investment banks, mutual funds, insurance companies, and pension funds. Institutional investors are unlikely to relinquish any control that they exercise over the boards of directors during the privatization process. So the path taken in the transition to capitalism will probably have a decisive influence upon the final result.

3.3   Where does good law come from?

The current economic crisis in the post-communist countries demands a political solution. The privatization agencies will inevitably respond to politics. For example, in Croatia the privatization fund's director is appointed by the President of the Republic, and the fund will have access to tax revenues supplied by the state. The intimate connection between politics and finance creates many possibilities for political favoritism and corruption in the allocation of investment funds.

In the long run, the government privatization funds must be liquidated or transformed into investment banks that are insulated from politics and operate on commercial principles. In the meantime, the course of privatization will be evolutionary in part and planned in part. The emphasis and direction of privatization will shift as political currents reverse themselves, voters gain more experience with capitalism, new issues become salient, and public priorities change.

Privatization requires much law making, so the process of making law must itself be analyzed and its workings anticipated. The economic analysis of legal process is a substantial body of theory. A few of its insights, beginning by distinguishing between legislation and judge-made laws merit attention. Property, torts, and contract law in the English-language countries find their origins in the common law. Common law is created by judges as they build upon precedent and pronounce legal rules in deciding particular cases. According to the original understanding of the common law, judges were supposed to identify social norms and enforce those that satisfy certain legal criteria (Eisenberg 1988). For example, communities develop standards of reasonable care with respect to potentially dangerous activities like driving cars.

Social norms arise from repeated interactions among people. Economic theory has offered various proofs that repeated games often have efficient solutions under specified conditions. Efficiency in repeated games requires low discount rates for futurity, an indefinite number of repetitions, and information concerning the past history of the moves made by other players. Consequently, the social norms that judges enforce tend to be efficient. The pressure in common law toward efficiency increases when judges adopt efficiency not just fairness as a goal (Cooter 1990). Economic analysis has made remarkable progress in demonstrating the efficiency of the common law. However, the pressures toward efficiency have not always prevailed against counter-pressures that also exist in the common law.[8]

The victories of Napoleon resulted in the abolition of common law in most of Europe and its replacement by codes and other statutes. To become law in democratic countries, codes must usually be enacted by the legislature. Judges subsequently have some scope to make new laws by interpreting codes. The interpretation of codes has similarities to the common law. A lively debate continues concerning how large the difference really is between common law and the interpretation of codes, both of which can be called "judge-made law".[9]

The discretion of the court to interpret and make law is determined in part by history, such as the existence of common law or a tradition of courts reviewing statutes to determine their constitutionality. In addition, the court's power is determined by the constitution, especially by distributing power among the other branches of government. It is not hard to show that courts have more interpretative power when the constitution gives veto power over legislation to several other independent bodies (see Ferejohn and Weingast, forthcoming, and Gely and Spiller 1989).

To illustrate, under Britain's unwritten constitution, the Prime Minister gets the legislation that she wants. If Britain's highest court interprets law differently from the Prime Minister, she can easily change the law. No one else has an

---

[8]To illustrate, the enthusiasm of American judges to extend tort liability is widely perceived as having created inefficiencies and caused a crisis in the law of torts. See Priest (1985).

[9]This point is discussed in the context of country reports from all over Europe in a symposium. See Cooter and Gordley (forthcoming).

independent veto. In contrast, in America three independent vetoes exist for proposed legislation: the House, the Senate, and the President. The Supreme Court can depart widely from the interpretation of legislation preferred by any one of them without provoking revision of the law provided that one of the bodies with independent veto power prefers the Supreme Court's interpretation to the revision proposed by the other two bodies. Hence, the courts make a lot more law by interpretation in America than in Britain.

Judge-made law develops gradually by accretion. The principle pronounced in one case is extended to anther by analogy. If cases are too dissimilar, the analogy fails, and the attempted extension of law loses legitimacy. Unlike judges, the legislature, which enjoys the sanction of a majority of voters, is not bound to proceed incrementally. Instead, legislation can strike out abruptly in new directions. Legislation is autonomous, and judge-made law is historical.

Another difference concerns incentives. Ideally, judges are insulated from political and economic life so that their decisions are disinterested. "Disinterested" means that the interests of a judge or his family, especially their wealth and power, are not affected in any discernable way by how he decides particular cases. This ideal is realized in many European countries and in U.S. federal courts. In contrast, the wealth and power of legislators is directly affected by how they vote on particular bills. Statutes and codes are enacted by interested politicians. Politicians tend to redistribute wealth toward favored groups. In many instances, regulation has been the device by which politically favored industries obtain monopoly profits that competition would dissipate in an unregulated market. The economic analysis of legislation has produced the skeptical belief that statutes pertaining to property usually redistribute wealth in favor of politically influential groups. In contrast, judge-made law is largely disinterested. That is why judge-made law remains important to preserving property rights. Protecting property against politics requires an independent judiciary with the power to make law by interpreting statutes.

Privatization in the post-communist countries is an abrupt change that must proceed largely through legislation rather than judge-made law. The economic analysis of legislation provokes pessimism concerning the likelihood that it will lead to anything resembling a pure property regime. Uncertainty about property rights multiplies the opportunities for political redistributions to politically favored groups. The hope for secure property rights in law must rest upon widespread, popular disgust with their abolition under communism.

4   Summary and Conclusion

Private property is a bundle of rights that gives owners discretion over the use of resources. Discretion implies that the owners are not answerable to other people or the state. This zone of privacy is an aspect of freedom and a bulwark against tyranny. In addition, private property creates incentives for efficiency and innovation. A pure property regime promotes efficiency by internalizing the costs and benefits of resource use, lubricating trade, and promoting efficient organization.

Some organizations can be an individual's property, and others preclude individual ownership by their nature. Discretion and individual choice are aspects of organizational property while politics and collective choice are aspects of most non-property organizations. Private property and capitalism are not sufficient conditions to determine the form of corporate organization. Rather than prescribing a particular form, private property and capitalism ideally provide a framework for competition among alternative forms.

In practice, this framework cannot be perfectly neutral, because markets for organizations are thin rather than being naturally competitive. Privatization in the post-communist countries must adopt financial institutions through laws that favor particular ways of choosing business leaders. Germany, Japan, and the US provide alternative models.

Economic analysis suggests that disinterested judges might direct law toward efficiency, but legislation is less likely to take this course. Rather, legislation is directed toward efficiency in fits and starts as government responds to shifting political currents. Privatization needs a strong, independent judiciary, but it can only proceed through legislation, which counsels skepticism about the likely results.

Constitutional historians of the United States have identified certain moments in history when politicians and the public have been able to rise above immediate self-interest and respond to a larger vision (Ackerman 1977). In effect, these theories postulate behavior outside the economic model of self-interest, which leads to the creation of a constitutional framework for capitalism and democracy. Perhaps some of the post-communist countries will enjoy such a moment in their history right now. The challenge to the newly democratic governments is to develop a privatization strategy that will generate political support among voters as they experience its effects.

6 The Transition to a Market Economy

Sir Alan Walters

1 The Successes and Failures of Central Planning

Before considering the transition to a market economy, we must consider the need for such a transition. Today the need is clear: socialist and communist systems have failed to deliver (in a literal sense) anything like the standard of material advance so often promised. Indeed it now seems that, relative to the Western economies, the Eastern bloc started declining from the end of the 1960s. But we should reflect that the recognition of the superiority of the market system is a rather recent phenomenon among professional economists, particularly development economists and those specializing in the Eastern bloc. Of course, we all recall the adulation of central planning by Gunnar Myrdal (a Nobel laureate) and his host of development planners. Perhaps less well remembered is the obloquy which was poured on the policy of Ludwig Erhard in 1947 when he instituted a transition from a centrally controlled system to a market economy. With three notable exceptions (Friedman, Haberler and Sohmen) Western economists condemned it (Balogh, never a man for half-measures, called it "evil") and said it would end badly. It obviously did not.

But more recent rosy assessments of central planning abound. Even as late as 1979 the World Bank published a long and detailed study of Romania — the most Stalinist of the Eastern bloc. The Bank found that from 1950 to 1975 the Romanian economy had grown faster than any other country in the world (9.8 percent per annum). The Bank attributed this startling performance to the fact

The author thanks the Center for Institutional Reform and the Informal Sector for financial support.

that government, through its system of central planning, had control of all resources. The Bank forecast a rosy future for Romania — growing at 8.7 percent per capita to 1990.[1] Nor was Romania an aberration. The Bank published in that same year of 1979 a most rosy history of, and prognostication for, Yugoslavia. Studies up to 1984 continued to show that central planning, albeit somewhat modified in places, delivered the goods.

This review is not intended to score points, but simply to remind us of the long addiction of economists to planning and regulation. Obviously the conversion for some economists in Soviet studies and in development has been rather sudden — like Orwell's orator from Oceania who, having been informed in mid-speech that alliances had changed, effortlessly switched names. However, it is likely that there will be a reaction against the "cruel injustices" of the emerging market economies. Complaints more than the normal mutterings have already appeared, and some yearn for a Scandinavian or Swedish solution. Economics is a meretricious profession, and surely it will cope.

2   Democracy and the Market Economy

A second major theme of current discussions is the association of a market economy with democratic systems and procedures. This general sentiment is widespread in the West and in the emerging market economies. We hear much about the need for democracy before the transition to a market economy can be effected. Participation in the market required participation in politics. In the author's view this sentiment is a fundamental error. What a market economy requires is first "light" government and, second, substantial individual freedom. Then, the distortions introduced necessarily by government finance and regulation will not distort private decision making. Resources will be distributed according to people's, not the ruler's, preferences and, even more important, private incentives will be the powerful engine that drives this market economy.

"Light" government and personal freedom may well exist in a state with no democratic participation at all. Yet, there can be a market system with all the prosperity that it implies. Perhaps the most obvious example of this is the Crown Colony of Hong Kong. There is no democratic system at all in that colony. It is ruled by British civil servants appointed by the London government. True, the Governor of Hong Kong on occasion consulted the "consultative council" of appointed colony worthies. But no one would pretend that anything like

---

[1] If the 1950-75 growth figure were compared with the published income per capita figure in 1975, all Romanians would have been dead in 1950. Even in the land of Dracula, claims for the resurrection of the dead should be treated with perhaps more caution than their statistics.

democracy prevailed there. Yet, Hong Kong is one of the most liberal (in the literal European sense) societies in the world with the lowest tax rates (maximum income tax marginal rate of 15 percent). Government is both small and "light". Freedoms to employ, to work, to trade, etc., are almost absolute. And clearly, Hong Kong has prospered mightily — rather more than Romania, to correct the World Bank. Nor is Hong Kong an isolated case. Singapore is an obvious twin. But less obvious is Pinochet's Chile. Even his best friends and Pinochet himself would not claim that Chile was a democracy from 1973 to 1990. But Pinochet did free the individual from all the stifling restrictions of socialism and reduced dramatically the size of government. And Chile prospered.

What about the isomorphic cases? Probably the occasions when the transition to a democratic society is associated not with a retention of, or transition to, a market economy but with an increase in *dirigisme* are much more common. The idea of a democratic tyranny is not oxymoronic. Jacobite societies seem to grow out of revolutions or decolonizations that give "all power to the people". But the important point is that political democracy (defined here as a "one man, one vote" system) does not **naturally** generate the freedoms which are the necessary conditions of a market economy. To avoid misunderstanding, however, let me emphasize that I am not condemning democracy. On the contrary, democracy with its wide participation is a form of government that, in the absence of severe tensions between different groups, can produce the most civil, compassionate and just societies. But we should not claim democracy as either sufficient or even necessary for a liberal society with a market economy.

3 Transitions

The transition to a market economy always and at all times involves a familiar list of policies and, although this volume has refined and developed the ideas behind these policies (and in some cases suggested new priorities), the outline would be familiar to an Erhard or a Thatcher or a Pinochet.

First is financial stabilization, reducing the budget deficit and the monetary emissions of the central bank. This stabilization may involve many complex policies — almost certainly a tax reform (such as the switch from a profits tax to a value-added tax, as suggested by R. McKinnon, Ch. 7) and expenditure controls, particularly in the reduction of subsidies. There is no consensus on pegged versus free exchange rates. This author is keen on promoting currency boards for the emerging market economies — similar to that which operates in Hong Kong. Then, the exchange rate is absolutely **fixed** as distinct from pegged or floating.

Second is deregulation, eliminating a myriad of government controls and establishing the framework for free contractual relationships. This priority involves the recognition of property rights and the development of a legal system suitable for a market economy. It also implies a diminished role for the central planners as more room is provided for private initiative and enterprise. But oddly enough it is widely recognized that there is a need for more restraint on industry, particularly the heavy state-owned firms, to reduce pollution. Other areas of deregulation include trade reform and currency convertibility.

Third is the reform and privatization of state-owned concerns. To this list should be added the reduction in monopoly power not only of industry but also of trade unions, and in particular the reform of labor laws. The reform of the banking system and the development of commercial rather than planning criteria in banking is also of the utmost importance.

Much effort has been devoted to determining the appropriate sequencing of the various reforms and the development of safety nets to deal with the interim unemployment and distress. Since the process is one of reducing aggregate demand, freeing resources and transferring them to more efficient uses, it is important that the price signals be right, that is to say consistent with international relative prices, and that the incentives be appropriately private. Clearly, planning incentives with very different prices can perpetuate distortions (see Clague, Ch. 1). The need to privatize first and reform the banking system has been emphasized by many observers. Yet, Minister Klaus of Czechoslovakia has argued that one could have little effect on the sequencing of the reforms: whatever governments may decree, reforms have their own momentum. This view has much to recommend it. For example, in spite of the determination to privatize industry very rapidly, very little has, in fact, been achieved in any of the emerging market economies. This assertion leads to some final observations on models and modes of privatization.

4　Privatization

The leaders of the emerging market economies have become convinced that privatization is the one hope for their salvation as efficient industrialized democracies. They have looked at the great success of the Thatcher privatizations — British Airways, British Steel, housing, Jaguar, even British Telecom and the water companies — and they have liked what they have seen. Nationalized British Airways and British Steel began the decade of the eighties as about the worst performers, in terms of productivity and profits (i.e. losses), among the OECD countries. By 1990 these privatized companies were among the best performing corporations in the West. Privatization was clearly thought to be **the** essential ingredient that worked such miracles.

So it was. But this conclusion is a misleading and dangerous simplification. This naive belief in the emerging market economies, encouraged on occasion by enthusiasts from the West, is that, with the large state-owned enterprises, all that is needed is to change the ownership from the state to private persons. The motivation of the new owners would engender those efficient systems of production so characteristic of the West and so lacking in the East. There was thought to be no point in trying to reform the existing state-owned enterprises while they remained in state ownership. They were managed by the *nomenklatura* — chosen largely for their party rather than their management credentials. One of the enduring features of all emerging market economies, whatever their state of reform, has been the persistence of *nomenklatura* management. It is doubtful that any political leader in Eastern Europe will seriously attempt the Herculean task of sorting the sheep from the goats among the *nomenklatura* They hope, instead, that privatization will do the sorting for them.

The state-owned enterprises have also been vastly overmanned by highly unionized labor. A distinguished Hungarian told me that the state would not dare carry out the appropriate downsizing. The *nomenklatura* managers would protest and, if necessary, botch the job by retaining sinecures and disrupting production, blaming "the inhuman policy of restructuring". The Hungarian asserted that the only way efficiently to reduce the work force was to privatize — and, he assured me, the private companies could then rid themselves of the make-work jobs that had been so prevalent in the enterprise in its nationalized state.

This prognosis and policy is dramatically different from the successful Thatcher reforms and privatizations. The main contrast is that under Thatcher **the reform of the nationalized corporation was carried through while it was in the public sector.** The reductions in work force, the elimination of unprofitable plant and equipment, and the sharp increases in productivity, quality and service were all achieved while the enterprises were owned by the state. Indeed the government appointed new managers, such as Ian McGregor and John King, with the explicit mandate to turn the enterprises into profitable and sound undertakings that could hold their own in the competitive private sectors. The managers and workers had the privatization timetable and, most important, diminishing access to the public purse to encourage their efforts. But privatization occurred only after the hard work of reform had been completed. What privatization accomplished was to ensure that the corporation would not slip back into the bad habits of the public sector — such as recourse to subsidies, monopoly privileges, and cheap capital.

The emerging market economies expect that they can somehow skip this phase of preparation and reform of the large public sector enterprises. One can sympathize. In Poland, Hungary, Czechoslovakia and the Soviet Union, the distrust of government and its bureaucracy is universal. How can one expect the institutions that got these countries into the mess to be the agency that now extracts them from it? But, of course, there has been a change of government, and slowly even the bureaucracy is changing its habits, if not its personnel. A government that is committed to a market economy and private enterprise should be able to institute reforms on the Thatcher model. Poland, Hungary, Czechoslovakia and Russia all have their incipient Kings, McGregors and Cyril

Sharps. The government should appoint and motivate them, and back them in the ruthless reforms so needed in these arthritic economies.

Of course, there are objections. One of the strangest and most poignant is that the Thatcher privatizations were too slow and too little. In economies where up to 90 percent of non-agricultural production is in the hands of the state, the stentorian process of Thatcher privatization would be politically far too slow. The Eastern Europeans want market economies **now** — or at least in four or five years. Marton Tardos, the distinguished leader of the Free Democratic Party in Hungary, estimated that, at the Thatcher pace of the UK, Hungary would take 100 years to privatize its economy. There was nothing inherent in the Thatcher approach, however, that dictated the pace of privatization. It was determined by legal, political and administrative factors. There was no insuperable technical reason (even including so-called capital market saturation) that prevented the program from being speeded up — as indeed occurred after 1984. Nevertheless, it is likely not feasible to carry out the wholesale privatization envisaged in less than 10 years.

Another set of objections arises from the fact that there is no capital market in any emerging market economy, so there is no way of valuing the worth of state-owned enterprises. This problem is compounded by the fact that for so long prices have been distorted so that they are very different from both world prices and true domestic costs. Who knows what the expected stream of profits will be from purchasing, for example, the Gdansk shipyard? It was reported that the shipyard workers thought the yard was worth $500 million, while Arthur Andersen, when assessing it for a possible purchase by Mrs. Barbara Johnson, a wealthy owner of Johnson and Johnson, valued it at between zero and $30 million. This disparity illustrates the enormous uncertainties, both economic and political, that bedevil any potential deal.

However, this example is also an argument for taking the Thatcher road and for not attempting to privatize until at least many of these political and economic uncertainties are resolved. Then, one can write an honest prospectus for each of them. But there is another reason for the emerging market economies' thrust to privatization, which is in principle nothing to do with the improvement of efficiency and management. There is an urgent need to assuage the thirst of the inhabitants for the transfer of the powers of ownership from the state and its bureaucrats to the people. The establishment of property rights which can be bought and sold or bequeathed to one's children is, perhaps, **the** essential element of a capitalist system. And the major form of property in emerging market economies is industrial capital, housing and land. What is more natural than to give the shares to this property away to the people? Ingenious ideas have been produced whereby individuals would acquire vouchers enabling them to buy shares in holding companies or mutual funds which would themselves hold shares in the erstwhile state-owned enterprises. The mutuals would be required to diversify their holdings to avoid the enormous risks involved in particular erstwhile state-owned enterprises. In the classic phrase of Thatcherism, it would amount to returning the assets of industry back to the people.

But what about management under this system? In effect, the management would be controlled by the managers of the several mutual funds or holding companies. Experience in Britain and the United States suggests that such institutional shareholders tend to be active portfolio holders rather than active managers. Although one may try various institutional tricks to get active and interested management, there is no working model of such a system. It would be a very risky experiment. The prospect of launching vouchers and an active market in mutual fund shares among the whole populace where such instruments have been quite unknown for nearly 50 years is mind-boggling. It may be seriously doubted whether the market would be at all transparent, and the opportunities for misrepresentation, market rigging, etc. would be enormous. One fears that capitalism would soon be discredited.

There is, however, a good case for a pilot scheme of vouchers. Perhaps all these worries are ephemeral. Perhaps my dire warnings are beside the point. Let us try it on a modest scale before launching it on the grand national scale.

5   Conclusion

Professional economists can help in the transition to a market economy. A study of other transitions, such as those of Germany, China and the UK, will provide, not a recipe for success, but general admonitions on what is likely to, and what is not likely to work. Our knowledge, though real, is patchy and ill-founded for promoting any grand designs.

PART II
Macroeconomic Policy and Financial Discipline

7 Taxation, Money, and Credit in a Liberalizing Socialist Economy

Ronald I. McKinnon

This chapter explains why price inflation and a general loss of macroeconomic control are almost endemic in a liberalizing socialist economy. In their rush to decentralize decision making, privatize, and dismantle the apparatus of central planning, reformers inadvertently upset the preexisting system for sustaining macroeconomic equilibrium. The ability of the reform government to collect taxes and control the supply of money and credit is unwittingly undermined by the process of liberalization itself. Thus, the first part of the chapter seeks to understand how the preexisting system of financial control under Stalinist central planning actually worked, and why it tends to break down.

After decentralization begins, one unfortunate consequence of this increased inflationary pressure is to reduce the demand for money in favor of excess stocks of physical capital: redundant inventories, excess capacity in fixed assets, and unfinished construction projects. Because of monetary instability, this (unnecessary) fall in the productivity of existing capital aggravates the disruptions in industrial output from more or less unavoidable restructuring — redirecting the Council for Mutual Economic Assistance trade, moving away from excess dependence on heavy industry, adopting more modern technologies, etc. The Eastern European "J-Curve" in industrial and agricultural production — where output falls when liberalization begins, but then is supposed to increase later — is worsened.

Thus, in the second part of the chapter, more deliberate monetary and fiscal measures for containing inflation in a socialist economy in transition are spelled out — and these may differ substantially from measures to control inflation in mature capitalist economies. Rather than a "big bang" where all centralized socialist controls are simultaneously dismantled, the chapter holds that there is a natural or optimum order of economic liberalization. Moves to dismantle the apparatus of central planning, decontrol prices, privatize property, free foreign trade, and so on need to be supported by a proper sequence of fiscal, monetary, and foreign exchange measures. In this short discussion, only the broad outlines of such a financial order can be sketched; a fuller treatment is now available (McKinnon 1991).

1   Financial Control Under Classical Socialism

The centrally planned Soviet economy, before the advent of *perestroika* and the current financial breakdown, is our model of classical socialism. Although not addressed at all in this chapter, the hierarchical system of command and control and its institutional structure in the traditional Soviet economy is extremely complex — as nicely summarized by Richard Ericson (1991). This chapter focuses on the main elements of the financial system, which were also adopted to a greater or lesser extent by the smaller countries of Eastern Europe and the socialist economies in Asia.

In the classical socialist economy, the financial system has two essential features that differentiate it from its capitalist counterpart. First, the system of taxation is largely **implicit** and uncodified. Second, the system of money and credit for enterprises is entirely **passive.** In the absence of central planning, the monetary system itself does not restrain the ability of enterprises to bid for scarce resources.

Consider the fiscal system first. Because the government owns all the industrial and agricultural property, surpluses are extracted from enterprises (and indirectly from households) with relatively little codification in formal tax law. For example, no system of consumer excises (sales taxes) need be formally codified if the preexisting system of price controls keeps the retail cost of consumer "luxuries" — liquor, tobacco, automobiles, etc. — arbitrarily high. Then enterprises producing these goods would run with large cash surpluses (government revenue) which reverted to the state. Of course, the government can also lose revenue if prices of some goods, say basic foods, are set below their costs of production. The implicit consumer excise tax rate on these goods is then negative.

Similarly, no law establishing a personal income tax is necessary if all enterprises essentially withhold household income at its source. As long as the state owns the capital stock, it must set or limit the wages of workers and managers to ensure that enterprises, on average, do generate cash surpluses. Otherwise, if managers or workers' councils can determine their own wages with an indirect claim on the firm's physical capital, they will pay themselves "excessive" wages that tend to decapitalize the enterprise (Hinds 1990b). With the necessary wage controls already in place, maintaining a parallel system of personal income taxation is an unnecessary expense.

Under classical socialism, having enterprise "profits" — really residual cash surpluses which do not allow for depreciation of fixed capital or the drawing down of inventories — simply revert to the state is not an inefficient method of taxation. (The state must then provide financing for authorized new investments by recycling funds back to enterprises.) In the presence of centralized price controls, output targets, and input allocations, which enterprises generate surpluses and which generate deficits is largely arbitrary anyway. Thus, appropriating cash surpluses is the only feasible method for the government to tax enterprises. As long as all decisions for allocating resources are actually made by the central planning agency, seizing enterprise profits *ex post facto* need not be particularly damaging to managerial incentives.

In contrast, generalized business taxes that work well in a liberalized market context, say a value-added tax, might not even be collectible in a classical socialist economy when price controls prevent the tax from being shifted forward to the final user. Similarly, levying a formal gross turnover tax directly on enterprises (as socialist governments do) may simply reduce residual profits, which would otherwise revert to the state. As long as the final prices of goods sold are controlled by the government, whether revenue is formally collected from a turnover tax or from residual profit remittances to the state is a distinction without a difference.

Even under centralized price and output controls, enterprise surpluses remain somewhat uncertain. Variability in the technology, uncertainty in the availability of inputs, unknowns in inventory accumulation make enterprise cash surpluses difficult to predict *ex ante*. Hence, enforcing revenue collection in the absence of formally codified tax law requires that these surpluses remain "blocked" as they are generated *ex post*. Under classical socialism, therefore, enterprise deposits with the state bank cannot even be spent for domestic goods and services without permission, nor are enterprises allowed to hold "cash" — coin and currency that could be spent without being traced. This internal or "commodity inconvertibility" of enterprise money in socialist economies is much more restrictive than mere inconvertibility into foreign exchange (McKinnon 1979, Ch. 3),[1] which of course is a more common phenomenon in nonsocialist economies as well.

Within a classical socialist economy like the Soviet Union's, therefore, there are two monetary circuits: the (blocked) deposits of enterprises held with the state bank before 1985 — sometimes in several designated accounts — and households' coin and currency. Households can spend their cash freely for goods and services without getting permission from the government — if they

---

[1]John Williamson (1991) further clarifies various concepts of internal and external currency convertibility.

can find them in the shops — or deposit it into personal savings accounts that can be later withdrawn without restraint.[2]   To prevent an overhang (at fixed retail prices) of domestically convertible household money which leads to more than the normal "tautness" in aggregate demand in the socialist economy, the amount of the blocked enterprise money which is converted through wage or other payments for personal services must be strictly limited. Indeed, having the state bank carefully monitor the conversion from enterprise to household money complements the system of wage controls.

By itself, the Stalinist system of enterprise money and credit is essentially passive on both the loan and deposit sides of the state bank's balance sheet. On the loan side, enterprises are restricted neither by interest rates (which are kept trivially low) nor by fixed credit lines. If any enterprise had insufficient funds on hand to purchase supplies as allowed under the plan, it could borrow without restraint from the state bank. On the deposit side, the demand for "money" by enterprises is indeterminate. Blocked cash accounts simply build up until they are expropriated or the government gives the enterprise permission to buy something. But with all spending mandated by *Gosplan,* whether or not the enterprise has "cash" on hand does not affect what it can or cannot do.

In summary, the financial system does not constrain enterprises from bidding for scarce resources under classical socialism. However, as long as the central planning mechanism imposes a rough balance between supply and demand for each product, this absence of financial restraint on enterprises is not debilitating to the macroeconomy. Moreover, as long as the old method of implicit tax collection — based largely on the expropriation of enterprise surpluses — generates enough revenue and limits wage claims, the government can prevent inflation by limiting the buildup of liquid (unblocked) cash balances owned by households.

2   The Breakdown of Financial Control in the Transition

Once liberalization begins, the formal apparatus of central planning is weakened as decision making and effective property rights devolve more to the (state-owned) enterprises themselves and perhaps to a newly enfranchised private or cooperative sector. Price controls may or may not be removed in this transitional period. However, by giving up control over state property, the government in effect gives away its tax base. Because of the implicit nature of the old system of taxation, no formal internal revenue service exists for clawing back revenue

---

[2]This normal monetary guideline of classical socialism was violated by the Soviet monetary "reform" of January 23, 1991, when large-denomination ruble notes were canceled and withdrawals from personal savings accounts were restricted.

from entities that are no longer controlled by the government. Enterprises can no longer so easily be used as revenue (cash) cows, or as vehicles for indirectly taxing households. The result in the Soviet Union and Eastern Europe, as well as China and many of the smaller socialist economies of Asia, is a sharp decline in the revenue of the consolidated government as liberalization proceeds.

Starting from classical socialism before 1978, China provides the longest continuous revenue series on a decentralizing socialist economy: through the massive agrarian reforms in 1979-84 where land was leased back to households to the development of township industries and those in "free" economic zones in the late 1980s. Table 3 shows that the consolidated revenue of the central, provincial, and local governments fell from over 34 percent of GNP in 1978 to only 19 percent by 1989. Table 3 also shows that virtually all of this decline can be explained by a fall in "profit remittances" from enterprises and that revenue from business product taxes — turnover and value-added taxes — held up rather better (Blejer and Szapary 1989).

TABLE 3
China: Government Revenue, 1978-1989
(In percent of GNP)

	1978	1979-81	1982-84	1985-87	1988	1989[1]
Total Revenue[2]	34.4	30.0	27.0	24.8	20.4	19.0
Revenue from Enterprises	20.6	17.1	12.5	8.3	5.6	4.0
Of which:						
Profit Remittances	(19.1)	(16.1)	(11.4)	(0.4)	(0.3)	(0.3)
Profit tax	(1.5)	(1.0)	(1.1)	(7.9)	(5.3)	(3.7)
Taxes on:						
Income and Profits[3]	21.5	17.8	13.3	7.9	5.3	3.7
Goods and Services[4]	11.3	10.6	10.1	10.6	9.1	8.6
International Trade	0.8	0.9	1.1	1.8	1.1	1.1
Other Taxes	—	—	1.5	3.2	3.0	3.0
Nontax revenue[5]	0.8	0.8	1.0	1.3	1.7	2.4

[1]Budget.
[2]Total revenue includes nontax revenue.
[3]Includes profit remittances.
[4]Includes product, value-added, and business taxes.
[5]Excluding profit remittances.

Source: Blejer and Szapary (1989)

This overall revenue decline forced the central and local governments to cut expenditures heavily — so that measured fiscal deficits were only 2 to 3 percent of Chinese GNP. But this figure understates the "true" fiscal deficit. Because government-financed investment expenditures fell so sharply, local governments in particular pressured the banks to lend to the enterprises they owned or controlled in order to increase infrastructure investments in their localities. Besides fostering unhealthy fiscal competition among governments for control over enterprises and thus revenue (Wong 1990), this "forced" extension of excessive bank credit to enterprises throughout the Chinese economy undermined monetary control from the mid 1980s into the 1990s.

Although the period for observing the fiscal effects of liberalization is shorter, the (less reliable) Soviet fiscal data tell a similar story. From 1985 when Mikhail Gorbachev took office through 1989, table 4 shows government revenue falling over 6 percentage points of GNP. About half of this fall is attributable to declining remittances from state enterprises; special factors, such as diminished sales of alcohol at home and petroleum abroad, account for the remainder. Because the Soviet government has not been very successful in cutting back expenditures as revenue declined, by 1988-89 "formal" Soviet fiscal deficits had already reached 9 to 11 percent of GNP. In 1990-91, the fiscal decline in the Soviet Union became more precipitate with burgeoning deficits on which there is little reliable information. As the struggle between the central government and the republics for control over revenue-generating enterprises intensifies, the republican governments have refused to hand over revenue to the Soviets. In addition, enterprise surpluses may themselves continue to erode as prices are decontrolled and competition increases.

Because interest rates are pegged below market-clearing levels, fiscal deficits cannot be financed by the direct issue of government bonds to the nonbank public. Thus, liberalizing socialist governments typically cover their revenue shortfalls partly by borrowing from the (state) banking system which funds itself by issuing modest-yield saving deposits and liquid cash balances to households, and partly by allowing the blocked deposit money owned by enterprises to increase. Because of this monetary overhang, incipient price increases are large should price controls be removed. Thus even reformist governments become reluctant to eliminate price controls over a wide range of goods and services, and normal market development is severely impeded.

Monetized government deficits are not the only culprit in the inflation process, nor is inflation *per se* the only reason why markets fail to work as the apparatus of central planning is dismantled. The passive system of money and credit makes the budget constraints on enterprises unduly soft. Loss-making enterprises — those which are very inefficient or have their output prices pegged too low — continue to borrow from the state bank to prevent unemployment in their work forces; this perverse flow of bank credit contributes to the loss of control over the money supply. In addition, once planning controls are

TABLE 4
USSR: Fiscal Development
(In Percent of GDP)

	1985	1986	1987	1988	1989 (estimate)
State budget revenue	47.3	45.8	43.6	41.7	41.0
of which:					
From state enterprises	14.9	15.8	15.0	13.2	11.9
Turnover taxes	12.6	11.5	11.4	11.5	11.8
State budget expenditure	49.7	52.0	52.0	51.0	49.5
of which:					
Investment in the economy	8.2	8.3	8.7	8.7	7.2
Subsidies	8.9	9.4	9.3	10.1	10.6
Overall balance	-2.4	-6.2	-8.4	-9.2	-8.5
Adjusted balance[1]	—	—	-8.8	-11.0	-9.5

[1]Includes cost of extra-budgetary agriculture price support but excludes balance of centralized fund operations.

Source: IMF (1990)

removed, profitable enterprises will be anxious to spend their previously blocked cash balances lest they be seized or refrozen — thus exacerbating the inflationary pressure.

But the inflation story for the economy in transition does not end here. The productivity of physical capital — both fixed assets and inventories of inputs and goods in process — could fall. Because of the absence of attractive monetary assets, whether liquid cash, or time deposits bearing a positive real rate of interest, newly liberalized enterprises will overbid for storable material inputs, foreign exchange, capital goods, etc. In effect, decentralized enterprises will carry "excess" inventories of all kinds as **substitute monetary stores of value** (McKinnon 1991). The abysmally low productivity of physical capital in socialist economies could worsen during liberalization, thus adding to the net inflationary pressure as the supply of goods for sale falls relative to the aggregate demand for them.

Finally, once central planning is dismantled but the uncodified tax system based on the seizure of accumulated enterprise surpluses remains in place, it can hardly fail to undermine managerial incentives. The syndrome of the "soft budget constraint" (Kornai 1986b) is aggravated: firms making incipient losses get compensated by subsidies (including cheap credit), and "successful" firms have their surpluses removed. In addition, the desperate need of government for revenue leads to continual and unpredictable reinterventions to control enterprises and to extract surpluses; and these reinterventions are made easier when the highly visible deposits of enterprises with the state bank are easily (re)frozen or seized.

Such reinterventions make it virtually impossible for a socialist government like the Soviet Union to commit to lasting tax or monetary agreements, or for enterprises to make long-term contracts with each other. Whatever tax, property, or credit arrangements are promulgated, they are continually overturned as economic events unfold. This chronic instability in the "rules of the game" may well be characteristic of any socialist regime where political and economic power is monopolized by one party (Litwack 1991). However, it is greatly aggravated if a government is fiscally straitened and must grab economic surpluses whenever they become visible.

3   Creating an Internal Revenue Service: From Profits Taxation to a VAT and Personal Income Tax

As a government divests state-owned enterprises while freeing wholesale and retail markets from price and output controls, how can financial equilibrium be better maintained? What domestic fiscal and monetary reforms would be necessary and sufficient to constrain enterprises and households from overbidding for the economy's scarce resources?

On the fiscal side, it is important to focus just on the central government by itself — although fiscal relationships among central, provincial, and local governments can be tangled (Wong 1990). At the outset of the liberalization, an organized internal revenue service (IRS), a major government bureaucracy for collecting taxes from households and liberalized enterprises, should be in place. Operating under stable tax laws, the IRS can collect revenue directly from households and from enterprises in the rapidly growing liberalized sector. Then, as the relative size of taxable surpluses from traditional enterprises in the unreformed state sector decline, the government's fiscal position need not deteriorate.

Besides collecting revenue, however, the way the new IRS works *vis-a-vis* liberalized enterprises — as distinct from enterprises remaining under government ministerial control — must be spelled out. The debilitating practice of seizing the cash surpluses of profitable enterprises while subsidizing loss makers must end. But the recent history of the reform socialist governments of the Soviet Union, China, and the smaller economies of Eastern Europe and Asia is one continual reintervention to seize high profits and to subsidize losses. This moral hazard in public policy is now so pronounced that major institutional changes in both the fiscal and monetary systems are necessary if government reintervention is to be credibly foreclosed. On the fiscal side, I suggest that **reforming socialist governments eliminate the taxation of profits generated within domestically owned enterprises in the liberalized sector.**[3]

Once output prices are decontrolled and production decisions are made freely — but not until then — a full-scale value-added tax (VAT) can be effectively imposed. Thus, new enterprises, or existing enterprises just entering the liberalized sector, would immediately register to pay their VAT as a condition for getting an operating license and legal protection from the State. For example, imposing a flat 20 percent VAT rate on all liberalized enterprises whether profitable or not is straightforward. Whatever their corporate form — cooperative, private, or owned by the central or local governments — their VAT liabilities would be unambiguous. Provided that the fledgling IRS also imposed a full-scale personal income tax, supplemented by consumer excises, taxing the profits of **liberalized** enterprises should be unnecessary for securing sufficient revenue.[4]

Traditional enterprises under direct state control, as described below, would remain subject to the old-style full taxation of residual profits. For accounting purposes, however, a "shadow" VAT might also be imposed on them. Although this shadow VAT reduced residual profits one-for-one much like the old socialist turnover tax used to do, the government would then have a better accounting measure of "true" profits and losses in traditional enterprises.

Unlike the old-line industrial ministries sponsoring specific industries, the new IRS would deal with households and liberalized enterprises throughout the economy. A VAT is levied at a flat rate on enterprises' gross sales less the tax embedded in purchased supplies. If profit taxation is officially abandoned, no accounting measure of enterprise profits is necessary for collecting the VAT; this circumstance would help shelter the IRS from pressure to seize "inordinate" enterprise profits. (Operating under a moderate-rate personal income tax, the IRS would still want to catch dividends paid out to individuals.) Moreover, because the incidence of the VAT is eventually passed forward to retail buyers, pressure to exempt liberalized loss-making enterprises, those which the state is no longer sponsoring, from paying this well-defined tax would be minimal.

---

[3]There remains a strong case for moderate domestic taxation of domestic profits that are repatriated in some form to foreigners. Not only would the socialist government need the revenue, but the foreign-owned firm can typically claim equivalent tax credits against its own corporate income tax liability in its home country.

[4]The pros and cons of different forms of taxation under classical socialism in comparison to a more liberalized economy are reviewed in McKinnon (1991).

4   Enterprise Financial Constraints in the Transition: A Tripartite Classification

Even with a fledgling IRS in place, the fiscal position of the reforming socialist government is likely too precarious, and its ability to collect tax revenue from the private sector too weak, to afford any massive giveaway of claims on earning assets. For fiscal reasons alone, an early attempt at a "big bang" privatization by giving common shares in large state-owned enterprises or in natural resource industries to households on a widespread basis could be seriously misplaced. However, this argument does not preclude a one-time restructuring of formal ownership rights in state enterprises more effectively to recognize the implicit claims of existing stakeholders — workers, banks, pension funds, and the public treasury — by the distribution of explicit equity shares that validate these claims (Lipton and Sachs 1990b). Nor does it preclude rapid effective privatization in agriculture — as the Chinese demonstrated with the break up of the communes and the advent of their "family responsibility system" after 1978.

However, breaking up large industrial concerns in the context of a "big bang" is a more dubious proposition (Murrell 1990b) — although one can move much more quickly to liberalize small-scale industry and agriculture. Indeed, capitalism is best grown from modest beginnings in small-scale enterprises that provide a sorting mechanism for successful and unsuccessful entrepreneurs (Kornai 1990). Many years might have to pass before domestic entrepreneurs with proven managerial expertise accumulate sufficient capital to buy state-owned industrial assets on a large scale. Correspondingly, massive sales of domestic assets to foreigners at the outset of the liberalization could even delay the development of domestic entrepreneurship — although joint ventures, in which domestic partners retain the principal ownership claims, can sometimes be useful vehicles for absorbing foreign technologies.

Before the transition to a full-fledged market economy is effected, therefore, both traditional enterprises with soft budget constraints and liberalized enterprises with hard budget constraints would likely coexist for some years, but under somewhat different monetary and tax regimes to maintain financial control more efficiently. Table 5 summarizes what financial arrangements would be consistent with the degree of liberalization or mode of operation of each class of enterprise. Three relatively gross classifications are distinguished.

First, **traditional enterprises** remaining under state ownership would remain subject to some price controls on their outputs, and perhaps to state materials allocations for some inputs (including credits from the state banking system). They could include both natural public goods such as utilities, energy-producing resource-intensive industries, and infrastructure activities like roads and irrigation facilities. In addition, industrial basket cases — those running with negative cash flows even when prices are fully liberalized, but which the government

TABLE 5
Alternative Financial Arrangements for
Enterprises in Transition

	Traditional[1] Enterprises	Liberalized Enterprises	
		State Owned[2]	Private
Taxation	Expropriation of surpluses[5]	Uniform value-added tax	Uniform value-added tax
Deposit Money: Domestic Commodity Convertibility[3]	Restricted	Unrestricted interest-bearing	Unrestricted interest-bearing
Credit Eligibility	State Bank	Nonbank capital market	Nonbank capital market
Wages	Government determined	Government determined	Market determined
Residual Profits	Accrue to government	Dividends to government -retained earnings for reinvestment	Dividends to owners[4]-retained earning for reinvestment or lending to other private interprises
Foreign Exchange	Restricted	Current account only	Current account only

[1]Traditional enterprises are those whose output and pricing decisions are still determined by a central government authority or planning bureau with centrally allocated inputs and credits from the state bank to cover (possible) negative cash flows.

[2]"State owned" can refer to any level of government. Nevertheless, the VAT and restrictions on bank credit would apply equally to liberalized enterprises owned or controlled in different jurisdictions.

[3]"Commodity convertibility" here means the freedom to spend for domestic goods and services or to buy and hold domestic coin and currency, but need not imply convertibility into foreign exchange.

[4]Dividends would be subject to the personal income tax when paid out to private owners, but retained earnings would not be taxed.

[5]Although residual profits revert to the state, they could include a "shadow" VAT levy in order better to understand the "true" profitability of traditional enterprises.

could not immediately close down for social reasons — would also fall into this "traditional" category.

This distinction between liberalized enterprises with hard budget constraints and traditional enterprises need not preclude substantial rationalization of relative prices in the latter. Indeed, although a "big bang" in the sense of a massive transfer of ownership claims to industrial property at the outset of liberalization should be eschewed, widespread **marketization** of economic transacting where government-controlled prices are set closer to market-clearing levels is both feasible and highly desirable. For example, in the energy sector, which one would expect to remain under state ownership and control much like a public utility, a sharp increase in the economy-wide price of energy to approximate world levels should be charged to all enterprises at the outset of the transition process. Otherwise, liberalized enterprises will begin using, or continue to use, energy wastefully. Even though traditional enterprises may not economize on energy use very rapidly, the reduction in their accounting profits as the price of energy is increased would be a better signal to the government of their true profitability. Higher energy prices would allow the government to collect (tax) the economic rents (surplus) associated with the exploitation of this natural resource more efficiently.

Second, in **state-owned liberalized enterprises,** output and input decisions would be freely determined by the enterprise management, who could also bargain freely over commodity prices in pursuit of higher profits after paying the value-added tax. State-owned manufacturing concerns could fit into this liberalized category as long as the government exerted its ownership claim over capital to maximize profits. Although managers of liberalized state-owned enterprises would operate freely in commodity markets, the government would continue to set wages and salaries for managers by direct participation in wage bargaining. The government would also determine the division of profits between dividends reverting to the state and earnings retained by these enterprises themselves.

Third, **private liberalized enterprises** would have no direct government restraints on their making output, price, wage and dividend decisions in the pursuit of higher profits. Along with their liberalized state-owned counterparts, these private or cooperative enterprises would be liable for the value-added tax but not for any separate profits tax. However, the IRS would also enlist their cooperation in withholding personal income taxes on any wages, interest, dividends, or capital gains paid out to individuals.

For each of these three enterprise classifications, the columns in table 5 list consistent tax, monetary, credit, wage, and profit arrangements. Down column 1, for example, traditional enterprises continue to be taxed by the expropriation of their surpluses (although this tax would include a "shadow" VAT calculation); their deposits in the state bank remain blocked and could be considered simply an extension of the government's treasury accounts. Being thus incapacitated in terms of their own financial resources, traditional enterprises would still be eligible for loans from the state bank at positive real interest rates to finance new investments or to cover ongoing losses. As under classical socialism, their freedom of financial action remains generally highly circumscribed. In contrast, columns 2 and 3 of table 5 also show that liberalized enterprises whether private or state-owned are subject to a uniform VAT but not to a profits tax.

5 Hardening the System of Money and Credit: Banks and Liberalized Enterprises

What system of money and credit for the newly liberalized sector would be consistent with this different tax regime? The answer depends partly on the initial conditions that the transitional economy faces. Suppose it faces a near "worst-case" scenario in two important respects. First, a fiscal deficit forces the government (and traditional enterprises) to continue borrowing heavily from the banking system despite the best efforts of the newly created IRS. Second, the state banking system itself, with an enormous bad loan portfolio from past lending to loss-making enterprises at the government's behest, has yet to be restructured to avoid similar moral hazard in future lending. The need for a complete recapitalization of existing divisions or branches of the state banking system, before normal lending on commercial terms can begin, has been stressed by Brainard (1990a). Both enterprise deposits with and loans from the state banks may have to be drastically scaled down. (The sorry history of bank lending in partially liberalized regimes — as in Yugoslavia, Poland, Hungary, and China in the 1980s — shows the severe moral hazard from overlending to enterprises that local or central governments wish to sustain or promote.)

At the macroeconomic level, the first assumption says that no room exists for noninflationary bank lending to the liberalized sector. At the microeconomic level, the second assumption says that monetary intermediaries, whose deposits must be insured to protect the payments system, cannot be trusted to lend safely on commercial terms anyway.

Nor could traditional enterprises with soft budget constraints be trusted to lend to or borrow from other enterprises — particularly those in the liberalized sector — on any substantial scale. The recent financial history of partial "liberalizations" in the 1970s and 1980s in many Eastern European countries is that loss-making traditional enterprises overborrrow from their suppliers by simply not making payments on their trade credits, thus throwing suppliers into financial difficulty. To prevent general industrial collapse, the State Bank is often forced to reintervene to provide (inflationary) credit to all concerned. In this model, free trade on commodity account would prevail between the traditional and liberalized sectors, but they would be insulated financially. To maintain control over the aggregate supply of internally convertible ("household") money, the government would have to monitor carefully and limit the cash deficits of the traditional (and general government) sector with households and liberalized enterprises.

Given these micro and macroeconomic constraints, how might domestic banking arrangements best evolve with respect to the liberalized sector? Imagine two successive stages in the transition.

Stage One: Liberalized enterprises are confined to self-finance and to borrowing from the nonbank capital market not involving traditional enterprises. Bank lending to liberalized enterprises is prohibited.

Stage Two: Commercial banks begin limited and fully collateralized short-term lending to liberalized enterprises according to the "Real Bills Doctrine". That is, they lend only to finance the build up of "productive" short-term assets, such as inventories or accounts receivable, that can be easily realized if assumed.

At the outset of Stage One, all urban and rural liberalized enterprises, whether state-owned, cooperative, or private, become ineligible for credit from banks (that is, from deposit-taking monetary intermediaries). Borrowing from the nonbank capital market could take place freely. But, apart from "normal" trade credit which itself must be circumscribed, this borrowing is likely to be quite small for some years. Instead, liberalized enterprises would depend mainly on their on their owners' initial equity and subsequent (untaxed) retained earnings for investment finance. These earnings could now accumulate in currency and demand deposits or in interest-bearing time deposits that were now fully convertible for domestic spending. Banking institutions would be rearranged so that the government could no longer conveniently monitor, appropriate, or freeze the financial asset positions of the liberalized enterprises. When a state-owned enterprise was declared to be "liberalized," it would lose the privilege of borrowing from the state bank but be compensated with the right to accumulate internally convertible domestic money and other financial assets.

A primary goal of Stage One is to encourage firms to use monetary assets as a store of value, rather than physical assets. As households and liberalized enterprises build up their liquid asset positions, excess inventories and other forms of low-yield capital would be voluntarily disgorged and replaced with more attractive monetary assets. In this way the average productivity of physical capital could increase from the outset of the liberalization, in spite of industrial restructuring.

Decreasing the demand for physical assets as a store of value will also help disinflate the economy. If monetary assets are to be attractive, however, the efficiency of the payments mechanism becomes critically important to all liberalized enterprises, whether private or state-owned. To facilitate free convertibility of enterprise deposits into domestic goods or currency, rapid check clearing and money transfers are essential. In effect, the monetary circuit of liberalized enterprises would be unified with that of households as both could hold coin and currency as well as domestically convertible deposits. (However, the monetary deposits of traditional enterprises would remain blocked; their funds could not be spent or converted into cash without permission.)

In addition, the government would set substantially positive real interest rates on time deposits in the mode of successfully disinflating developing economies — such as Taiwan in the late 1950s and Korea in the mid-1960s. What the socialist government can afford to pay on deposits, however, is limited by its own fiscal position and its success in increasing the yields on the government-owned assets that dominate the loan side of the state bank's balance sheet. To achieve high real financial growth in households and liberalized enterprises, setting real deposit rates in this 3 to 6 percent range is consistent with the experience of other countries (McKinnon 1991), provided that these deposits are not subject to being blocked.

Such reliance on self-finance is the simplest technique for imposing financial restraint on liberalized enterprises while simultaneously increasing the productivity of physical capital. Bankruptcy would be virtually automatic if the internal cash flow of a liberalized enterprise became negative for any significant length of time. The effective wages paid to workers and the (implicit) yield to all owners of the firm's equity would vary directly with the firm's success in the open market. Self-finance avoids the issue of moral hazard in lending by government-owned or insured banks. It also has the great advantage of bypassing the difficult problem of how to establish a more elaborate corporate structure, with different forms of accountability to outside lenders.

However, self-finance works for liberalized enterprises if and only if output prices have been decontrolled fully, and firms can negotiate freely over input prices and wages. As long as no liberalized enterprise can borrow from the state bank, nor from traditional enterprises which still have access to credit from the state bank, then all liberalized enterprises will be in the same competitive position. In competitive equilibrium, therefore, profit margins should be sufficiently wide for liberalized enterprises, on average, to finance their own ongoing investments.

Are there historical examples of this widening of profit margins in a regime of self-finance? The successful liberalization of Chinese agriculture from 1979 to about 1985 relied almost exclusively on Chinese farm households building up their own cash positions to finance on-farm investments.[5] For enterprises to build up sufficient cash, however, depends on the absence of any significant tax on current profits and on having broad money bring a positive real deposit rate, that is, not be significantly taxed by inflation. In the early years (1979-84) of

---

[5]This example and others are discussed further in McKinnon (1991).

China's agricultural liberalization, the price level was quite stable, although inflation later became a serious problem.

To be sure, self-finance has its limitations. Large scale infrastructure investments for roads, pipelines, and major irrigation facilities, etc. would have to remain in the government (traditional) sector, although with a better set of commodity prices and positive real interest rates to guide decision making. Then, too, even successful liberalized enterprises with excellent investment opportunities would have to wait a bit longer (compared to borrowing externally) to generate internal funds sufficient to exploit those opportunities unless they could attract additional equity finance. Nevertheless, by building up or drawing down bank deposits at positive real interest rates, liberalized enterprises and households would be engaging in a limited form of inter-temporal arbitrage. Without access to external credits, liberalized enterprises would aim for rather larger average stocks of liquid assets (including deposits) to cover unexpected contingencies, such as shifts in their terms of trade, that might suddenly reduce current cash flows.

As the nonbank private capital markets develop — say, rural credit cooperatives or urban markets in short-term commercial bills — the severe credit constraints on liberalized enterprises would relax naturally. But these private lenders would also face bankruptcy if they made bad loans or charged interest rates below market levels. Compared to lending by the state-owned or state-insured banks, moral hazard in lending would be dramatically reduced. The government role would be to serve as ultimate enforcer of all debt contracts through the judicial system and to give the liberalized sector a stable unit of deferred payment by securing the price level.

Suppose such monetary control is established and fiscal deficits are reduced to the point that the government plus traditional enterprises no longer fully absorbed the lending resources of the state banking system. The price level has stabilized. Moreover, enforcement of debt contracts in the liberalized sector is secured, and open markets in some debt instruments, such as commercial bills, have begun to develop in the nonbank capital markets. Then, and only then, is Stage Two feasible: to begin fully collateralized bank lending to the liberalized sector on strictly commercial terms. The prior existence of a commercial bill market could provide a natural vehicle for providing that collateral; in fact, established bill brokers might be the most technically qualified applicants with sufficient capital to be granted private commercial bank licenses. Checkable and interest-bearing deposits could be offered to the general public provided that these authorized banks invested in a diversified portfolio of commercial bills with well-defined secondary markets and with more or less the same term to maturity as their deposits.

Alternatively, appropriately recapitalized divisions of the state bank could be designated as "commercial"; these divisions would mobilize additional saving by offering higher yield time deposits and then using the funds to begin "for profit" lending to the liberalized sector. However, tight regulations on collateral for securing their loans — perhaps inventory bills of lading or accounts receivable — would have to be in place to prevent moral hazard through the non-repayment of loans from developing all over again.

In the optimum order of liberalization, therefore, the development of ordinary commercial banking may well have to be deferred for some years after liberalization begins and to wait until overall monetary and fiscal control is secured. Putting the matter more negatively, premature efforts to break up the monolithic state bank (associated with classical socialism) into a central bank and more loosely regulated commercial banks (associated with mature capitalist economies) could lead to a disastrous loss of overall monetary control and a worsening of moral hazard in bank lending in transitional economies. This pattern occurred in Poland in 1988-89 with the partitioning of the state bank aggravating the underlying inflationary pressure[6] and is happening in the Soviet Union in 1990-91 with the formation of hundreds of wildcat "commercial" banks controlled by the old state enterprises (McKinnon 1991).

6   Foreign Trade and Foreign Exchange

The optimum order for liberalizing quotas, tariffs, and exchange controls in foreign trade in parallel with the freeing of domestic trade is as complex as it is important. This chapter has focused on domestic financial policy: how to reconstruct the public finances and the system of money and credit in a step-by-step transition from classical socialism toward a market economy.

In the order of liberalization, financial arrangements governing the foreign exchanges should parallel and complement these domestic tax and monetary arrangements. For example, traditional enterprises whose deposits remain blocked for domestic transacting could hardly be allowed to .exercise convertibility of this money into foreign exchange. In contrast, the money of liberalized enterprises could be freely convertible for current-account transacting, for importing or exporting, provided that the country's foreign commercial (tariff) policy was simultaneously well-defined under a unified exchange rate. These distinctions appear in the last row of table 4.

However, the severe domestic credit constraints imposed on the liberalized enterprises as a matter of policy would be undermined if such enterprises could freely borrow (or deposit) abroad. Until the domestic capital market matured

---

[6]I am indebted to Professor Arnold Harberger for pointing out this ill-advised feature of financial reform in Poland prior to the more successful price-level stabilization of 1990.

with borrowing and lending at market interest rates, foreign exchange convertibility on capital account would be inappropriate, even for liberalized firms.

What about tariffs, quotas, and commercial policy in foreign trade? Again the pace of liberalization would depend heavily on the socialist economy's initial conditions: the preexisting system of protection and the degree to which it influenced resource use.

In a traditional centrally planned Stalinist economy, protection for domestic manufacturing is almost entirely implicit. From exchange controls and the apparatus of state trading, disguised subsidies to users of energy and other material inputs are coupled with virtually absolute protection from competing foreign manufactures. Although no formal tariffs appear in any legal codes, the implicit structure of tariff equivalents "cascades" downward from very high levels for domestic production of finished consumer goods through manufactured intermediate products through industrial raw materials and energy, which are negatively protected because of implicit export taxes (or import subsidies).

This highly cascaded structure of implicit tariffs in socialist economies raises effective protection in finished goods to the point where most manufacturing will exhibit negative (or very low) value added at world market prices. In such circumstances, a precipitate move to free trade could provoke the collapse of most domestic manufacturing industries no matter how the exchange rate is set and no matter that some of this industry might eventually be viable at world market prices.

Thus, reforms to make commercial policy more explicit should accompany efforts to make the currency convertible on current account. In McKinnon (1991), the simultaneous "tariffication" of quantitative restrictions on competing imports and the elimination of implicit export taxes on energy and material inputs as the economy moves quickly to a market-based system are suggested. Once made explicit, the highest tariffs in the cascade can then be phased down step-by-step to zero (or a low uniform level) over a pre-announced five to ten year time horizon. The newly marketized economy would then converge to free foreign trade at a more deliberate pace — one that better recognized the problem of overcoming distortions from the preexisting system of protection.

7   Concluding Note on the Eastern European "J-Curve"

Before moving quickly to decentralize domestic economic activity or to privatize state property, a comprehensive explicit system of personal and business income taxation should be in place. In addition, the system of money and credit should be transformed into one that actively constrains the ability of enterprises to bid for scarce resources — while at the same time providing them with attractive monetary assets which they can freely accumulate. Otherwise, the liberalizing socialist economy faces the possibility of an immediate inflationary explosion.

Similarly, a precipitate move to free foreign trade without taking adequate account of the preexisting implicit system of industrial protection, and the severe distortions in resource use arising therefrom, risks the possibility of a rapid collapse in industrial output much like that experienced in East Germany and Poland in 1990-91.

Instead, one can conceive of a more deliberate pace of liberalization conditioned by the ability of the government to reform its monetary, fiscal, and foreign trade policies to support market liberalization properly (McKinnon 1991). Not only would the initial sharp downturn in economic activity characteristic of all the Eastern European economies at the present time be mitigated, but liberalizing reforms themselves would stand a better chance of being sustained into the indefinite future.

8 Stabilization and Liberalization Policies for Economies in Transition: Latin American Lessons for Eastern Europe

Sebastian Edwards

1 Introduction

In many ways 1989 and 1990 have been magical years with the end of the Cold War and the beginning of an exciting period of political and economic reconstruction in Central and Eastern Europe and an era that promises great opportunities for the world economy. As nations of Eastern Europe abandon the doctrines and policies of communism, they face the immense challenge of implementing an efficient and effective transition to a market-oriented economic regime. What makes the transitional issue particularly difficult is that the peoples of Eastern Europe have placed their hopes of a dramatically rapid improvement in their standard of living on the implementation of market-oriented reforms. To the extent that these reforms fail, or if the transition is perceived as being unduly costly, disillusionment and frustration will settle in, generating serious social and political unrest with unpredictable consequences.

In designing policy packages for the transition to free markets, the Eastern European countries face three main problems: first, how to stabilize their economies, achieving internal and external macroeconomic balance; second, how to implement the structural and market-oriented reforms in an orderly and effective way; and third, how to proceed with the privatization process. With

An earlier version of this chapter was presented at the American Economic Association meetings in Washington D.C. in December 1990, as well as at the Prague Conference. The author is grateful for comments from discussants at the meetings and from Geoff Carliner, Julius Santaella, Gordon Rausser and Chris Clague. He is also indebted once again to Mike Savastano for helpful discussions. Support from the Institute for Policy Reform is gratefully acknowledged.

respect to stabilization policies, in the majority of the countries the most important controversies refer to: (1) how to solve a situation of monetary and fiscal disequilibrium. In some nations — Poland, Yugoslavia and the Soviet Union, for example, this discussion has also dealt with how to eliminate a situation of monetary overhang; (2) whether the anti-inflationary program should be based on an exchange rate or monetary anchor; and (3) the extent to which the labor market should be reformed and de-indexed.

In terms of structural, market-oriented reforms, the key questions are how fast and in what sequence the opening of the external sector and the creation of a domestic financial market should take place. In this area the issue of bankruptcy laws has also been hotly debated. Finally, with regard to privatization the key discussions have centered on whether firms should be sold or given away to the public, how fast this transfer should take place, and to what degree foreign investors should be allowed to participate in the process.[1]

Among the formerly socialist economies attempting to make the transition to a market economy, the macroeconomic situation inherited from communism differs quite substantially from country to country. At one extreme are Yugoslavia and Poland, which confronted spiralling inflation on the eve of their stabilization programs launched in January, 1990. At the other extreme is Czechoslovakia, which avoided fiscal deficits and inflation under communism and was able to begin its transition program under conditions of a fair degree of macroeconomic stability (see Thomas, Ch. 16). Even in Czechoslovakia, however, substantial upward revisions in prices have been inevitable, necessitating currency devaluations and wage controls. The other countries of Eastern and Central Europe — Hungary, Bulgaria, Romania, and the USSR — have encountered fiscal deficits and inflation in varying degrees and will need to confront issues of macroeconomic balance as well as those of structural reforms and privatization. This chapter will focus mainly on stabilization problems during the transition and will draw its Eastern European examples primarily from Poland and Yugoslavia, but the lessons drawn are applicable to most of the countries that have recently begun their transitions.

The liberalization and stabilization programs in Poland and Yugoslavia exhibit a number of striking similarities (see Coricelli and Rocha 1991). Both countries freed prices, devalued abruptly, and decided to rely on a major price level adjustment to solve the monetary overhang problem. The two countries immediately declared (partial) convertibility of their currencies and subsequently fixed the nominal exchange rate in an attempt to provide an anchor for the price system.

In Yugoslavia the fixed nominal rate was abandoned after one year; a (substantial) devaluation was implemented in the first week of 1991. In Poland, on

---

[1]On controversies regarding the Eastern European reforms, see Hinds (1990b), Lipton and Sachs (1990a) and Nordhaus (1990).

the other hand, a nominal devaluation was implemented in May, 1991, when the zloty was adjusted by 15 percent with respect to the dollar and pegged with respect to a basket. Both countries increased interest rates to control aggregate demand, and announced (but not quite implemented) tough bankruptcy laws. Additionally, they both partially de-indexed wages to reduce inflation inertia. Also, in both nations, there have been announcements of sweeping privatization that have not yet materialized in any significant way (Coricelli and Rocha 1991).

In spite of some clear successes, such as a reduction in inflation in the second and third quarters of 1990, the (initial) elimination of the black market premium and the generation of a trade surplus, both Poland and Yugoslavia are currently facing some serious problems. Although inflation is lower than in the first months of the programs, it is (especially in Poland) still significantly higher than expected. In Yugoslavia the republics have challenged the central authorities including the austerity adjustment programs, and the country is on the verge of a civil war. Unemployment has climbed rapidly, and industrial production has plummeted. After an initial period of excitement, it is becoming apparent that the path to a market-oriented system will be long and difficult. In light of these results, a number of observers are asking themselves whether other (former) socialist nations, and the USSR in particular, should follow similar programs or if, on the contrary, they should follow alternative paths.

Although strictly speaking the Eastern European experiments have no direct precedents, there are some historical episodes that can shed some light and provide important lessons on particular aspects of the free market transformations. For instance, the post-World War II European experience with monetary overhang and monetary reforms offers potentially important lessons on how to tackle a situation of major monetary disequilibrium cum rationing. Also, the large number of stabilization attempts in Latin America during the last four decades provides a wealth of lessons — both positive and negative — on different aspects of anti-inflationary programs.

From an historical and comparative perspective the largely successful stabilization and liberalization experiences in Chile and Mexico in the last 15 years offer particularly important lessons for Eastern European leaders and their advisors. In both of these countries, inflation has been significantly reduced, the external sector has been practically opened to free trade, dynamic domestic financial markets have been created, vigorous privatization programs have been enacted, and an increasingly strong record of growth has been established. In fact, Chile, Mexico (and Bolivia) have recently been able (partially) to conquer extreme inflations.[2] An important difference between the Chilean and Mexican experiences is that in Chile stabilization was very gradual, while the reduction of inflation to manageable levels was achieved quite rapidly in Mexico. In Chile it

---

[2]The main difference in these three cases is that in Mexico and Chile stabilization has been accompanied by recovery and growth while Bolivia has remained basically stagnant.

took 25 quarters to reduce inflation from its peak to below 5 percent per quarter, but it took only 6 quarters to accomplish this task in Mexico.[3]

The purpose of this chapter is to discuss some Latin American lessons on stabilization that can be useful to understand better the policy options available to the former socialist nations. Although the analysis focuses on stabilization, there is some reference to privatization and other market-oriented policies. Throughout the discussion the case of Chile receives the most attention. The reasons for focusing on Chile are several. First, in 1973 Chile faced initial conditions that in some respects are as close to those of Eastern Europe as they can possibly be: in mid-1973 Chile faced a severe situation of monetary overhang, almost every price was controlled by the government, black markets were rampant, production had stagnated, the fiscal deficit bordered 25 percent of GNP, every sector of the economy was severely distorted, and most key sectors of the economy (including banking, commerce, exports, and large manufacturing firms) were owned by the state. Second, during the last 15 years Chile experimented with a series of alternative policies, providing a fascinating laboratory of sorts where some mistakes were made. Third, in contrast with many other Latin American episodes, Chile's policies in the 1970s and 1980s dealt with both stabilization and liberalization (including a major privatization program). Fourth, Chile represents a successful transition from a highly inflationary and tightly controlled economy into a market-oriented and stable one. The degree of success of the Chilean experience is clearly underscored by the fact that the newly elected democratic government of President Patricio Aylwin has decided to maintain in place the vast majority of the economic reforms implemented during the Pinochet regime.[4] And finally, as is documented in section 3 below, the stabilization program implemented in Chile bears some remarkable similarities to that undertaken in Poland and Yugoslavia.

Although the Latin American experience offers some important lessons for Eastern Europe, it is crucially important to bear in mind that there are some fundamental differences between the two regions. In fact, if these differences are not considered there is a danger of mechanically applying analyses derived for a particular historical setting. Perhaps the most important difference between the two regions — and in particular, between the Chilean episode and Eastern Europe — is political. While Chile's reforms were undertaken by dictatorial rule, the Eastern European programs are being carried out by (mostly) democratic

---

[3]Notice, however, that this comparison is in a way unfair since the peak quarterly rate of inflation was much higher in Chile than in Mexico. In Chile, this peak was achieved in the second quarter of 1974, in which inflation reached 98.3 percent; in Mexico the peak was in the second quarter of 1983 with a rate of inflation of 23.4 percent.

[4]On the way the new democratic government has dealt with the Pinochet economic legacy, see Edwards and Edwards (1991).

governments. This difference should not be underestimated in comparing the specific experiences in these two regions. Some of the policies implemented in Chile may prove to be too unpopular to sustain in a democratic regime.

Another key difference between Chile and Eastern Europe is that in 1973 Chile had already in place a large number of fundamental market-oriented institutions. In fact, in spite of decades of government intervention and controls, Chileans had basically lived under a controlled market system. The challenge faced by the Eastern European nations is tremendous: creating market institutions from scratch is a task of Herculean proportions that should not be underestimated.

The rest of the chapter is organized as follows: section 2 deals at an analytical level with four of the most important macroeconomic problems faced by the former socialist economies embarked on stabilization programs: (1) alternative ways of dealing with the monetary overhang and rationing; (2) fiscal equilibrium and the reduction of inflation; (3) the use of fixed nominal exchange rates as an anchor in the anti-inflationary policy; and (4) the role of indexation and labor markets in the adjustment process. Section 3 discusses some important Chilean (and Mexican) lessons regarding these four important areas of the stabilization programs. This section argues that there are some very important stabilization lessons from Latin America for Eastern Europe. Section 4 provides conclusions, including some remarks on structural reforms and privatization policies.

2   Stabilization and Liberalization in Eastern Europe: Problems, Controversies and Policies

The initial conditions faced by reformers in Eastern Europe and the USSR can best be described as chaotic and unsustainable.[5] In the majority of the countries in the region, the combination of a growing monetary disequilibrium with declining labor productivity had been translated into widespread rationing of consumer (and other) goods and seriously misaligned relative prices. This problem was compounded by the fact that increasingly large fiscal deficits were (or are currently) monetized, thereby putting additional pressure on the macroeconomy, generating an extremely critical balance of payments condition, and making the repressed inflation particularly difficult to handle. Table 6 contains some basic data on the performance of these economies in the second half of the 1980s. The fact that in a number of these countries the observed rates of inflation were rather low in 1989 is not necessarily a sign of financial stability; in

---

[5]A serious problem in evaluating the initial conditions in the Eastern European countries is that the data available are extremely poor.

TABLE 6
Economic Conditions in the USSR and Eastern Europe in 1989

	Estimated Real GDP (1986=100)	Growth in Industrial Output 1989*	Inflation Rate in 1989
Bulgaria	99.9	0.0%	11.4%
Czechoslovakia	104.0	0.0%	1.8%
Hungry	101.4	-3.6%	6.9%
Poland	97.9	-4.2%	640.0%
Romania	99.5	n.a.	n.a.
USSR	105.5	0.0%	5.7%
Yugoslavia	98.4	-1.0%	2795.0%

*Refers to adjusted (as opposed to official) data.
Source: Directorate of Intelligence, Central Intelligence Agency (CIA).

many cases, it is a reflection of the fact that the substantial accumulated monetary increases were not always allowed to reflect themselves in price increases.

Stabilizing the economy is, without a doubt, a clear priority in any reform program for the (former) communist countries. Most authors have, in fact, agreed that in any sequencing discussion, the implementation of an anti-inflationary program should precede most other measures. There is much less agreement, however, on **how** to implement such a stabilization program and on how to deal, among other things, with money overhang, the fiscal disequilibrium, the exchange rate and the labor market. In this section some of the most important controversies surrounding stabilization in former socialist countries are analyzed. In the next section the discussion broadens to analyze how the recent stabilization experiences in Chile and Mexico can facilitate a better understanding of some of the problems faced by the Eastern European policy makers.

The implementation of stabilization programs is particularly difficult because, contrary to most modern experiences with macroeconomic crises, the USSR and many of the Eastern European nations faced (or currently face) both a **stock** and a **flow** macroeconomic disequilibrium.[6] The stock disequilibrium, which generated a **monetary overhang,** has been the result of years of rapid

---

[6]The different speed of reform across countries makes generalizations rather difficult. While some countries have already eliminated the stock disequilibrium, others are still struggling with this problem.

money creation under generalized price controls and declining productivity. This stock disequilibrium has provoked a situation where the actual (observed) income velocity is substantially below **desired** velocity of money and where queues and rationing are an everyday fact of life. The flow disequilibrium, on the other hand, has been the result of large (and increasing) fiscal deficits that have been monetized.

There is virtual consensus among analysts that in those countries facing both a stock and flow monetary disequilibrium, a necessary early step in the reform process is the elimination of the money overhang. At the same time, there seems to be a clear understanding that the elimination of the stock excess supply of money will not eliminate *per se* the inflationary pressures in the system. The elimination of inflation will require in addition significant fiscal adjustment that will greatly reduce, if not put a complete end to, the fiscal deficit and inflationary monetary finance.

2.1   Eliminating the monetary disequilibrium: Price adjustment or monetary reform?

A situation of monetary overhang, or repressed inflation, results when increases in the stock of money take place in an environment of generalized price controls and rationing. In these circumstances not only does the economy face disequilibrium relative prices, but in addition the actual real stock of money (M/Py) exceeds the desired stock of money $(M/Py)^*$ — where the usual notation has been used:

$$\left(\frac{M}{Py}\right) > \left(\frac{M}{Py}\right)^* \tag{1}$$

In these circumstances goods are rationed through queuing and/or a secondary black market. Clearly, then, there are "virtual" prices that clear the market for which there is no monetary disequilibrium. The existence of these "virtual" prices, of course, does not eliminate the fact that these countries face a serious situation of repressed inflation.[7]

An obvious, but nonetheless important implication of equation (1) is that there are four potential ways of solving a situation of monetary overhang: (1) a reduction of nominal money balances M through some type of monetary reform;

---

[7]Some authors have argued that there is no such thing as a monetary overhang. According to this view, even under repressed inflation there is a virtual price level — closely associated to black market prices — that clears the monetary market. Although this is definitionally correct, this view ignores the fact that many transactions take place at official prices and that consumers hold money while waiting for goods to show up in government stores.

(2) a (supposedly) once-and-for-all increase in the domestic price level P; (3) an increase in domestic real output y; and (4) a rise in the desired quantity of money $(M/Py)^*$.[8] The last two alternatives — a major increase in real output and a significant increase in the demand for money — are impractical, and implausible; moreover, even if y and $(M/Py)^*$ do increase, they will not do so with the speed required to solve the overhang problem in the short run. For all practical purposes the result is a (discrete) price adjustment or a monetary reform as the only two practical ways to eliminate the money overhang. In both options it is implicitly assumed that **relative** prices are allowed to adjust rapidly and to regain equilibrium.

Interestingly enough, while in the post-World War II period most European nations opted for the monetary reform route, at present, the Eastern European nations that have embarked on adjustment have chosen to rely on the price level adjustment approach. As pointed out in section 1, both Yugoslavia and Poland decided to handle the overhang by simultaneously freeing the vast majority of prices, declaring (partial) exchange rate convertibility and engineering a major nominal devaluation. Some authors have criticized the use of this approach for solving the overhang in these countries and suggested that the best path for the Soviet Union is to undertake a significant and sweeping monetary reform (see Dornbusch and Wolf 1990).[9]

Naturally, at the textbook level both of these alternatives are perfectly equivalent. While the monetary reform operates through the numerator of (M/Py), the price level adjustment operates through the denominator. In real world economies, however, this equivalence does not hold. First, there are marked differences with respect to the administrative requirements for each policy. While a monetary reform requires a complicated and major logistic operation, the adjustment through prices is (almost) automatic.[10] Additionally, when implementing a monetary reform, it has to be decided whether currency will be blocked, or confiscated. If blocked, for how long, and if confiscated, how much,

---

[8]Naturally, a combination of these four mechanisms would also work. See Lipton and Sachs (1990a) for a theoretical analysis of some of the most important aspects of monetary overhang.

[9]In modern Latin America the recent Collor de Mello stabilization plan in Brazil constitutes the only experience with monetary reform. However, partial reforms where a proportion of the public debt has been either blocked or transformed into lower value titles have taken place in a number of countries including Argentina and Chile. When the first version of this chapter was written, the Soviet Union had not yet implemented the 100 and 50 ruble bill confiscation process. As is pointed out below, this process must have been the most clumsy monetary reform ever engineered.

[10]The degree to which the adjustment is automatic through the price level is particularly clear when the exchange rate is allowed to float. In both Poland and Yugoslavia, however, the exchange rate was fixed after the devaluation. This issue is treated below.

and in what fashion? All of these are of course difficult and time-consuming decisions. In fact, in practical terms the most difficult problem associated with the implementation of a monetary reform is that the authorities need an approximate knowledge of the magnitude of the overhang. Miscalculations in this area can lead to serious losses in credibility. The difficulty in estimating the approximate magnitude of the overhang is particularly serious in the case of Eastern European countries, where the historical data are not reliable and where the structural and institutional reforms will affect the demand for money in an unpredictable way.[11] This problem is neatly illustrated by the fact that there are several divergent estimates on the extent of the monetary overhang in the Soviet Union. While some authors argue that an elimination of the excess supply of money in that nation will require the doubling or even tripling of the price level, others have claimed that a 50 percent adjustment will probably be enough (see the October/November 1990 issue of *The International Economy;* see also Nordhaus 1990, and McKinnon 1991). A particularly serious problem occurs when the monetary reform is not accompanied by a very rapid price liberalization and by a serious attempt at curbing the fiscal deficit. In this case, as in the recent USSR bill confiscation attempt, the relaxation of repressed inflationary measures will be extremely short-lived, with the phenomenon of monetary overhang recurring quickly and with even greater force.

An additional problem related to a monetary reform is that the reform itself may greatly affect the confidence in the domestic monetary system. To the extent that the public fears additional future confiscations or blockades, it will substitute away from domestic money and move toward real assets and foreign bank deposits. To the extent that this substitution occurs, the monetary reform *per se* will generate additional macro-disequilibria and fuel inflation. A final serious problem confronted during monetary reforms relates to the issue of fairness and distributive effects. The most straightforward way of tackling this issue is by allowing each individual to exchange up to a certain amount of old money (currency and deposits) into new money. In this way, the poorer segments will be relatively protected. This type of exchange was not carried out in recent Soviet reform, generating serious loss of confidence in the monetary system.

On the other hand, the price-level adjustment alternative is not free of problems. In particular, it is unlikely that the price level will experience only the required corrective once-and-for-all jump, without any additional perverse effects on the rate of inflation. In fact, to the extent that there are (implicit or explicit) multi-period contracts and indexation, the major price-level jump required to eliminate the overhang is likely to set in motion serious inflationary

---

[11]Dornbusch and Wolf (1990) argue that it is possible to compute the (approximate) magnitude of the overhang by combining historical data on some benchmark (normal) year and estimates of black market activities.

pressures that will perpetuate themselves for several periods.[12]   Moreover, to the extent that the initial price-level jump generates expectations of further large price changes, desired velocity will increase, and economic agents will try to anticipate (expected) future inflation, thereby putting additional pressure into the system. Dornbusch and Wolf (1990) have recently argued that attempts to solve the monetary overhang through a price level adjustment can easily degenerate into unstable situations that can even lead to hyperinflation. The fact that in both Poland and Yugoslavia, after the initial price-level adjustment, over 50 percent of deposits are still maintained in foreign currency can be interpreted as the public's lack of confidence in the future of the stabilization program.

Recently some analysts, including the staff of the International Monetary Fund, have argued that it is possible to link the elimination of the money overhang to the privatization process. This linkage would entail exchanging the excess nominal money holdings for property titles to (some) of the newly privatized firms.[13]   These proposals, however, miss the point that the elimination of the monetary overhang is a prerequisite for proceeding with almost every step in the reform process. This conclusion means that the resolution of the **stock** monetary disequilibrium has to take place very rapidly and cannot wait for the legal and administrative requirements for a successful privatization to be implemented.

In sum, then, at least in principle, both basic methods for handling a situation of monetary overhang entail some risks. While a monetary reform, especially one that errs on the estimated magnitude of the overhang, can generate serious dislocations including a loss in the credibility of the domestic monetary system, a price level adjustment can generate additional inflationary forces that, at least in theory, can explode into a hyperinflation. In fact, according to Dornbusch and Wolf (1990), four of the countries that opted for the price level adjustment in the post-World War II period ended up facing major hyperinflations. What is clear, however, is that if the monetary reform route is chosen, it is important not to use the pretext of the reform itself for delaying the freeing of prices and, thus, the correction of relative price distortions. Naturally, if prices are freed within the context of a monetary reform, their adjustment will be significantly less dramatic than if the program relies on price jumps only. In section 3, the Chilean experience with the use of price level adjustments to solve its monetary overhang in late 1973 is discussed in detail. What makes the Chilean experience particularly important is that until the recent stabilization attempts in Eastern Europe, it constituted the only episode of monetary overhang elimination since the aftermath of World War II.

---

[12]This perpetuation of inflation will arise even if there is partial indexation. Naturally, the more generalized indexation is, the more serious this problem will be.

[13]Hinds (1990b) also discusses this possibility. He is, however, quite critical about its applicability.

2.2   Fiscal discipline and the end of inflation

The elimination of monetary overhang will not put an end to inflation in Eastern Europe or the Soviet Union. Indeed, inflationary pressures will come to an end only if the monetization of the fiscal deficit is eradicated: either fiscal deficits are reduced to levels compatible with foreign financing, or they are plainly reduced to zero. Naturally, a comprehensive approach to fiscal balance will require tackling the problem from both the revenue and expenditure side. In the second half of the 1980s, however, the fiscal deficit increased significantly in most of the region (see table 7).

In Poland and Yugoslavia, the stabilization programs contemplated massive expenditure cuts — mostly through the elimination of subsidies to state-owned firms — and an increase in revenues through the collection of dividends from public enterprises and higher compliance and efficiency in tax collection. In both cases the initial fiscal adjustment was substantial, allowing a closing of the gap between revenues and outlays.[14] In both cases, however, after an initial success, maintaining fiscal discipline has been extremely difficult in light of regional and political unrest.

Perhaps one of the most serious macroeconomic problems faced by the Eastern European authorities is the creation of an efficient and effective tax system. For decades, these economies have functioned on the basis of an **implicit** tax system where direct controls over wages, prices and enterprise earnings provided the bulk of government revenue. As the system moves away from direct government intervention and toward market-generated price signals, these sources of government revenues will disappear. Standard tax systems — which rely on both direct and indirect taxes — will have to be implemented. This implementation, of course, is not an easy task. It is important, however, to institute a tax system early on that will be able to raise revenues in an efficient way. In that regard, a broad value-added tax, such as the one adopted in the last decade or so in many Latin American nations, would possibly provide the most effective cornerstone of a modern tax system.[15]

---

[14]See Rocha (1990) and Coricelli and Rocha (1991). Many stabilization programs including those undertaken to date in Eastern Europe rely on an increase in the efficiency in tax collection as an important source for closing the fiscal gap. The main idea is that once the initial measures (such as the freezing of the exchange rate) reduce inflation, there will be an increase in real revenues (a reverse Oliveira-Tanzi effect). Although there is some merit in this belief, there is a serious risk of overestimating the actual importance of this phenomenon. This rise will be especially great in cases where the monetary overhang is handled through a price level adjustment, and where due to the existence of indexation and medium term contracts, inflation will remain high for some time.

[15]See Kopits (1991) for a thorough discussion of options and progress in this area of the reform programs.

TABLE 7
Fiscal Balance as Percentage of GNP/GDP
in Selected European Countries*

	1985	1989
Bulgaria	-1	-3
Czechoslovakia	-1	-9
Hungary	1	-2
Poland	-1	-1[a]
Romania	3	8
USSR	-2	-10
Yugoslavia	1	n.a.

*A negative sign indicates a **deficit,** while a positive sign indicates a **surplus.**
[a]1988.
Source: Kopits (1991).

A serious problem faced by most countries embarked on a stabilization program is that during the transition inflation tends to erode real tax revenues (the Oliveira-Tanzi effect). An efficient antidote to this problem, and one that has been tried in some Latin American nations such as Chile, is to enact an **indexed** tax system where corporate and other taxes are subject to inflationary correction. An additional advantage to indexing the tax system is that it will tend to add credibility to the stabilization program.

The reduction or elimination of subsidies to public firms is another important channel through which the fiscal gap has traditionally been closed.[16] This measure, which has recently been undertaken in both Poland and Yugoslavia, often results in severe losses for firms and in an increase in their debt, some of which eventually becomes bad debt. A potential problem is how to handle these losses and low-quality debt once the decision to privatize is made. One possibility is to sell the firms, including the bad debt, at a relatively low price. This low price reflects the fact that the companies' financial conditions are not fully healthy. This sale option was, by and large, the procedure used during the first round of Chilean stabilizations in 1973-80 (see Edwards and Edwards 1991). Although this procedure may be the most efficient way to proceed — since it allows the privatization to proceed quite quickly — it is usually politically risky.

---

[16]In fact, for many years IMF stabilization programs have included the elimination of subsidies as one of their most important components (see Edwards 1989b).

When public firms are sold at low prices the authorities are often accused of "giving away" the national patrimony. An alternative procedure is to "clean" the firms to be privatized from bad debt before they are offered to the public. A potential problem with this approach is that the public enterprises' bad debts are sometimes transferred to the Central Bank, transforming a fiscal deficit into a quasi-fiscal deficit.[17] If, indeed, as part of the pre-privatization strategy, the authorities decide to free public firms of bad loans, a more effective procedure is to transfer them to a specially created institution or holding company that will only have losses. The government, then, will have to finance these losses from its general budget. In this way the system greatly gains in transparency and efficiency.

2.3   De-indexing labor and other markets

A common characteristic of very high (as opposed to hyper) inflation episodes is that the system acquires considerable inertia. This inertia usually arises from (implicit or explicit) indexation and the existence of staggered contracts. The existence of these inertial forces (partially) explains why, even in cases where the monetary overhang and the monetization of the fiscal deficit are eliminated, inflation takes a long time to subside. Thus an important initial step in stabilization programs is to de-index the economy, trying to transform agents' behavior from being backward-looking to being forward-looking. A broad de-indexation process, affecting not only wages but also debt and other contracts, is usually preferred. However, maintaining a tax system that is resilient to inflation has been an important component of successful programs. In both Poland and Yugoslavia, the de-indexation of wages has been an important component of the initial stabilization package.[18]

The de-indexation of the labor market would also play an important role in providing much needed flexibility to the labor market during the adjustment period that follows the freeing of prices and the implementation of other reforms such as the opening up of international trade. In fact, it is well known that an important prerequisite for reducing the unemployment costs of trade liberalization is to eliminate most wage rigidities including indexation. The reason for this statement is that in countries with labor-intensive exports, a trade liberalization will, under most circumstances, result in a reduction in the real wage rate in the short run. Over the longer run, however, as investment in new equipment takes place, wages will tend to increase until in the new equilibrium wages will

---

[17]This transfer occurred in Chile during the second round of privatization in 1985-87. See Luders (1990).

[18]See J. Williamson (1985) for a series of interesting case studies on attempts to de-index during a stabilization program.

tend to exceed those prevailing before the reforms.[19] If the real wage is not allowed to decline in the short run, however, a significant increase in unemployment will take place. In that regard, it is highly likely that if wages had **not** been de-indexed, the increase in unemployment in Poland (from zero percent in late 1989 to approximately 5.5 percent in September, 1990) would have been even larger.

2.4   An exchange-rate anchor?

In both Poland and Yugoslavia, after the initial maxi-devaluation and the establishment of partial convertibility, the nominal exchange rate was fixed as a way of providing an anchor for the price system. Although exchange-rate-based stabilizations have had a long history, they remain controversial. Many authors see a serious danger of real exchange-rate overvaluation associated with these policies. This danger could indeed materialize if, after the initial devaluation and the pegging of the nominal exchange rate, inflation continues to go on at a pace significantly higher than world inflation. In this case, domestic goods would quickly lose international competitiveness, and a serious balance-of-payments situation could arise.

The most common cause of real exchange-rate overvaluation in exchange-rate-based stabilization programs is that the pegging of the nominal exchange rate is **not** accompanied by the required correction in the fundamental determinants of inflation, such as the fiscal deficit and money creation. However, even if adequate fiscal and monetary policies are put in place, there is still a serious risk of overvaluation if the economic system exhibits some inertia. This possibility can be illustrated with the following simple model of an economy with partial backward indexation based on Edwards and Edwards (1991):

$$\hat{P}_t = \alpha \hat{P}_{Tt} + (1 - \alpha) \hat{P}_{Nt} \tag{2}$$

$$\hat{P}_{Tt} = \hat{E}_t + \hat{P}_{Tt}^* \tag{3}$$

$$D^N \left[\left(\frac{P_N}{P_T} \right)_t, Z_t \right] = S^N \left[\left(\frac{W}{P_N} \right)_t \right] \tag{4}$$

$$\hat{W}_t = k \hat{P}_{t-1} \tag{5}$$

---

[19]This statement is based on the plausible assumption that in the short run capital is sector-specific. Only slowly through time can capital be reallocated across sectors. On these issues see Edwards (1988).

$\hat{P}_t$ is the percentage rate of change of the domestic price level; $\hat{P}_{Tt}$ is the percentage rate of change in the price of tradeables expressed in domestic currency; $\hat{P}_{Nt}$ is the rate of change of nontradeable goods prices; $\hat{E}_t$ is the rate of devaluation, and $\hat{P}^*_{Tt}$ is the rate of change of the international price of tradeables; D^N and S^N are the demand and supply functions for nontradeable goods; W_t is the nominal wage rate, and $\hat{W}_t$ is its rate of change in period t; and finally, Z_t is aggregate real expenditure.[20] Equation (2) states that the rate of change of the overall price level is a weighted average of the rate of change of tradeables and nontradeables prices, with α and $(1 - \alpha)$ being the weights. Equation (3) links the domestic price of tradeables to the world price via the nominal exchange rate. Equation (4) is the equilibrium condition in the market for nontradeable goods. Demand depends negatively on relative prices and positively on aggregate real expenditure. Supply of nontradeables, on the other hand, depends negatively on the product wage rate. Equation (5) is the rule of wage indexation and states that in every period nominal wages are adjusted in a percentage k of past inflation. If, as was the case in Chile, there is full backward indexation, $k = 1$, and $\hat{W}_t = \hat{P}_{t-1}$.

Under the assumption that as part of the stabilization program the nominal exchange rate is pegged ($\hat{E}_t = 0$), and aggregate expenditure does not change ($\hat{Z}_t = 0$), we obtain the following equation for domestic inflation:

$$\hat{P}_t = \left(\frac{\alpha\varepsilon + \eta}{\eta + \varepsilon}\right)\hat{P}^*_{Tt} + \left(\frac{(1 - \alpha)\varepsilon k}{\eta + \varepsilon}\right)\hat{P}_{t-1} \tag{6}$$

where η is the price elasticity of demand for nontradeables (that is, $\eta < 0$), and ε is the supply elasticity of nontradeables with respect to the product wage ($\varepsilon < 0$). This equation clearly captures the fact that under these circumstances the domestic rate of inflation will exhibit inertial behavior. The importance of this inertial force will depend not only on the extent of indexation, k, but also on the parameter $(1 - \alpha)\varepsilon/(\eta + \varepsilon)$. In the case where there is 100 percent backward indexation ($k = 1$) the domestic rate of inflation will eventually converge to the world rate of inflation of tradeables, $\hat{P}_{Tt}$.

Defining the real exchange rate, e, in the standard way:

$$e_t = \frac{E_t P^*_{Tt}}{P_t} \tag{7}$$

we find that its evolution through time will be given by:

$$e_t = \frac{\varepsilon(1 - \alpha)}{\eta + \varepsilon}(P_{Tt} - kP_{Tt-1}) \tag{8}$$

---

[20]Naturally, this simple representation assumes that the monetary overhang situation has already been resolved.

This means, then, that to the extent that the world rate of inflation, $\hat{P}_{T_t}$, falls short of lagged inflation multiplied by the coefficient of wage indexation, the real exchange rate will be subject to an appreciation process ($\hat{e}_t < 0$). The higher is k, the higher will be the likelihood of a real appreciation, and eventually, of overvaluation.[21]

During 1990 both the Polish and the Yugoslav economies experienced important real exchange-rate appreciations that slowly but surely reduced the degree of competitiveness of their exports. In Yugoslavia, this process resulted in the abandonment of the fixed rate in early 1991. Poland, on the other hand, implemented a "corrective" devaluation in May 1991, after which the zloty was once again pegged. This time, however, it was pegged relative to a basket of currencies. It is still difficult, however, to predict whether Poland will run into a situation of overvaluation. These difficulties in evaluating the real exchange-rate situation are due, in part, to the fact that given the peculiarities of Central European trade in the past, it is difficult to use historical series to make real exchange-rate comparisons. Section 3 describes this subject in light of the Chilean and Mexican experience.

The rationale for relying on exchange-rate-based stabilization programs is based on two interrelated ideas: first, a fixed nominal exchange rate imposes discipline on the monetary and fiscal authorities as well as on manufactured goods producers; and second, a pegged nominal exchange rate reduces the expectations of inflation. Some recent work on stabilization in advanced nations has argued that the credible adoption of an exchange-rate system with limited flexibility such as the exchange-rate mechanism of the European Monetary System, will by itself reduce inflationary pressure through a change in inertial forces (see Giavazzi and Giovanini 1989). The key issue, of course, is whether the unilateral adoption of a fixed rate is indeed **credible.** If the fixed rate lacks credibility, the public will speculate against the fixed rate and the Central Bank, thereby making the inflationary situation even more difficult.

Whether a specific program based on a pegged exchange rate has credibility is, to a large extent, an empirical issue that will vary from country to country and across historical settings. However, it is still possible to make some general comments on the subject. First, the degree of credibility of the policy will largely depend on the perceived coherence of the program. If the public sees that

---

[21]An important feature of this model for understanding some of the potential problems associated with the Polish and Yugoslavian programs is that to the extent that there are increases in aggregate demand ($Z_t > 0$) fueled by increased transfers from abroad, the forces toward appreciation and eventual real overvaluation would increase significantly. In fact, the abandonment of the fixed nominal rate in Yugoslavia after one year was the result of real appreciation fueled by a combination of inertia and increases in aggregate expenditure.

there is genuine progress on the fiscal and monetary fronts and that some agreements between unions and firms are established, the degree of credibility on the sustainability of the fixed exchange rate will increase. Second, credibility will be much greater if there are **institutional** constraints that will require the government to maintain its commitment to a fixed rate, and thus to fiscal discipline. This type of institutional constraint is present in countries that join the European Monetary System or (to a lesser extent) that have an independent Central Bank, but not necessarily in nations that unilaterally decide to peg their nominal exchange rate, such as Poland and Yugoslavia did in 1990. The discussion of the Chilean and Mexican experiences provides greater detail on this issue of credibility.

Recently, some authors have investigated some of the most important **real** consequences of stabilization programs based on pegging the nominal exchange rate. In a comparative study of several Latin American episodes from the 1960s through the 1980s, Kiguel and Liviatan (1990) found that most exchange-rate-based anti-inflationary programs have been characterized by both an expansion of real activity in the initial months of the program and by a non-trivial degree of real exchange rate appreciation. Calvo and Vegh (1990) have developed an optimizing model of a small open economy to compare formally the inflationary and real effects of exchange-rate and monetary-based stabilization programs.[22] With a cash-in-advance constraint, currency substitution and capital mobility, they find that a credible exchange-rate-based stabilization generates an output expansion through the permanent reduction of domestic interest rates. However, if the program lacks credibility, the initial expansion of output is followed by a substantial recession. They also argue that the less credible the program is, the more significant will be the real effects of the stabilization program.

3   Some Latin American Lessons for Eastern Europe: Money Overhang, Exchange-Rate Anchors and De-indexation

Although Chile did not become a full-blown socialist country under President Salvador Allende, the initial conditions faced by the Chilean free-market reformers (sometimes called the "Chicago boys") were in more than one respect similar to those encountered in Central and Eastern Europe: (1) A significant repressed inflation had generated a major monetary overhang, whose elimination some experts estimated would have required a rise in prices of approximately 500 percent by mid-1973.[23] (2) The economy was plagued by generalized

---

[22]This comparison is done from a different perspective in Fischer (1986).

[23]See Bardon (1973). Corbo and Solimano (1990) also find that in Chile there was a significant monetary overhang at the end of the Allende period.

scarcity, long queues and rampant black markets. (3) The fiscal deficit — which was fully financed by money creation — reached 26 percent of GDP in 1973. Although "official" annual inflation was 700 percent in September, 1973, all the available evidence indicates that the economy still faced a major "stock" disequilibrium. (4) A program of nationalization of domestic and foreign-owned firms had resulted in a two-fold increase in public sector value added between 1970 and 1973. As in Poland, unemployment was virtually nonexistent, while labor productivity was rapidly declining (see Edwards and Edwards 1991).

The main goals of the Chilean economic team in 1973 were to defeat inflation, to reestablish external equilibrium, and to transform the economy from a tightly centralized system into a market-oriented regime. Although the political systems were very different, there are some remarkable similarities between Chile's market-oriented economic policies and those of Poland and Yugoslavia. (See table 8 for a synoptic comparison between Chile's and Poland's policies.) As in Poland and Yugoslavia, Chile eliminated the vast majority of price controls during the first week of the reforms — more than 3,000 prices were immediately freed; prices of 39 "necessities," however, remained under loose control for some time. A very large devaluation (over 90 percent) was used as a way of dealing with the monetary overhang and, as in Poland, partial currency convertibility (for commercial transactions) was rapidly established. An external sector trade reform immediately eliminated all import licenses, prohibitions, and quotas, and by 1979 had slashed import tariffs to a uniform 10 percent. As in Poland, the initial reaction to these policies was a dramatic and historically unprecedented increase in non-traditional exports. For example, in 1974 the US dollar value of non-mineral Chilean exports increased 200 percent with respect to 1973.

There are still more similarities. As in Yugoslavia and Poland, the Chilean authorities implemented an exchange-rate-based stabilization, in which the fixing of the nominal exchange rate in the context of an economy open to international competition was the cornerstone of the anti-inflationary program. Also, as in the recent Eastern European programs, in a further effort to eliminate inflationary pressures, wage indexation was initially greatly reduced (followed later by 100 percent backward indexation), and the labor market was reformed.

The rest of this section briefly discusses some of the most important aspects of the Chilean stabilization and draws lessons for Eastern Europe. Four issues discussed in the preceding section are highlighted: (1) the elimination of money overhang; (2) the fiscal deficit and the flow macro-disequilibrium; (3) the indexation of the labor market; and (4) the use of the nominal exchange rate as an anchor. On this last important issue, the effects of the Chilean and Mexican exchange-rate-based stabilization programs are formally compared.

TABLE 8
Policies for Stabilization and Market-Oriented Reform:
A Comparison Between Chile in the 1970s and Poland in the 1990s

Chile	Poland

A. Price and Wage Rate Policies

- More than 3000 previously controlled prices were freed in October of 1973. Initially only 30 goods continue to have controlled prices.

- From Oct. 1973 to July 1975 partial and lagged wage indexation; between July 1975 and Aug. 1981, full *de facto* indexation

- Most prices freed during first week of January 1990.

- Limited and lagged wage indexation.

B. Exchange Rate Policy

- Sept. 12, 1973 official devaluation of the peso by 85%. Number of exchange rates reduced from 13 to 3 and then to 1. Partial convertibility (current account only).

- A crawling peg system was followed until Feb. 1978. From Feb. 1978 to June 1979 the rate of devaluation was preannounced at a rate below ongoing inflation. In June 1979 exchange rate was **fixed** to the dollar to provide an anchor to the anti-inflation program.

- Jan. 1, 1990, official devaluation of the zloty by 46%. Exchange-rate unification. Partial convertibility (current account only)

- Exchange rate is fixed to dollar to provide an anchor to the stabilization program.

C. Fiscal and Monetary Policies

- In 1974 a fiscal reform was enacted that indexed the tax system, implemented a broad VAT at a 20% rate, and eliminated most exemptions. Broad expenditure cuts. Fiscal deficit was reduced from 25% of GDP in 1973 to 2% in 1975.

- Fiscal adjustment attempted, mainly through reduction in expenditures on subsidies. Target for 1990 calls for an adjustment of the fiscal accounts of 5% of GDP.

Table 8 continues

TABLE 8
(continued)

Chile	Poland
• Significant tightening in monetary control was attempted early on. However, during 1974 reserves accumulation became an important source of money creation. Interest rates were freed and were very high until 1980.	• Control of net domestic assets of Central Bank. • Interest rates raised by more than 4 times to 35% per month.
D. Trade Policy • Rapid elimination of quotas, licenses and prohibitions.	• Rapid elimination of quotas and licenses.
• Sweeping tariff reform that slashed tariffs from approximately 100% in 1973 to 20% in 1976 and 10% by 1979.	• Reduction of import tariffs.
E. Privatization • Rapid process of privatization of banks and firms nationalized during the Allende period. Banks privatized first. Foreigners' participation limited in the privatization process. However, a flexible direct foreign investment statute was enacted.	• Plans drawn, little done (yet).

3.1 Money overhang and the initial stabilization program

The economic policies of Dr. Salvador Allende during 1970-73 generated a classic situation of repressed inflation.[24] Former Unidad Popular Minister Sergio Bitar has described the situation as follows:

---

[24]For an extraordinary insider's account of the economic policies of Allende, see Bitar (1979). For a recent analysis of the conduct of macroeconomic policy during this period see Dornbusch and Edwards (1991). See also Larrain and Meller (1991).

The black or parallel market emerged in Chile in 1972, and became increasingly important during 1973. Economic disequilibria grew more rapidly than the new control mechanisms...The excess of aggregate demand and...monetary expansion increased during the first half of 1972...Relative price distortions also fueled the black market...(especially) in the textile and construction sectors...

(Bitar 1979, pp. 196-7)

Although during the last months of the Allende presidency the official rate of inflation had reached 15 percent per month, at the time of the coup (September, 1973) there was still a substantial monetary overhang. Bardon (1973), for example, estimated in August, 1973 that to eliminate the overhang the price level had to increase between 400 and 560 percent. More recently, Corbo and Solimano (1990) have estimated, on the basis of demand-for-money regressions, that in the third quarter of 1973 the magnitude of the monetary overhang was approximately equal to 50 percent of total money demand.

One of the most important priorities of the military economic team was the elimination of the monetary overhang and black markets. Interestingly enough, at that time there was no thought whatsoever about the possibility of a monetary reform; from the very beginning, the decision was made to free almost all prices and to let the jump in the price level take care of the overhang. This price liberalization was, in fact, carried out at the same time as a 90 percent devaluation was engineered and (partial) convertibility for commercial transactions was established. As a result of this policy, prices increased in October, 1973 by almost 90 percent.

The immediate effect of this measure was the overnight disappearance of black markets and rationing, followed by a precipitous fall in the premium in the parallel market for foreign exchange. As transactions moved back into the "overground" economy, tax collection rapidly increased, providing a partial alleviation to the fiscal deficit, which in 1973 had reached the extraordinarily high level of 23 percent of GDP. All of these events, of course, bear a remarkable similarity to recent Eastern European episodes.

The freeing of prices and the devaluation of the nominal exchange rate were soon supplemented by a battery of other measures. Subsidies to public sector firms were eliminated, public employment was cut, wages in the public sector were reduced in real terms, and a process of privatization, which resulted in the transfer of 251 firms to the private sector in 1974 alone, was initiated.[25] Trade liberalization and financial reform were also initiated. During 1974, most quantitative restrictions on imports, including a 10,000 percent prior deposit, were

---

[25]Of these, 202 were actually returned to their owners and 49 were sold. See Chapter 4 of Edwards and Edwards (1991) for details.

eliminated, and an initial round of tariff reduction took place. An important component of the early policies was the attempt to shift the focus of wage setting from backward looking to forward looking. This issue is discussed in greater detail in section 3.3. In terms of exchange-rate policy, after the initial devaluation the government enacted a crawling peg system aimed at maintaining the real exchange rate relatively constant (see Edwards and Edwards 1991).

As a result of the initial public-sector measures the fiscal deficit was reduced by more than one half in 1974. Most of this fiscal adjustment came from a reduction in expenditure. In spite of this progress, at the end of 1974 the fiscal deficit still stood at almost 11 percent of GDP.

Although the strategy chosen by the economic advisors to eliminate the money overhang succeeded in achieving its objective, it did so at a large cost. The combination of an enormously large price jump, a major devaluation, and price freedom in a country with a 40-year tradition of price controls, generated substantial expectations of further inflation in the private sector. In a perceptive article, Ramos (1977) argued that as soon as firms had the possibility (for the first time in many years) of setting prices freely, they decided to **anticipate expected** future cost increases by raising prices by more than what the fundamentals dictated.

These expectations of high and rapid inflation were validated during the first quarter of 1974, when the government mandated a wage adjustment of 60 percent and implemented a devaluation with respect to the U.S. dollar of 41 percent (see Ramos 1977). From that point onward, Chilean inflation exhibited a significant degree of inertia that was mainly determined by expectations and their validation through both exchange-rate devaluations and money creation.[26] There is little doubt that the unleashing of these substantial and chaotic expectations of inflation in the aftermath of the price jump of October, 1973 were largely responsible for the extraordinarily long time it took for the Chilean inflation rate to subside. This slow speed of stabilization is particularly puzzling once it is recognized that for all practical purposes by 1977 the fiscal-deficit problem had been completely solved. It is not possible to know what would have happened if a monetary reform — accompanied, or shortly followed by the freeing of prices — had been implemented in 1973. One can only speculate that in this case inflationary expectations would have been lower and that possibly the transition to lower and more stable inflation would have been more rapid.

---

[26]It is interesting to note that computations of the **steady state** rate of inflation justifiable by the fiscal deficit were significantly lower in every one of the initial years than the actual inflation. In 1974, for example, the "justified" rate of inflation was between 200-250 percent while actual inflation exceeded 370 percent. The difference between these two figures can (partially) be explained by inertial forces. In 1978 the government decided to face expectations dramatically through the adoption of an exchange-rate-based stabilization that culminated with the fixing of the peso to the US dollar in June, 1979. The most important characteristics of this program are analyzed in subsection 3.2 below.

3.2   Tax reform, the fiscal deficit and inflation

In early 1975 a sweeping tax reform was implemented in Chile. The principal features of this reform include the replacement of a cascade sales tax with a flat-rate 20 percent value-added tax; a full indexation of the tax system; an elimination of the remaining tax exemptions and subsidies; a unification of the corporation and non-corporation income taxes into a flat-rate business tax; and the integration of the personal and business income taxes (Edwards and Edwards 1991).

The initial stabilization program did not consider using the exchange rate as an anti-inflationary tool. In fact, it was decided to maintain a crawling peg exchange-rate system that consisted of periodically adjusting the nominal exchange rate at approximately the same rate as lagged inflation.

In June, 1976, as a means of breaking inflationary expectations, the government revalued the peso by 10 percent with respect to the US dollar. In March, 1977, to break further expectations, the nominal exchange rate was again revalued by 10 percent. As before, this appreciation was followed by periodic devaluations that tried to compensate firms for the loss of competitiveness generated by the tariff reduction process. By late 1977 inflation was still very high in absolute levels — 87 percent per annum.

The revaluations of the peso of 1976 and 1977 marked the first steps toward a major change in the Chilean stabilization strategy and in the authorities' concept of the role of macroeconomic policy. In early 1978 Chilean stabilization efforts moved from being fiscal based to exchange rate based. Some important aspects of this policy, including its credibility, are discussed in subsection 3.4.

3.3   Labor markets and indexation

On the labor market front, the government tried early on to incorporate some corrective forces.[27] The automatic wage adjustment due in October, 1973 was postponed until January, 1974. During that year, an effort to provide forward-looking wage adjustment was instituted. This wage adjustment resulted in mandated wage increases well below the accumulated rate of inflation.[28] Starting in July, 1977, however, a one-hundred-percent-plus backward indexation mechanism was put into place. As inflation was (slowly) declining during this period, this backward-looking procedure assured that wages would automatically increase in real terms.[29]

---

[27]A crucial element in labor market developments during this period is the dismantling of the Chilean labor movement. For political reasons the immense majority of union leaders were persecuted. Union activities were reduced to mere symbolism.

[28]As a result, in 1976 real (average) wages were 16 percent below their 1970 level and 30 percent below the peak year of 1971.

[29]Edwards and Edwards (1991) provide detailed information on every mandated wage adjustment.

Not only were wages fully indexed by 1976, but most other contracts also included indexation clauses. Many transactions were denominated in dollars, and with the exception of 30-day CDs, all financial transactions were subject to inflation adjustment. There is little doubt that the rapid reintroduction of 100 percent backward indexation can partially account for the slow rate at which inflation was reduced.

3.4   Anchoring the system through the nominal exchange rate

In February 1978 the administration of the exchange rate completely took over as the most important anti-inflationary tool. At that time, a novel policy of pre-announcing a **declining** rate of devaluation for a fairly long period of time (up to a year) was introduced as a way of further reducing the rate of inflation. This system, popularly known as the *tablita,* deliberately set the initial rate of devaluation at a lower rate than ongoing inflation. With trade reform having virtually eliminated the most important trade barriers, it was expected that this system of pre-announced devaluations would have two important effects on inflation. First, it was thought that it would diminish inflationary expectations. Second, and more important, it was expected that the system would work in a way similar to a textbook-type fixed-exchange-rate regime imposing price discipline on the economy. It was thought that domestic inflation would rapidly converge to the level of world inflation plus the rate of devaluation of the peso.

In June, 1979, with inflation standing at an annual rate of 34 percent, the government put an end to the system of a pre-announced declining rate of devaluation and fixed the exchange rate at 39 pesos per dollar. It was expected that this move to a fixed rate would reinforce and accelerate the purchasing-power-parity-type convergence of domestic to world inflation.

When the *tablita* was adopted in early 1978, and again when the peso was pegged to the dollar in June, 1979, it was decided **not** to alter the wage indexation mechanism. Paradoxically then, while the authorities expected price setters and other agents to form forward-looking expectations, they maintained a crucial market linked to a rigidly mechanical backward indexation regime. This decision resulted in the maintenance of an important component of the inertial forces in the system.[30]

---

[30]Besides the adoption of a fixed-exchange-rate regime, another important development took place during 1979. Steps toward the liberalization of capital flows were taken when in June of that year commercial banks were allowed greatly to increase their ratio of foreign liabilities to equity. This relaxation of capital inflows resulted in massive borrowing from abroad and paved the way to Chile's debt crisis. The massive inflow of foreign capital was one of the fundamental causes of real exchange rate **overvaluation** in Chile (see Edwards 1985). An early warning of the danger of excessive capital inflows is in McKinnon (1973).

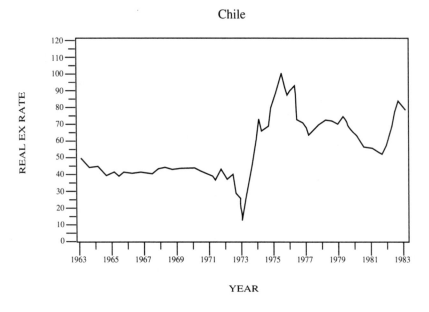

Chile

YEAR

FIGURE 2

3.4.1 Exchange-rate pegging and real exchange-rate overvaluation Contrary to what was expected by the architects of the open economy stabilization plan, after the exchange rate was fixed in mid-1979, the domestic rate of inflation did not rapidly converge to its world counterpart. In fact, the use of the exchange rate as a stabilization tool helped generate a steady real overvaluation.

Figure 2 shows the evolution of Chile's (bilateral) real exchange rate from 1963 through 1983. Three things stand out from this figure. First, following the fixing of the nominal exchange rate in mid-1979, the real exchange rate experienced a sustained appreciation. Second, when the rate was pegged (and even when the *tablita* was first adopted in 1978), the real exchange rate was relatively low (appreciated) with respect to its 1975-76 levels. Consequently there was not much of a cushion for the exchange rate to fall without generating an overvaluation during the transition to price stability. This experience contrasts with that of Mexico, where prior to embarking on the exchange-rate preannouncement program and the Solidarity Pact the real exchange rate was **undervalued**.[31] Consequently, the subsequent real exchange-rate appreciation observed in Mexico has not resulted until this time in a situation of real exchange- rate overvaluation.

---

[31]On the Mexican stabilization package see Beristain and Trigueros (1990). For a discussion of the evolution of the real exchange rate in Mexico see Edwards (1990).

The third interesting characteristic of Figure 2 is that there is a clear structural break in the real exchange-rate behavior in Chile. Throughout 1974-84, in spite of broad fluctuations, the real exchange rate was at all times significantly higher than at any time during the previous 10 years. Two main "real" events that greatly affected the behavior of "fundamentals" are behind the major real depreciation that took place between 1965-73 and 1979: First, there was a drastic liberalization of international trade, which eliminated all quantitative restrictions and reduced import tariffs from an average of more than 100 percent to a uniform 10 percent level (Edwards and Edwards 1991). Second, there was a steep, and apparently permanent, deterioration of Chile's terms of trade. During 1975-79 the average real price of Chile's main export, copper, was 41 percent below its 1965-73 average.

An important aspect of exchange-rate based programs refers to the need to monitor real exchange-rate movements to assess whether situations of overvaluation are emerging. Such monitoring, however, is not an easy task. As the fundamental determinants of the equilibrium real exchange rate change, as has been the case in Poland and Yugoslavia, it becomes exceedingly difficult to know with any degree of certainty whether the real exchange rate is moving closer to an overvaluation situation. Under these circumstances it becomes extremely important to monitor very closely developments in the external sector to capture early on any possible signs of overvaluation. In the cases of Chile and Argentina, in the late 1970s the abundance of foreign capital made the evaluation of real exchange-rate conditions even more difficult, since many of the superficial signs of overvaluation such as a loss in international reserves and a black market premium were not present.[32] This situation is indeed a possible danger in Eastern Europe where temporary substantial increases in capital inflows may provide a false sense of boom, hiding potentially dangerous situations of overvaluation.

The steady process of real overvaluation since the pegging of the peso greatly hurt the performance of non-copper exports. In 1981 the dollar value of non-traditional exports dropped by 15 percent, while traditional non-copper exports declined by 16 percent. In fact, for those firms in the Corbo and Sanchez (1985) study the overvaluation of the peso was one of the most severe blows received throughout the first ten years of the experiment with market-oriented policies.

When the first version of this chapter was written in late 1990, it was pointed out that there was a great danger in using an exchange-rate anchor in Yugoslavia and Poland. The abandonment of the program in Yugoslavia and the May, 1991, devaluation in Poland lend support to this view. Poland, however, has once again pegged its nominal exchange rate (to a basket). Although it is too

---

[32]In principle, temporary increases in capital inflows will result in real exchange-rate overvaluation. See Edwards (1989a) for a theoretical model and some empirical evidence.

early to tell whether this new peg will be sustainable, it is important to emphasize again that the dangers of overvaluation are still present, and are particularly serious in circumstances where the fiscal deficit is not fully under control.

3.4.2   Exchange-rate anchors and credibility: A comparison between Chile and Mexico   One of the goals of adopting a pre-announced rate of devaluation (which could be zero), as was done in Poland and Yugoslavia, is to alter the public's expectations. Indeed, if the adoption of a nominal exchange-rate rule is credible and if the private sector believes that the predetermined nominal rate will impose (or assure) discipline, it will tend to alter its behavior. Ideally, in an economy suffering from significant inertial forces, a credible adoption of an exchange-rate rule will alter the process of expectations formation from being backward looking to being forward looking. This change means that, with other things given, the implementation of a credible exchange-rate-based stabilization program will reduce the degree of persistence built into the inflation process. Contracts, under a credible exchange-rate pegging will take into account the change in the exchange-rate regime, and this change in behavior will then be reflected in the data on price changes.

A potentially fruitful line of attack for empirically analyzing the degree of credibility of exchange-rate-based programs is to investigate whether, once the exchange-rate rule is adopted, the degree of inertia of inflation is indeed reduced. Formally this investigation can be carried out by estimating an equation of the following form:

$$\pi_t = a_0 + a_1 \pi_{t-1} + a_2 (D\pi_{t-1}) + \sum b_j X_{jt-k} + u_t \tag{9}$$

where π_t is the rate of inflation in period t, D is a dummy variable that takes the value of 1 during the period when the exchange-rate-based program is in effect, and the X_j's are other determinants of inflation. In this equation the coefficient a_1 captures the degree of inertia of the inflationary process before the exchange-rate-based program and the coefficient $(a_1 + a_2)$ is our measure of persistence once the exchange-rate anchor is used. Under a credible program, then, we would expect the coefficient a_2 to be significantly negative. A zero value (or a positive value) of a_2 would suggest that the program lacked credibility and that it failed to alter the public's expectations and perception of the system's dynamics.

A number of variations of equation (9) were estimated using quarterly data for Chile. In these estimates two alternative dummy variables were used: the first one, D1, took a value of one between the second quarter of 1978, when the program of pre-announcing the rate of devaluation was first implemented, and the first quarter of 1982. In the second case, D2, the dummy variable took a value of one between the third quarter of 1979 and the first quarter of 1982. That is, D2 covers only the period when the nominal exchange rate was strictly

fixed. With respect to the other determinants of inflation (the X_j in equation (9)), current and lagged values of a number of variables were considered, including the rate of devaluation, the rate of growth of domestic credit, and the rate of growth of money. Although most equations were estimated for the period between the first quarter of 1974 and the first quarter of 1982 — that is, the last quarter of a fixed exchange rate — a number of other time periods were also considered.

In every regression run the coefficient of $D\pi_{t-1}$ turned out to be positive (although statistically not significantly different from zero), indicating that the adoption of the exchange- rate rule did not alter the degree of inflationary inertia in the system. The following is an example of the type of result obtained (t-statistics in parentheses):[33]

$$\pi_t = -0.031 + 0.754\pi_{t-1} + 0.249 D2\pi_{t-1} + 0.123 DEV_t$$
$$\quad (-0.869)\ (8.923)\quad\ (0.669)\qquad\quad (1.352)$$

$$+ 0.076 DEV_{t-1} - 0.133 GM_t + 0.266 GM_{t-1} \qquad (10)$$
$$\quad (3.001)\qquad\ (-0.990)\qquad (2.255)$$

$$\bar{R}^2 = 0.965,\ DW = 1.910$$

Durbin's $h = 0.298$, Period: $74Q1 - 82Q1$

where DEV is the rate of devaluation and where GM is the rate of growth of M1.

In order to test further whether the adoption of the fixed exchange rate in June, 1979 had an effect on the inflation process, a number of tests on the structural-stability-of-inflation equations of the type of (9) were performed. If indeed the shift from an accommodating adjustable exchange-rate regime to a rigidly predetermined one is credible, it would be expected that the inflation equation would capture a change in regime. However, these stability tests were supportive of the dummy variable results reported previously, showing no structural break in the inflation equation. For example, in the case of equation (10) the Chi-square statistic for structural stability had a value of $[\chi^2(6) = 2.23]$, indicating no evidence of a change in the inflationary regime in mid-1979.

---

[33]This equation was estimated using ordinary least squares. When instrumental variables were used the results were very similar.

The above evidence, then, suggests that the adoption of a predetermined exchange rate in Chile was not associated with a change in the nature of the inflationary process that one expects from a credible policy.[34]   In particular, expectations and contract practices (e.g., indexation) do not seem to have been affected in a significant way. This result, of course, was particularly true for the case of wage contracts, which largely remained backward indexed to 100 per-cent of past inflation. Consequently, the degree of inflationary inertia remained basically unchanged after the adoption of the exchange-rate-based program.

Equations of the type of (9) were also estimated for Mexico. The Mexican program differed from the Chilean one in a very important respect: while in Chile the stabilization program was based solely on fiscal restraint and a prede-termined (and then fixed) nominal exchange rate, in Mexico incomes policies became a central element of the anti-inflationary package supplementing the exchange-rate rule and the fiscal adjustment. Indeed in late 1987 with the estab-lishment of the *Pacto de Solidaridad,* unions, entrepreneurs and the government worked out a politically and economically feasible plan for defeating inflation: price and wage guidelines became important elements of this program (see Beristain and Trigueros 1990).

The key question, then, is whether a program which combines the use of the exchange rate as an anchor with incomes policies is more credible — and thus more able to alter the dynamics of inflation — than a program that relies exclu-sively on the exchange-rate anchor.[35]   To investigate this question a number of equations based on (9) were estimated using quarterly data for Mexico for the period 1979-90. As in the Chilean regressions the dummy variable was defined for two alternative periods: D3 takes a value of one between the second quarter of 1988 and the second quarter of 1990, while D4 takes a value of 1 from the first quarter of 1989 (when the *Pacto* was first renewed) and the second quarter of 1990.

Contrary to the case of Chile, in every equation estimated for Mexico the coefficient of $D\pi_{t-1}$ turned out to be significantly **negative,** indicating that the adoption of the pre-announced exchange-rate system, and the other policies in the *Pacto,* were credible, significantly changing the dynamics of inflation. The following equation illustrates the type of results obtained:

---

[34]This evidence, of course, does not mean that the fixing of the exchange rate did not have some effect on inflation.   Naturally, to the extent that devaluation enters the infla-tion equation, a lower DEV will generate a lower π.

[35]The implicit assumption is that in both cases the fiscal side has been corrected. This assumption is valid for both Chile and Mexico.

$$\pi_t = 0.002 + 0.845\,\pi_{t-1} + 0.197\text{D3}\,\pi_{t-1} + 0.077\text{DEV}_t$$
$$\quad\ (-0.417)\ (20.778)\quad\ (-4.222)\qquad\ (3.551)$$

$$+\,0.059\text{DEV}_{t-1} + 0.046\text{GM}_t + 0.059\text{GM}_{t-1}$$
$$\quad\ (2.233)\qquad\quad (1.476)\qquad (1.852) \tag{11}$$

$\bar{R}^2 = 0.964$, DW = 1.621

Durbin's $h = 1.321$, Period: $79Q1-90Q1$

The estimated autoregressive term for the *Pacto* period is equal to 0.648, only 75 percent of its value during the rest of the period. Although it is not possible to make generalizations at this point, these contrasting results between Chile and Mexico are quite suggestive, indicating that the adoption of an exchange-rate rule on its own need not alter the dynamics of inflation.

4   Concluding Remarks

Some of the most important stabilization policy problems faced by the USSR and the Eastern European nations have been analyzed in this chapter: (a) the monetary overhang; (b) the fiscal deficit; (c) the de-indexation issue; and (d) the question of exchange-rate anchors. With respect to each of these areas some lessons stemming from the Latin American experience with stabilization and anti-inflationary policies have been discussed. Of course, Latin American policies should not be applied mechanically to Eastern Europe. In fact, differences in initial conditions and the political environment make this analysis mostly suggestive. The most important conclusions of this study can be summarized as follows:

1. The reliance on a major price-level jump to eliminate the monetary overhang in Chile in October, 1973, proved to be costly. Expectations of inflation became high and chaotic, with firms and other agents adjusting their prices in anticipation of expected further inflation. These expectations, plus the rapid full indexation of the economy, were translated into a system with a high degree of inertia, and thus in an extremely long path toward price stability.

It is not possible to know what would have happened if an alternative policy had been followed. One can only speculate that some type of monetary reform — possibly one based on combined currency blocking — would have resulted in a smoother and less traumatic transition.[36] Under this alternative policy the

---

[36]Arguably the blocked funds could have been used to create some long-maturity instruments in the emerging financial market.

monetary reform would have been immediately followed by a liberalization of (most) prices and a devaluation. The freeing of prices would have allowed a correction of relative price distortions but presumably would not have resulted in the type of traumatic jump in the price level that was, in fact, observed. Also, after the monetary reform the required discrete devaluation would have been smaller than what was actually observed.

2. There is no doubt that fiscal adjustment is a crucial requirement for achieving stability. An important component of this adjustment is the creation of a tax system that is not vulnerable to inflation itself. The sophisticated inflation adjustment clauses introduced into the Chilean tax system in late 1974 greatly helped that country to eliminate the public sector imbalances. The creation of this type of system in Eastern Europe would appear to be an important element for achieving a stable macroeconomic environment.

3. In successful experiences the efforts to de-index the labor market, i.e. to decouple wage increases from past inflation, have been maintained throughout the stabilization program. In Chile, the return to full backward-looking indexation in late 1976 added considerable inertia to the inflationary process. Whether a de-indexation program will indeed be feasible will depend on political consensus. Whether this type of policy is politically possible in Eastern Europe is not yet clear.

4. The adoption of an exchange-rate-based stabilization program, where the nominal exchange rate is either pegged, or its rate of change is predetermined at a rate below ongoing inflation, carries a serious danger of provoking a major overvaluation. This result can occur even if the fiscal deficit is fully under control as in the case of Chile. Some countries have dealt with this problem by starting the stabilization program at a point of undervaluation, as in Mexico in 1988.

5. The most important goal of the adoption of a predetermined nominal exchange rate as part of a stabilization program is to alter the dynamics of the inflationary process. More specifically, a credible adoption of an exchange-rate rule will reduce the degree of inertia in the system. An empirical comparison between the Chilean and Mexican cases shows that while in the former the adoption of the exchange-rate rule did not affect the inertial forces built in the system, in Mexico the degree of persistence in inflation was significantly reduced. The main difference in these two experiences is that in Mexico the exchange-rate rule was supplemented with other incomes policies.

9 The Design of Financial Systems for the Newly Emerging Democracies of Eastern Europe

Joseph E. Stiglitz

If capital is at the heart of capitalism, then well-functioning capital markets are at the heart of a well-functioning capitalist economy. Unfortunately, of all the markets in the economy, capital markets are perhaps the most complicated and least understood. Few governments leave capital markets to themselves — they are affected by a host of regulations and government policies. Moreover, the structure of capital markets appears, in some important respects, vastly different among major capitalist economies. Are the differences inessential, perhaps a consequence of different historical experiences but having no more substance beyond that? Are they important, each reflecting an adaptation to the particular cultural or economic circumstances of their own countries? Or are some more conducive to economic success, with the solid economic performance of some countries being a consequence of their well-designed capital markets, and the poor performance of others being in part a consequence of ill-designed capital markets?

To a large extent, the form of capital markets observed in the more developed countries is the consequence of an historical process. Technologies have changed everywhere, especially those affecting capital markets. These markets are transactions intensive; banks are involved in recording millions of debits and credits a day. The computer revolution has, first and foremost, lowered the costs of such transactions. It is not apparent that the capital markets inherited by the more developed countries are the appropriate ones for the technologies of the twenty-first century. But change is not without cost, and the evolution of financial systems, even when confronted with quite serious problems, appears to be a slow process.

Financial support from the Institute for Policy Reform is gratefully acknowledged.

The newly emerging democracies of Eastern Europe face difficult choices in designing capital markets. The choices they make will have a bearing not only on the efficiency with which capital is allocated, but also on the macroeconomic stability and performance of their economies. In one respect, they have an advantage over more developed economies: they may have wider scope for choice, less encumbered by current institutional forms. But the necessity of choosing itself places a heavy burden on them, as the choices they make now may not be easily undone. Institutions once established are not easily or cost-lessly altered.

The objective of this chapter is not to lay out a blueprint for the ideal set of capital markets, but rather to help frame the discourse. On another occasion, when asked to talk about agricultural policies for these economies in transition, I found myself in the uncomfortable position of an American saying, "Do as we say, not as we do." Our agricultural policies do not obviously follow from a model of economic rationality. And so it is in discussions of capital markets. Parts of the capital market in the United States are, to put it mildly, in disastrous shape. One major part of our financial system, our Savings and Loan Associations, has gone belly-up. The S & L debacle has cost the taxpayers hundreds of billions of dollars. Beyond this financial loss is a real loss: resources were mis-allocated. The government's losses are only a part of the total losses to society. If one takes a middle ground in the estimate of the loss, $300 billion, then it is as if almost one year's investment of the United States was completely squandered. It is hard to fathom mistakes of this magnitude.[1] While the S & L debacle is the most obvious problem with our financial markets, other parts of the US banking system are also not healthy.

For the present discussion this US experience at least has the benefit of making clear the causes and consequences of ill-functioning capital markets.

1   The Functions of the Capital Market

To help frame the discussion, this chapter will first review the central functions of capital markets. These have been variously described as:[2]

---

[1]This figure may overestimate the true social loss. Much of the loss is in real estate, and some of these expenditures were for the purchase of land. The banks' borrowers (and thus, with default, the bank) made speculative mistakes. They overpaid for the land. But these are pure transfer payments. Of course, these transfer payments affect the level of real savings of the economy, and thus have a deleterious effect on the economy's growth path.

[2]For a more extensive discussion of these various functions see, e.g. Stiglitz (1985), Greenwald and Stiglitz (1991), Stiglitz and Weiss (1991), Fama (1980), and the references cited in these papers.

a. Transferring resources (capital) from those who have it (savers) to those who can make use of it (borrowers, or investors): in any capitalist economy, there is never a perfect coincidence between those who have funds and those who can make use of those funds.

b. Agglomerating capital: many projects require more capital than that of any one saver or any small set of savers.

c. Selecting projects: there are always more individuals who claim that they have good uses for resources than there are funds available.

d. Monitoring: ensuring that funds are used in the way promised.

e. Enforcing contracts: making sure that those who have borrowed repay the funds.

f. Transferring, sharing, and pooling risks: capital markets not only raise funds, but the rules which determine repayment determine who bears what risks.

g. Diversification: by pooling a large number of investment projects together, the total risk is reduced.[3]

h. Recording transactions: generally running the medium of exchange.

In this description, capital markets not only are involved in intertemporal trade but also in risk. The two are inexorably linked, partly because intertemporal trades involve dollars today for promises of dollars in the future, and there is almost always the chance that those promises will not be fulfilled. Thus, even if one would like to separate the two, as a practical matter, in all capital markets, the two are combined.

The various functions described are linked together, but in ways which are not inevitable. For instance, banks link the transactions functions and the functions of selecting and monitoring. With modern technologies, the transactions function can easily be separated. In cash management accounts, or CMAs (run by the various brokerage houses in the United States), money is transferred into and out of "banks" instantaneously. The brokerage house's bank performs the transactions function, but no balances are kept, and accordingly no loan function (such as selecting and monitoring projects) is performed.

Some investment banks perform selection functions, in effect certifying bond or equity issues, but playing a very limited role in subsequently monitoring the borrower. Today, mutual funds provide risk diversification services, with little attention to many of the other services of capital markets.

The variety of financial institutions illustrates the advantages that come from specialization as well as the possibilities of economies of scope. Thus, one of the traditional arguments for the interlinking of the medium-of-exchange function of banks and their loan functions was that in the process of mediating

---

[3]This function can be viewed (like some of the other functions) as "economizing on transactions costs, including information costs". Individuals can diversify without using financial intermediaries, but at greater costs.

transactions, they acquired considerable information which might be of value in loan assessment and monitoring. This argument still has considerable validity, though the presence of a large number of alternatives for processing transactions vitiates some of the information content; observing a small fraction of the transactions of a potential borrower may have little if any information value.

Some of the interlinkages among functions arise from particular characteristics of information: judgments about whether a particular loan candidate is worthy have a lot more credibility when the persons or organizations making the judgments are willing to put up money than when they are only willing to make a recommendation. Monitoring is enhanced when there is a likelihood that the borrower will be returning to the lender for additional funds.

At the same time, it is important to bear in mind the distinctions among the various financial institutions and the roles they play. Thus, while the capital market as a whole raises and allocates funds, much of the activity in bond and stock markets involves trading existing assets. The stock market, in particular, is a relatively unimportant source of funds in the United States and the United Kingdom — two of the countries with the most developed equity markets (see Mayer 1989). New firms typically raise their capital through venture capital firms, and established firms finance themselves through retained earnings, resorting to bank loans and debt if they should require outside funding. Though the liquidity provided by the stock market to shareowners may affect the incentives for firms to reinvest retained earnings, the equity market itself does not exercise a primary role in raising and allocating investment funds.

What are the distinctive aspects of capital markets that result in government regulation in almost all countries? Capital markets are different from ordinary markets, which involve the contemporaneous trade of commodities. As noted, what is exchanged is money today for a (often vague) promise of money in the future. This distinction plays an important role in explaining why capital markets cannot be, and are not run as, conventional auction markets, and why as a result there may be credit (and equity) rationing (see Stiglitz 1988a, 1988b; Stiglitz and Weiss 1981; Greenwald, Stiglitz and Weiss 1984; and Myers and Majluf 1984). It also explains some of the important roles that financial institutions perform, described in the previous section, such as monitoring and selecting: in conventional markets, there is no need to select; the item goes to the highest bidder.

2   Primary Roles of Government

An analysis of the role of the government begins with an examination of the primary capital market regulatory roles that government has already assumed. There are four distinct roles.

2.1 Consumer protection

The government is concerned that investors not be deceived. Thus, if a bank promises to repay a certain amount upon demand, the government wants to ensure that it will repay that amount. Information about the financial position of the firm is a public good, meriting government intervention.[4] Of course, there are private incentives for disclosure (at least by the better firms; see Stiglitz 1975, or Grossman 1981); and in many areas, private rating agencies, such as Best for insurance, Moody's and Standard and Poor's for bonds, and Dun and Bradstreet for other investments, do play a role. The question is whether they are adequate; most governments have decided that they are not.

Government attempts to protect consumers have taken four forms:[5] (1) By ensuring the solvency of financial institutions,[6] governments make it more likely that financial institutions keep the promises they have made (e.g. banks will return the capital of depositors upon demand, insurers will pay the promised benefits when the insured-against accident occurs). (2) Deposit insurance and government-run guaranty funds protect consumers in the event of insolvency. (3) Disclosure laws make it more likely that investors know what they are getting when they make an investment.[7] (4) The market is regulated to ensure that certain individuals (insiders) do not take advantage of others. In the United States, there are a variety of such regulations, from those prohibiting inside trading to those regulating the operation of the specialists (market makers) to those attempting to prohibit unsavory practices such as cornering a market.

The government's interest in consumer protection in this area goes beyond looking after the interests of investors. It is concerned that without such protection, capital markets might not work effectively. If investors believe that the stock market is unfair, they will be not be willing to invest their money. The market will then be thin, and firms may have greater trouble raising capital. Episodes when investors have been cheated — from the South Sea Bubbles of the eighteenth century on — have been followed by a drying up of equity markets. Honest firms trying to raise capital are hurt by the potential presence of scoundrels; there is an externality. Government policies in protecting investors are thus aimed at making capital markets function better.

---

[4]In addition, there may be an economy of scope between the enforcement of fraud laws and this kind of regulation. It is easier to enforce against fraud if there are clear (and compulsory) standards of disclosure.

[5]Beyond fraud laws, which prohibit outright deception.

[6]How government attempts to insure solvency is discussed below.

[7]In the United States, there are laws intended to make sure that borrowers know the true rate of interest they pay on loans and that purchasers of equity know the true risks which they are undertaking in making an investment.

2.2   Government enhancing the solvency of banks

The United States has periodically been plagued with bank runs, perhaps more frequently than have other countries. There are three sets of instruments that the government has employed to enhance the solvency of banks.[8]

2.2.1   Insurance   Government insurance for depositors was one way of trying to restore confidence in banks, and thus prevent bank runs. The government has undertaken this insurance role for two different reasons. One is to enhance the viability of the banking institutions, by increasing consumer confidence, making runs less likely. In this role, the insurance reduces the likelihood of illiquidity causing a bank default of a basically solvent firm. Here, the question is whether the other mechanisms (to be described below) suffice, or whether there is much value added by government insurance. The second role is consumer protection. Today, **in principle** it is virtually impossible to justify the latter role, as individuals can put their money in money market funds, investing in Treasury bills, for which there is no default risk (apart from that which might arise as a result of fraud).

Given that the government does provide insurance, the government, like any other insurer, has a vested interest in making sure that the insured-against event does not occur — that is, the government in its capacity as insurer has a vital interest in insuring the solvency of those that it has insured. This interest provides one (but only one) of the rationales for government intervention.

2.2.2   The lender of last resort   Another mechanism for preventing bank runs was provided with the establishment of the Federal Reserve, a lender of last resort, ensuring that banks could obtain funds if they had a short-run liquidity problem. With this assurance, it was hoped, bank runs would be less likely. Obviously, this mechanism does not resolve problems for a truly insolvent bank; its only intent is to prevent short-run liquidity problems from bringing down a bank.

2.2.3   Regulations   A variety of regulations is designed to prevent banks from becoming insolvent. Such regulations are (or should) be based on the following principles. (a) Monitoring banks is costly and necessarily imperfect. (b) Accordingly, the regulations must be designed to make it more likely that those in control of banks make the kinds of decisions which enhance the solvency of the institution; and to make it possible to detect problems before the bank

---

[8]The government takes a less active role in ensuring the solvency of most other financial institutions, with the possible exception of insurance. Insurance firms are highly regulated, and the government in most states has established a guaranty fund to protect those who purchase insurance against the consequences of insolvency of insurance firms.

actually becomes insolvent. The regulations must further be based on the recognition that there are important asymmetries of information between the bank and the bank regulators, that the "books" of the bank are largely in the control of the bank, and that accordingly, the information presented to the bank regulators may be "distorted". For example, banks are in a position to sell undervalued assets, and to keep overvalued assets at their book value. When banks systematically engage in this practice, then "book" value will systematically overestimate true value.[9]

The objective of increasing the likelihood that those in control of banks take solvency-enhancing decisions is aided by requiring that the bank have substantial net worth — so that it has much to lose in the event of losses — and by restricting the kinds of loans and investments (e.g. insider lending and purchases of junk bonds) which the bank may make.

2.3 Government attempting to enhance macroeconomic stability

One of the reasons that the government has been concerned about bank runs is that the collapse of the banking system has severe macroeconomic consequences. Banks (and other financial institutions) are a repository of specialized information concerning their borrowers; when these banks fail, there is a concomitant decline in the economy's information-organizational capital. This decline translates into a decrease in loan availability. Note that this problem would not arise if capital markets were just auction markets. But they are not. A decrease in information not only impairs the efficiency with which funds get allocated; it may also lead to more extensive credit rationing, so that the effective cost of capital is greatly increased.

One of the functions that banks (and other financial institutions) are engaged in is certifying who is likely to repay loans, i.e. whose promises to pay should be believed. If too many people are so certified — if there are too many who can get funds, and they decide to exercise that option — then the demand for goods can easily exceed the supply. Since the price system (interest rate) often does not function to clear the capital market, there can be, within the market system, no automatic market-clearing mechanism. This fact provides an important role for a central bank.

2.4 Competition policy

In the United States, perhaps more than in other countries, there is (or at least has been) a concern that without government intervention, the banks would be able to exercise undue concentration of economic power. Many of the restrictions

---

[9]Tax considerations may limit the extent to which they engage in these practices. But when a bank is in danger of insolvency, regulatory considerations are likely to dominate tax considerations.

imposed on banks, such as those relating to interstate banking (American banks formerly were allowed to have branches only within a state), and those relating to what activities banks can engage in, were intended to limit their ability to exercise economic power.

Because government intervention is so pervasive, one might argue that it is difficult to tell what institutions might eventually evolve to provide some of the same services and protection currently provided by government. Proponents of "free markets" might contend that it is only impatience with the speed at which market institutions solve their own problems, not their capacity to solve those problems, which accounts for the large role of government. The few pieces of evidence there are, however, do not lend support to this argument. Chile experimented with relatively unregulated banking and disastrous results. The United States has had long periods in its history of relatively lax regulation. In the recent troubles confronting several major insurance companies within the United States, the rating agencies, whose sole economic role is to track the financial viability of these insurance companies, simply did not foresee the problems until they were all too visible for **everyone** to see, and customers cashed in their policies in droves. To be sure, badly designed government policies may exacerbate some problems (the extent of defaults within the S & L industry can be traced to a badly designed set of regulations and provisions), but there is no evidence that the elimination of **all** regulations would make matters better. (Several European countries do seem to function well without government-provided deposit insurance; this regulatory role may be an example where government actions have "crowded out" private actions which would have provided comparable services. But the fact that this is true for one particular government-provided service hardly provides a convincing case that it is true for all government services and regulatory activities. There are fundamental market failures underlying these government activities, which are described in the following paragraphs.)

This, perhaps by now familiar, litany of the roles that government regulation plays in financial markets is one way to approach the problem of government regulation. The other way is to ask if there is any reason to believe that free and unfettered capital markets result in efficient resource allocations. Until fifteen years ago, there was a quick and easy answer: Adam Smith's invisible hand theorem stated that competitive markets would ensure efficient resource allocations. But research over the past decade analyzing in depth the functioning of the capital market has found that, due to the imperfect information, the capital market is an exception to this theorem. With imperfect information, markets are, in general, not constrained Pareto efficient (see Greenwald and Stiglitz 1986, 1988). There is no presumption in favor of unfettered markets.

One of the major reasons for this conclusion is that much of the return in capital markets consists of rent seeking. Knowing Exxon has made a major oil discovery a minute before anyone else does may make you a fortune buying Exxon stock, but it does not increase the efficiency with which society's resources are allocated (see Hirschleifer 1971). Much of the innovation in the financial sector entails recording transactions more quickly, but is society really much better off as a result? Someone might receive the interest which would otherwise have accrued to someone else, but have more goods been produced? Or have they been allocated more efficiently?[10] Suppose one hundred dollar bills fell at our feet, one bill next to each of us. Suppose we were busily engaged in some productive activity. If we could agree, it would pay all of us to wait until we finished the activity, and then to each bend down to pick up the bill at his or her foot. But this result is not a Nash equilibrium: if others were working, it would pay each of us to bend down to try to pick up as many dollar bills as possible. Of course, when we all do it, we each get our own hundred dollar bill; we have lost the production we would otherwise have had and are all worse off as a result.[11]

In short, there is no *a priori* basis for arguing that the government should not intervene in the capital market; and there seem to be strong arguments for government intervention. In any case, some government intervention is likely. The question then is what kinds of financial institutions to establish, and what role government should play.

3   Perspectives for the Newly Emerging Democracies: Issues of Transition

Most of the problems discussed in the previous section are generic: they arise in virtually any economy, though with more force in some than in others. The problems take on a particular color within the newly emerging democracies of Eastern Europe, and it is upon these distinctive features that attention is focused.

Two separate sets of issues may be distinguished — those relating to the form of the financial institutions that will eventually emerge in these countries and those relating to the particular problems associated with the **transition** from their current situation to a market economy. Of course, the two problems are in a sense inseparable: views about the ultimate destination impinge on how some of the short-run problems ought to be addressed, and answers provided to the short-run transition problems will almost undoubtedly have a major impact on the ultimate destination. Indeed, this interaction is important: decisions made in the short run may not easily be reversed.

The rest of this section discusses the problems associated with the transition, with particular emphasis on the instances where the manner of their resolution is critically dependent on the conception of the eventual structure of the financial system.

---

[10]See Stiglitz and Weiss (1991) for a formal model.

[11]I am indebted to Larry Summers for this example.

There are five related central problems facing these economies in the process of transition. The first is well-recognized: (1) how to establish **hard budget constraints.** The importance of the other four has only gradually been recognized: (2) historically, the banks and other so-called financial institutions did not perform any of the central functions (other than mediating transactions) that are associated with financial institutions. In effect, completely new institutions have to be created; yet in most of the countries, rather than creating new institutions, there has been an attempt to adapt old institutions. The extent to which their **historical institutional legacy** will impair them remains to be seen: will the old modes of thinking impede their ability to recognize their new economic functions? At the very least, a process of reeducation is required. (3) Under the old regime, not only did banks not perform the same role (e.g. screening loan applicants), but those taking out loans did not view them in the same way: after all, given that the government owned both the bank and the enterprise, it was like the left pocket owing the right pocket money. Both sides of the transaction looked upon it as simply an accounting exercise. These perceptions raise important questions about what we are to make of the **inherited loan portfolios** of the financial institutions. How these inherited debts are treated has obvious consequences for, and is obviously affected by, the process of privatization. (4) The former socialist economies inherit a situation in which the state had an economic monopoly. Moreover, the state did not use **competition** as an instrument of policy. On the contrary, there were state monopolies in many industries (including the financial sector). Developing effective competition may prove to be a difficult task. (5) The relationship between finance and **corporate control** has increasingly drawn the attention of economists (see Stiglitz 1985). Special problems are likely to arise in those socialist economies which decide to privatize by means of schemes which result in a wide distribution of equity ownership, and these problems have implications for the role and design of financial institutions. The first three of these issues are discussed below. The final two are discussed in the next part, where the focus is on the ultimate shape of the financial system.

Underlying much of the discussion of the design of financial systems for the newly emerging democracies is the extent to which reliance should be placed on the reform and reorganization of existing institutions, the extent to which reliance should be placed on the creation of new institutions, the extent to which a clean slate should be declared, with old debts and credits created under a very different economic regime being wiped out. Many of the issues that form the basis of this debate turn on politics and expectations and bring us beyond the scope of economics. Still, there are basic economic issues that are relevant to this discussion. It is upon these economic issues that attention is focused. Much of the discussion will center around the reform of existing institutions rather than the distinctive problems of creating new institutions.

Perhaps the first problem one encounters in the reform of current financial institutions is that of their solvency. Many of the financial institutions have been run with soft budget constraints: deficits have been made up by the government.

Soft budget constraints within the financial sector can have disastrous effects for the entire economy. Soft budget constraints, like a disease, can be highly contagious. If the banks face soft budget constraints, they will not impose discipline upon their borrowers. If a borrower has a zero or negative net worth, he may not care if he makes a loss: even if the government will not make up the difference, he may be able to borrow to keep himself operating.

There is a more direct mechanism by which the disease of soft budget constraints is spread: firms are constantly extending trade credit to suppliers and customers. If some firms are not on a tight leash, they may not put their suppliers and customers on a tight leash. If there is a widespread belief that the State stands behind State firms, and will honor their debts, then any State firm is in the position of being able to create credit.

3.1 Hardening the budget constraint through privatization

The difficult question is how best to harden the budget constraint. There are no easy answers. This section addresses some problems with some of the often proposed solutions. The seemingly simplest solution is privatization. Once a firm is in the private sector, it has no more "entitlement" to the public purse. It must sink or swim.

3.1.1 Problems of valuation The problems of privatization have been widely discussed. Some of those problems which arise acutely in the privatization of the financial sector merit attention. Assume, for the moment, that the government were to decide to sell the financial sector in open competition. One central problem is that of valuing the assets of financial institutions. The risks associated with valuing those assets imply that, with risk-averse bidders, the State is likely to get considerably less than the actuarial fair value. This likelihood, of course, holds true for all privatizations. But the risks are, in a fundamental sense, different from the risks associated with privatizing industrial firms. One of the central aspects of the risks associated with valuing a bank's assets is how, in the process of privatization of the "firms" that owe the bank money, the liabilities of those firms are to be treated. These are issues which, at this juncture, have not been resolved. Thus, the central valuation risk is a political risk, and it makes little sense for the government to transfer — at a cost — that risk to the private sector.

Moreover, the consequences of valuation errors are likely to be particularly severe. On the one hand, if the bidders overestimate the value of their assets, the financial institutions will be undercapitalized. Undercapitalized financial institutions have strong incentives to undertake undue risks. Excessive risk-taking is the familiar moral hazard problem, the consequences of which were all too clear in the case of the S & L debacle in the United States, as the near-bankrupt firms gambled on their resurrection. Moreover, if such undercapitalization is widespread, then the likelihood of a government bailout becomes very high, and the financial institutions knowing this possibility will act accordingly: in this instance, privatization will not effectively harden budget constraints.

If the bidders underestimate the value of the assets, there will be charges of a government giveaway. It may be hard for governments to resist the temptation to recapture these profits by, for example, a special tax on the enterprise.

3.1.2   Insolvency of financial institutions   In the case of either a significant under- or overvaluation of the assets, the success or failure of the financial institution will not convey much information — other than about the luck (or lack of it) of the bidders, or their skill (or lack of it) in predicting political winds. If a bank appears to be solvent, it may not be because it is making good lending decisions. It may only be because its assets were undervalued.

By the same token, the government faces severe problems in deciding what to do with a bank facing a liquidity crisis. First, it must ascertain whether it is insolvent. Determining insolvency gets back to the basic problems of asset valuation discussed earlier. The value of its loan portfolio depends in large measure on government policies: will the government honor the loans taken out by state enterprises? Will it insist on those purchasing state enterprises "honoring" these debts? And even if it is ascertained that a bank is insolvent, should one presume that it is incompetent and should therefore be shut down?

Not necessarily, particularly if there have been drastic changes in economic circumstances that could not reasonably have been anticipated. But this kind of insolvency is precisely the position in which many Eastern European institutions find themselves. Moreover, the grounds for granting loans by state-run banks may have had little to do with standard commercial principles. Banks under socialism do not perform the central functions of screening and monitoring that they do under capitalism.

Assume one concludes that the insolvency is not a mark of incompetence: what then? There is perhaps valuable organizational capital[12] which would be lost if the bank were dissolved. One needs a once-and-for-all capital infusion. Without some method of ensuring that such a capital infusion would not be repeated, again incentives would be distorted.

3.1.3   Public distribution of shares: a negative capital levy?   The same problems would arise — even more strongly[13] — if the banks were privatized, but

---

[12]Earlier it was suggested that there may be "negative" organizational capital: the outmoded ways of thinking associated with banking under socialism may tinge the banks in the new economic situation and thus impair their ability to perform their new, different, and more important economic role.

[13]Because, unlike the case where the bank is sold, there has been no outside assessment of the value of assets and liability, as unreliable as those assessments might be, and no infusion of additional equity from the outside, which one might normally be expected to occur in the event of privatization of a bank.

the shares distributed publicly. This distribution is, in effect, a lump sum grant, or a negative capital levy.[14] Traditional tax theory has argued for the desirability of capital levies, were it not for the distortionary consequences arising from the expectation that they might be repeated. Proponents of these negative capital levies argue that the gains in managerial incentives from privatization more than outweigh the subsequent costs arising from the distortionary taxation which will be necessary to raise the requisite revenue. But a partial privatization, with the government retaining a substantial fraction of the shares, would presumably do as well: in most large private corporations in the United States, managerial pay is only weakly related to managers' contributions to firm performance (see Jensen and Murphy 1990).[15]

To mitigate the negative capital levy effect, the government might, alternatively, treat the current assets of a non-financial firm being privatized as debt of the firm to the government. But then the government itself would be involved in the difficult question of valuation with all the untoward consequences of misvaluation which have previously noted.

3.1.4   The timing of privatization of financial institutions   In short, the potential viability of any newly privatized bank may depend as much on its competence in valuing the old assets — or on luck, as prices and market values change in hard-to-anticipate ways — as on the competency of the institution in performing its **ongoing** roles (described earlier in this chapter). Particularly during the early stages of the transition, where government laws, regulations, and policies affecting the private sector are not clear, market values may change in hard-to-predict ways. For instance, the government might decide that the high debt of some firms represents an impediment to their ongoing operation and either repudiate that debt or assume that debt as its own obligation. These alternatives

---

[14]Any tax which has the property that there is nothing **current** that the individual can do to avoid or reduce the tax is non-distortionary. In general, such taxes are referred to as lump sum taxes. They can be levied uniformly (in which case they are, quite naturally, called uniform lump sum taxes); or they can be levied differentially, on the basis of some characteristic. When individuals are required to pay a once-and-for-all sum based on the amount of capital, it is called a capital levy. Of course, if it is anticipated, a capital levy is distortionary, for people will take the lower after-tax returns into account in deciding how much to save. (Of course, all taxes, distortionary or non-distortionary, have real effects; but the real effects associated with lump sum taxes, including capital levies, are just income effects — the consequences of taking away income from individuals, as any tax must necessarily do.)

[15]And again, the difficulties of valuing the financial institution's existing assets make it difficult to ascertain whether the financial institution is doing a "good" job.

have obviously drastically different obligations for the holders of this debt paper.[16]

In the days of socialism, financial structure made no difference (here at last was a domain in which the Modigliani-Miller theorem was correct though for quite different reasons: all obligations were simply obligations of one part of the government to another[17]). Firms produced what they were told to produce; finance simply accommodated these "orders" (for a more extensive discussion of this situation, see McKinnon, Ch. 7). In market economies, financial structure makes a great deal of difference (see Stiglitz 1988a). Again, there is no incentive or sorting reason to impose the inherited financial structure of firms upon the ongoing operations of the firm. Some kind of recapitalization is required. While privatization represents one form such recapitalization can take, government assumption of debt (as in the restructuring of the S & L's in the United States) and debt-for-equity swaps (as in the restructuring of some third world debt) may represent interim measures to be taken as the government re-examines some of the more fundamental issues associated with privatization. But these recapitalizations, as desirable as they may be, can have profound effects on the outstanding liabilities of these firms to the financial institutions. There seems a case for resolving these uncertainties before proceeding with the privatization of financial institutions. If privatization is postponed, some alternative interim method of hardening budget constraints may be required. Professor McKinnon (Ch. 7) provides one thoughtful possibility.

Leaving for the moment the question of the timing of privatization of the financial institutions, there are some important caveats to bear in mind in the design of the "privatization package".

3.2   Other issues in the hardening of budget constraints

There are obvious macro as well as micro advantages of enforcing tough budget constraints. The excessive expansion of credit can clearly lead to inflationary pressures. However, hardening the budget constraint too rapidly, or in the wrong way, can lead to a separate set of problems.

Tough budget constraints have obvious incentive effects — provided they can be met. But beyond their incentive effects, they are important as selection

---

[16]An important issue in the transition process is how to deal, more broadly, with these inherited obligations. Inflation is obviously one way of reducing their importance, but this option obviously has its own disadvantages. A fuller discussion of this issue is beyond the scope of this chapter.

[17]This description undoubtedly oversimplifies the situation, particularly in those countries, like Hungary and Yugoslavia, where there were bankruptcy laws and firms had some autonomy, and the government as a consequence did not serve as the ultimate guarantor of all loans.

mechanisms. Those who cannot meet the market test are weeded out. This selection mechanism only makes sense if market prices are right. But in the transition period, market prices are likely to deviate markedly from their longer run equilibrium values. Moreover, in assessing viability, some value must be attached to the capital which is used. But when the machines that have been installed are inefficient and of low quality, how are they to be evaluated? The market for used machines is thin. If undervalued, it may be too easy to meet the market test. If overvalued, it may be impossible for the firm to survive.

Secondly, the standard macro model focuses on the effect of monetary (credit) constraints on aggregate demand. But such constraints also have effects on aggregate supply. If firms cannot get sufficient working capital, then production will be cut back.[18] If interest rates are raised sharply, and there has not been a recapitalization, high debt firms may be thrown into bankruptcy. But these problems have nothing to do with their current operating efficiency, only with an inherited financial structure.[19] If the reduction in aggregate supply exceeds that of aggregate demand, the monetary (credit) constraints can actually be inflationary. More broadly, it is important that credit be cut off to those for which the return is lowest. But in the transition process, that distinction is difficult to ascertain.

There are problems with controlling both the allocation of credit and its total volume. When there is a single bank, the volume of credit is, in principle, easy to control. But a central part of establishing a market economy is having at least a few competing banks and other financial institutions. In the United States and many other capitalist economies, the government relies on indirect control mechanisms for controlling the quantity of credit: open market operations, discount rates, and reserve requirements. Even in the United States, the relationship between these instruments and the volume of credit becomes tenuous when the economy faces considerable uncertainty, as in the event of a downturn. In newly established financial systems, there is likely to be even greater uncertainty about these relationships, and thus indirect control mechanisms may be viewed as an excessively risky way of controlling the volume of credit. On the other hand, the Central Bank may not be in a position to allocate credit targets efficiently among the various banks. One suggestion is "marketable quantity

---

[18]See Greenwald and Stiglitz (1990) for a model which analyzes simultaneously the effect of capital market conditions on aggregate demand and supply. Calvo and Frankel (1991) have emphasized the role of these supply effects in the transition process.

[19]While there is some debate about the significance of the costs of bankruptcy, in the process of transition, when all of society's resources are being reorganized, the disruption in the use of resources following a bankruptcy may be particularly costly. The external costs of bankruptcy are especially large when there is only one supplier of a good, as was often the case under central planning.

constraints". The Central Bank would control the quantity of credit, either auctioning off the right to issue loans or granting the rights to various banks, with the proviso that banks could trade the rights among themselves. Such marketable quantity constraints combine the certainty of quantity targets with the allocational efficiency of market mechanisms.[20]

4   Perspectives for the Newly Emerging Democracies: The Ultimate Shape of the Financial System

There are some basic issues concerning the design of the financial system which must be faced as part of the transition, but which are as much issues of the ultimate shape of the financial system. The discussion is divided into three sections. The first deals with the role of competition, the second with the set of regulations that are concerned with the solvency/liquidity of the banking system, and the third which focuses on issues of corporate control.

4.1   Banks and competition
There are two separate but related issues: competition among banks and banking practices which affect competition among firms. The United States has clearly been worried about the possible deleterious effects of banking practices which limit competition among firms. Recent reforms in the banking system have encouraged more competition within the banking system — far more competition than in other countries — and there are proposals to dismantle some of the regulations which were intended to limit the economic power of banks.

The problem of establishing viable competition is a bone of some contention. There are some who believe that allowing foreign competition is all that is required: there are enough firms in the international marketplace to ensure that competition within a current will be strong, if only these international firms are allowed to compete. There are some (such as Baumol, Panzar and Willig 1982) who have argued that to ensure economic efficiency and zero profits, all one needs is **potential** competition — the threat of entry — not actual entry.

---

[20]Such marketable quantity constraints have been introduced in the United States for the control of certain kinds of pollution. Weitzman (1974) provides an analysis of the advantages of the use of quantities versus prices as control mechanisms in the presence of uncertain benefit and cost functions. Such an analysis can be extended to the problem under consideration here. The kinds of criticisms raised against the use of the price system for the allocation of credit (Stiglitz 1988b) can be raised here, for the use of the price system in allocating the rights to allocate credit among financial institutions.

Others[21] see a variety of barriers to entry of a kind that have been well documented within capitalist economies, resulting in at best imperfect competition. This author is inclined to the latter view. Adam Smith had it right when he described the natural inclination of businessmen as attempting to restrict competition: "People of the same trade seldom meet together, even for merriment and diversion, but the conversation ends in a conspiracy against the public, or in some contrivance to raise prices."[22] These tendencies may be all the stronger among individuals who have formerly worked closely together, as seems often to be the case when large state enterprises are divided into competing firms. Anecdotes of firms getting together to stabilize the market and to prevent disorderly competition do not prove the point, but they at least alert us to the existence of a problem.[23] It is all the more difficult to make competition effective because of the past lack of competition and because firms within an industry have been encouraged to cooperate rather than compete. They have developed a nexus of social relationships which promote such cooperative (noncompetitive) behavior.

Banks can, and have, served the function of limiting competition in product markets. They are in an ideal position for coordinating decision making. Moreover, it is even in the bank's narrow interest as a lender to limit competition: the fiercer the competition, the more likely the less efficient firms within the market will go bankrupt, and thus, the more likely that some loans will not be repaid.

While the vitality of capitalism does not depend on the existence of perfect competition in the textbook sense, a high level of competition is essential to ensure both economic efficiency and that the fruits of that efficiency are passed on to consumers. Farmers will find little relief if instead of receiving low prices for their goods from the government, they receive low prices from monopsonist food processors. In either case, low prices will depress production and inhibit development of the agricultural sector.

There is a general presumption that competition among banks is no less desirable than competition in other sectors of the economy. But while **some** competition among the banks is desirable, excess competition may have its own problems. Banks, perhaps even more than other institutions, depend on their reputation. Reputation is an asset worth preserving — provided that there is an economic return. But for there to be an economic return, competition has to be

---

[21]See Salop (1979). A vast literature has emerged within what is sometimes called the "new industrial organization theory" describing the variety of ways by which firms can create strategic barriers to entry and can use restrictive practices to facilitate collusion.

[22]*Wealth of Nations,* I.x.c.27.

[23]On the other hand, the fact that firms make profits does not prove that competition is limited, as some critics of markets within the socialist and former socialist economies seem to suggest. There are profits to be had from making markets work more efficiently, from supplying what is needed. Not all profits are monopoly profits.

limited. The limitation may come from natural economic forces — establishing a reputation may act as a barrier to entry (see Eaton 1986; Shapiro 1983; Schmalensee 1982; or Stiglitz 1989b).[24] It is worth noting that in the United States, one of the effects of deposit insurance was to reduce or eliminate this barrier to entry, facilitating entry and competition. But the resulting competition, and the ensuing reduction of reputation rents, encouraged banks to pursue short-sighted policies which contributed to the S & L debacle and the current banking crisis.

There seems a real possibility of either excessive entry — driving rents to zero, and thus eliminating the incentives for maintaining a reputation — or of insufficient entry — leading to insufficient competition within the financial sector. Nor does the government's ability to set the "right" level of entry inspire confidence. Out of this dilemma, no clear prescription emerges, simply a word of caution: the financial sector needs to be carefully watched, for evidences of significant "errors" in either direction.

4.2   Regulations for a banking system

There is now widespread recognition (for the reasons given earlier) that even in the best run of capitalist economies, banks need to be regulated. Earlier, the general form and objectives of this regulation were discussed. To translate these objectives into concrete proposals for the financial institutions of the newly emerging democracies would be beyond the scope of this chapter. But a couple of key issues merit attention. These relate to the twin problems of "market failure" and "government failure," both of which are well illustrated by the problems which have confronted the Savings and Loan Associations (S & L's) and banks within the United States.

The standard diagnoses attribute the problems facing American financial institutions to eight factors:

1. Deposit insurance, which removed the incentive of depositors to monitor banks.

2. Inadequate capital requirements, which resulted in insufficiently capitalized institutions having an incentive to take excessive risk. (Some financial institutions found themselves with negative net worth, were they to be evaluated at market values; the low net worths were partly the result of bad investment decisions, partly the result of changes in interest rates which decreased the value of their assets, which consisted largely of long-term debt at fixed interest rates.) Firms with negative or low net worth gambled on their resurrection.

---

[24]Though this argument holds, to some extent, in many other markets, it holds with particular force in financial institutions where what is being exchanged is dollars today for promises of dollars in the future. A buyer of a TV can see quickly what he is getting; if the TV wears out in two years, the producer will quickly lose his reputation. With financial markets, the promises are frequently much longer term.

3. Inadequate restraints on how financial institutions could invest the funds which were entrusted to them, allowing those who wished to gamble on their resurrection to do so. Indeed, in an attempt to **help** the failing S & L's the Reagan administration had, in the early 1980s, actually loosened the regulations.

4. Inadequate incentives for banks not to engage in risk-taking: their premiums on deposit insurance were not adjusted according to the risks being undertaken. Indeed, a process of Gresham's Law was at work: firms that offered high interest rates could attract more funds (since depositors only cared about the interest rate — with deposit insurance all were equally safe); and to pay the high interest rates, financial institutions in effect **had** to undertake high levels of risk.

5. Inadequate monitoring by regulators.

6. Inadequate accounting procedures: assets were not valued at current market value, so that firms whose net worth was low or negative — and who, therefore, had an incentive to engage in excessive risk-taking — were not shut down.

7. Regulatory forbearance: regulators, having noticed a problem, had every incentive to try to "patch things up" rather than face an immediate crisis.

8. Corrupt bankers.

The last problem is more a consequence rather than a cause: bankers used to rank among the more boring and more steadfast members of the community. It was the incentives and opportunities provided by the banking climate in the 1980s that attracted, if not corrupt individuals (by most accounts they were responsible for a relatively small fraction of the total losses), then at least more "entrepreneurial" activities (to put a positive light on their risk-taking actions). They should not be blamed for pursuing their self-interest, for taking advantage of incentive opportunities provided by the system, even if it meant the government had to bear much of the risk and they reaped much of the potential reward.

The problems facing the regulators are inherent: they have less information than the banks, and they will therefore always be at a disadvantage. (The problems are exacerbated by the low pay regulators receive, both absolutely, and relative to that received by those they are regulating. But these restrictions in pay are part of the almost inherent limitations on government, referred to earlier.)

The effect of deposit insurance on monitoring is a red herring: individuals have neither the capacity nor the incentive, even in the absence of deposit insurance, to monitor effectively. The fact is that monitoring is a public good; individuals do not have access to the relevant information, and they are not in as competent position to judge as regulators should be. Rating services go only a little way to fill the gap. They certainly have not performed in stellar fashion in the current crisis.

Any insurance firm, when it provides insurance, knows that insurance may give rise to a moral hazard problem: it attenuates incentives to avoid the insured-against accident. It attempts to impose "regulations" to mitigate these effects; fire insurance companies attempt to mitigate the losses of fire by insisting that commercial insurers have sprinkler systems. The regulatory system should be designed to take account of the fact that the government and depositors have limited abilities to monitor banks. They should be designed to alter incentives, to exercise control at points where observability is easy, and to reduce the magnitude of residual risk-bearing by the government. Government regulations of insured accounts can be viewed in the same way that any insurer attempts to reduce his exposure: capital requirements, restrictions on interest paid to attract funds, and restrictions on risky investment all reduce the likelihood of defaults which will necessitate the government paying up on the insurance it has provided. Ownership restrictions, limiting potential conflicts of interest and the abuse of banks' fiduciary responsibilities, reduce "temptation" and, therefore, once again, the burden on monitoring.

With capital requirements set at a sufficiently high level, many of the other problems are alleviated: since the government will be bearing less risk, the consequences of adjusting premiums to the risk being borne become less important,[25] and the consequences of failing to value the bank correctly also become less important[26] — problems will still be detected before it is too late, that is, before the government's risk exposure has increased. Incentives for excessive risk-taking by banks will be reduced, and the banking system will seem less attractive to the kind of risk-loving entrepreneurs who found their haven in the S & L's in the 1980s.

As noted earlier, some of the indirect restrictions which may be effective are those on ownership of banks. But on this last point, the present author is less confident, for reasons discussed next.

4.3   Banks and corporate control: two views

The desirability of maintaining strong walls between the financial and production sectors of the economy runs counter to what many observers see as the very successful models of financial structure of Japan and Germany. These

---

[25]The government would, in any case, have a difficult time adjusting premiums to reflect risk: is it likely that the government could charge higher premiums for deposit insurance in one state than in another, declaring that in its estimate the risks are greater? A number of recent proposals have suggested ways in which the government can employ market mechanisms to provide "objective" determinations of the appropriate premium levels. For instance, the government can "sell" a portion of the insurance in the re-insurance market, using the prices determined there as the basis for levying premiums.

[26]Banks complain that marking to market assets is "unfair" since, in practice, not all assets are marked to market; some assets, such as the physical assets the bank owns, typically are not revalued. But there is less justification to this complaint than at first seems the case: under current practice, banks have, in effect, the option of revaluing assets at their own discretion. An asset which has increased in value can be marketed, and thus the capital gain recorded; and an asset which has decreased in value can be kept on the books at the original value. Accordingly, "book" value can present a strongly biased view of the firm.

provide very viable alternative models for designing financial systems, models which are particularly attractive in the context of "people's capitalism" to which some of the emerging democracies may be evolving. There are many viable financial structures. On the other hand, there are also many non-viable financial structures. The United States has one with certain marked problems, and it seems to be embarking upon reforms in that system that will exacerbate those problems.

The Japanese financial system is usually characterized as involving production groups, each with a bank at the center. These banks are closely involved with production firms. When Mazda had trouble, its bank stepped in, changed management, and successfully turned the company around. There is competition across these groups and cooperation within each group.

The Japanese model has received considerable attention as resolving a problem plaguing American managerial capitalism. With widely diversified shares, managers have considerable autonomy. Good management is a public good: all shareholders benefit if the firm is run better. No shareholder can be excluded from these benefits. Each shareholder thus has an inadequate incentive to monitor the firm. Indeed, there are great barriers to small shareholders doing an effective job. The alleged control mechanisms work most imperfectly — management is seldom replaced through the voting mechanism, and there are fundamental problems with the takeover mechanism (Stiglitz 1972, 1982, and 1985; and Grossman and Hart 1980).

While banks nominally do not have control, they may actually exercise more effective control. They have a credible threat of withdrawing credit; information problems mean that credit markets are inherently imperfect, and when one firm withdraws credit, others will not normally rush in.[27] Moreover, credit is normally more concentrated than equity (there is normally a lead bank, the number of banks in a lending syndicate is limited, and they have a variety of reciprocal relationships which help reduce the importance of free rider problems). Thus, banks have both the incentives and the means to exercise control.[28]

In this perspective, the appropriate way to view the firm is as a multiple principal-agent problem — the various principals being all those who provide capital to the firm as well as the workers (essentially, anyone who would be adversely affected by, say, the bankruptcy of the firm). In this view, the manager is the "agent" of all these principals. While the bank may not induce the firm to take actions which maximize the welfare of these other groups—ensuring that there

---

[27]For a theoretical analysis of why this phenomenon occurs, and of the incentive effects of credit termination, see Stiglitz and Weiss (1983).

[28]See Berle and Means (1933) and Stiglitz (1985). Part of the reason for the concentration of debt is that, given the limited extent of risk, risk diversification is less important than in the case of equity.

is a relatively low risk of bankruptcy may not maximize expected returns to shareholders— the control which they exercise does confer external benefits on other groups, at least in ensuring the solvency of the firm. When the bank also is a shareholder, one could argue that the bank is more likely to pursue actions which enhance the overall return to capital. This shareholder role is one of the essential advantages of the "Japanese model". There is a single bank which has the incentive to exercise the critical monitoring function; and because it also has an ownership stake, it does so in a way which reflects both the interests of lenders and owners of equity.

One might imagine that if the shares of the large enterprises within the newly emerging democracies were widely distributed, there would be real problems of managerial control. The worst kinds of abuses — the kind that have been documented in the case of RJR-Nabisco — could become prevalent. The Japanese system **may** limit these at the expense of an agglomeration of enormous amounts of corporate power. Some of these abuses will be limited by ensuring that there are several such groups and that there will be competition among them. (Thus, one's view of the desirable financial structure may be affected by how effectively one believes antitrust laws will be enforced.) International competition may provide further discipline. Yet, one cannot be blind to the possibility that the concentration of large amounts of capital under the control of relatively few individuals (even if they do not "own" the capital) can be used to obtain political influence, possibly to restrict competition (though always, of course, in the name of some other more sacred principle).

Perhaps a hybrid system — one in which there are holding companies, performing, in effect, managerial roles over those who are part of their group, and **separate** financial institutions — would provide the needed checks and balances.[29] The financial institutions would provide an important role in monitor-

---

[29]Some people envisage the holding companies as having a role only in the transition process. They see a process of concentration with some ownership shares eventually being sufficiently large to play an effective role in control. There is little evidence on the speed with which such concentration would occur, or indeed, whether it would ever occur, in which case the holding companies would become a permanent part of the scene.

[30]To some extent, designing financial institutions that "work well" with those of Western Europe may be as important as any of the factors listed, if the Eastern European countries want to be integrated quickly into Europe.

[31]It is perhaps worth noting that the United States quite explicitly tried to restrict the extent to which one firm could own or control other firms (at least in related industries), because of its concern over the resulting potential for collusive behavior. On the other hand, having firms own other firms (as seems to be prevalent in Japan) may provide a more effective system of "peer monitoring". See Arnott and Stiglitz (1991) for a discussion of the role of peer monitoring in mitigating moral hazard problems.

ing the monitors; and at the same time, the separation would serve to limit some-what the concentration of economic power.[30,31]

In recent years within the United States, venture capital firms have played a vital role in providing finance, particularly to new high technology industries (especially in computers, and bio-medical and related areas). There, the monitoring and selection functions are intimately interconnected with the provision of capital. Whether there is a greater potential scope for these firms, and whether variants of these firms could be adapted to the process of privatization, is not yet clear.

4.4   Equity markets

The choice of focusing attention primarily on banks, not on equity markets, has been deliberate. To a large extent, equity markets are an interesting and fun sideshow, but they are not at the heart of the action. Relatively little capital is raised in equity markets even in the United States and the United Kingdom. One cannot expect equity markets to play an important role in raising funds in the newly emerging democracies. Equity markets are also a sideshow in the allocation of capital. Robert Hall once said that the *Wall Street Journal* finally got it right, when it split the financial section from the business section. The two are only very loosely connected. Managers do not look to the stock market — to the views of the dentists in Peoria or the retired insurance salesmen in Florida — to determine whether another blast furnace should be built, or whether further exploration for oil should be undertaken. The stock price is relevant — they look at the effect on the stock market price. But it does not, and should not, drive their behavior. It simply provides too coarse information to direct investment decisions. And in the transition process of the Eastern European countries, it is even less likely that equity markets will play an important role in providing information which is of relevance for investment decisions.

On the other hand, if the stock market becomes important, instability in the stock market[32] can contribute to macro-economic instability in ways which are by now familiar. The policy implications of this danger (e.g. for transactions taxes on the stock market) remain a subject of considerable debate (see Stiglitz 1989b; and Summers and Summers 1989).

While the stock market enhances liquidity, and the enhanced liquidity makes investment in equities much more desirable, the stock market is not an unmitigated blessing. There has been concern, for instance, that to the extent managers do pay attention to stock market prices, it leads them to behave in an excessively shortsighted manner (presumably because stock prices are excessively sensitive to short run returns). Advocates of this view — which can be traced at least back to Keynes — look for ways to encourage long-term investment in securi-

---

[32]Of the kind that can result from speculative bubbles.

ties, perhaps using the tax system to discourage short-term trading (e.g. a turnover tax). Though this is not the occasion to enter into that debate, it should be noted that there is little evidence that such taxes, which have been implemented in several countries, have had any adverse effects on market volatility or, indeed, on the ability of the market to perform any of the other functions which it performs.

5   Conclusions

Financial markets play a central role in any capitalist economy. The design of capital markets affects the ability of the economy to raise capital and to allocate it efficiently. Beyond that, the design of capital markets affects the efficiency of enterprises in all other sectors of the economy. Even if one has little confidence in the efficiency or effectiveness of the "market for corporate control," the monitoring function of financial institutions provides essential discipline on managers, a discipline function which is particularly important in economies in which shares are widely held.

While there is an array of financial structures found in different capitalist economies from which the newly emerging democracies can choose, it is not evident that any represent the "optimal" financial structure, or indeed, that any of them has fully adapted to the new technologies which have revolutionized the processing of information. In the case of some capitalist countries, the defects in the financial systems are all too apparent. The newly emerging democracies have ahead of them a delicate balancing act: once they settle upon a financial structure, they will find change is difficult and costly. Vested interests arise which will quickly attain political and economic influence. The dangers of too impetuously settling upon a financial structure seem clear. But privatizing and establishing a well-functioning market economy require effective capital markets. Delay is costly. At the very least, it is hoped that in this chapter may prove some help in thinking through some of the key aspects in the design of financial markets and institutions.

PART III
Government Policy Toward the Private Sector: Antitrust Policy and the Safety Net

10 Anti-Monopoly Policies and Institutions

Robert D. Willig

There is increasing consensus that the creation of a free market economy requires a policy regime that like a quilt is made up of many interwoven pieces whose unity and spread are critical to its effectiveness. There is less awareness, however, that appropriate anti-monopoly policy is integral to the quilt's design. The purpose of this chapter is to make this case, both as a matter of logic and as a lesson derived from experience.

It is surely understandable if attention to anti-monopoly policy were to be overlooked amidst the daunting agenda facing the emerging market economies, which includes:

1. Creation of secure rights to private property
2. Establishment of a code of commercial law
3. Privatization and restructuring of state enterprises
4. Bringing stability and convertibility to the currency
5. Relaxation of trade barriers
6. Reform of business regulation and pricing constraints
7. Creation of capital and credit markets

While the fundamental importance and difficulties of these steps cannot be overstated, it would, nevertheless, be a serious error to omit anti-monopoly policy from the list of free-market essentials or to leave it for last as an afterthought.

Brazil's experience during the summer of 1990 in its exploration of competition policy underscores this point. On the very day that the reform-minded government ended the longstanding system of micro-regulation of the prices of milk at all stages of distribution, the leadership of the dairy industry declared that if the government would no longer fix their prices, they would have to do it for themselves. After a highly visible public meeting, they decided to award themselves a lucrative raise by setting the newly fixed levels of milk prices well above the old ones. Within 24 hours, *de facto* price regulation was re-instituted, and the highest levels of government became feverishly engaged in writing stop-gap anti-monopoly rules as a precursor to the permanent legislation that is still under debate.

Brazil's lesson is that a newly emerging free market economy needs anti-monopoly law and needs it quickly. This lesson can be fully generalized and is not lessened in its force by the special circumstances associated with the revolutionary changes occurring in East and Central Europe.

Competition is the engine that makes market economies work. The core of competition is the existence of sufficiently many sellers independently offering choices, or standing ready to offer choices, to buyers. To make sales, producers must then outdo their active and potential rivals in quality and price. Buyers can protect themselves against sellers that offer excessively high prices or excessively low quality by offering their business in return for better deals from alternative active rivals of those sellers or from potential entrants. Success thus depends upon efficient production of goods and services that consumers or business buyers want, along with aggressive pricing at levels consistent with efficient costs. Great success goes to those who risk their efforts and capital to invest in creating new desirable choices for tomorrow.

While this description of competition is so simple to appear more a caricature than a characterization, it is supported by state-of-the-art research, and it is sufficiently rich to frame some of the essentials of anti-monopoly policy. The succeeding sections develop some of these basic elements of anti-monopoly policy in the context of emerging market economies, drawing on the experiences of the United States as a source for comparisons, for mistakes to avoid, and for successes to adopt.

1   Competitive Code of Conduct

At the core of competition are sellers' independent offers for the business of buyers, among which buyers are free to choose. Unfortunately, typical sellers would find it more profitable to make coordinated offers instead of independent ones. In general, with mutually effective commitments to coordination, sellers can hold prices well above costs, can refrain from costly measures to enhance service, and can escape pressures to cut costs and improve products. And typical sellers would have strong financial incentives to reach such anti-competitive agreements with one another.

Thus, even with the institutions in place to support a capitalist economy, competition is far from a foregone conclusion. Competition, and the consumer benefits it brings, requires a code of business conduct to assure that apparently rival offers are truly independent. The code of business conduct must therefore outlaw cartel coordination. It is anti-monopoly law that establishes the competitive code of conduct.

Of course, an appropriate body of anti-monopoly law will be far broader than just a rule against cartel behavior — covering at least such other areas as monopolization, or abuse of dominance, mergers, acquisitions, joint ventures, and horizontal and vertical constraints. Nonetheless, in the same fashion that independent rivalry is central to competition, proscription of cartel behavior is central to appropriate anti-monopoly law.

A code of competitive conduct is especially vital in a nation new to the free market form of economy. Under central planning, or in an encompassing state-owned sector, normal acceptable business culture entails discussion, agreement, and lobbying with respect to collective pricing; rigid and exclusionary patterns of distribution; and agreements on market allocation. Rivalry is viewed as wasteful, or at best, peripheral to the workings of the system. The desired norm is efficiency through agreements that assign roles without needless or divisive overlap such as agreements that eliminate independent action and choices.

Thus, the creation of a free market economy that relies on competition requires drastic revision of the business culture. The previous norm that was a natural concomitant of centralization and state ownership must be replaced with the radically different code of competitive conduct.

That this is a difficult and problematic challenge is evidenced by portions of US experience with deregulation. In the late 1970s, substantial reform of railroad regulation gave carriers the freedom to compete for traffic against trucks, encouraged them to compete with one another, and significantly lessened the role of regulation in decisions on rates and services. The individuals leading the US railroads were unable to adapt quickly to the new business environment. Only new leadership proved to be capable of taking independent, aggressive, and creative actions for the purpose of attracting business away from trucks and from other railroads. Analogously, as many sectors of the telecommunications industry were opened to competition in the 1980s, new executives with backgrounds in marketing and in non-regulated sectors rose quickly to displace those who had been standouts in the old regime. In both of these US industries, successful competitive conduct seemed to require leadership from individuals with experience in that mode of business.

The most upsetting example was recently uncovered by the Department of Justice in the US trucking industry. Before regulatory reform during the 1980s, trucking firms collectively set prices through rate bureaus for their thousands of types of movements. The reforms ended this system, permitting rate bureaus to propose collectively only General Rate Increases to the regulatory agency, the Interstate Commerce Commission (ICC). However, it now appears that the rate bureaus agree on price increases that are implemented without regulatory control under the rubric of "independent actions". Billions of dollars of transportation costs are involved here, and the US Department of Justice has petitioned for an end to all antitrust exemptions for these rate bureaus.

Evidently, noncompetitive business culture and modes of conduct are very difficult to change and slow to adapt, even in the context of the largely competitive US economy. Fostering a competitive code of conduct in an economy emerging from socialist central planning is, then, truly a daunting challenge.

2   Vulnerability of Local Markets

One possibility is that concern over noncompetitive domestic conduct (and structure, for that matter) will be obviated by international competition once the new capitalist economies are fully open to trade. Some comfort can be validly taken from this possibility. To the extent that domestic buyers have ample independent choices available from cost-effective foreign sources, domestic cartel behavior would cause little harm to domestic buyers. Indeed, to this extent, cartel behavior would provide little benefit to domestic suppliers, and their commercial success would rest on their ability to compete in the relevant international market.

However, it is unclear how complete will be trade liberalization, how immune from noncompetitive conduct will be domestic distribution channels for imports, and how cost-effective will be foreign suppliers to domestic buyers. Moreover, as the chapters by McKinnon (Ch. 7) and Harberger (Ch. 17) discuss, sound policy may entail deliberate protection of emerging market economies from the full rigors of international competition in the early phases of the transition. While it is clear that such protection would deny to domestic buyers valuable sources of goods and services, and create opportunities for domestic sellers to exercise monopoly power they would not possess with free trade, these authors, nevertheless, identify countervailing benefits for the growth of domestic entrepreneurship and productive capabilities.

Of course, the more the sectors of an emerging market economy are isolated by protection from international trade, the more they are vulnerable to monopolization and to the concomitant injuries to domestic buyers. But more generally, even without the isolation that results from deliberate protection, many important markets may be naturally local in character. In this respect, despite the dramatic differences between the US economy and those of the emerging capitalist nations, there may be a pertinent lesson from the US experience. Over the last two years, the Department of Justice has obtained convictions for price fixing of soft drink bottling, milk delivered to institutions, bus bodies, concrete pipe, moving and storage services, dentistry, road construction, trash collection, billboard space, building construction, fencing, auto parts sold to General Motors, hinges, gasoline, delivered ice cream, and commercial auctions. It is striking that this list is comprised of goods and services that are mostly sold in local markets. The list serves as an effective reminder of the diversity and importance of local markets, and, therefore of the vulnerability of an open economy to anti-competitive conduct.

3 Tough and Clear Rules Against Cartel Behavior

In view of the critical importance of competitive conduct to an emerging free market economy, there is a strong case for an anti-monopoly law that includes "bright-line" rules against cartel behavior along with criminal sanctions. Only in this way can the government deliver the clear and powerful statement of what business conduct is expected and what is forbidden, and, thereby, make plain the linkage between the drive for free markets and the requisite new business code of conduct. To avoid a measure that would be draconian and inhumane, the criminal sanctions could be announced early in the transition but phased in according to a preset schedule over several years.

Apart from their role in punctuating the vital message of competition, criminal sanctions for cartel behavior are very important for deterrence and for whistle-blowing. Here, too, US experiences may be instructive.

Recently, a group of dentists became the first medical practitioners to be indicted for criminal antitrust violations. To illustrate deterrence at work, a few weeks later the newsletter of the American Medical Association, distributed all over the country, ran a lead story describing the case: "The primary physician reaction to this has to be 'this could happen to me.' Those who fix fees, boycott health insurers, or allocate patient territories face the same felony penalties as the dentists, imprisonment and heavy fines" (*American Medical News,* October 5, 1990).

Many price-fixing cases come to the attention of the Department of Justice from employees who are ordered by their bosses to conspire with competitors, and who avoid criminal liability by turning instead to a local government official. This underscores how important it is for anti-monopoly rules to be widely publicized and to be supported by the availability of a local presence of the enforcement agency.

A Department of Justice study shows that a disproportionate number of firms caught colluding are relatively small and privately held. One explanation might be that only in such firms are the possible gains from collusion likely to be earned by those who personally bear the risks of the penalties from being caught. It would follow that firms that are diffusely and publicly held are unlikely to collude because the managers' potential gains are outweighed by their personal risks. The larger firms in the US economy may, thus, be effectively deterred from cartel conduct.

4   Structures of Anti-Cartel Laws

The new anti-monopoly laws of the emerging market economies clearly reflect appropriate concerns that cartel-like behavior could undermine the workings of competition and prevent the benefits of free markets from being realized. However, the specific provisions of these laws do not unambiguously create the tough and clear rules against cartel behavior that one can argue are vital.

The Polish anti-monopoly law, "The Law of 24th February, 1990, On Counteracting Monopolistic Practices," prohibits a total of fourteen "monopolistic practices," including price-fixing and market allocation agreements. However, none of these prohibitions apply if the practices in question "are necessary to conduct economic activity and they do not induce the substantial limiting of competition." Among other practices appearing in the same articles of the law are predation and "selling commodities in a manner leading to offering a privileged status to certain economic entities or other entities." The Anti-Monopoly Office is empowered to issue cease and desist orders, to void contracts that violate the articles of the law, and to order firms that have profited from monopolistic practices to lower their prices for a period of time.

Czechoslovakia's Competition Law, passed January 30, 1991, renders "impermissible and null" agreements which fix prices or output, divide markets, commit the parties to discrimination or tying arrangements, or deny to others access to a market. A variety of exceptions can be applied for, and there is a general exception where the parties to an agreement have collectively less than 5 percent of the market. The law contains specific provisions for the registration of cartel agreements with the applicable competition agency giving them official blessing.

The Hungarian Competition Law also appears to include provisions for the registration of cartels, in the same tradition of the German Cartel Office that influenced Czechoslovakia's law. The Hungarian law appears to take a tougher stance in its prohibitions of vertical agreements and arrangements than in its treatment of horizontal cartel-like agreements.

Thus, the anti-monopoly laws of these emerging market economies do not lay down clear prohibitions against cartel behavior and certainly provide for neither criminal penalties nor a transition to such a regime. Instead, they follow the spirit of the European Community (EC) competition laws in these regards, perhaps looking forward to the time when harmonization will be important for a formal relationship with the EC. While this structure of anti-monopoly law does not seem well suited to the task of creating from a statist economy a free market economy based on competition, the US experience provides some pertinent parallels and lessons.

One hundred years ago the United States faced the task of restoring competition to its economy — a challenge not completely unlike that facing the emerging market economies today. The United States' first federal antitrust law, the

Sherman Act, was passed in 1890 against a background of cartelization and monopolization of the American economy by the great "trusts" of the era. The trusts were legal entities that avoided market pressures to compete by centralizing control of production and sales within an industry. Trusts were notorious in key industries such as oil, corn, the railroads, tobacco and whiskey.

The trusts engaged in conduct that provoked widespread resentment and political calls for reform. They engaged in secret rebates to favored customers (usually other trusts), price-cutting to drive out competitors, and other forms of exclusionary conduct. In addition, there was corruption and bribery of public officials. By 1888, the resentment against trusts was so strong that both of the major political party candidates for President promised to seek national antitrust legislation, and two years later the Sherman Act was signed into law.

During the first ten years after enactment of the Sherman Act, antitrust continued to gain support in popular opinion, but the law was not vigorously enforced, and the government suffered some losses in court. It was not until after the turn of the century that the government brought significant and effective antitrust cases. Enforcement of the Sherman Act eventually rid the country of trusts and restored a competitive market structure, but the rather unremarkable record of the Justice Department in the early years of antitrust enforcement is in part a testimony to the grip that the trusts had on the nation's power bases.

American antitrust law derives most importantly from the Sherman Antitrust Act; the Clayton Act, passed in 1914; and the Federal Trade Commission Act, passed in 1914. These statutes, which establish the basic legal principles of competition, are worded very broadly; their meaning today is the result of a century-long evolutionary process of interpretation and application by federal courts. Although the statutes have been variously interpreted and their purposes vigorously debated, there is currently a solid consensus that antitrust should protect competition, not competitors, and that the antitrust laws should be construed to permit, not to hamper, business arrangements that promote efficiency. These fundamental principles prompted Supreme Court Justice Black to describe the United States' antitrust laws as a "charter of economic liberty aimed at preserving free and unfettered competition as the rule of trade."

Section 1 of the Sherman Act is the basis for both criminal and civil antitrust enforcement. It prohibits concerted conduct that unreasonably restrains trade. There are two basic requirements for finding conduct that affects interstate or foreign commerce to be unlawful pursuant to Section 1.

First, there must be an agreement — a "contract, combination, or conspiracy" — among two or more parties. Section 1 does not apply to unilateral actions. It is often difficult to tell whether there has been an agreement in a particular case, and proof of an agreement has become one of the most frequently litigated antitrust issues. Agreement may be proven by either direct or circumstantial evidence, and may be either explicit or tacit. Mere "conscious parallelism," which takes place when two or more firms knowingly take a similar course of action without an agreement to do so, does not constitute an "agreement" under Section 1 of the Sherman Act.

Second, the agreement must be one that is an "unreasonable" restraint of trade. Early in the application of the Sherman Act it was recognized that virtually all agreements — even a simple contract by which one firm commits to buy from a second firm rather than the second firm's rival — restrain trade in some way. As a result, the United States Supreme Court adopted as the fundamental principle of the Sherman Act (as well as antitrust generally) that practices are unlawful only if they "unreasonably" restrict competition by creating anti-competitive harm that outweighs efficiency gains.

In deciding whether an agreement is unreasonable, the courts have developed two basic forms of analysis. Under the *"per se"* approach, inherently anti-competitive practices are held to be illegal; no analysis of their actual competitive effects is required. Agreements among competitors to fix prices, rig bids or divide markets are illegal *per se* under the Sherman Act, Section 1.

Under the "rule of reason" approach, by contrast, particular agreements are analyzed in detail and are held illegal only if it can be shown, based on the facts of the individual case, that the anti-competitive effects outweigh any competitive benefits resulting from the challenged conduct, such as some efficiency-enhancing integration of their operations. If the pro-competitive effects are not sufficient to offset the anti-competitive effects of a questioned agreement, courts are likely to view the agreement as a restraint of trade under the Sherman Act.

As a matter of publicized policy, as well as law, the Department of Justice generally brings criminal cases against those who commit *per se* offenses under Section 1 of the Sherman Act, and these often lead to substantial fines and imprisonment. In contrast, rule of reason cases are almost always conducted under civil procedures, where the Court is asked to issue an injunction and perhaps to levy fines as well.

Thus, there is substantial variance between the current status of antitrust practices in the US concerning cartel behavior and the apparent wording of the laws of the emerging market economies in East and Central Europe. However, there is much less divergence between that wording and both the language of the Sherman Act and the legal practices that were followed early in its history.

While it may be important to recognize that the transition to a competitive economy would be effectively hastened by tough and clear rules against cartel behavior, and that the new competition laws of the emerging market economies do not provide them, it is even more important at this juncture to recognize that these laws do not preclude this policy approach. Instead, one lesson of the US experience is that antitrust laws that are broadly worded can support tough and clear rules. In the US, such rules have evolved through legal precedent and enforcement policy.

In the emerging market economies, perhaps tough and clear rules could be effectuated under the applicable statutes through publicized statements of enforcement guidelines by the anti-monopoly agencies. *Per se* treatment of price fixing and market allocation could be articulated as enforcement policy, and the maximum penalties under the law could be applied to these offenses as a matter of policy commitment. The language of the competition laws of the emerging market economies that establish the analogue of the US rule of reason could be applied to practices that are more likely to entail genuine efficiencies, such as forms of horizontal agreements involving real production integration or the creation of new products.

5 The Danger of Overly-Expansive Anti-Monopoly Laws

In contrast to the thesis that emerging capitalist economies need clear and tough rules against cartel behavior, one must be fully aware of the dangers of expansive anti-monopoly rules. Anti-monopoly laws with broad provisions permitting intervention against dominant-firm behavior and "price gouging" pose the danger of chilling the very investment and entrepreneurship that emerging economies sorely need.

It is very difficult and time consuming to separate efficient, pro-consumer behavior by a firm with a large market share from behavior that tends to harm consumers by destroying competition. It is equally challenging to define, no less uncover, price gouging. However optimistic one may be about the accuracy of enforcement efforts along these hazy lines, all should agree that such enforcement activism has the dangerous potential to discourage business activity whose reward might include a "dominant position" or the ability to charge a "high" price. In a new market economy with many needs to be met, sectors to be developed, and niches to be filled, it would not take rare success for a domestic or foreign investor to create such a market position.

Expansive anti-monopoly authority would, hence, be likely to subject many successful entrepreneurs to discretionary government intervention. Regardless of the skills and integrity of the officials involved, such power may be a deterrent to the needed entrepreneurship, and, thus, be counterproductive to the overall transition to a prosperous free market economy.

6 Conclusion

It is very encouraging that the emerging market economies have recognized that anti-monopoly policy is integral to the process of transition. Poland, Czechoslovakia, and Hungary have passed competition laws and have established expert agencies to implement them. It is gratifying that the officials of these new agencies have sought advice from anti-monopoly officials from the more mature market economies and that they are pursuing their responsibilities with dedication and awareness of the importance of their roles. The conclusion of this chapter is a simple one. The next step in the process of implementing effective and beneficial anti-monopoly policy should be that the agencies formulate and publicize enforcement guidelines. These guidelines need to take a tough and clear stance against cartel-like horizontal practices and provide commitments of caution and confinement of discretion when it comes to interventions on the basis of firms' market shares and price levels.

11 The Safety Net During Transformation: Hungary

David M. Newbery

1 Background

The countries of Eastern Europe face multiple discontinuities in their economic management. Not only are they attempting systemic transformation, but they face a severe terms-of-trade shock caused by the collapse of CMEA[1] trade and a shift to hard currency payments for oil. Some countries, notably Hungary and Poland, have the additional problem of servicing their high external debt with high real interest rates and pessimistic prospects for international trade. Any one of these problems might give cause for disquiet over the prospects for economically disadvantaged members of society, and in a period in which consensus-building is critical for the success of political transformation, adverse impacts on vulnerable sectors of society could undermine support for the process of transformation.

One can address these problems by first asking how systemic transformation might affect income distribution. In some fortunate countries (Czechoslovakia?) this issue might be the only major source of dislocation, but in most Eastern European countries one must also ask what additional impact the structural adjustment required to meet the terms-of-trade shock and/or the debt burden might have on income distribution and the ability of the government to protect

Support from the Institute for Policy Reform and the British Economic and Social Research Council is gratefully acknowledged. I am grateful for helpful comments from István Székely and the participants of the CEPR workshop *Economic Transformation in Eastern Europe,* London, February 22-23, 1991. A number of charts containing detailed quantitative information have been omitted from this version of the paper.
[1]Council for Mutual Economic Assistance.

vulnerable groups. One can then ask what methods are available to provide safety nets and protect vulnerable groups, whether existing policies are likely to be adequate, or whether they will need to be supplemented or reformed, and if so, in what directions. In the interests of concreteness, the discussion will concentrate on Hungary, though it is hoped that the analysis has wider application.

2 Systemic Transformation and Income Distribution

Figures 3 and 4 compare the income distribution by decile in Hungary and the UK before and after taxes and transfers. The heavy bars represent gross income before taxes but including pensions, unemployment benefits, and other cash transfers. To this measure of gross income are added benefits in kind (free medical services, education, etc.) from which are subtracted direct and indirect taxes and national insurance payments (for state pensions) to give final income. Note that in each case the population average is taken as 100 and the scales are identical to facilitate direct comparisons about the income **distribution** while abstracting from differences in income **levels**.

Several differences stand out from the comparison between Hungary — an economy which has passed through the first stage of transformation by introducing a system of direct and indirect taxes similar to those used in market economies — and the UK, which has had such a system in force (with frequent though structurally more minor reforms) for many years. The first difference is that the UK system of benefits in kind is considerably more progressive than in Hungary. UK benefits decrease in absolute terms as one moves up the income distribution, while in Hungary they are far more uniform (and also proportionately larger). UK taxes are somewhat more progressive than Hungarian taxes and also absolutely a larger fraction of income.

The second difference is that while the before-tax income distribution in the UK is substantially less equal than in Hungary, so also is the post-tax and transfer income, in spite of the more progressive system of transfers. The bottom decile in Hungary receives a final income which is nearly 75 percent of the average, while in the UK it is below 50 percent. The top decile in Hungary has less than 150 percent of the average, while in the UK the top decile has more than 200 percent.

The obvious explanation is that the UK reflects the attempt to mitigate the naturally inegalitarian outcomes generated by a market economy by means of a quite progressive system of taxes and transfers. These taxes and transfers are intended to take into account distributional considerations while not prejudicing efficiency or income levels too severely. Hungary has not fully adjusted prices and wages to market equilibrium levels, and thus has not yet had to face up to the full problem of correcting the potentially large inequities which might ensue. Under the former system of bureaucratic socialism, employees of state enterprises

Per household income, taxes and benefits
Hungary 1989

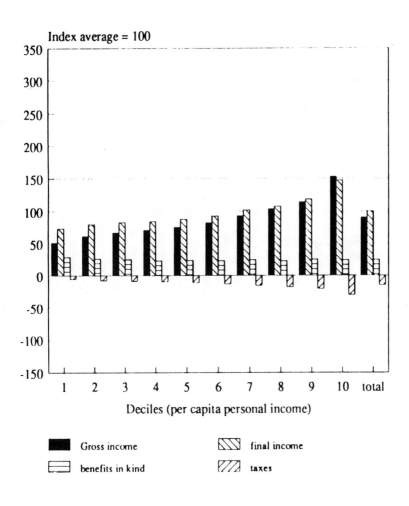

Index average = 100

Deciles (per capita personal income)

■ Gross income   ▨ final income

▤ benefits in kind   ▨ taxes

upa and Fajth (1990)

Fig. 3

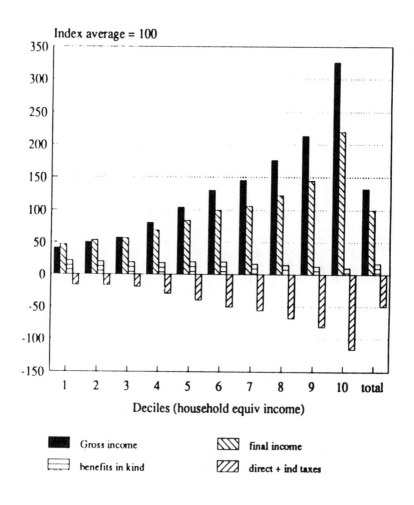

Per household income, taxes and benefits UK, 1987

Index average = 100

Deciles (household equiv income)

■ Gross income   ▨ final income
▭ benefits in kind   ▨ direct + ind taxes

Economic Trends 1990

Fig. 4

were paid incomes which were not subject to income tax, while the enterprise was subject to a range of essentially confiscatory levies designed to appropriate the surplus, which was then redistributed to firms in proportion to their investment requirements. Indirect taxes and subsidies were intended to adjust further the revenues of enterprises while maintaining consumer prices at levels deemed appropriate.

In a centrally planned Soviet-type economy, taxes are not used to redistribute income. Individuals receive wages at rates deemed appropriate for their needs, and a large fraction of their needs are met by direct provision (free education, health, etc.) or at subsidized, below market-clearing rates (housing) by direct allocation. In such a system income taxes on individuals are not needed, since their take-home pay is controlled. In a bureaucratic socialist economy such as Hungary, the plan, as such, no longer plays such a clear-cut role, but the Plan Office certainly exercises considerable influence over the allocation of resources and distribution of income by direct enterprise-level intervention, often retroactively adjusted.

Contrast this with Western thinking, which argues that the competitive market will achieve an efficient allocation of resources but is unlikely to achieve a just distribution of income, nor is it likely to provide an adequate supply of public (or collective) goods such as defense, environmental services, and the like. The benchmark is thus taken as the competitive market allocation (more accurately, as the efficient allocation which such an ideal market would achieve), and taxes are judged by the efficiency with which they achieve their objectives. Taxes create distortions, and the fall in the value of the output compared with the undistorted equilibrium is a measure of the cost of raising revenue — and is usually termed the deadweight cost of the tax, or the excess burden. Taxes are justified if the value of the revenue raised is greater than the cost of raising the revenue, including this extra deadweight cost. The revenue may be required to pay for infrastructure or other public or non-marketed goods or to transfer income to poorer or more deserving recipients. In a planned economy, a tax is judged by the success with which it steers decisions toward those planned. In a market economy a tax is usually judged by the extent to which it is the least costly way of raising revenue (to be used for a whole variety of purposes), though some taxes are specifically designed to correct a market failure — such as the damage caused by lead in petrol, for example.

Current economic analysis emphasizes the desirability of aiming at efficiency in production, confining the inevitable distortions to the consumption side of the economy as far as possible. Provided that firms in the economy are competitive and are exposed to foreign competition, this efficiency will be achieved by taxes which are neutral to firms, such as value-added taxes and (properly designed) profits taxes. The main emphasis is then placed on income taxes and commodity taxes designed to raise the required amount of revenue for public expenditure and redistributive transfers, while best meeting distributional objectives. Taxes and expenditures are then adjusted in the budget primarily to achieve macro-economic stability and to adjust the tax structure where improvements are identified.

The Hungarian tax reforms of 1988-89 were intended as a crucial first step in the transition to a market economy. Enterprises were required to gross up wages and to withhold income taxes so that the after-tax income of employees was essentially unchanged (though inflation reduced real wages during this period). In the fullness of time, if enterprises are successfully persuaded to compete in product, labor, and capital markets, they will presumably adjust wage payments to reflect differences in marginal productivity, and wage dispersion will increase. Successful entrepreneurs will similarly increase their incomes, as will those with scarce skills such as accountants, bankers, financial analysts, and others in the productive services sector, while those who are unskilled, or in relatively unprofitable sectors (mining?, heavy industry, and those sectors heavily dependent on CMEA trade) will suffer a decline in relative and perhaps also absolute income. On this score, then, there are grounds for concern about income distribution, especially in the lower deciles (at least to the extent that low household income arises from low pay for their economically active members).

Another aspect of Hungarian income distribution which is distinctive but not revealed in aggregate figures is the high relative standard of living of rural to urban workers. In 1985, households of manual workers spent 49,768 forints per head while those of the cooperative peasantry spent 50,414 forints per head.[2] Inactive urban households spent 46,476 forints while those in villages spent 40,374 forints, virtually identical. In most other countries of Western Europe, rural and agricultural incomes are considerably below urban levels. It is interesting to speculate how the removal of food subsidies might affect the urban-rural income differentials. Higher food prices will lead to a decline in quantity demanded, which might have a depressing effect on farm-gate prices, lowering rural incomes, and somewhat offsetting the increase in urban food prices. The figures for January-August, 1990, bear this supposition out, and show that compared to the same period one year earlier, agricultural sales are down by 11 percent, and agricultural prices are up by 28 percent (compared to those of industry which are up only 19 percent), while the consumer price index is up 27 percent (National Bank of Hungary 1990). Devaluation and the attempt to stimulate agricultural exports to replace some of the industrial exports no longer demanded by CMEA partners might eventually offset this decline to some extent. But it is hard to see how the rather high relative standard of rural living will survive

---

[2]Hungary (1987, p. 306). Note that there are subsidies to electricity, transport, etc., which are only available to urban dwellers, so that the differences in real incomes may have been masked by the reported money incomes. Note also that rural incomes often include the income of workers who also work in the industrial sector.

the tendency to increased commercialization of agriculture and the decline of rural labor demand.

Other changes that might be anticipated in the move to a freer labor market have to do with participation rates and unemployment. Participation rates for women have risen in both Hungary and the UK, but are systematically higher in the former than in the latter, which itself is high by Western European standards. To a considerable extent, this difference reflects the very different social attitudes toward women working in socialist countries, and the extent to which the state is willing to support these participation rates by providing nursery and other child care facilities.

It is an interesting and important question whether these attitudes will change and whether support facilities will deteriorate with the shift to a market economy, or whether Hungary represents the equilibrium toward which Western market economies are evolving, and which will continue to be supported largely by social attitudes and expectations. If there is a decline in female participation, then this decline is likely to affect adversely families with young children, and much will then depend on the effectiveness of the system of child support. The next section examines the effectiveness of the system of transfers and benefits in addressing distributional objectives.

3 Transfers and Benefits

For poorer families in Hungary, the primary benefits in kind received are education subsidies, while for the richer families housing subsidies dominate. To a considerable extent this pattern reflects the reality that when households are ranked by per capita income, larger families with more and/or younger children and fewer working adults are poorer, and they naturally benefit more from education.

One way to judge the extent to which various transfers protect the poor is to measure the extent to which they are targeted on the lower income deciles. Table 9 gives in the first column (headed "shares in total") the percentage of all subsidies allocated to each category, and in the remaining four columns the percentages of the total subsidy paid out under each heading which are received by the bottom two and top two deciles. Thus, of the 100 percent spent on kindergartens (2,776 forints per average household, or 3.4 percent of total subsidies), 19.5 percent went to the poorest decile and only 5.4 percent to the richest decile. If the lowest decile receives more than 10 percent, or the lowest two deciles receive more than 20 percent, then one can say that expenditure is preferentially favoring the poor, otherwise one could not argue that the subsidies were targeted on the poor. "Social items" (1.4 percent of the total or 1,154 forints per household on average) and "other housing investment subsidies" (3.9 percent or 3,168 forints per average household) stand out as obviously targeted on the poor, while

TABLE 9
Decile Shares in Totals,
Hungary 1989
Percent

	shares in total	bottom decile	second decile	ninth decile	top decile
social items	1.4	40.8	37.0	0.0	0.0
nurseries	1.2	25.6	9.1	1.5	2.9
kindergartens	3.4	19.5	16.3	5.2	5.4
other housing investment subs	3.9	16.3	10.7	10.4	15.6
primary schools	10.8	15.9	14.7	6.8	4.6
school books	0.1	12.7	12.5	7.5	5.2
water/sewge private dwels**	1.9	10.0	10.6	9.3	9.8
outpatient (other health)	6.2	8.8	9.4	10.4	11.7
hospitals	10.6	8.7	9.2	10.2	11.4
milk	0.5	8.7	9.0	10.4	10.6
medicine subsidies	4.9	8.7	9.3	11.1	11.4
secondary schools	5.7	8.6	9.7	8.5	4.3
transportation**	4.5	7.9	8.0	12.3	10.2
dairy products	0.9	6.8	8.1	11.8	13.5
culture, sport**	7.7	6.5	7.3	12.8	16.0
heating**	6.6	6.3	7.6	12.5	12.9
deprec of state dwels**	1.2	5.7	7.6	14.4	14.5
rent**	2.8	5.7	7.6	14.4	14.5
water/sewge state dwels**	0.7	5.7	7.6	14.4	14.5
cafeterias	1.7	5.0	6.7	14.0	14.6
mortgage payment	16.9	4.8	6.0	17.3	21.5
other training	0.9	4.3	6.4	12.6	15.7
theatre, etc**	0.9	3.8	5.3	15.7	20.4
vacation	1.6	2.9	5.6	13.6	16.1
higher eduction	3.0	2.7	8.8	10.6	13.2
all subsidies	100.0	7.1	7.6	14.0	16.1
personal net income		4.7	6.2	13.9	20.5
noncash social inc and subs		9.2	9.5	11.4	12.5

* social income in kind and subsidies
** primarily benefiting urban households

Source: Kupa and Fajth (1990, Chapter II, Table 1.2.2.i)

four out of the top seven (which qualify as having more than 10 percent targeted on the lowest decile) are all subsidies associated with children, who are more likely to be found in poorer households. If they are counted as part of the safety net, they amount to 23 percent of total subsidies and social income in kind, while if they are not, the remaining items amount to 7.2 percent of the transfers.

One explanation, consistent with the evidence in Figures 3 and 4, is that the system of wage determination was sufficiently egalitarian that few transfers needed to be specifically targeted to the poor, or designed to supplement low incomes, as in most Western countries. It was presumably thought sufficient to make transfers conditional on status (number of children, whether engaged at home in child care, etc.) in order to supplement incomes adequately. It is difficult to believe that this system will continue to be adequate as wages, employment and prices equilibrate toward market-determined levels. Looking on the bright side, if only 23 percent of total transfers can be claimed to be "pro-poor" or well-targeted to supplement low incomes, then the remaining subsidies and transfers do not serve that purpose, and might reasonably be reallocated towards income supplementation.

3.1 Pension payments

In 1986, 21.5 percent of the Hungarian population was over the retirement age (partly because the retirement age is 60 for men, and 55 for women). In Britain in 1988 the proportion of the population above UK retirement age was 18.2 percent,[3] and above the Hungarian retirement age was 23.4 percent. The Hungarian population is declining slowly, so the proportion of elderly might be expected to be somewhat higher than in the UK, but it is actually lower, due to the considerably lower life expectancy in Hungary.

Pension payments accounted for 62 percent of total social income in cash in 1978 and 61 percent in 1989, in spite of the 25 percent increase in the number of pension recipients. The rapid inflation in the latter part of the 1980s eroded the higher pensions except for the older pensioners. The government appears to have done a good job of indexing lower pensions, and one can interpret this as a conscious attempt to protect poorer pensioners from the adverse effects of recent reforms. Given the pressures on the budget and the large share already accounted for by pensions, though, the natural solution is to make a commitment to raise the pension age in line with life expectancy (which has been declining, but which will surely at some stage begin to improve); otherwise, any improvements in living standards which show up in improved health are likely to precipitate a pension funding crisis, given the projected declining population size. To the

---

[3]The proportion of the population actually receiving retirement pensions was 17.6% of the population (UK 1990b, Table 3.21).

extent that prime age workers are tempted to emigrate, the fiscal situation would become even worse.

3.2   Unemployment insurance

The unemployment rate remained below 2 percent, even after the recent reforms, until the end of 1990, reflecting an understandable lack of political will to restructure large firms, harden budget constraints, and accept the bankruptcy of non-viable concerns. Unemployment has recently begun to increase rapidly, however. Employment and output have both fallen sharply in each of the last two years. As the reform continues, more bankruptcies can be expected and will inevitably cause more unemployment, as the Polish experience indicates. With luck, a reasonable fraction of those laid off will move into the private sector. The government accepted the case for setting up an unemployment insurance scheme to facilitate the required restructuring in 1988, and some 56,000 unemployed workers were receiving payments at the start of 1991. The willingness of workers to join new enterprises in relatively untried activities in the private sector is clearly enhanced if they believe they will be assured of an income related to contributions and hence wage (and also duration of contributions) if their enterprise lays them off (or goes bankrupt). The absence of such a system would likely make workers less willing to change employers, and their reluctance would reduce the flexibility of the labor force. It would also be likely to set up political pressures to protect jobs and resist reform. It has been suggested that the Great Depression in Britain would have been a politically revolutionary period but for the existence of the recently introduced unemployment insurance.

Insurance-based unemployment schemes such as that set up in Hungary typically pay an amount related to previous income, regardless of current financial position, and are usually of limited duration, as their function is to facilitate the transition between jobs. Again, if the experience of Western countries is a guide to the future prospects in the East, it is unlikely that unemployment insurance will be adequate to deal with problems of low pay and lengthy unemployment spells which typically hit some sections of the population with greater frequency than others (e.g. unskilled or older workers).

3.3   Income supplementation rather than consumption subsidies

The natural solution to the problem of low pay and high unemployment in certain sectors of the population (and to other problems) is to provide income supplementation based on need (measured by family structure, income, and possibly assets[4]). There is in any case a standard public economics argument for

---

[4]In Hungary, anonymity of asset holdings and bank deposits may rule out means-testing of assets of the kind used in Britain.

moving away from subsidies on particular goods (food, transport, etc.) toward income transfers related to income level, provided the country has a comprehensive system of income tax. It does not then have to rely on a differentiated system of indirect tax to redistribute income. Subsidies to goods are likely to be poorly targeted and will benefit the rich who consume them as much (and probably more, as they are likely to consume more) than the poor. This targeting concern is illustrated quite clearly in Table 9, which shows that only 7.1 percent of all subsidies go to the lowest decile, while 16.1 percent go to the highest. Housing subsidies in particular benefit the rich far more than the poor, while consumer subsidies are fairly uniform across the income distribution. Means-tested supplementary benefits, on the other hand, are by definition targeted on those with low income.[5]

Another powerful objection to consumer subsidies is that they distort choice and may undermine competition. If energy for domestic use is income inelastic (as is electricity consumption in Britain), it might appear to be an attractive candidate for subsidy. Energy has traditionally been heavily subsidized in Eastern Europe, though notably less so in Hungary than elsewhere. Low energy prices lead to profligate energy use, which is particularly inappropriate given the recent shift to trading energy at world market prices and the current environmental concerns. Energy prices have risen slightly more than the general price level, though less than food, so further increases may be necessary. It is important to remember that Hungary had removed the larger part of fuel subsidies in the early 1980s and was much better placed than countries like Poland and Czechoslovakia. Indeed, the main impact of the move to hard currency trading at world prices of oil imported from Russia was a sudden sharp fall in the equalization tax received by the government which before 1991 brought domestic prices up to world prices. In Hungary, the main problem is the publicly supplied district heating which is not metered at the consumption level and so provides few incentives for efficiency.

Public transport is also heavily subsidized, and this subsidy may be defended on grounds of market failure — private car users do not pay adequately for the congestion they cause in towns. But subsidized inter-urban bus transport in Hungary has undermined the market for private bus companies just at a time when the British experience suggests that transport is an ideal sector for deregulation and privatization. The natural solution, which is fiscally attractive as well, is to increase the taxation of private cars (on gasoline and by annual license fees) while removing the subsidy from public transport (except for

---

[5]That is not to say that means-tested benefits are unproblematic, for the means-testing can give rise to high marginal rates of taxation, poverty traps, and low take-up rates, as well as being expensive. See Atkinson and Hills (1991) for a recent and useful survey of social security in developed countries.

carefully identified cases). It seems that the Hungarian government aims to do so, though early attempts to raise gasoline prices led to disturbances and were retracted.

Many of these subsidies are being abolished, and in any case the degree of consumption price distortion was probably lower than in other Eastern European countries; for example, the ratio of food prices to non-food consumer prices in Poland had to double in 1990. Provided the real incomes of those receiving various income supplements, child allowances, pensions, etc., are appropriately indexed, the fiscal saving will be somewhat less than the previous levels of subsidy but will still be positive, while the safety net is retained. Indeed, an explicit commitment to index well-defined targeted transfers might strengthen the safety net and reduce the fears caused by inflation.

3.4 Housing, mortgages and rents

Most developed market economies find the tax treatment of housing one of the more problematic and politically sensitive policy areas. Most market economies wish to encourage a "property owning democracy" in which the majority of the population owns a house and have thereby a greater commitment to political stability and fiscal responsibility. These same governments typically tax interest income ("unearned income" in the revealing terminology of the UK Inland Revenue) in part because at the time income taxes were first introduced, wealth was highly concentrated, and interest income was highly correlated with wealth and living standards. Given this interest income tax, the natural way to encourage widespread home ownership is to allow mortgage interest payments to be deducted from income to determine assessable or taxable income — thereby giving a tax subsidy for borrowing to purchase a home. This policy has a compelling logic if interest income is taxed, as it makes the after-tax interest rate (roughly) equal whether lending or borrowing, and thus does not distort portfolio decisions. If interest income were taxed but borrowing were not deductible, then prospective home buyers would be advised to liquidate their financial assets in order to finance house purchases, to reduce their tax liability.

A second common feature of tax systems is that the imputed income (i.e., the rent that would have to be paid if the house were rented) is typically not subject to tax, while the income from other financial assets is taxed. Combined with the effect of mortgage tax relief, house buying becomes the most financially attractive investment for the majority of the population, and this feature makes borrowing more attractive than saving. It further makes the private rented property market relatively unattractive, as these rents are taxed. In the UK, the share of private rented housing has fallen from almost half at the turn of the century to about 10 percent, while owner occupation has risen to two thirds of the total stock of dwellings. Renting from local authorities accounts for just over 20 percent. The effect has been to reduce labor mobility among the poor, as there are long waiting lists for local authority housing, and few alternatives, if buying is ruled out as too expensive for temporary relocation.

Finally, the system of interest taxation and mortgage relief is particularly perverse during inflationary periods. If the real rate of interest is 5 percent before tax, and the rate of inflation is 10 percent, money rates of interest will be 15 percent. At a 33 percent tax rate, the after-tax rate of interest will be 10 percent nominal, or zero real. Taxation will then take 100 percent of the real return of the asset, and tax relief will make borrowing costless. It is hard to believe that either of these is desirable, but both have characterized the tax systems of most countries and have also been written into the Hungarian income tax system (though the tax on interest income is now only 20 percent of the nominal amount, so that 100 percent taxation of real interest requires a 20 percent rate of inflation at a 5 percent real interest rate).

The problem of inflation is particularly acute and biased in its effect in Hungary as existing mortgage holders were offered a choice between two attractive alternatives. The first was to write down 50 percent of their loan and pay the market rate on the rest (currently 32 percent floating rate), while the second was to pay 15 percent (possibly floating) on the whole loan.[6] New house buyers are required to pay market interest rates, subject to various subsidies for young families and first time buyers. It might have been better to have specified a real cost of borrowing. For example, if the 3 percent mortgage interest rate had been interpreted as appropriate to an economic system intended to have zero inflation, then borrowers might continue to be charged 3 percent interest on their outstanding debt, but the debt would be revalued periodically (perhaps semi-annually) in line with the retail price index. The initial payments would not be a crippling fraction of total income for new house buyers, and would rise as prices (and their incomes) rose. If, for example, a family buys a house costing five times the annual family income, then annual payments of about 33 percent of current income (assumed to rise in line with inflation) would repay the original 100 percent mortgage over 20 years at a 3 percent real interest rate. But if the family had to repay at an initial nominal interest rate of 30 percent the first year's payment would amount to 150 percent of income — resulting in considerable forced saving.

---

[6]There are two qualifications — the first is that everyone had to pay a minimum of 1500 forints per month for the first year, and the second is that the legality of changing the existing contracts of 3 percent nominal is being examined by the Constitutional Court, which might uphold the original contact (until Parliament obtains the required majority to make constitutional changes to this law). Some 500,000 mortgage holders have opted for the first option as of March, 1990.

In Hungary, with a strong tradition of private construction (supplemented by state provision),[7] the main problem will be the design of the tax and mortgage interest system as well as of the taxation of housing services. In other countries with a larger share of state-owned housing, privatization (i.e. selling these houses to their tenants) is an obvious strategy (and in the UK was the largest and most successful privatization). For the Eastern European countries, privatization will become financially attractive only if rents are raised to commercial levels, a politically difficult task. A compromise, popularized in Britain and now also introduced into Hungary, is to offer state-owned housing to sitting tenants at a substantial discount, which reflects the present discounted value of the subsidized rent until the house is voluntarily vacated and becomes available for sale at a commercial price. But even this approach requires new leases to be at rent levels that are not subsidized. The determination of such rents is made more difficult by rapid inflation but should be related to the real rate of interest, rather than the nominal rate (as the property value will rise in line with inflation).

If the experience of Britain is a guide to the effects of wide-scale privatization of state-owned housing, homelessness is likely to rise rapidly. Between 1981 and 1989, almost 1.5 million local authority and new towns dwellings were sold to occupiers (out of a total housing stock of about 22.5 million). The number of homeless households that were placed in accommodations by local authorities under the Housing Act, 1985 doubled over the same period to nearly 150,000 (UK 1991, p. 141). Housing benefits now account for nearly 4 percent of total government expenditure, and nearly 8 percent of social security benefits. Again, this increasing percentage suggests the need to move from general subsidies on housing (currently biased toward the higher income deciles) toward a more carefully targeted system of support that is integrated with other forms of social security.

4   Terms-of-Trade Shocks and Structural Adjustment

Hungary and Poland face the additional problems of servicing their high foreign debt while adjusting to a collapse of CMEA trade (especially with Russia and East Germany) and a dramatic increase in the cost of energy imports (especially oil and gas), now payable in hard currency at current world market prices, rather than at the old Bucharest formula price, which lagged behind current prices. Thus they face problems familiar to Latin American and other deeply indebted

---

[7]The average annual number of private houses built between 1976 and 1985 was 58,000 while the average number of state dwellings was 24,000 (Hungary 1987, p. 338). Recent figures suggest that public housing construction has fallen further since then.

less developed countries, which are typically required to undertake structural adjustment programs to finance their external obligations. The World Bank's 1990 *World Development Report* is specifically concerned with poverty and the effects of trade shocks and structural adjustment on the poor. A major point coming out of that report is that while historically there has been very little extreme poverty in Eastern Europe (World Bank 1990, Table 2.1, p. 29), the transformation raises issues similar to those faced by other developing countries. As a result, the lessons learned there might be of some relevance.

What does economic theory have to say about the likely effect of structural adjustment on poverty? Much depends on the original objectives of the government and on the political constraints under which it labors. At one (ideal) extreme one can imagine a government imbued with a strong egalitarian sense which raises revenue not only to finance normal government activities (law and order, defense, infrastructure, etc.) but also to redistribute income optimally, as in the utilitarian theories of optimal tax theory (Atkinson and Stiglitz 1980, Newbery and Stern 1987). Structural adjustment invariably requires a reduction in consumption relative to production as the country endeavors to bring its fiscal and trade deficit under control and to meet its external debt payment obligations. In such cases revenue for redistributive purposes (as opposed to debt repayment) becomes scarcer and more costly. The government has to worry more about the efficiency costs of revenue raising and less about the redistributive benefits, and so redistributive activities must be scaled back, at least temporarily. In the worst case, the maximum revenue the government can raise is just enough to meet its expenditure obligations, and the design of taxation is motivated solely by efficiency considerations, not at all by equity. The poor will necessarily suffer during such an adjustment.

At the other (more realistic) extreme, the government was not raising and spending revenue primarily to benefit social welfare but to advance sectional interests (such as civil service employment, producer interests, the welfare of the urban proletariat, the army, etc.). Much will then depend on the political bargains that can be struck in the course of agreeing on the structural adjustment program with the IMF and/or World Bank. It is entirely possible that the external constraints can be used to alter the balance of domestic power and reduce allocations to some pressure groups, releasing resources for deficit reduction and poverty alleviation. The *World Development Report* appears to be quite optimistic about such possibilities while, at the same time, being quite sensitive to the realities of political economy. Thus, it makes the point that finely targeted poverty programs may be the most cost-effective way of protecting the poor but that this expenditure "can reduce public interest in the vigorous implementation of government programs to help the poor. For example, in the late 1970s, Sri Lanka replaced a universal food subsidy with a less costly targeted food stamp program. In time, the benefits of the new program declined. The middle classes no longer benefited from the scheme, and although the new program was more cost-effective, it lost crucial political support." (World Bank 1990, p. 92)

The case studies examined by the *Report* suggest three conclusions (p. 118): already existing well-targeted programs should be maintained; absent these programs, new carefully targetted programs should, if possible, be introduced; and in the face of opposition, all programs should be scaled back to release funds for the introduction of other, possibly better targeted programs.

What do these conclusions imply for Eastern Europe and for Hungary in particular? First, it is probably fair to say that previous governments were at least as egalitarian as any elsewhere, and they had devised a redistributive system that ensured that poverty was remarkably low for countries of this level of income. To that extent, many well-targeted programs already exist and should be preserved or strengthened to deal with the market realities of inflation, unemployment, and the removal of various consumer subsidies. The irony is that where the country was already pursuing very egalitarian policies, adjustment will almost inevitably mean that they will have to be scaled back. Putting it at its bluntest, if the object of the reform is to unleash some of the repressed forces for greater efficiency and higher incomes, the tax and reward system will have to become less progressive, and this lack of progressivity will probably harm those at the lower end of the income distribution. Second, the existing system of supports was often administered through the enterprises, and as these are commercialized and/or privatized, they will have less incentive (and, in the stringent market conditions likely, less ability) to administer these supports. New infrastructure for handling social security programs will be required, and it may be difficult to set up adequate machinery in the short run. As many of these programs are probably best handled by local government, and as the revenue base of local government is still in a transitional state, there are likely to be additional difficulties in re-establishing these programs in the more market-oriented environment of the 1990s.

The same point can be made in a different way. The reform process will eventually lead to positive gains, but it is unduly optimistic to suppose that these will arrive early on in the transition. If output available for domestic consumption does not increase much over the first few years, then gainers will gain initially at the expense of losers. Clearly there are going to be some who gain, possibly very substantially (and this gain might be seen as an essential step in recreating the middle class whose capital and enterprise are required to sustain the growth of the private economy). It follows that some will lose and that they are likely to be the more vulnerable. The key political issue is whether the most vulnerable can be protected during the transition, with the brunt of the burden borne by the middle-income deciles — in practice the workers in the state-owned enterprises — or whether the middle-income deciles will be protected at the expense of the extremes. Inaction is likely to mean that the poor will bear a disproportionate share of the costs of transition, as positive steps will be required to set up the necessary infrastructure and revenue sources for their protection.

5 Policy Issues During Transformation

Some of the policy choices relating to setting up unemployment insurance and reforming the tax and social security system have already been addressed. Others, such as the removal of food and other consumer subsidies, have been dealt with at the theoretical level — it was concluded that subsidies to goods should be replaced by indexed means-tested supplementary benefits paid in cash, possibly contingent (in the case of housing) on existing expenditures (rents). The key remaining questions relate to the speed of reform and issues of sequencing. Is the Polish "crossing the chasm in one jump, not two" the right way to reform prices and subsidies, or is the gradual approach favored by the Hungarians preferable?

Two potent arguments support the swift elimination of distortions. The first is that one wants decisions to be guided by the right set of prices as quickly as possible so that investment decisions, in particular, are not distorted or based on incorrect transitional prices. The second is that the credibility of the reform process may be undermined by a slow adjustment. The following argument is developed by van Wijnbergen (1990): The government can choose between "cold turkey" (prices immediately decontrolled) or "gradualism" (prices may be fully decontrolled next period, but are only partially adjusted toward market-clearing levels this period). Voters will decide whether to continue with the reform process after observing the performance of the economy (measured, in this model, by the size of the supply response) in the first period. In the gradualism approach, if initial prices are kept low, then it will be profitable to hoard in the expectation of making capital gains when prices are liberalized in the future. This hoarding will reduce the supply elasticity (goods will not come to the market). If the first period prices are closer to market-clearing levels, the incentive to hoard will be lower, and the supply response of goods brought to market will be higher. In the cold-turkey approach there is no incentive to hoard at all, and the supply response is at its highest. This argument suggest that the lower the initial prices, the less likely the program is to succeed in obtaining support for its continuance. This claim is correct, but it requires some delicacy to show that when the risk of failure is made endogenous, the result continues to apply.[8]

If efficiency and credibility argue for immediate liberalization, what of the safety net arguments? The argument for cold turkey is that safety nets will be needed eventually if prices are to be liberalized. These safety nets should ideally be set in place as early as possible and tailored to market realities in which

---

[8]The issue is that with low initial prices, the risk of failure is large, so the risk is that hoarding will be unprofitable as next period the old prices will be restored, and hoarding will be discouraged; with higher initial prices the risk of success is higher, making hoarding more attractive. Allowing for the effect of hoarding on the success of the reform alters, but does not reverse the thrust of the simple argument.

prices and wages vary more violently than under the former socialist system. This argument requires basing safety-net allocations (minimum pensions, family allowances, supplementary benefits, etc.) on incomes and current price levels (i.e. indexing), in which case the time path of adjustment should not be an issue. Any alternative might mean that gradualism was less painful than immediate liberalization, but only by concealing and deferring the problem, which would be better addressed explicitly and immediately.

There is another, macroeconomic argument in favor of rapidly replacing subsidies by less costly targeted means-tested cash transfers. Tax reform reduces the effective rate of profits tax from nearly 100 percent to something nearer to 40-50 percent. This reform will tend to reduce revenue. If wages are grossed up sufficiently and income taxes are now paid by workers, then some of the former profits tax will come back in the form of income tax. The problem is likely to come from loss-making firms. Although in aggregate, after-tax profits plus losses may not change much, since the losses are likely to be borne directly or indirectly by the state, and the profits are likely to be available to firms to invest or distribute, the net effect is likely to be an increase in demand and a fall in net government revenue, requiring higher taxes or lower subsidies elsewhere. Higher taxes would defeat the purpose of trying to reduce the role of the state in economic activity, hence the need for reductions in untargeted subsidies.

It has already been argued that inflation, coupled with fixed and low nominal interest rates for past mortgages, involves a substantial new subsidy to households. It has also been argued that this new subsidy is likely to require restructuring of mortgage interest payments and rents. If these are based on real interest rates, and if the former rents had not been kept at artificially low levels for lengthy periods (as in the Soviet Union), then the impact on households need not be too severe. Even where rents were formally very low, moving to a real-interest-based rate need not involve unreasonable fractions of family income (though proportionately the increase might be large). In 1985 active Hungarian households spent typically less than 9 percent of total expenditure on housing (compared to between 15-23 percent in Britain). Rent amounted to 512 forints per person for manual workers compared to total expenditures of 49,768 forints, or 1 percent of total expenditure, which is remarkably low, even allowing for the reasonable fraction of owner occupation (Hungary 1987, p. 306). The fact that the correct level of rents or mortgage payments would not be unreasonably high does not, of course, mean that a movement to such a level would be politically popular.

5.1   Pensions

As almost all pensions are paid by the state, the only issue is that of indexing the level to reflect appropriately the new level of prices. The main problem here is that the average price level may conceal considerable differences in the levels of items like rent. Where some rents remain frozen but others adjust, the average will conceal important differences. One option is to recognize explicitly a rental or housing element in the pension which is based on individual circumstances. Until now the solution has been that rental payments by pensioners were frozen, but this option will need modification if rents are to be moved to market levels.

5.2   Food subsidies and rations

In Hungary, most consumer prices are probably not far from equilibrium levels as a result of gradual reforms over a lengthy period. In the Soviet Union, this relationship is far from true. Is there a case for combining the elimination of food subsidies with ration entitlements? If these were combined with a free market in food, with the rations sufficient for some bare minimum, then consumers would typically buy additional quantities of food at free market prices and the rations would act like lump-sum transfers of purchasing power. They would be administratively costly, would act as untargeted and therefore expensive general subsidies, and might be prone to corruption. As a result, it is hard to think of good reasons not to move to market wages (which will be related to the new price level) and indexed safety-net payments. The main reasons might be political (to make the change to free market prices acceptable) or because the authorities have no confidence in their ability to set up the necessary system of income-based safety nets. Rations would not seem to be necessary or desirable in Hungary or Poland, for example, however good the case might be made for their use in the Soviet Union.

5.3   Low-income producers

Liberalization is likely to lower the returns to many activities, and if those activities are to continue, wages will have to fall. Self-employed workers in such activities will suffer a direct fall in income. The experience of Britain is relevant here. Initially, many producer services such as cleaning, provision of meals, laundry services, rubbish collection, etc. were provided in-house in the state sector (hospitals, schools, etc.). Privatization and contracting out of such services resulted in considerable cost savings, but these were in large part obtained by a drop in the wage rates of the workers, who moved from the state sector (at wages determined by the activity of the institution) to the private sector (which, for unskilled labor, paid lower wages). The same decline in wages may occur in the agricultural sector, though without knowing how farm-gate prices of agricultural goods are likely to change it is difficult to be sure.

What, if anything, should be done to protect the incomes of such workers? The standard answer is that the system of social security should be designed to provide safety nets for families of low-income workers, rather than attempting to maintain wage levels. If the cost of employing these workers is kept above the market equilibrium level, then employment will be depressed, and the cost of meeting the distributive goals will be higher. A good tax system aims at production efficiency (and thus paying market-determined wages) while redistributing income through the income tax (and possibly indirect tax) system.

5.4   Sequencing, privatization and the role of property rights

The sequencing of reforms affects not only their credibility and sustainability, but also the distribution of adjustment costs. Key issues to address are the order in which foreign trade and domestic prices are liberalized, and whether either or both should be delayed until large enterprises have been broken up into smaller units ("demonopolization"). The case for moving as quickly as possible on demonopolization and foreign trade liberalization has already been made on efficiency grounds (Newbery 1991). What would be the impact of this sequencing on income distribution? The adverse effects of keeping large combines in being are readily identified. They stifle competition and make it difficult for small enterprises to gain access to the banking system, which, if it is to be persuaded to impose hard budget constraints on the large firms, will be subject to tight monetary policy. This tight monetary policy in turn will tend to favor large as opposed to small customers of banks and make the repayment of trade credit advanced by small firms to large buyers delayed or problematic.

One of the most promising sectors for small enterprises and privatized firms to enter is that of retailing, wholesaling, distribution and transport. Where the large firms retain powers over imports (as often happens) then again competition is stifled and entry prevented. The Polish policy of subjecting wages in large enterprises to tight controls while liberalizing prices and wages in the private sector has the advantage in this context of encouraging exit from the state to the private sector in pursuit of higher wages. But this advantage may be thwarted if the private sector is discriminated against by the residual power of the large firms.

Privatization of small enterprises (by management buy-outs) is arguably the best way of stimulating labor demand to offset the large declines in employment likely in the state-owned enterprises, while privatizing large enterprises intact is likely not only to be difficult but to have the opposite effect. Where enterprises can be dismantled into smaller units, the solution is obvious. Thus, for example, the average number of trucks per firm in Hungary is 566, in Poland 137, in Germany 4, and in Holland and France, 7 (Bennathan, Gutman and Thompson 1991).

Private enterprise requires a clear legal definition of property rights which are defended by the courts and police. While this requirement is recognized in Eastern Europe, this recognition is less evident in the Soviet Union. Even in Eastern Europe, the issue is clouded by arguments over restitution and compensation. A pessimistic scenario is that ambiguities over property rights in periods in which private property is potentially available leads to alternative extra-legal systems of imposing and defending property rights, of which various kinds of mafia organizations are the most worrying. The historical record suggests that while it takes unusual and turbulent circumstances to establish such rival extra-legal organizations, once established they are difficult to dislodge, and they result in territorial cartelization and the exercise of market power (quite apart from other less savory activities). The recent activity of territorial gangs controlling access to food and black market goods in Moscow is a good though worrying illustration. While state monopoly in a socialist society may be able to protect the weak, mafia monopolies are unlikely to do so. It may be that the rapid, unambiguous creation and defense of private property is one of the most urgent tasks for preserving existing safety nets while unleashing repressed productive forces.

12 Institutions for the New Private Sector

Anne O. Krueger

As Eastern European countries grapple with the problems of transition to a market economy, important questions arise as to the lessons that may be learned from the experience of other countries. In recent years, there have often been announcements of major economic reform programs in developing countries; some have been adopted, a few successfully. A natural starting point is, therefore, to examine the lessons, if any, from the experience of developing countries for the transition of Eastern European countries today.

When I anticipated a visit to Prague — my first visit to an Eastern European country in the process of transition — I was strongly convinced that the problems of Eastern European countries are quite different from those of developing countries confronting the need for policy reform. It is frequently observed that formerly communist economies do not have the institutional structure necessary to support a market economy and that few people have had experience with markets. It seems to follow, therefore, that the process of transition starts from a very different basis in Eastern European countries.

While that observation is obviously correct in an important sense, my visit here has made me question it. In the developing countries that have attempted to reform their economic policies, there has been a sizeable, if not overwhelming, state sector coexisting beside the private sector. Public sector enterprises have typically had significant inefficiencies of operation. Most of those governments undertaking reforms have avowed their determination to reduce the size of the state sector but have not been very successful in doing so. Moreover, the size of the state sector has not been the fundamental problem, nor the problem on which the success of reforms depended. Rather, the problem is that most economic growth that occurred prior to reform took place in response to incentives artificially created by government.

219

Entrepreneurs, therefore, were agile in dealings with government officials and in "working the system". While the institutions of the market were **apparently** in place, in fact these institutions evolved to seek profitable opportunities from government favors: influencing government regulations or the allocation of permits was frequently the prerequisite for profitable operation.

Numerous government policies created this environment for private entrepreneurs. Some of the most powerful incentives have originated in policies designed to encourage domestic industry. In many countries, imports have been prohibited once domestic production of a commodity has been undertaken. New industries have been encouraged through favorable access to (rationed) credit at negative real interest rates, preferential tax treatment, and preferential treatment in receiving foreign exchange licenses for imports. Most of these encouragements have been at least partly discretionary on the part of government officials. Producers in society have, therefore, become accustomed, by and large, to reacting to events in the nation's capital rather than responding to signals emitted through shifts in supply and demand in the world market.

When policy reform was undertaken in developing countries, therefore, there were institutions in place. But if reforms were to succeed, those existing institutions had to adapt to significantly altered circumstances. It is not obvious that adapting existing institutions is easier than creating new ones. Admittedly, a legal structure is in place, private property rights exist, and there is a certain degree of certainty governing contracts. But the institutions have evolved a pattern not only of responding to the wrong incentives but even of looking to the wrong place (to government) to discover to what to respond!

In Chile, in Turkey, earlier in Korea, and in the UK under Mrs. Thatcher, a major achievement of reform has been to diminish the role of the state's influence over incentives confronting individual decision makers in the market. Governments have moved from an instigating and initiating discretionary role in creating incentives to what may be called a supportive role. In supporting a market economy, there are many legitimate governmental functions: provision of infrastructure, setting (and enforcing) the rules of the game, improving the quantity and quality of education and health services, etc. Governments which have successfully reformed their economies have shifted attention to this latter set of tasks. When, in addition, it has been decided to encourage certain activities, such as export growth in Korea, the encouragement has been largely nondiscretionary: producers who exported were entitled to stated incentives. In these circumstances, decision makers must look to market signals for their incentives, and the private sector can then behave privately and in a socially productive manner.

In this sense, there is a great deal in common between reforms in developing countries and those in Eastern Europe. In each instance, institutions must be adapted or created to generate new earnings streams. When those earnings streams are created in response to incentives which more appropriately reflect the trade-offs with which society is confronted, real incomes can grow very rapidly.

What, then, is the experience from developing countries? It is, by and large, that growth has taken place primarily through the emergence of new activities, not through the adaptation of older ones. In Turkey, despite the government's stated determination to privatize, almost all state economic enterprises continue to operate in the public sector and to produce at a much lower estimated economic efficiency than private firms. But the growth of the late 1980s has originated largely from new economic activities that were started since incentives changed; the state-enterprise **share** of output has declined. Even within the private sector, some small firms grew very large, while some large firms stagnated. While some producers continued to use the same combination of inputs as before, shifting output mix and lengthening production runs to the newly profitable export market, a much larger fraction of growth originated from new economic activities.

In Korea, for example, total investment in the first dozen years after reforms began in the early 1960s was 5,387 billion won at 1970 prices. This investment contrasts with total cumulative investment up to 1961 after the Korean War of only 586 billion won. Likewise, manufacturing value added averaged 924 billion won annually in the early 1970s, contrasted with 103 billion won in the early 1960s. The traditional manufacturing industries (food, beverages, tobacco, textiles, wood products, printing and publishing) fell from 63.3 percent of manufacturing activity to 36.8 percent in that same period. (The data are from Kim and Roemer 1979.) Even within the more traditional manufacturing industries, it was primarily new firms that expanded greatly during the 1960s.

A reasonable estimate would be that some 80-90 percent of Korean GNP in the early 1970s was created by factors of production that were doing something different than they had been in 1960. This estimate includes people moving from agriculture to industry, new investment, people switching jobs in the 1960s, etc. Probably only 10-20 percent of GNP was produced by farmers who were tilling the same land as in the 1960s and workers employed in factories producing the same sorts of products as in 1960.

If this estimate is correct, it implies that it is extremely difficult for existing firms to adapt — although some do, to be sure — and providing a more conducive environment for adaptation can ease and accelerate the transition process. But that, in turn, implies that policy emphasis should surely be on creating the appropriate environment for the generation of new earnings streams.

That conclusion, however, suggests that Eastern European countries may be at a disadvantage. Focus seems to be upon privatization of existing assets, which is obviously a contentious and difficult issue. It is politically important because the existing assets now belong to the state, and people feel that those assets should be returned to the people in a "fair" manner. The difficulty is that there is no such thing as "fair," and searching for the least unfair process will inevitably be time-consuming and divert attention away from the more important problem of creating new earnings streams.

Just as entrepreneurs in developing countries turn to the capital city to seek valuable licenses, so potential entrepreneurs in Eastern Europe probably turn their attention to seeking larger shares of privatized assets when the real challenge is to create new ones. It may, therefore, be that the biggest drawback Eastern Europe may have is an understandable but nonetheless misplaced fixation on the old assets. Had the Turkish reforms in the 1980s consisted solely in privatizing state economic enterprises, they would have failed!

Important questions are what the old assets are worth and whether they are worth enough to be occupying as much time, attention and scarce resources of politicians, finance ministries, and ministries of ownership as they have, in fact, been given. It is highly plausible that attention should have been primarily on rapid adoption of a commercial code, establishment of assured legal procedures, and other arrangements to assure small businesses that if they succeed, they will, indeed, be rewarded.

What evidence we have to date on the value of state assets comes from the former East Germany, where the factories and machinery are today worth a lot less than had been generally thought. Given that evidence, what reason is there to believe that the existing physical facilities in Eastern European countries are worth so much?

This disparity leads immediately to the question of the timing of transition. Insofar as the creation of new earnings streams by people in different places or doing different things is the objective, it is important that those people be adequately rewarded for making changes. Those rewards occur only when there is reasonable certainty about the stability of incentives with which they are confronted. And that need for certainty, in turn, implies that speed in creating a new structure is of the essence. There is a potential for a vicious circle. The longer people are uncertain and the longer there is uncertainty that reforms will take hold, the weaker will be the response to whatever has taken place. The weaker that response, the more political opposition there is likely to be to the reforms. That opposition, in turn, will further increase uncertainty as well as the difficulty of achieving agreement on reform. There is probably also a virtuous circle: once new incentives are established with certainty, the responses (often not visible because they are likely to be from small individuals and firms) will often begin generating new earnings streams fairly quickly. Those earnings streams can, then, generate political support for economic policies, which in turn reinforces credibility that the existing incentive structure will continue, thus further stimulating responses to it.

Minister Vaclav Klaus of Czechoslovakia has said that you cannot decide upon timing and sequencing of the transition because it is a process, and that is certainly true. But one reason it is a process is because resources, especially of key decision makers, are limited, and they can focus only on a few things at a time. In that regard, it is much easier to remove existing controls and laws that restrict and prevent behavior than it is to create new institutions, such as a tax collection system. Speed in removing obstacles is, therefore, essential. Creation of a stable macroeconomic environment and a certain legal framework for the protection of asset values generated by new earnings streams can clearly be accomplished more quickly than old assets can be disposed of. Small and medium-sized firms can be privatized fairly quickly (Fischer, Ch. 13). Doing all these things rapidly and letting new earnings streams be developed can also remove some of the contention from the disposition of the old assets (if indeed they are assets and not liabilities).

There is one other reason for speed. The longer the transition takes, the more time is provided for pressure groups opposing change to emerge. That potential opposition argues strongly against such measures as "temporary" protection against imports, special treatment for entrepreneurs asserting that they "need" subsidies or other assistance, and other discretionary assistance to industry.

Standing still further back and asking where the Eastern European countries are likely over the longer run to fit into the economic map of the world, it seems evident that their economic future lies in appropriate utilization of human resources. Eastern Europe's location and its highly educated labor force both suggest this conclusion. Over the past several decades, this comparative advantage was twisted by the creation of heavy industry, and the economies have become autarkic. Integrating them into the world economy is going to require moving resources into new endeavors which are intensive in human capital, and it is highly doubtful whether large, state-owned factories can be privatized in ways which will accomplish that task.

Creating an open foreign trade regime, which will in itself provide some much needed competition to state-owned industries, supporting small entrepreneurs as they seek foreign markets, preventing anti-competitive practices among domestic producers of nontradable goods, and providing improved infrastructure in support of economic activity, are the major challenges facing the governments of Eastern European countries.

PART IV
The Privatization Process

13 Privatization In East European Transformation

Stanley Fischer

The creation of a viable private sector, owning and managing the bulk of the economy's assets, is the essence of the transformation problem in formerly socialist economies. And since virtually all production is currently carried out in the state sector, privatization of state assets is an essential step in the creation of the private sector.

Advice from most Western institutions and economists on how to privatize has rapidly converged on a standard approach. Small firms should be privatized by sale almost immediately, perhaps with some financing provided by the state. Larger industrial firms should be corporatized as soon as possible, moved out of the shelter of the ministries that now in principle control them, and put under the direction of corporate boards; shares should be distributed to some combination of current workers in the firms, current management, mutual funds, holding companies, banks, insurance companies, pension funds, citizens, and the government.[1] Plans envisage the corporatization phase being completed within a year or two. In most variants the initial post-corporatization ownership structure is

Support from the Institute for Policy Reform is gratefully acknowledged.

[1]For a review of such plans, see Borensztein and Kumar (1990), and Milanovic (1990); see also details of proposals and analysis in Blanchard *et al.* (1990), Feige (1990), Frydman and Rapaczynski (1990a), Grosfeld (1990), Lipton and Sachs (1990b), and Tirole (1991). Tirole (1991) draws on the industrial organization literature in analyzing principles that should guide the privatization process. The absence from this chapter of plans presented in languages other than English is unfortunate; the richness of the debate within each country can be discerned by reading authors familiar with those literatures, for example Kornai (1990) on Hungary.

transitional, because the government retains a large ownership share, and because the holding companies (or their equivalent) are to be phased out. The period from corporatization to full private ownership of firms that are to be privatized is generally expected to last several years, and in some instances, up to a decade.

Ownership reform in agriculture, housing, and land has drawn less attention than industrial and commercial restructuring. The issues are less difficult in the cases of housing and land than for operating enterprises; in agriculture, there is already a significant private sector to build on in Poland, and some private sector activities in other formerly socialist economies. While Bulgaria and Romania passed land reform laws early in 1991, there has as yet been little privatization of land.

The standard advice does not draw complete agreement. Kornai (1990), along with others, argues that state assets should be sold and not given away. The role of the holding companies or mutual funds has not been entirely clarified (Hinds 1990a): privatization plans for Czechoslovakia place less emphasis on holding companies than those for Poland, which in any case are more eclectic concerning the role of financial institutions than some earlier proposals.[2] Hungary is relying more on privatization from below, initiated by the firm, than other countries. Some, basing their advice on the finding by Vickers and Yarrow (1988) and others that successful privatization in the UK required the privatized firm to operate in a competitive environment, believe that demonopolization should precede privatization. Other questions remain open. What is the role of foreigners? How should firms that are not yet privatized be managed? Is it necessary, as argued for instance by Brainard (1990b), to build up the banking system before privatizing? What other sources of finance can be created?

The debate over privatization has been intensely practical, conducted in real time with real interactions between the academic literature and policy. By early 1991 major legislation had been passed in Bulgaria, Czechoslovakia, Hungary, Poland, Romania, and Yugoslavia, and, of course, the former East Germany; significant small case privatization and some large firm privatization is taking place.[3] While it cannot yet be claimed that there is a wealth of experience of privatization in formerly socialist economies on which to draw, the experience — and certainly the legislation — is growing.

This chapter re-examines the main issues in privatization in the formerly socialist economies, drawing on experience of privatization in Poland and

---

[2]Contrast, for instance, the proposals in Lipton and Sachs (1990b) with the program of the Government of Poland (1990).

[3]Developments in Hungary, Poland, and Yugoslavia through late 1990 are reviewed in Milanovic (1990).

Hungary and to some extent in Czechoslovakia.[4] In section 1, the standard approach is set out in more detail, and the privatization of small and medium scale enterprises is discussed. In section 2, the privatization of the core of large industrial and commercial firms is addressed. The privatization of financial intermediaries, housing, agriculture, and land, are discussed briefly in section 3. Conclusions are presented in section 4.

1   The Standard Approach

The sheer scale of the privatization needed in the formerly socialist economies makes the problem very different from that faced by other countries that have undertaken major privatization programs. Table 10 presents data on the share of the state sector in value added in commercial and industrial activities in different countries during the 1980s. The largest completed privatization program so far is that of post-Allende Chile, which moved firms producing about 25 percent of GNP into the private sector, some of them firms that had only recently been nationalized. The much studied UK program shifted only about 4.5 percent of GNP and employment out of the state sector.

Reforming governments have opted for the principle of rapid privatization. This choice reflects their commitment to move decisively from socialism to capitalism, avoiding as far as possible any detours into a third way. The experience of privatization in almost all developing countries has been disappointing:[5] the loss of patronage and political rents attendant on privatization reduces its attractiveness to the political system.[6] This experience, along with the political need for a credible reform program in the face of the unprecedented scale of the privatization necessary in formerly socialist economies, accounts for the decision to go for rapid privatization. Even though credibility demands that an irreversible program be put in place as rapidly as possible, it is clear that the process of privatization will take many years. It is also likely that the relative decline of

---

[4]The privatization process in Yugoslavia, where implementation has been heavily affected by political instability, is not described. The Yugoslavian approach was interesting because labor management and ownership were most heavily entrenched there. See Milanovic (1990).

[5]See the special issue of *World Development,* May 1989, that focuses on developing countries, but also examines lessons from the United Kingdom.

[6]Any political economy model of slow or halting privatization would have also to account for the fact that state sectors stopped growing in the 1980s, and that many of them began to recede. Any such model would include a political tradeoff between the efficiency of production and the availability of rents; the perceived terms of that trade-off must have changed in the 1980s.

TABLE 10

Share of State Sector in Value Added

Czechoslovakia (1986)	97.0
East Germany (1982)	96.5
USSR (1985)	96.0
Poland (1985)	81.7
China (1984)	73.6
Hungary (1984)	65.2
France (1982)	16.5
Italy (1982)	14.0
West Germany (1982)	10.7
United Kingdom (1983)	10.7
United States (1983)	1.3

Source: Milanovic (1990).

the state sector will after a few years result more from an increase in production by new private firms than from privatization.

The issue of the ownership rights of current employees confronts all the reforming countries, particularly because the decentralization programs of former communist governments typically moved in the direction of worker management. The issue arises most forcefully in considering spontaneous privatizations, in which current employees in one way or another privatize the firm for their own benefit. The standard approach argues that existing workers have no special claims on the firm's assets on fairness grounds. For instance, why should industrial workers obtain larger claims on capital than workers in less capital-intensive industries, such as teaching? Or, why should workers in successful firms become wealthier than those in less successful firms? Although it is likely in the latter case that workers in more successful firms have on average worked harder and invested more than those in less successful firms, the general point is correct. However, political power as well as fairness shapes privatization programs, and it has already been decided that existing workers will receive special treatment, at least in Poland and Hungary.

Similarly, the issue of the rights of former owners is a live one in several countries, most notably East Germany, Hungary, and Czechoslovakia. Explicit legal treatment of the rights of former owners not only strengthens the credibility of a country's commitment to the rights of private property, but also prevents the legal confusion over ownership that could arise if the issue were left to be settled later in the courts. However, redress should be provided to former owners in a way that does not slow the privatization process: compensation should **not** take the form of giving the original owners the rights to the property itself, but rather the right to compensation by the state. New owners cannot get on with running their businesses if they face the possibility of claims for restitution by former owners. /

The standard approach summarized in table 11 is not monolithic. It is standard in rejecting a case-by-case approach to privatization along UK lines — on the grounds that the process would take far too long, in separating as the heart of the issue the core of large commercial and industrial enterprises, and in insisting on rapid progress in establishing the principle and the fact of private ownership. It has not yet devoted as much attention to the privatization of other assets and industries. There are, however, many important details on which different plans, including those already embodied in legislation, differ. Borensztein and Kumar (1990) list six different distributive plans;[7] if they were writing now they would have to add the programs passed by the Czechoslovak and Polish parliaments which do not exactly coincide with any of their six.

Small commercial and industrial firms: Existing small firms, typically in retail trade and distribution, are being privatized fast. The privatizing agency may be the local rather than a higher level of government. Very rapid progress has been made in this area in Poland, where most shops had been privatized by the end of 1990; governments in Czechoslovakia expect to sell over 100,000 small firms in 1991 — with auctions having begun in February; and Hungary expects to privatize most of retail trade in spring, 1991. / More public sales of small firms, especially in transportation and distribution, can be expected as larger vertically integrated firms are restructured, and parts are sold off separately. The number of new privately owned small firms in the reforming countries far exceeds the number of privatized firms. For example, by one estimate there were 200,000 small firms in Poland in November 1990, of which more than 80 percent were newly created rather than privatized.[8]

Despite the rapid increase in the number of firms, problems of both financing and red tape are frequently reported. Any banking system would have difficulty in appraising small firms headed by new entrepreneurs wanting to operate in a new and highly uncertain economic environment, all the more so would the underdeveloped banking systems of the formerly socialist economies. The red tape is a holdover from socialism and underdevelopment, and has to be attacked as soon as possible. The financing problem for privatizations can be mitigated if the state or local government provides term loans or leases that enable the purchasers to pay for their assets slowly. The financing problems of new firms will have to be addressed through rapid banking sector reform, for instance by creating

---

[7]These six are presented under the headings: citizen shares (Feige); vouchers (Romania); financial intermediaries (Frydman/Rapaczynski); financial intermediaries (Lipton/Sachs); privatization agencies (Blanchard); and self-management.

[8]These data are taken from Jackson (1990), who warns of their likely imprecision.

TABLE 11
The Standard Approach

A. Small commercial and industrial firms

Privatize fast, by sale, if necessary with special financial arrangements, including leasing.

1. "Micro" enterprises, such as small retail stores
can be sold very rapidly.

2. "Small and medium" scale enterprises can either be
(a) first corporatized and shares then disposed of
through sale to an individual or group, or
(b) the assets sold or leased after liquidation of the state
enterprise (as in the 1990 Polish legislation).

B. "Core" of large industrial and commercial firms

1. Commercialize, setting up corporate boards.
Issue: Membership of boards and control of firms.

2. Privatize by distributing or selling shares.
Issues:
   a. Speed of privatization, types of firms privatized, and extent of restructuring before privatization.
   b. Share sales or free distribution.
   c. To whom (roles of foreigners & former owners).
   d. Role of financial institutions (mutual funds, holding companies) between corporations and households.
   e. Does the government hold back shares for later sale, and role of stable core of investors.

C. Financial institutions, housing, land, agriculture

---

new banks or separate entities within existing banks to finance new firms, perhaps using externally provided finance.

There is an intermediate class of "small and medium" scale enterprises, about 5,500 of them in Poland (where the core group of the largest companies consists of 500 firms). Polish legislation proposes an extremely eclectic approach for the privatization of these companies, to be carried out by representatives of the government, with the firms taking the initiative. The legislation envisages some firms being corporatized and shares distributed. The privatization may be initiated by a prospective buyer, who will buy a significant bloc of shares; employees will be entitled to some of the shares for free. Other shares may be sold through auction, public offer, or negotiated sale, with stock exchange listings to follow. Alternatively, small and medium scale firms may be liquidated and the assets disposed of through sale, through absorption of the assets into a new company, or through lease, which may also offer the right of purchase. The legislation envisages few restrictions on these sales, aside from the setting of a minimum price. Under this heading, firms could also be sold to their current employees. Important issues that will arise in the privatization of the largest firms, such as the treatment of the firm's debt, will have to be handled here too. Presumably the firms that are more heavily indebted are likely to be liquidated before being disposed of, though it is not yet clear how the creditors will be compensated, if at all. The eclecticism of the approach to the privatization of these small and medium scale enterprises in Poland is justified by the need to move fast.[9]

While the privatization of small firms has received less attention than that of large firms, its importance should not be underestimated. Future growth is more likely to come from firms in this size class than from the larger firms, so that the rapid progress that has already taken place in the development of microenterprises and the rapid pace of privatization that is possible for small and medium-scale enterprises can make a key contribution to the development of market economies in the formerly socialist economies.

2   Core of Large Industrial and Commercial Firms

The core of largest firms (500 firms in Poland, 5000 in the USSR) accounts for the bulk of industrial output. Typically, these firms are larger and more vertically integrated than they would be in a market economy. In considering such firms, it is necessary to distinguish those that are close to being natural monopolies and are publicly owned in many market economies, such as the railroads and

---

[9]The eclectic approach described in this paragraph is being followed also for larger firms in Hungary (see Bokros 1990), as will be discussed below.

telephone companies, from firms that have no such claim, such as heavy industry. The latter are likely to face competition from new entry and from imports, while the former are not. Given the need to develop a regulatory framework for the quasi-natural monopolies[10] and the time pressures on competent government bureaucrats, the privatization of such firms should be left for later.

2.1   Corporatization

Corporatization (or commercialization) of the core firms is expected to take place quickly. In Poland, it is estimated that over half of the largest 500 firms will be corporatized in 1991 and the remainder in 1992. At the end of the corporatization process, the firm has a legal structure similar to that of most state-owned enterprises in market economies. The board of directors will be primarily responsible to the government,[11] which will appoint the bulk of the members. Workers are also to be represented on corporate boards in several countries; while this representation can be seen as a vestige of worker management, it is also a feature of German corporations.

The performance of the newly corporatized firms will depend on the quality of both management and corporate boards. Current management is likely to be retained initially, but both management consultants and management contracts can be used to improve the quality of current management. Technical assistance funds should be available to help finance the use of foreign consultants and managers. Management training on a large scale is also beginning; foreign financing should be available for this purpose. There is, nonetheless, no doubt that the quality of management should improve over time as more experience is gained of working in a market environment.

The quality and independence of the boards of directors will also be an important influence on the performance of the firm and the completion of its privatization. Given their knowledge of the operations of the firm, it would seem natural to put the bureaucrats who were formerly responsible for the firms onto the boards. Where exceptional individuals are involved, that will help; otherwise, the temptation should be avoided. New directors can be trained, as is happening in Poland. Foreign experience can be drawn on by putting one or two foreign businessmen on the more important boards. The quality of the boards

---

[10]They are described as quasi-natural monopolies because there is a potential role for competition in many such industries — such as telephone communications.

[11]The government agency to which the state-owned enterprises will be responsible differs from country to country. Czechoslovakia and its constituent states will set up Funds of National Property to which the assets will belong and which will be responsible for privatization. In Poland, the commercialized firms will belong to the Treasury, but their privatization will be carried out by the Ministry of Ownership Transformation. In Hungary, the State Property Agency has to approve privatizations.

will improve with experience, and government will have to keep a watchful eye at the early stages.

There is a general issue of the extent to which firms and industries should be restructured before privatization. This "triage" phase of the privatization program has not received much attention, but the difficulties that beset the *Treuhandanstalt*, which draws on a large stable of former West German business executives, suggest that it could take longer and be much more difficult than expected. Some of the newly corporatized firms will lose money. It is not at all clear how the government will decide which firms to subsidize before privatizing and which to close down or liquidate. Given that many of the largest firms in formerly socialist economies are vertically integrated to an excessive degree, there is a good case for attempting a relatively rapid restructuring of the firm before privatization. The separate pieces will probably be easier to sell than the whole. Restructuring of an industry will not be necessary so long as the firms that are privatized face potential competition from abroad and from new entries. As argued above, firms that are likely to remain monopolies should be privatized relatively late, after a regulatory framework is in place.

The government and corporate boards will also have to decide how far to restructure firm balance sheets before privatization.[12] The firms' liabilities to banks, inter-enterprise credits, and the treatment of implicit or explicit pension liabilities will be at issue. Direct sales of some firms are anticipated in all countries, and in these cases balance sheet restructuring will be part of the negotiations to help determine the sales price.

There is less need to restructure the balance sheet where firms are being given away, provided the shares in different firms are distributed equitably over the population. However, the management of newly privatized firms will have enough on their plates in operating in the new market environment without also having to engage in extensive debt negotiations, so that cleaning up of balance sheets would be helpful — and offsetting cancellations of inter-enterprise credits should not be too expensive for the government.

2.2 Sale or distribution of shares

The first choice after commercialization is whether to sell shares, give them away, or both. This decision involves trade-offs among the speed of privatization, the amount of revenue that can be raised, and the ownership role of foreigners. Because of the difficulties of company valuation, a commitment to rapid sale on a large scale would imply low revenues. Because domestic financial intermediaries are weak and there are few individuals with the necessary resources, rapid sale would imply a large ownership share for foreigners. Accordingly, most countries envisage rapid free distribution of some shares to

---

[12]This issue is the key problem in privatizing banks, and will be discussed below.

the public. Thirty percent is being distributed in Romania, a complicated formula applies in Poland, and Czechoslovakia is using its voucher scheme to distribute between 40 and 80 percent of each privatized company to the public.

Free distribution of shares would be unattractive if the main motive for privatization were to raise government revenue. The revenue motive has been important for governments in other countries, including the UK, and added revenue would no doubt be welcome to formerly socialist economy governments at the start of the reform process. Nonetheless, revenue is not the main goal; rather, it is to move firms rapidly into the private sector with the intention of increasing their efficiency and that of the economy. With an eye on future revenues, governments generally plan to hold back some shares for later sale.

In Poland, shares will be distributed 30 percent to the public, 20 percent to the pension system, 10 percent each to commercial banks and workers, and the remaining 30 percent will be held by the government. The distribution to the pension system makes sense as a means of funding existing pension liabilities and, thereby, reducing future calls on general revenues. Further, by funding the pension system, the government encourages the principle of funded rather than transfer pension schemes.

It would be a mistake to give shares to banks at this stage of the reform process. Two arguments can be made in favor of bank share ownership. First, the banks have some financial expertise, so that their ownership of equity will help improve the efficiency of the stock market. Second, share distribution to banks is a means of building up banks' assets and correspondingly their capital in advance of the balance sheet restructurings and writedowns that have to come. Since some of the assets written down will be loans to the firms whose shares are being distributed, there is some logic in compensating the banks in advance. However, share distribution gives the banks assets of highly uncertain value at a time when the value of their assets is in any case unknown and when the main need is to restore the safety of banks and confidence in them. Bank share ownership would also give them inappropriate incentives to lend to firms in which they have ownership shares. It would be preferable to hold the shares that have been earmarked for banks in a separate general fund, which could be used later to infuse funds into banks that need them and to restructure bank balance sheets with safer assets.

In Czechoslovakia, vouchers for the purchase of shares will be distributed to all citizens, with the government retaining at least 20 percent to deal with claims on the firms made by former owners. The proportions are reversed in Romania, where the government retains 70 percent. Although there are fiscal reasons for the government to retain shares, the more it does so, the less credible is its commitment to move rapidly to a private ownership market economy.

The voucher schemes have to be completed by a pseudo-market to establish the initial voucher prices of firms. Triska and Jelinek-Francis (1990) discuss alternative schemes for the initial allocation of shares, favoring a pro rata allocation method in which the number of shares individuals receive in a given company is equal to their pro rata share in the total bids for that firm.

While this method would clear the market, some alternative schemes being considered would not, at least not as rapidly. A *"tatonnement"* is proposed for Czechoslovak privatization: initial prices will be set for 2000 companies, individuals will then tender vouchers for shares in individual firms, prices will be changed on the basis of the excess of supply or demand of shares, and the process repeated. Despite its conformity with the textbooks, this process has few benefits to recommend it. The information on which individuals base their bids for shares must be extremely imperfect, and the final prices correspondingly poor guides to investment decisions. It would be preferable to distribute shares in mutual funds to individuals, on an equitable basis, and allow the mutual funds to trade in the shares of individual companies. Individuals would be allowed to sell mutual fund shares after a specified period, say two years.

2.3 The role of foreigners

The potential role of foreigners has been a matter of concern in all the formerly socialist economies. Countries want the benefits of foreign expertise and foreign finance. But they are concerned that, in the absence of domestic sources of finance, foreigners will acquire a large part of industry at fire-sale prices. Accordingly at the same time as countries seek foreign expertise, in the form of technical assistance or management contracts, they make provisions to control the share of foreign ownership. For instance, in the auctions of small firms in Czechoslovakia, foreigners were not allowed to bid in the first round. Similarly, the distribution of ownership shares or vouchers to citizens or residents limits the initial extent of foreign ownership.

These limits may appear redundant at present when there is no large flow of foreign finance into the formerly socialist economies. However, some limits are justified because large-scale foreign purchases at low prices could discredit the entire privatization process. Further, governments have shown their interest in negotiating or encouraging joint ventures and other means of foreign participation. Constraints on foreign ownership can be relaxed once the privatization process is well established.

2.4 The Hungarian difference

Practice in Hungary will differ from that in the other countries in two major respects. First, there will be greater reliance on privatizations initiated by the firms themselves. These "privatizations from below" continue to be referred to as spontaneous privatizations (see Bokros 1990). However, the spontaneous privatizations that led to an outcry in Hungary and other countries in 1989 usually referred to a particularly favorable deal that involved either the current management or other members of the *nomenklatura*. Since 1989, all Hungarian privatizations have had to be approved by the State Property Agency, which has exercised its right of refusal in almost one third of the cases it has considered. The State Property Agency also intends to initiate privatizations and will consider proposals originating from potential purchasers. Hungary hopes to privatize one third of state assets within the next three years.

Second, Hungary has hardly accepted the principle of free distribution of shares. Kornai (1990) argues strongly that property **should** be purchased, and that the basis of the new system will be undermined if it starts with a free gift. Bokros (1990) allows for some distribution of vouchers but refers to free distribution of shares as a marginal solution that is part of a social compensatory scheme rather than a serious attempt at privatization, adding (p. 7) "it is not considered seriously as part of any 'grand design' even by social researchers and leftist intellectuals." The arguments in favor of free distribution on an equitable basis are that the property has already been paid for by the population and that those currently able to purchase assets may have obtained their wealth illegitimately. Countering the argument that property acquired freely is unlikely to be treated seriously, Hinds (1990a) points out that individuals who inherit property do not seem to mistreat it. While the argument against free distribution is not compelling, Hungary does avoid the complication of the free distribution schemes that some form of concentrated ownership or control has then to be introduced, for example the holding companies.

The pragmatic Hungarian approach is making progress more rapidly than the alternative approaches being followed in other countries. There is a trade-off between the speed with which the privatization process takes place and the fairness of the process. Speed matters.

2.5   The development of a stock market

All privatization programs envisage a major role for a stock market. While there has been considerable skepticism about the absolute efficiency of the US stock market in the academic literature (e.g. Shiller 1989), the question is one of relative rather than absolute efficiency — and here it is difficult to envisage any other arrangement that will perform the information processing and corporate control functions that a stock market provides. However, the importance of the stock market varies across countries, with the banks playing a relatively more important role especially in Germany.

It will take some time to develop stock markets with the necessary depth and efficiency. Trading should be restricted up to that time. Hungary has already instituted a stock market. Poland has decided to follow the French model of the stock market, stock registration, and clearing, in part because of the technical assistance offered. The stock market opened for business July 2, 1991. A securities commission is also being set up with training assistance from the United States SEC. The Securities Commission will register securities to be traded, license brokers and mutual funds, promulgate and enforce regulations, and attempt to educate the public.

2.6 Mutual funds and holding companies

It is unlikely that an efficient stock market can be developed until shares begin to be exchanged for money rather than vouchers or other shares. The share or voucher distribution schemes lead to widely dispersed share ownership and raise concerns about both the efficiency of the stock market and the role that share-owners can play in corporate control. If all shareholders are small, none of them has much incentive to do the research that will lead to efficient asset pricing. Further, small widely dispersed shareowners cannot exercise control over corporate boards and management, because they lack the financial resources to back their judgment with sales or purchases of shares.

Two approaches have been suggested to deal with these problems. The first is to develop institutional investors, such as pension funds and mutual funds. The second is to set up self-liquidating holding companies. For simplicity, these are referred to as the mutual fund and holding company proposals respectively. It is taken for granted that it would be desirable in any case to encourage institutional investors such as pension funds, and that encouragement can be provided immediately under any approach in which shares are distributed rather than sold. Pension funds will also develop over the course of time as newly privatized firms have to provide pensions for their employees. The sooner these institutions can begin trading in the stock market for money, the more rapidly the stock market can develop.

The difference between the mutual fund and holding company approaches is that the mutual funds are expected to take a more passive role in management. The creation of mutual funds will solve the problem of uninformed investors. The mutual funds can be set up either (a) by allocating shares in companies to them, and then allocating shares in mutual funds to individuals, or (b) by allocating vouchers to individuals to bid for shares in mutual companies. Scheme (a) would be preferable, since there can at the beginning be very little information on the basis of which individuals would bid under scheme (b). Some thought has also been given in Poland to the establishment of financial intermediaries, such as mutual funds, that will obtain outside capital (including foreign capital) and purchase shares rather than be given them (Jedrzejczak 1990). In any case, foreign experts are expected to take part in the management of financial institutions, including mutual funds.

Mutual funds would exercise discipline over company management by sales and purchases of shares. Managers should be given stock options to ensure that stock price movements affect their actions, though the question of whether they would act in an excessively shortsighted (supposedly American) rather than long-term (supposedly Japanese) fashion is open. A sufficient number of mutual funds — at least 15 in the smaller countries, more in the Soviet Union — will have to be created for the stock market to operate efficiently. The efficiency of the market will depend also on the composition of the funds' share holdings. Each firm should initially be owned by more than one mutual fund, but shares should be distributed in a way that allows mutual funds to specialize in gathering information. After a short while, the mutual funds should be allowed to purchase or sell whatever shares they want. Over the course of time, specialized funds can be expected to develop.

Two important questions arise: when trading for money can begin and how liquidity is to be infused into the stock market. Mutual funds would need initial financial capital to be able to buy and sell shares for money rather than other shares. The source of this capital is not clear; the state could provide mutual funds with initial capital, or other institutions such as pension funds, or individuals, could invest in the mutual funds. It would probably be advisable to limit both the volume of trading and the participation of individuals in the early days of the stock market. For example, the mutual funds could be kept as closed-end funds, and individuals allowed to sell only some portion of their initial holdings, during an initial period such as the first year after the stock market is opened, or after shares are distributed (since not all shares will be distributed at the beginning).

Unlike the mutual funds, holding companies would take an active role in the management of companies. Being represented on corporate boards, they could supervise management decisions and personnel. Shares would be distributed so that each firm is allocated predominantly, but certainly not exclusively, to one holding company. To prevent monopolization, the holding companies should not be specialized in particular industries. The number of holding companies should be sufficiently large to make collusion difficult. This condition would require at least 20 companies in a country like Poland.

The holding companies would be set up not only to concentrate information in the stock market, but also because effective management in a market economy — particularly financial management — will be scarce in the early transition stages in the formerly socialist economies. The holding companies would be expected to include the best corporate managers and also to draw on foreign experts in managing companies.

There are two major fears about the holding companies: first, that if they are badly run, they can create more difficulties than they solve; and second, that they will end up essentially reproducing the ministries that they are designed to replace. There is no way of ensuring that the holding companies are run well. They face a formidable management task in bringing a large number of companies into the market economy and in closing the firms that will not make it. Management incentives that tie compensation to stock market performance or the profitability of their firms will help but cannot substitute for management skills that operatives in market economies have acquired through on-the-job and academic training over long periods.

It is inevitable that the holding companies would in part be managed by those who have managed companies in the past. The holding companies could also have enormous power. There is, therefore, a real possibility the holding companies would end up acting like the ministries that they are in effect replacing. This danger can be mitigated by ensuring that there is competition among holding companies within each industry and by supervising the holding companies. However, their possession of superior information makes supervision difficult.

Blanchard (1990) suggests that the holding companies should be self-liquidating, required to sell off their companies over the course of time and with a specified end date. They would, thus, serve as privatization agencies. This suggestion is worthwhile for preventing the economic dominance of holding companies, even though the example of the industrial groups in Japan tempts the thought that holding companies may also be an efficient way of organizing industry. There is no need to use only one or the other method — mutual funds, or holding companies — exclusively. Larger firms can be privatized individually, smaller ones can be privatized through holding companies (with the shares distributed to holding companies without creating cartels or monopolies), and mutual funds can hold shares of both the larger companies and holding companies.

2.7 The remaining shares

In each of the share distribution proposals, the government retains a significant percentage of ownership, sufficient to make it the largest shareholder. A benevolent government would be able to use this power to improve firm performance, but there is no reason to expect the governments of reforming economies to behave differently from other governments. It is unwise for the government to continue to hold these shares for very long. Governments should commit themselves to divesting through some mechanism as soon as possible, when it is clear that a company is operating successfully in the private sector.

Lipton and Sachs (1990b) suggest that the government seek out a "stable core" of investors who will constitute the ownership and management nucleus of each company and sell its shares to them. The possibility of the government at any time being able to sell off 30 percent of the shares, at a price of its choosing, would subject any other negotiations for share sales to great uncertainty. Thus, it would be appropriate for the government to seek out purchasers during the early phases of privatization, in collaboration with the corporate management, but not to continue to exercise its implicit control after the firm is established in the private sector.

2.8 Financing needs

One major difficulty with the proposal to distribute rather than sell shares is that companies are very likely to need financial capital as they begin operating in a market environment. Depending on how the government treats the proceeds of sales, companies that are sold can acquire this capital automatically. This automatic acquisition is certainly one advantage of the Hungarian approach.

Alternatively, other sources of finance could be made available through the banking system. Brainard (1990b) argues that financial sector reform is essential for rapid transformation. Rapid financial sector reform would certainly assist the privatization effort. However, it cannot take place very rapidly, because the value of existing assets and liabilities of the banks will not be known until the economy settles down to a more rational set of prices and the restructuring of the real side of the economy is complete. The fear, based on experience, is that banks will make loans designed to save existing assets rather than develop new ones if they are encouraged to lend before their balance sheets are cleaned up.

Banks can help newly emerging companies by segregating financing of new investments from their ongoing relationships, and governments may want to funnel financial assistance from abroad through the banking system.

3   Other Privatizations

Financial intermediaries, housing, agriculture, and land, will all have to be privatized before the economies of the formerly socialist economies can be regarded as having made the transformation to private market status. These economies have moved to two-tier banking with the central bank separated from commercial banks. Unless the government is willing to guarantee the value of assets transferred at the time of privatization, the banks will not find buyers until their balance sheets are cleaned up. Cleaning up their balance sheets is likely to take significant injections of funds and time. But the banks should in any case not be privatized until an adequate regulatory apparatus is in place. Because this regulatory framework, too, will take time to establish, progress is urgent. Rapid development of the regulatory framework is needed also so that new banks, including foreign banks, and other financial institutions can begin to develop.

While there is some private housing in all the formerly socialist economies, the bulk is state owned, and there has been little attempt at privatization in the last few years. It is well understood that until rents are raised to realistic levels and wages adjusted accordingly, there is little incentive for renter to buy their houses or apartments. Because there are so many units to privatize, because cooperative arrangements in apartment buildings will have to be developed, and because mortgage financing will have to be provided, the sale of housing is likely to be very slow. It is, nonetheless, surprising that it has received so little attention so far.

Agriculture is substantially private in Poland but remains mainly collectivized in Czechoslovakia and Hungary. There has been little progress in decollectivization and in land reform, and there is no agreed strategy in these areas. By some reports, there has also been relatively little pressure for reform from within the agricultural sector.

4 Concluding Comments

The progress that has been made in analyzing privatization options in the formerly socialist economies and moving the analysis into legislation is remarkable. So is the progress that has been made in dealing with the privatization of small commercial and industrial firms. It remains true though that privatization of large-scale firms has barely begun and that the evidence is not yet in on whether the ambitious Czechoslovak and Polish approaches will result in more rapid privatization than the more piecemeal Hungarian approach. There are great uncertainties about how the Czechoslovak and Polish approaches will work, particularly when the stock market can begin to play a role, whether the holding companies or mutual funds will be successful, and how rapidly it will be possible to move on a major scale from commercialization to privatization. It should also be emphasized that privatization has soon to be tackled in other areas — financial institutions, housing, and agriculture and land.

Given the magnitude of the task, it would be a mistake to discourage any potentially viable form of privatization that is not theft. The pragmatic approach being followed in Hungary and in the privatization of medium-scale firms in Poland gives promise of faster privatization than any monolithic alternative.

What if privatization turns out to be slower than hoped? That will be a setback to hopes for the rapid creation of a private sector. But the success of small-scale privatizations, and the extraordinary growth of very small firms, suggests that the key to the long-run transformation of the formerly socialist economies may lie less in the privatization of the very large industrial firms — some of them dinosaurs — than in the development of new firms and the growth of existing smaller firms. For that reason, rapid progress in other areas, such as the creation of a suitable legal environment, price decontrol, industrial deregulation, and trade liberalization, is as important to the development of a vibrant private sector as privatization of large firms.

14 The Political Economy of Transition in Eastern Europe: Packaging Enterprises for Privatization

Gordon C. Rausser and Leo K. Simon

1 Introduction

An abstract model of the transition from a centralized command economy to a market economy focusing on privatization is a novel orientation for this chapter. In much of the literature on privatization in Central and Eastern Europe, either a case is argued for a particular transition proposal or specific aspects of the privatization problem are isolated and considered in detail.[1] By contrast, this chapter abstracts from the details and presents a general conceptual perspective that provides an overview of the entire transition. Speaking metaphorically, the transition is seen through a wide-angle lens. Moreover, the **process** of transition compared to the existing literature on this subject, is a particular concern. The model focuses on the **way** in which government policies and enterprise-level

The authors thank Anna Meyendorff for suggesting that our multilateral bargaining model could usefully be applied to the transition process in Eastern and Central Europe. Greg Adams and Richard Ball provided able research assistance. We are indebted to Chris Clague, Glen Harrison, Robert Powell, Scott Thomas, Jean Tirole, and Brian Wright for helpful comments on an earlier draft. We have benefitted greatly from conversations with numerous economists from Czechoslovakia and Poland. Leo Simon acknowledges support from the Center for Institutional Reform and the Informal Sector.

[1]See Beksiak *et al.* 1990; Blanchard 1990; Blanchard and Layard 1990; Borensztein and Kumar 1990; Dewatripont and Roland 1990; Frydman and Rapaczynski 1990a,b; Kornai 1990; Hinds 1990b; Jedrzejczak and Majcherczac 1990; Laffont and Tirole 1990; Lipton and Sachs 1990a,b; Mejstrzik 1990; Roland 1990; Tirole 1991; Varady 1991; von Furstenberg 1990.

decisions are made and relatively less on the specific **content** of these policies and decisions.

This chapter does not offer an implementable proposal, comparable, say, to Lipton-Sachs (1990b). Rather, it suggests an internally consistent, logically complete, skeletal structure. This chapter is intended to complement rather than substitute for papers in which specific proposals are presented. The abstract structure is customized in different ways. Different proposals are embedded into the model and then their properties and implications evaluated, compared, and contrasted. Reference to proposals currently being debated in both Czechoslovakia and Poland will illustrate this chapter's relationship to current literature.

The chapter's purpose is to develop a framework that integrates the major issues currently being debated in the literature to assess the relative strengths and weaknesses of alternative proposals. In particular, the model should facilitate understanding of the relationship between the political and the economic aspects of the privatization problem; between the short-run and the long-run aspects; between decisions that must be determined at the level of central government and those that are specific to each enterprise; and between the legislation of transition policy and its detailed implementation.

There has been vigorous debate over the "big policy questions" and the "grand design" of privatization programs. The basic questions include: the speed and sequencing of reform; macroeconomic and stabilization policies; the pros and cons of vouchers and other massive privatization schemes; and the importance of fostering free entry and competition from domestic and foreign sources. By contrast, very little attention has been paid to the process by which the "nitty-gritty" details of privatization will be implemented. For every enterprise that is privatized, a multitude of details must be decided upon: how will the enterprise be structured; who will control it; and what sweetening provisions will be included to induce buyers, particularly foreigners, to purchase enterprises with less than stellar prospects. The aggregate impact of all these details on the chances for a successful transition could be very significant. It would, of course, be manifestly foolish to attempt to prescribe in advance answers to each of these details; on the other hand, an important research problem is to consider alternative ways of structuring the process by which all of these detailed decisions are resolved.

The advice offered by Western academics to policy makers will inevitably fail to take into account certain important aspects of the process. These lacunae are likely to be more serious when the advice is formulated in the absence of any vision of the transition process as a whole. On the other hand, an overall conception of the entire process may serve as a disciplinary check on individual proposals by drawing attention to gaps in these proposals and to points at which their designers' intentions may be thwarted by the manipulative behavior of self-interested participants. Ideally, such an overall conception would provide an exhaustive, conceptual classification of the decisions that have to be made, the players that will have to make them, the institutional structures within which policies will be negotiated and implemented, and a set of performance criteria against which the process can be evaluated. This chapter should be viewed as a tentative first step in this direction.

The conceptual model has been designed with five basic premises in mind: multilateral bargaining, political economy, heterogeneity, decentralization, and pluralism.

1.1 Multilateral bargaining

In a world in which economic rights are ill defined, a bargaining problem naturally arises. Throughout Central and Eastern Europe, this problem can be conceptualized as a multifaceted conflict between multiple interests representing workers, management, claimants to property rights based on prior ownership, foreign investors, representatives of different groups in the distribution chain, etc. The issues in question include not only ownership rights over land and assets, but also the rights of different interests relative to each other and to the state.

It is useful to distinguish two different kinds of bargaining problems. There are issues that must be negotiated at the level of central government: for example, what will be the nature of the regulatory and legal infrastructure within which these privatized enterprises will operate? Other issues concern the disposition of individual state-owned enterprises and must be negotiated on a case-by-case basis. In particular, what will be the precise nature of each corporate entity that is being packaged for sale to private buyers? Who will control it? How will it be structured? What kind of compensation schemes will be in place for management and workers? What special provisions will be in place that affect the relationship between the privatized entity and other firms, including established and new competitors, firms that are up and down stream in the distribution chain, etc.? In the discussion that follows, the focus will be on bargaining problems of the latter kind. One presumes that, because of the complexity and diversity of the issues during the transition, the state is not in a position to resolve them by fiat. Rather, over the transition, the state is presumed to be one negotiator among many.

Bargaining problems of this kind can be resolved in a variety of ways. At one extreme, an explicit institutional structure may be established by the state to facilitate an orderly negotiation of the issues. This institution would specify: (a) the interests that should be represented in the bargaining process; (b) the space of issues over which these interests can negotiate; (c) what degree of consensus is sufficient to conclude negotiations; (d) who will represent "the state," the founding ministry or some agency established specifically to deal with privatization; and (e) what will happen if negotiations break down? At the other extreme, the state may provide no procedural guidelines whatever as to how the issues should be resolved. In this procedural vacuum, the economic rights in question may simply be expropriated by whichever party — typically the current management — is strategically located to do so.

A fundamental premise of this chapter is that the procedures implemented for resolving these bargaining problems will have a profound impact on the ultimate performance of the post-privatization economy. Relative to the general trend that appears to be emerging in Central and Eastern Europe, there should be more opportunities for decentralized negotiation. One can hypothesize that if certain kinds of enterprise-level decisions are negotiated within the context of an appropriately specified institution, the interaction between the various interests represented at the bargaining table — each acting in a self-interested way — will provide a self-policing mechanism that will tend to mitigate flagrant transgressions of the public interest. Though individually these transgressions might all be relatively minor, their cumulative effect may seriously degrade the quality of the transition.

While there is considerable potential for corruption and narrowly self-interested behavior at every stage of the transition process, this potential seems particularly acute when the privatization plans for each enterprise are negotiated. The prospects for influencing the fine details of this part of the process directly, through legislation and traditional methods of bureaucratic control, are dim. Such pessimism is based on several factors: the enterprise-level negotiations are unlikely to command sustained public excitement and, hence, will lack political "sex appeal"; the range of issues and circumstances are too heterogeneous and complicated; there are too few precedents; and finally, there is far too little time.

Our process-oriented perspective does suggest an indirect, "hands-off" way to exercise some control over this phase of the process: by imposing some explicit structure on the enterprise-level, multilateral bargaining process, the government can introduce some checks and balances into the negotiations. For example, of the three "primary" parties at the bargaining table — management, employees of the enterprise, and the state agency responsible for privatization — the first two parties have every incentive to design privatization plans that inhibit competitive pressures, while the third will inevitably be more concerned with effecting a successful sale of the enterprise than with issues such as the competitiveness of the resulting market structure. From the standpoint of the public interest, then, the outcome of multilateral bargaining is bound to be sub-optimal, provided that participation in the process is restricted to the three primary parties. Moreover, the directions in which these outcomes will deviate from the optimal are more or less predictable. A natural policy response is to include at the bargaining table some additional player or players whose interests can be expected to balance the "collective interest" of the primary players and, hence, mitigate the inherent biases in the primary bargaining environment. Rules can be established for selecting well-informed representatives of taxpayers and consumers. Compensation could be offered to these representatives of interests that benefit from competitive outcomes. The Multilateral Bargaining model described in section 2 provides a useful analytical tool for investigating the effectiveness of this approach to policy making. Using simulation techniques, one can experiment by adding different combinations of players to the primary group and observing how the outcome of the bargaining process is affected.

The theoretical basis for our viewpoint on multilateral negotiations was developed in three recent papers (Rausser and Simon 1991a,b,c), which introduce a formal game-theoretic model of Multilateral Bargaining. This model is briefly reviewed in section 2. In other contexts, the Multilateral Bargaining (MB) model has been used descriptively (Rausser and Simon 1991a,b), to explain how, during the process of multilateral negotiations, coalitions are formed, deals are struck, and compromises are reached. In this chapter, the model serves the additional, prescriptive role of guiding recommendations about how to design an actual negotiating framework to solve the kinds of bargaining problems described above. To be sure, the model reflects a general assessment of how the major issues should be framed and analyzed.

1.2 Political economy

A second basic premise is that any policy recommendations must be both economically and politically consistent. This consistency requires a specification of the relationship between short-term economic developments and longer-term political ramifications. Obviously, economic policy objectives cannot be pursued in isolation, since the prevailing political configuration will constrain the set of options available to planners of the transition process. On the other hand, economic developments can shift the balance of political power. As the post-privatization economy develops, new interests will acquire economic power, and new institutions will emerge to strengthen the power of groups that wish to defend these institutions. Meanwhile, the public at large will register its approval or disapproval with the progress toward a market economy by increasing or decreasing its support for the government. These changes in the prevailing political configuration will have an impact on the continuing policy debate determining, to some extent, the kinds of economic reforms that will be sustainable in the long run. The dynamic interaction between these economic and political facets of massive privatization programs must be taken into account. Indeed, one can expect that models which ignore political-economic feedback effects will have a natural tendency to overestimate the prospects for a successful transition.

The following example illustrates the kind of political-economic interaction that could adversely affect the reform process. Policy makers in Central and Eastern Europe appear to be overly complacent in their reliance on foreign competition as the main disciplinary device that will force monopolists to operate efficiently. Indeed, Polish officials cite their country's liberal tradition in the area of trade policy when questioned about the viability of this approach to anti-monopoly policy. Our dynamic political-economic perspective leads to skepticism about this heavy dependence on competition from abroad. If, as seems very likely, the post-privatization industrial structure turns out to be highly over-concentrated and inefficient, then the main effect of threatening foreign competition will be to unleash a powerful confluence of political forces in favor of protectionism. Owners of the domestic enterprises will lobby to defend their rents, managers will lobby to defend their privileges, and workers will lobby to defend their jobs. Because the problem of unemployment never really arose under communism, the potent tension between introducing free trade and maintaining employment levels never became apparent.

What can be done to preempt this kind of powerful impetus toward protectionism? Obviously, there is an urgent need for liberal trade legislation, but further steps will have to be taken beyond legislation to ensure that it is sustainable in the long run. Foresight is required to identify those economic interests that stand to benefit from liberal trade policies. Governments may find it worthwhile to attempt to structure the development of political and economic institutions so that the interests that have been identified can function as effective political counterweights to the protectionist interests.

1.3   Heterogeneity

Given the heterogeneous nature of state-owned enterprises, there is no one method of privatization that will dominate all other methods in every instance. The state-owned enterprises awaiting privatization come in a wide variety of different forms: there are small firms and large firms; firms with dramatically different debt-equity structures; firms that produce tradeables and others that produce nontradeables; firms that are flourishing and others that are floundering, requiring either liquidation or reorganization; firms with different degrees of asymmetric information among interested parties; firms with different propensities for corruption; etc. Given this vast array of different circumstances, a range of alternative privatization methods should be available, and a systematic procedure should be developed for matching each state-owned enterprise with the most appropriate privatization regime.

The spectrum of alternative regimes might range from relatively *laissez-faire* regimes, allowing enterprise managers considerable flexibility to package their enterprises any way they please, to highly structured regimes, involving audit and oversight requirements. The more structured regimes would be better equipped to prevent corruption and guard against the possibility that provisions antithetical to the public interest would find their way into the privatization plans. Of course, these regimes would also involve a great deal more time and expense than the less structured ones. To exploit the potential efficiency gains from heterogeneity, then, the more resource-intensive regimes should be reserved for cases in which the need for special safeguards is greatest. It follows that some systematic procedure must be developed for classifying enterprises according to their potential for corruption and manipulation and for assigning enterprises to regimes in accordance with this ranking. The development of the ranking procedure could be a formidable task.

1.4 Decentralization

A fourth premise is that the fine details of the privatization process cannot be resolved **at a distance.** Should one expect any centralized bureaucratic implementation of the fine details of, for example, the Polish privatization program to be any more successful than the central planning techniques whose poor performance fueled the drive toward privatization in the first place? In Oliver Williamson's (1991) terminology, this premise argues for more hands-off governance of the privatization process. Such a position is entirely consistent with the arguments advanced long ago by Hayek (1945), who noted that, for economists the core task is

... precisely how to extend the span of our utilization of resources beyond the span of control of any one mind; and, therefore, how to dispense with the need of conscious control and how to provide inducements which will make the individuals do the desirable things without anyone having to tell them what to do.

Concretely, this premise leads to the question: to what degree should the transition process be decentralized? Obviously, the process cannot be decentralized completely, since some aspects of the problem are intrinsically global in nature. Others depend on factors that will differ widely from enterprise to enterprise. A heterogeneous approach to these aspects is essential as has previously been noted. However, the central authority will almost certainly be poorly equipped to make the appropriate heterogeneous judgments on a case-by-case basis. The only viable alternative, then, is to have certain kinds of decisions be negotiated locally, at the level of each enterprise.

At a minimum, enterprises need governance structures that are not controlled by the central government. It also seems clear that the greater the differences between individual enterprises, the more important it is to expand the role of local decision makers in setting the specifics of the governance structure. Indeed, there are many elements that **can only** be resolved at the local level. For example, who should sit on the board of directors of each enterprise? How should the particular responsibilities associated with running each individual enterprise be divided between the board of directors and the management? At least in Poland, the current privatization program assigns to the central authority too much responsibility for determining many of the enterprise-specific aspects of the transition process; in particular, the program leaves too little discretion to enterprise management, workers, and boards of directors. Given the Polish government's demonstrated bias towards centralization, one can expect that even for obviously enterprise-specific decisions, unless responsibility for resolving them is explicitly delegated to local decision makers, there will be a tendency for the central authority to involve itself too heavily in the decision process.

1.5 Pluralism

A fifth and final premise is that political and economic benefits are to be gained by involving a larger number of interests in the privatization process. The public perception of **fairness** will be enhanced if the privatization process is characterized by a greater degree of pluralism. In addition, the more interests that are represented in the process, the more difficult it will be for some interests to collude in the pursuit of narrow, self-interested goals that are in conflict with the public interest. In academic proposals for privatization in Central and Eastern Europe, as well as in the proposed and current laws (Czech and Slovak 1990, Czechoslovakia 1990, Poland 1990a,b), too few interests are represented in the transition process. This situation is paradoxical given the presumed importance of diffusing the distribution of ownership and of establishing pluralistic democratic institutions. Certainly, if there is an increase in the number of interests that are represented, then transaction costs will also increase. Up to a point, however, the benefits will outweigh these costs. Moreover, the costs will be short term, while the benefits will be long term. For example, one obvious benefit of broader-based participation is that political support for the privatization process is more likely to be robust in the face of the inevitable setbacks that will be experienced, so that the trend toward a market economy is more likely to be sustainable.

Another argument for pluralism is the familiar one that, when organizations wield considerable political power, a system of checks and balances should be built into their structure. For example, there is an expectation that in several countries, especially Poland, a relatively small number of holding companies will emerge to provide centralized oversight and control over large numbers of privatized corporations. This group of companies is likely to develop into a powerful economic force, and its political influence is bound to be commensurate. If control of these holding companies is vested in a small group of individuals with narrow, very homogeneous interests, then this concentration of economic and political power could have detrimental consequences for the country at large. Accordingly, before these holding companies become established, attention needs to be directed toward broadening the range of interests represented at the higher echelons of their management.

For example, each holding company will build up a pool of "generalist" corporate directors, who will be assigned to the boards of directors of various enterprises in which the holding company has an interest. As a group, this pool will have tremendous power, so that all interests in society should have the opportunity to participate in their selection. By contrast, the Polish government's 1990 proposal assigns exclusive responsibility for the selection process to the Ministry of Ownership Transformation. If the Ministry itself is controlled by a non-representative group such as the ex-*nomenklatura*, then this provision may create an opportunity for this group to take over the entire holding-company apparatus.

1.6 Outline of the model

The framework in which these five premises can be operational is important. The transition process can be modelled as a dynamic negotiation procedure, which is formalized as a four-phase non-cooperative game. The four-phase game is summarized below and presented in more detail in section 3. Three of the four phases are formulated as Multilateral Bargaining games, using different specifications of the MB model introduced in Rausser and Simon (1991a) and reviewed in section 2. In phases I and IV, the participants in the bargaining process are members of the central government, and various interest groups that have access to these members. In phase III, multiple bargaining sessions are conducted in parallel.

Phase I of the game is called the **cabinet-level negotiation phase.** In this phase, members of the central government interact with nationally representative interest groups to determine the general institutional structure and to select certain "transition regimes" from a given universe of alternative regimes. Each transition regime is a different method for preparing an enterprise for privatization. For example, there might be a distinct transition regime corresponding to each of the "classical" methods of privatization used in Western economies as well as to each of the radical methods for massive privatization currently under discussion in Central and Eastern Europe (see Lewandowski and Szomberg 1989). The final task in phase I is to specify guidelines for assigning enterprises to regimes.

In phase II, which is called the **assignment phase,** the actual matching of enterprises and transition regimes takes place. The matching process can be modelled in a variety of ways depending on the nature of the guidelines set in phase I. At one extreme, the guidelines could be exhaustive, so that the matching process is entirely centralized. In this case, phase II would be redundant. At the other extreme, the matching process is entirely decentralized — the current management of each individual enterprise could have complete autonomy to choose its own regime. An intermediate case would involve, for each enterprise, a transmission of information between the central authority and local interests. Parties with an interest in an individual enterprise would reveal information to the center. This information, together with the guidelines set out in the previous phase, would be used to assign the enterprise to a regime.

Phase III is the **enterprise-level negotiation phase.** Negotiations take place at the level of each enterprise to determine the precise nature of the package that will be presented for sale to the public. The nature of these negotiations — who participates, what issues are addressed, etc. — will vary depending on the transition regime to which the enterprise has been assigned. The negotiations may include issues such as ownership interest, control, high-powered versus low-powered incentives or, more generally, the governance function for each enterprise. The participants may include representatives of some or all of the interests mentioned above — management, workers, taxpayers — and others besides.

Once phase III has been completed, the post-privatization economy unfolds for a short period of time, leading to changes in the distribution of political power. In phase IV, called the **renegotiation phase,** policy makers at the central level reconvene to renegotiate some of the issues debated in phase I. At this point, modifications and reversals of earlier policy decisions about institutional structure may result from the changes in the configuration of power. Finally the economy unfolds again, now for a longer period of time, resulting in a random vector of "long-term performance measures". The various players in the game derive their ultimate utility from the values of these performance measures.

2   The Multilateral Bargaining Model

This section provides a review of the multilateral bargaining (MB) model that was introduced in Rausser and Simon (1991a). The model will be applied in section 3 to represent, in a stylized way, the process by which decisions relating to the transition are negotiated. The MB framework is extremely general and can be customized to represent a wide range of decision-making institutions ranging from dictatorship, through bilateral negotiation to highly pluralistic structures. A brief interpretation of the model, a heuristic description of its structure, and a statement of its main properties are presented here. Concrete illustrations of the model and of its comparative static properties are in section 3.

The MB model is a non-cooperative game in extensive form, with a finite number of players and a finite, but arbitrarily large, number of "rounds". It is a generalization of the famous alternating-offer bilateral bargaining game known as the Stahl-Rubinstein model (Stahl 1972, 1977; Rubinstein 1982). In the Stahl-Rubinstein model, players take turns to propose a division of a "pie". After one player has proposed a division, the other can accept or reject the proposal. If the proposal is accepted, the game ends, and the division is adopted. If it is rejected, the second player then makes a proposal, which the first player then accepts or rejects. The game continues for a finite, or possibly infinite, number of rounds. Apart from generalizing this model to incorporate many players and multi-dimensional pies, the model differs from Stahl-Rubinstein in just one respect. In this game, the proposer is chosen randomly "by nature" in each round of bargaining, according to a pre-specified vector of "access probabilities".

The model can be interpreted in a variety of different ways. One possibility is to view it as a stylized representation of the kind of "backroom" negotiations which take place between members of the "inner circle" of a complex organization.

In particular, suppose there is an important meeting scheduled for the plenary body of this organization (e.g., a parliamentary debate on a significant bill or a shareholders' meeting). Prior to this meeting, intense activity within the inner circle might be expected: coalitions would be formed, deals would be struck and compromises would be negotiated in informal, private, off-the-record meetings between the influential members of the organization.

As an example, imagine the negotiations between senior members of the President's staff over the selection of a particular minister. The following scenario seems like a plausible description of what might happen. A number of different staff members, and possibly the President as well, are concurrently lobbying their colleagues, each attempting to build support for his or her own preferred candidate; somehow, one of the staffer's candidates is eventually singled out from the others and is formally proposed for the ministerial position. If enough support has been generated for the candidate, then ratification will be *pro forma.* Otherwise, the lobbying process will begin again until agreement is finally reached.

The model conforms rather closely to this informal process. There is, however, one aspect of the process that is difficult to describe analytically: how does one staff member's candidate come to be singled out from the others? In this model, a "black box" solves this problematic issue and the model simply assumes that nature chooses among proposals randomly. It seems natural to presume that each staffer's proposal is more likely to be singled out, the greater is that staffer's relative political power within the organization. The idea is formalized by assuming that nature's random choice is governed by a vector of **access probabilities.** The probability weight assigned to each participant is interpreted as a measure of his or her relative political power.

The model is now summarized in a very heuristic way. The reader is referred to Rausser and Simon (1991a) for a formal treatment. A number of players meet together to select a **policy** from among a given set of alternative policies. The specification of the game includes a list of **admissible coalitions.** An admissible coalition is interpreted as a subset of the group that has the authority to choose a policy on behalf of the whole group. For example, in a **majority rule bargaining game,** a coalition is admissible if and only if it contains a majority of players. More generally, however, the set of admissible coalitions might have a variety of structures. In fact, for reasons that will become apparent, the game imposes the restriction that there is some player who belongs to **every** admissible coalition. This player will be referred to as **essential.** For example, in the heuristic scenario presented above, it is natural to assume that no minister can be appointed without the approval of the President. If this scenario were to be represented by the MB model, then the President would be modelled as an essential player.

In general, the requirement that some player be essential seriously restricts the applicability of the model. One can argue, however, that in the present context the assumption is satisfied quite naturally. The MB institution enters into this four-phase model in two ways. First, it represents the process of cabinet-level decision making in phase I. In this context, a coalition of cabinet members will be considered admissible if the support of all its members is sufficient to guarantee that any proposal will be accepted by the cabinet as a whole. Intuitively, it is unlikely that even a majority coalition will be admissible in this sense unless some of the government leadership belongs to the coalition. In this case, then, the government leadership is an essential player. Second, the MB model is used to represent the enterprise-level negotiations in phase III between the state and the various groups that have an interest in each enterprise's privatization plan. In these negotiations, the essential player is naturally the state agency whose approval is required before any privatization plan is accepted.

The game consists of a number of **negotiating rounds.** Each round has three parts. In the first round of the game: (1) each player chooses a policy and an admissible coalition; (2) nature chooses one of the proposals at random; the probability that each player is chosen is equal to the player's access probability. The player selected by nature is called the **proposer;** (3) each member of the proposer's coalition decides whether to accept or reject the proposer's policy. If all members accept the policy, it is **implemented** and the game ends. If one member rejects it, the players proceed to the second round, and the above procedure is repeated. If no agreement is reached after the final round, the game ends and players earn a **disagreement payoff.**

The model can be illustrated by applying it to an elementary version of the spatial voting problem familiar to political scientists (see Fiorina and Plott 1978). Suppose that there are five players, labeled 1, 2,...5, and that the set of admissible coalitions consist of any three of these players. They meet together to select a number between 1.0 and 5.0. Once a number has been chosen, each player receives a **payoff** of five units **minus** the distance between the chosen number and the integer identifying the player. For example, if the number 3.5 is chosen, player #3 earns a payoff of $5 - |3-3.5| = 4.5$. Players are assumed to be risk neutral.

Each player's objective is to obtain the highest possible **expected** payoff. When a player selects a policy, she must balance her own preferences for different policies against the likelihood that she can put together a coalition that will endorse her selection. Clearly, when a player considers whom to invite into her coalition, she has a natural incentive to choose players whose preferences are similar to hers. For example, other things being equal, player #1, who is extremely left-wing, is more likely to choose the left-to-centrist coalition consisting of herself with players #2 and #3 than to ally with the right-wing players, #4 and #5.

The policy that is ultimately agreed upon by the group will be called the **solution** to the MB game. The properties of this solution are quite striking. First, it is unique. Second, it is conceptually quite straightforward to compute. (Of course, in problems that are more complicated than our simple example, a substantial amount of computing time may be needed.) Third, if the number of negotiating rounds is sufficiently large, the solution is almost independent of the identity of the player who proposes it and of the precise number of negotiating rounds. The solution to this particular example is extremely easy to compute and the technique is illustrated below. The reader who is uninterested in the technicalities should skip to the beginning of section 3.

Assume that each player has an equal "access probability," i.e., each is chosen by nature to be the proposer with probability 0.2. Also assume that, if the last negotiating round of the game is reached and players fail to agree, then each player receives a "disagreement payoff" of zero. As is usual in problems of this kind, it can be solved by starting from the last round and working forward. First, consider the decision problem facing a player in the last round of the game. Note that, if **any** number between 1 and 5 is agreed upon, then every player receives a positive payoff which is preferred to the disagreement payoff. Thus, **each** player knows that, if nature selects her to be the proposer in the last round, she can propose her favorite policy (i.e., her own number) and **any** coalition will endorse it. Thus in the last negotiating round of the game, player #1 will propose the policy 1.0 and similarly for the other players.

Now consider the situation facing players in the penultimate negotiating round of the game. In the previous paragraph, a calculation was made for what will happen if players fail to agree in this round: they will proceed to the last round and receive a random payoff depending on the player that is selected by nature: specifically, each integer from 1 to 5 is chosen with probability 0.2. The **expected** payoff for each player conditional on disagreement is easy to calculate. For example, player #1 earns payoffs 5, 4, 3, 2, and 1, with equal probability, yielding an expected payoff of 3 units, while player #3 earns payoffs 3, 4, 5, 4, and 3, with equal probability, yielding an expected payoff of 3.8 units. Player #2's expected payoff turns out to be 3.6. To compute what she should do in the penultimate round, the only information a player needs are these expected payoffs.

For example, consider player #1. If she proposes her favorite alternative (i.e., 1.0), it is bound to be rejected, since player #3 would prefer to take her chances in the last round than accept 1.0 in the penultimate round — preferring an expected payoff of 4 units to a sure payoff of 3 units — while players #4 and #5 would also reject this alternative. Thus, in the penultimate round of the game, player #1 is obliged to negotiate a compromise solution. It is easy to verify that the best she can do is to propose the policy 2.0 and the coalition consisting of herself and players #2 and #3. Player #2 will certainly accept this proposal, and player #3 will be just as willing to accept it also. Using this logic, players #1 through #5 will propose the numbers, 1.8, 2, 3, 4, and 4.2, respectively, in the penultimate period. Conditional on reaching the penultimate round, then, the expected payoffs that players will receive are 3, 3.92, 4.12, and 3.92, 3, respectively.

Repeating the computations for the third-to-last period, the players will propose in this period, 2.12, 2.12, 3, 3.88, and 3.88, respectively. By now the pattern will be clear. If the total number of negotiating rounds in the game is sufficiently large, then the proposals that each player will submit in the **first** round of negotiations will be very close to 3.0.

3   An Abstract Model of the Transition

In this section the model of the transition process is presented. As noted earlier, very little structure is imposed on the model *a priori;* rather, it is intended to be a malleable, skeletal framework that can be molded readily into many shapes. Apart from introducing the model, there are two objectives in this section. The first is to demonstrate that our overall structure can be customized usefully to address a wide variety of different problems. Accordingly, a catalog of ways to specify the basic components of the model is presented, along with an explanation of how the formal concepts should be interpreted: who the players are, what kind of decisions will be negotiated, and how the variables such as access probabilities should be interpreted. A second objective is to illustrate some of the properties of the multilateral bargaining model.

3.1   Phase I: The cabinet-level negotiation phase

Recall from section 1 that in this phase members of the central government interact with nationally representative interest groups. Their tasks are organized into two categories: they will determine the general institutional structure of society and set guidelines that will be used in phase II to assign each enterprise to one of many alternative "transition regimes".

The description of the cabinet-level MB game will include a vector of **access probabilities,** interpreted as measures of the **distribution of political power** prevailing at the outset of the game. For example, "the workers" as a group would have a significantly lower access probability in Czechoslovakia than in Poland. On the other hand, from the different ways in which these countries have resolved the issue of restitution of prior claimants' property rights, one can infer that the "prior owners" group should have a significantly higher access probability in Czechoslovakia than in Poland.

The set of coalitions that are declared to be admissible in a particular MB game is another reflection of the distribution of political power. Recall that a coalition will be called admissible if its members collectively have sufficient political power to ensure that any proposal that they sponsor will be adopted by the central government. One can assume that no coalition of interests in society can implement a policy decision without the approval of the leadership of the government.[2] This assumption is formalized in the model by the restriction that the government leadership is an **essential player,** or a member of every admissible coalition.

Two types of decisions are made in this first phase of the model. First, players must select a vector of **institutional policy variables.** Each institutional policy vector is a complete description of the commercial and legal environment within which individual enterprises will operate. Each vector must encode a vast array of information about items including: legal institutions such as conflict of interest laws, commercial code, bankruptcy law, and the administration of justice; commercial institutions such as capital markets and stock markets; investment in infrastructure industries such as telecommunications, data services, transportation, and education; and government policies on matters such as anti-trust regulation, foreign trade and capital mobility. In addition, each institutional policy vector must completely describe the timetable for developing new institutions and restructuring old ones.

A component of institutional structure that has received considerable attention is the financial/management institution referred to as a **holding company** or **mutual fund.** To specify the proposed structure of one of these institutions completely, a number of institutional policy variables is required: will they function merely as passive investors, or will they take an active role in the management of the companies that they invest in? How many will be formed? Will they be mandated by the central privatization agency or merely encouraged by tax incentives? How will they be controlled? How will they be staffed?

The second task for the negotiators in this phase is to choose an **assignment rule** that specifies criteria according to which each enterprise will be assigned to some **transition regime,** i.e., some method for accomplishing the privatization of the industry. There is, of course, a vast array of possible transition regimes, ranging from the "classical" methods used by the Thatcher government in Britain to the radical mass-distribution methods currently being debated in Central and Eastern Europe. Abstracting from the details of these alternatives, each of them can be presented as a particular specification of a common formal structure. Specifically, each transition regime is characterized by a complete list of structural parameters for an enterprise-level MB game.

A universe of **local decision vectors** and a list of potential **local participants** in the enterprise-level MB games are first identified.[3] A transition regime is then specified by four elements: (a) a subset of the universe of **local decision vectors;** (b) a vector of **access probabilities** for the local participants; (c) a collection

---

[2]Obviously, this assumption presumes a degree of stability in government that may not be present in reality.

[3]In the discussion, the adjective "local" is shorthand for "specific to a particular enterprise".

of **admissible coalitions** for the local MB game; and (d) a **disagreement outcome**. Note that one need not specify explicitly which groups are included or excluded from the local negotiations. This information is contained in (b) and (c); a group is implicitly excluded if it has an access probability of zero and is not a member of any admissible coalition.

The local decision vectors: Each local decision vector completely describes an enterprise that is packaged for privatization. The set of local decision vectors for a given transition regime delimits the range of possible outcomes that can result, given that transition regime. The purpose of the negotiations in phase III is to select one of these alternatives. For example, for the transition regime corresponding to the classical British-style approach to privatization, each local decision vector would correspond to a different corporate prospectus for the enterprise that is about to be floated. In particular, the local decision variables might specify information about factors such as: the distribution of ownership, including details about admissible foreign involvement; the prices at which different classes of shares will be offered; the structure of corporate control; and so on.

Local participants and their access probabilities: As in the cabinet-level MB game that was played in phase I, the participants at the local level are functionally defined **groups** of individuals. One can divide these groups into three categories. The first category consists of the representative of the state (e.g., the representative could be an official from the founding ministry or from some specifically created bureaucracy such as a State Privatization Agency). As in phase I, one assumes that the state representative is concerned not only with the public interest but also with political considerations and personal gain (Rausser and Zusman 1992). In particular, the possibility that either the management or the workers can "capture" the state representative is of interest.

The second category consists of groups that in some sense are assumed to be immune to the possibility of capture. While it is somewhat arbitrary to assume that some but not all groups are corruptible, there are at least two grounds for distinguishing certain groups. First, there may be some groups for which the value of maintaining a reputation for impartiality is high relative to the potential benefits from corruption. Second, the potential for corruption may be positively correlated with "familiarity": parties who have had few prior dealings with each other may be relatively unwilling to enter into a conspiracy, for fear that one party will expose the other. Members of this second category might include for example, international accounting and management firms, or institutions such as the World Bank or the European Bank for Reconstruction and Development (Tirole 1991).

The third and major category consists of the usual kinds of private interest groups. This category might include such groups as the management of the enterprise; the employees of the enterprise; individuals with prior ownership claims to the enterprise; environmental and consumer advocacy groups; trade organizations, including representatives from industries that will either supply the enterprise or purchase and distribute its products; foreign corporations; and the various investor groups, i.e., commercial banks, pension funds, financial intermediaries, and holding companies that are discussed in many of the major proposals. Also included in the universe of participants is an abstract, residual group representing "all other small investors". (The representative of this group might be a member of the local government of the community in which the enterprise is located).

Each transition regime specifies a vector of access probabilities for the local participants. In many regimes, these probabilities will be zero for all but a few groups. For example, in a "spontaneous privatization" regime, there might be only two or three players with non-zero access probabilities: the founding ministry, the management, and possibly the employees. Unfortunately, access probability vectors corresponding to proposed designs are unclear because available proposals fail to specify which groups are expected to participate in the local decision-making process.

The set of admissible coalitions: One can assume that the state representative is an essential player. In many regimes, the management may also be essential, and possibly the workers as well. On the other hand, in classical kinds of regimes, involving a great deal of information disclosure, independent auditing firms will typically be essential.

The disagreement outcome: There are several natural candidates for a disagreement outcome. One is simply the status quo. If the local negotiations end in disagreement, the enterprise will remain in state hands for some period of time. Another is that the state will implement its own "boilerplate" privatization plan for the enterprise. Either of these alternatives will presumably be unsatisfactory for all concerned, and so induce the participants in the local negotiations to make the compromises that will be necessary to reach an agreement. More generally, our MB model suggests ways in which the disagreement outcome might be used as a policy instrument to steer negotiations in one direction or another by changing the relative costs of disagreement for the different participants. Of course, the instrument will be effective only to the extent that enforcement of the disagreement outcome is considered by the participants to be a credible threat.

3.2 Phase II: The assignment phase

In this phase, state-owned enterprises are matched with transition regimes. One can assume that each **state-owned enterprise** is completely described by some vector of **attributes.** These attributes specify such diverse aspects of the enterprise as: (a) the nature of the products produced by the enterprise, a description of its plant and equipment, and the technology it utilizes; (b) a description of its financial status; (c) the place of the enterprise within its industry, including its market share and the nature of its competition; (d) some indication of the risk profile of the firm; (e) the distribution of information within the enterprise, i.e., whether critical data is widely available to many different groups, or whether some group such as management has a significant informational advantage;

(f) the nature of "measurement errors" in monitoring the performance of the enterprise (Holmstrom and Milgrom 1990); (g) the relationship between the enterprise and the state bureaucracy, e.g., whether workers and/or management have a cooperative or an adversarial working relationship with the founding ministry; (h) the "distance" between management of the enterprise and the founding ministry; and (i) any potential synergies between the enterprise and some prospective foreign investor.

The initial specification of the four-phase model includes a list of state-owned enterprises together with their identifying attributes. Typically, the central privatization agency will be only partially informed about the attributes of the various enterprises. By specifying an appropriate set of admissible signals that enterprises can transmit and by designing an assignment function with appropriate incentive properties, the central privatization agency can induce enterprises to reveal information that will facilitate the selection of a suitable transition regime.

The assignment process may take a wide variety of specific forms, ranging from fully centralized to fully decentralized. At the centralized extreme, the signaling aspect will be trivial; enterprises will simply be assigned to regimes without regard to any communication from the enterprise. At the decentralized extreme, the matching aspect will be trivial; enterprises will simply specify the regimes that they prefer, and these choices will prevail. Between these extremes, one can imagine many varieties of "revelation mechanisms" of varying complexity.

In the proposals currently under discussion, there are examples of both of these extremes but apparently no explicit discussion of any intermediate kind of assignment rule. For example, in both Poland and Czechoslovakia, enterprises are distinguished primarily on the basis of size and secondarily on the basis of whether or not a foreign investor seems to be at hand. Czechoslovakia has a "small" and a "large" privatization plan, while Poland distinguishes between "small," "medium," and "large" enterprises. It appears that in both countries the classification of enterprises into size categories will be entirely centralized. Both countries allow for exceptional cases in which foreign investors acquire enterprises through one of the classical privatization regimes. It appears that the enterprises themselves will be entirely responsible for declaring whether they are exceptional cases.

The two extreme alternatives of complete centralization or decentralization are unlikely to be optimal with respect to any reasonable criterion function. On the one hand, the central privatization agency will generally have less access than the enterprises themselves to information that is critical for the purposes of selecting a transition regime. On the other hand, a significant moral hazard arises when the choice of regime is delegated to the enterprise itself. Since neither full centralization nor full decentralization is an optimal alternative, expending some effort toward developing an intermediate kind of assignment rule is warranted. To illustrate the potential in this regard, two highly simplistic vignettes are proposed which are intended only to be suggestive.

The first vignette addresses the issue of collusive behavior during the transition process. Perhaps the simplest and cheapest possible way to package an enterprise is to allow closed bilateral negotiations between the management of an enterprise and the founding ministry. Indeed, the proposed method for large-scale privatization in Czechoslovakia relies heavily on the preparation by management of a "privatization project". This method seems to amount to a bilateral negotiation process. There is, clearly, a high potential for collusion here between the two parties. One response to this risk would be to incorporate an objective overseer into the negotiation process.[4] Certainly, it would be too costly and too time-consuming to insist on oversight in every instance. A more feasible alternative would be to require oversight only in situations where the risk of collusion is highest. Specifically, when all local participants have positive access probabilities and when information is equally available to all (think of a crowded and well lighted street) then there is no need for external policing; when the street is dark and sparsely populated, then the need for monitoring and policing is greater.

The potential for collusion depends largely on the personal propensities of the parties involved, and this kind of information will certainly be unavailable to the central authorities. There may, however, be objective and potentially verifiable indicators that are positively correlated with the risk of collusion. An obvious hypothesis is that collusion is more likely between two agents, the better they know each other. If this hypothesis is valid, a comparison of the two agents' group affiliations will provide an informative signal about the risk of collusion. More abstractly, one can imagine constructing a "familiarity index" for pairs of agents and scoring each pair based on publicly verifiable information.[5]

---

[4]In terms of the model, choose a transition regime in which some group with oversight responsibilities is included as an essential player.

[5]This familiarity index can form the basis for the design of an assignment mechanism. Assume that the group affiliations of the ministry representatives are public information. The manager of each enterprise would transmit a verifiable signal about his present and past group affiliations. The central privatization agency would compare each manager's affiliations with those of the corresponding government official, score each pair on the familiarity scale, and then assign each enterprise to a regime with or without an independent overseer, depending on whether the pair's familiarity score exceeded or fell short of some threshold level. This level would be determined as part of the negotiations in phase I of our model. Its magnitude should depend on society's collective willingness to pay (in terms of time and money) for a reduction in collusion. A society that collectively views collusion as a minor problem relative to the cost of preventing it would choose a relatively high familiarity threshold. The more seriously society views the problem, the lower the threshold should be.

The second vignette addresses the problem of asymmetric information among participants in the localized MB game. A widely recognized problem of transition design is that in certain enterprises some participants — either management or the workers, or both — will have access to critical information that is not publicly available. To prevent the informed participants from exploiting their informational advantage, it may be necessary to assign these enterprises to transition regimes in which an auditor is an essential player. Once again, however, the central privatization agency is unlikely to be able to rank enterprises based on the degree of local asymmetric information. If enterprises are to be distinguished on this basis, then, the local participants themselves must be induced to reveal the information about the degree of information asymmetry in their enterprises. Clearly, it will be difficult to induce informationally advantaged groups to reveal their superior knowledge. In principle, however, it should be possible to elicit the truth by soliciting signals from **all** local participants. There will, however, be serious mechanism design problems to be addressed. Since informationally disadvantaged groups will not in general be required to bear the full cost of oversight, it will be difficult to ensure that enterprises are assigned to regimes with oversight only when the social benefits justify the additional social cost.

3.3   Phase III: The enterprise-level negotiation phase
In this phase, local participants at the level of each enterprise play an MB game. For each enterprise, the structural parameters of the game are included in the characterization of the transition regime to which the enterprise is assigned. It is important to emphasize that the role played by the multilateral bargaining model in this phase is quite different from its role in the other phases. In phase I, the MB model was used as a stylized description of **existing** decision-making institutions. In this phase, however, the nature of the local decision-making process is itself a decision variable; it is included as part of the design of the transition regimes. More specifically, it is beyond the scope of transition design to prescribe how interest groups should negotiate with each other at the level of central government. On the other hand, it is certainly appropriate for transition designers to specify alternative structures of the negotiation process between local participants. Of course, these designers must take into account the actual political configurations that exist at the level of each enterprise, or the structures they propose will not be sustainable. However, there is clearly some scope for modifying this existing configuration at the margin through an appropriate institutional design.

To illustrate the potential usefulness of the MB model as a tool for investigating alternative negotiating structures, consideration is given to some highly simplified and artificial scenarios which are intended only for instructional purposes. (The remainder of this section is somewhat more technical than the rest of the chapter. Readers who are uninterested in the inner workings of the MB model might choose to skip to the beginning of subsection 3.4.)

First, for the simplest possible case, assume that there are only two participants in the localized negotiations — management and the founding ministry — and that both are essential players. Assume that each participant has a distinct "ideal point" in the space of local decision vectors, i.e., a vector that he or she strictly prefers to all others. Assume also that payoff functions are continuous and strictly quasi-concave. If the "contract curve" is constructed in the usual way, it will be a curve joining these two points. It is a simple exercise to verify that the solution to the MB game must lie on this curve and that an increase in one player's access probability will shift the solution along the curve in the direction of that player's ideal point.

Now, complicate the example by adding an additional participant, for example, a representative of the workers. Assume that each player has a positive access probability. If all three players are essential, the analysis is much the same as before. Construct the triangle joining the ideal points of the three players (i.e., the convex hull of the ideal points). Once again, it is straightforward to check that the solution to the MB game must lie strictly inside this triangle and that an increase in the access probability of one player will shift the solution closer to that player's ideal point.

The problem becomes more interesting if the workers' representative is not an essential player while the first two players remain essential. In this case, the solution will once again lie on the contract curve joining the first two players' ideal points. In general, however, it will be different from the solution that would be obtained if the workers' representative were excluded from the negotiations. Moreover, the solution will be closer to management's ideal point, the greater the commonality of interest between workers and management relative to the communality of interest between the workers and the ministry. Finally, if the workers have more in common with management than with the ministry, then an increase in the workers' access probability will shift the solution along the original contract curve in the direction of management's ideal point.

The scenarios above are sufficiently simple that the model does little more than confirm what seems intuitively obvious. The model can, however, provide more tangible benefits in more complex situations. For example, suppose that there are many participants in the local negotiations. Assume that the government is concerned only with maximizing the overall "quality" (i.e., potential economic efficiency) of the packaged enterprise while the other interest groups are less interested in overall quality than in maximizing their own private benefits. Many questions can be asked about the relationship between the structural characteristics of the MB game and the political and economic efficiency of the resulting product. First, what is the relationship between quality and the "size" of the space of local decision variables? In particular, is quality greater if participants are allowed to negotiate over the distribution of ownership shares or if this distribution is imposed from above as part of the specification of the transition regime? Second, is quality enhanced or degraded when the minimum size of an admissible coalition (or the required number of signatories to a privatization plan) is increased?[6] Similar questions to these have been studied in a different context (Rausser and Simon 1991b,c). The answers were perhaps surprising, though with hindsight the arguments are relatively transparent. First, quality is enhanced if players are allowed to negotiate over ownership shares. Second, quality is degraded by increasing the minimum size of the coalition.

There are a host of other questions that are much more complex to analyze. For example, how does the quality of the transition process vary with the distribution of access probabilities (political power) among the various participants? Since, at the local level, the vector of access probabilities is, at least at the margin, a policy variable, the answer to this question will be of considerable interest to transition designers.

3.4   Phase IV: The renegotiation phase

Between phases III and IV, the economy evolves randomly over a short period of time. The properties of the stochastic path depend on all the variables that were negotiated in phases I and III. As observed in the introduction, the economic, social and political topography will be in flux during this evolutionary period. Some existing groups will become more powerful, others will become less so, and new power centers will emerge as newly created institutions acquire vested interests in the status quo. To illustrate the importance of changes in political power, consider three examples. First, if the managers as a group gain financially from the privatization process, their political power will increase commensurately; if the privatization process is perceived to be successful and if the managers are perceived to be partly responsible, then their power will be enhanced even further. On the other hand, to the extent that their recent financial fortunes are viewed by the public as unfairly acquired, their power base will be eroded. Second, consider the newly formed holding companies. If these groups play the dominant role that is expected of them in Poland, then as a group they will certainly develop into a significant political force, introducing a new set of economic interests to the political equation. Third, political support for the government leadership will increase or decrease depending on public evaluation of the way the transition process has been implemented, as well as on early indicators of the success or failure of the privatization process. Regardless of these early indicators, an opening of the political system to the broader representation by alternative local participants in phase III may be the most effective means for sustaining the public policies implemented in phases I and II. The diffusion of power that comes with open access and participation at the local level

---

[6]Alternatively, suppose that one policy variable available to the transition designer is the number of required signatories to the negotiated agreement between the enterprise and the ministry. How is quality affected by increasing or decreasing this number?

should result in more transparency and enhance the credibility of the entire transition process (Rausser and Thomas 1990).

All of these developments will be captured in a summary way in phase IV by changes in the structural characteristics of the cabinet-level MB game, i.e., the vector of access probabilities, the set of admissible coalitions, and the disagreement outcome. These changes may lead to a renegotiation of decisions agreed upon in phase I. To the extent that the distribution of political power favors groups whose interests conflict with those of society as a whole, the outcome of this renegotiation process will compromise progress toward the long-run goal of a market economy. On the other hand, to the extent that the government's position is bolstered by early indicators of a successful transition, the resulting increase in the government's access probability will strengthen its negotiating position and allow it to consolidate its program toward reform.

Clearly, decision makers in phase I should take into account these feedback effects when they evaluate alternatives in phase I. It is useful to mention one example here; several others are discussed in the following section. A view that appears to be widely held is that those enterprises in which private investors show most interest should be assigned to a classical Western-style transition regime and should be sold off to the highest bidder. The arguments in favor of this view are transparent: at least some enterprises will be sold, so that progress toward privatization will be seen to be made, and some sales revenue will be generated for the state.

The arguments against this approach are less transparent. They are presented then in a particularly grim scenario. If the approach just described is adopted, then the tendency will be for the most eligible enterprises, i.e., those with the highest potential and least risk, to be sold off to foreigners and domestic wealth-holders. The remaining enterprises, i.e., those with little potential, will be privatized through radical voucher/giveaway methods to the public at large. As the better enterprises continue to do well in the post-privatization economy, while the weak enterprises continue to flounder, there will be widespread public dissatisfaction with the inequitable situation. The government and the pro-privatization forces will lose political support and, in the renegotiation phase of the model, anti-market forces may be powerful enough to slow down or reverse the drive toward privatization. In essence, when the implications of phase IV are fully taken into account, decisions that in phase I seemed rational from a myopic perspective may be called into question because of their negative long term consequences.

4 Conceptual Issues

This multiphase, process-oriented model offers a novel perspective on several aspects of the privatization process which are presented in this section. The discussion is organized around the following themes: (1) the speed versus the quality of the transition; (2) centralized versus decentralized transition designs; (3) pluralism; and (4) policy credibility. For each of these themes, an attempt has been made to summarize the views currently being expressed in the literature, to present this chapter's perspective on the issue and to relate these perspectives to the model.

4.1   The speed versus the quality of the transition

There is a tradeoff that must be resolved between, on the one hand, the speed and cost of the transition and, on the other, the "quality" of the resulting process. For example, in phase II of the model, the key local decision variables could all be negotiated entirely in private, in bilateral meetings between the founding government ministries and the current management of each enterprise. Privatization could be implemented very rapidly using this method, but the distributional and efficiency costs might be exceedingly high. The potential for collusion between the negotiating parties would be very great, and managers would be able to package their enterprises in ways that maximized their personal gain without much regard for the implications of their actions for the future economic viability of the enterprise. At the other extreme, a broad-based, open, and pluralistic negotiating environment would result in a more equitable disposition of the enterprises, but the process could be slow and costly, especially if it involved extensive outside auditing or independent overseers to monitor proceedings.

4.2   Centralization versus decentralization

Once an enterprise has been assigned to a particular regime, should the remaining aspects of the packaging problem be resolved by negotiations at the enterprise level, or should they be subject to tight central control? This issue involves some delicate, political-economy questions. One argument for central control might be that, in certain cases, the configuration of power at the enterprise level may be so unbalanced that politically disadvantaged groups may be unable to protect their interests, while these groups may be better able to defend themselves in a centralized forum. The reverse argument may be equally valid under certain conditions. It may be the case that less privileged groups can be mobilized at the local level to exert influence on matters that concern them deeply. Because of coordination problems, these same groups may be quite ineffective at the central level.

Clearly, there is unlikely to be an entirely satisfactory answer to this question that applies uniformly across enterprises. Thus, the menu of transition regimes should include a variety of options involving differing degrees of centralized control. The mechanism by which enterprises are matched to transition regimes should be capable of distinguishing enterprises in which the various local participants are unable to advance their interests from those in which participants are able to protect their own interests.

Are less privileged groups better able to defend their interests at the local or the central level? Obviously, the answer will depend on the particular local environment. That is, local power configurations may vary widely so that, in some cases, the center can protect them better than they can protect themselves; in others, the situation may be reversed. For example, one important variable is the relationship between participants who are powerful at the local level and their contacts in the founding ministry; to the extent that the ministry is "captured" by the locally powerful groups, the interests of the remaining groups will be at risk. If the ministry maintains its independence from these powerful groups, the rights of the less privileged are more likely to be protected. A second important variable relates to the distribution of information. To the extent that information is highly asymmetric, the interests of informationally disadvantaged players will be at risk.

4.3 Pluralism

In Czechoslovakia, the approach to privatization is relatively decentralized, but there is not much explicit institutional support for a pluralistic determination of the transition. Officially, in Czechoslovakia, any party can propose a privatization project. However, the founder is not obliged to take notice of each of the different proposals. There is not much in the way of explicit insistence on an open debate. It appears that a party can submit a project at the last minute before some deadline, imposing a lot of pressure on the founder to accept without giving the proposal much consideration.[7] In Poland, there is even less explicit provision for pluralism. By contrast, the need for an explicit pluralistic approach seems particularly great in these countries because of the potential for collusion between the *nomenklatura* in the enterprises and the ex-party members who remain powerful with the founding ministries.

4.4 Policy credibility

An issue related to political-economic feedback is credibility or consistency of official policy. This issue is important because domestic and foreign companies will watch these newly emerging economies for signs that the environment is stable enough to make the country a good investment risk. Overturning in phase IV policies set in phase I may be taken as a signal to outside investors that the environment is unreliable. Foreigners will require a greater potential return as a requirement for investing, and this additional leakage will detract from growth of domestic wealth.

It is presumed that consistency is positively correlated with participation at phase III. The chain of events might be as follows. If the important parties

---

[7]By way of comparison, consider the Public Hearing model familiar in the United States where competing alternatives are posted for a fixed minimum amount of time, hearings are scheduled, and responses to written objections are required by law.

believe that they have been consulted at key points in the decision process, they will be more willing to accept a wide range of outcomes without withdrawing their support. Even if participation has no direct positive effects, a bad draw from nature, which leads to poor performances by specific industries or the economy at large, will be less likely to lead to disaffection among the general public, to significant reduction in support for the center in phase IV and, ultimately, to revisions in policy that dampen or even reverse the trend toward reform.

5   Concluding Remarks

In this chapter, a game-theoretic model of the process of transition from centrally planned economies to market economies in Eastern Europe has been presented. The design of the model reflects the influence of a number of basic premises. In the final analysis, the major conclusions are methodological rather than substantive. Specifically, more effort should be directed toward the development of a general conceptual framework that provides an overview of the entire transition process, viewing it through a wide-angled lens. An ideal formulation would provide an exhaustive, conceptual classification of the decisions that have to be made, the players that will have to make them, the institutional structures within which decision making will take place and a set of performance criteria against which the process can be evaluated. A particularly important requirement of the ideal formulation is that it be "logically complete," in the sense of specifying an explicit decision-making process for dealing with "residual contingencies" not dealt with elsewhere in the formulation.

The importance of modelling the dynamic interaction between the economic and political facets of massive privatization programs has been emphasized. One must be mindful that there will be a natural tendency to overestimate the prospects for a successful transition unless these interactions are taken into account. Given the heterogeneous conditions facing state-owned enterprises, no one method of privatization will dominate all other methods in all instances. In addition, if the ultimate goal is to establish a pluralistic, decentralized, market-oriented system, then the transition process itself should have similar characteristics. Many experts in the area apparently disagree with this premise; they advocate a centralized, bureaucratic implementation of the process. Why should a centralized approach to privatization be any more successful than the centralized planning techniques whose poor performance fueled the drive away from communism in the first place? Finally, political and economic benefits can be gained by involving a large number of players in the privatization process. One obvious benefit of broad-based participation is that political support is more likely to be robust against the inevitable setbacks that will be experienced as the newly privatized economy gets under way.

15 Privatization in East-Central Europe: Avoiding Major Mistakes

Jan Winiecki

Economic theory tells us that of the various forms of ownership, private ownership is the most efficient. But theory tells little about how to get from where East-Central Europe is at present to an economy with predominantly private ownership. The ongoing privatization debates reflect uncertainty regarding the proper paths to privatization, as well as conflicting goals and interests. Goals, paths and interests are, in fact, interrelated, adding to the complexity of the problem.

In recognition of this complexity, this chapter will not offer yet another allegedly guaranteed formula for success. It is, rather, a (probably non-comprehensive) list of major mistakes that can be made with respect to privatization coupled with recommendations on how to avoid them. The existence of some trade-offs among potential mistakes, however, implies that not all of them can be completely avoided.

The relative success of the East-Central European countries in avoiding these mistakes will be evaluated. The chapter deals only with the post-communist economies of the region. East Germany is excluded from comparative evaluation for obvious reasons, while Yugoslavia is included (even if it does not fit exactly the "post-communist" formula at the federal level).

1 Avoiding "Capitalism Without Capitalists"

One of the pitfalls on the path to a capitalist market economy is associated with the muddle over the relationship between private property and the market. The

The author acknowledges financial support from the Center for Institutional Reform and the Informal Sector.

271

muddle is ideological in its origins. The democratic left is now ready to accept the market (see Le Grand and Estrin 1989). In fact, after the collapse of state planning, it has little choice!

However, a corollary of the market economy is private ownership (for critiques of market socialism, see Baechler 1990 and de Jasay 1990). But left-leaning economists, not being able to accept both market and private ownership at the same time, have been busy for some time devising various schemes aimed at the creation of "capitalism without capitalists" (Winiecki 1990a).

Although these ideas originate mostly in the West, some of their protagonists have found adherents within East-Central European governments and major political groups. The most fashionable of these illusion-spinning schemes are state holdings, or state investment banks, or "state-somethings" that are to be allocated a majority of shares in state enterprises turned into joint-stock companies (see Gomulka 1989; Nuti 1988 and 1989; Iwanek and Swiecicki 1987; and Swiecicki 1988). Bureaucratically appointed managers of such institutions would, then, be expected to simulate the behavior of managers in privately-owned firms in the stock market. They would be given the same rights as shareholders, except that they would not benefit from capital gains or pay the price of capital losses.

At the level of interaction between the state bureaucracy and state enterprise managers, these schemes can be criticized in terms of public choice theory. Politicians and bureaucrats are not impartial umpires deciding on the issues in a disinterested manner. They have their own interests (re-election for the former, empire-building and/or leisure on the job for the latter) which influence their relations with state enterprise managers.

It is an illusion to expect that "playing at the stock market game" may be more important for both sides of the interaction than these other interests. Monsen and Walters (1983) concluded in their study of West European state enterprises that they had "not been able to discover a single case of a top executive of a European nationalized company who was replaced for failing to earn a required rate of financial return. By contrast, there are dozens of cases of managers who have resigned in protest, been fired, or were not reappointed because of a major disagreement with their governments over policy."

At the level of conflict of interest between owner (the state) and manager, illusions of "capitalism without capitalists" can be criticized in terms of property rights and agency theory. Private ownership links investment decisions to capital gains and losses and is thus more efficient than state ownership, which has much more room for opportunistic behavior on the part of managers.

There is a world of difference between the shareholder who uses his own knowledge or hires a specialist to play the stock market with his own money and a bureaucrat who risks the state's (i.e. taxpayer's) money. As Kornai (1990) aptly points out, "simulated joint-stock companies, the simulated capital market, and the simulated stock-exchange" all "add up to...Wall Street — all made of plastic."

All of the East-Central European post-communist countries have resisted the temptation to go for a fake rather than a genuine article. In this resistance they have shown greater maturity than some of their Western advisers. Not all of them, however, have avoided another ideological trap, namely that of a "third road" in the form of self-managed (or labor-managed) firms and their more recent successor, employee share ownership (see the critique in Gruszecki and Winiecki 1991).

These illusions have been — not surprisingly — strongest in Yugoslavia, where it is planned to sell up to 60 percent of share value to employees in each enterprise. The non-transferability of shares is to be introduced for an unspeci-fied period. Employee-owned firms of that sort are only marginally better in efficiency terms than labor-managed firms (Gruszecki and Winiecki 1991). Their successes, alleged or real, should be seen in the context of the market dominance of privately-owned firms that force efficient behavior on employee-owned firms.

If employee-owned firms become the dominant form of ownership, however, their deficiencies, known from property rights and agency theory, will leave a strong imprint upon their performance — and on that of the economy as a whole. In Yugoslavia all "third road" attempts stem also from the interest of the communist ruling elite to perpetuate themselves in power. They are also increasingly perceived as a vehicle of Serbian domination over the more capital-ist-oriented northern republics: Slovenia and Croatia.

In Poland, however, a lobby in favor of self-management in the recent past and of employee share ownership currently is strongly linked to the victorious Solidarity, unfortunately giving these concepts enhanced credibility. The Polish government has wisely resisted attempts at making either of these ideas a domi-nant form of denationalization, but the pressure continues to be strong. Hungary is the country where these "third road" illusions are weakest.

2 Three Most Damaging Mistakes

There are many ways in which privatization could go wrong, quite apart from opting for "capitalism without capitalists" or some "third road". Three errors, in particular, are likely to be the most damaging for successful privatization, name-ly: (1) concentrating upon the means or methods of privatization before consid-ering its goals; (2) neglecting the time factor; and (3) disregarding the politics of privatization.

Some countries, lured by the glamour of British-style privatization through public sale of shares of enterprises, have concentrated on this particular method to the detriment of clear thinking of what they want to achieve. If the goal has been "people's capitalism" (with as wide a dispersion of ownership as possible), then British-style privatization would be a conceivable means to achieve it. But the United Kingdom already had a well-established capitalist class, while the East-Central European countries do not. Since the kernel of the capitalist market system is, not surprisingly, capitalists — people who take capital risk — the transition to the capitalist market economy should entail measures that support the emergence of capitalists.

A sale of small lots of shares to the general public is not helpful in this respect. At least some other means, such as sale of small and medium-sized enterprises to private individuals or small groups of individuals, or sale to foreigners of some enterprises or controlling blocks of shares, should also be considered.

The first Polish non-communist government gave its highest priority to designing the rules for British-style privatization. But the rather not unexpected result was that it had continuously to scale down its public-sale-based privatization plans, from 150 privatized enterprises in 1990 to 50 and, finally, to 5 enterprises privatized by January, 1991. At that rate privatization would last several hundred years. Privatization of commercial real property (shops, restaurants, pharmacies, etc.) is proceeding at varying speed in different areas, while the sale of small state-owned enterprises has not really even begun.

Hungary did not completely avoid the lure of the tried and tested British-style privatization. However, the government has understood well the need to foster a domestic capitalist class, and has, therefore, been more active in selling small and medium-sized enterprises to domestic entrepreneurs. At the same time, it also has understood the need for ownership control over management and is generally concerned about finding buyers of a controlling block of shares.

Czechoslovakia, a late starter, has followed a markedly different privatization path, particularly with regard to larger state-owned enterprises. It began the process of selling off small state enterprises and commercial property in early 1991. Yugoslavia, with its unfinished political change and communist influence, has in its privatization program given a high priority only to the conversion from labor-managed firms to employee share ownership.

The second major mistake is to forget that various methods of privatization require differing time spans for implementation — and time is a scarce commodity for countries in transition to the market system. A propensity for state enterprise managers to overinvest and generally use more resources in times of expansionary macroeconomic policy is well known. An economy with a predominantly state ownership is unbalanced by definition and is also inflation prone. (Recent Polish experience showed that in times of restrictive macroeconomic policy, such an economy is unbalanced and recession prone; see Winiecki 1990b.) Accordingly, privatization should proceed rapidly to change the highly unsatisfactory ownership structure in favor of privately-owned firms.

It is here that the British-style privatization reveals its major weakness in the East-Central European context. Asset valuation, preparation of prospectuses for would-be buyers, advertising campaigns, and, finally, public subscription all require time. The privatization of one or two dozen enterprises in the United Kingdom took more than a decade.

Could the East-Central European countries with their thousands of state enterprises, not to mention their rudimentary financial markets, follow that pattern? After persisting in this illusion for some time, the Polish government (both the previous Mazowiecki and the present Bielecki one) began to search for more rapid means of privatization that could be applied in parallel with public sales of shares. Czechoslovakia recognized from the start that public sales could last for decades, if not centuries, and opted for a free (or almost free — there are nominal charges only) distribution of a large part of state industrial assets to its citizens according to a voucher scheme entitling them to receive shares in enterprises of their own choice up to the value of the voucher. Only Hungary has stuck to the idea of the "businesslike" (i.e., sales only) privatization that may last for decades.

Kornai (1990) has cautioned that *embourgeoisement* is a long process and has warned against "instituting private property by a cavalry attack". However, an acceleration of this process should not be regarded as impossible (see Beksiak, *et al.* 1989; see also Gruszecki and Winiecki 1991). If the alternative is half a century to a century of privatization, shortcut privatization is not only possible but also highly desirable. The costs of decades of dominance of state ownership will certainly be higher than those resulting from unavoidable problems associated with the free distribution of state assets to citizenry. Quite a few analysts in East-Central Europe and elsewhere have agreed with this conclusion.

The last major mistake to be considered concerns the neglect of building a constituency for privatization. After all, it is a major political change and, as such, coalitions supporting the change are needed. "People's capitalism," the wide distribution of the ownership of financial assets, is an approach that may under proper circumstances (as in the United Kingdom, for example) receive wide acceptance. However, the impoverished populations of the post-communist countries are clearly unable to buy, even at discounted prices, the bulk of state industrial assets.

Therefore, free distribution to the population is preferable for reasons of both political efficacy and equity. Free distribution would generate more political support than sale, which would give too large a share to the hated communist *nomenklatura*.

Political efficacy considerations suggest yet another rationale for free distribution of state assets to the population. The population at large may be the only constituency that can be organized to resist the claims of a less numerous but already better organized constituency: employees of large state-owned enterprises who prefer the free distribution of assets to employees over distribution to the population at large.

The previous Polish government failed to recognize the importance of building a political constituency, although its single-minded pursuit of British-style privatization did not give it much of a chance to find one. Hungary fares better only because employee ownership is not so popular there, but the insistence on the sale of assets rather than free distribution limits grass roots support for privatization. Czechoslovakia, with its free distribution scheme, seems to have generated greater popular support for privatization. In Yugoslavia, the idea of selling rather than giving shares in enterprises to their employees did not win much enthusiasm. Workers are already receiving the benefits of ownership without having to pay for the shares.

Summing up, when it comes to avoiding the most damaging mistakes, Czechoslovakia is clearly in the lead, with Hungary next, Poland coming in a poor third, and Yugoslavia bringing up the rear. Not only has Yugoslavia made all three mistakes discussed here (as has Poland to some extent), but it is on an altogether wrong track — an as yet incompletely defined "third road".

One caveat is necessary at this point. It is not possible to avoid all mistakes simultaneously. For example, if Czechoslovakia decides to speed up the privatization process by the free distribution of a large part of state industrial assets (through the voucher scheme), then it will privatize sooner than other post-communist countries of East-Central Europe. Most probably, the privatization will also be smoother due to greater political support. But this choice entails costs as well as benefits. Free distribution leads to large dispersion of ownership with all the attendant costs of weaker control by owners over managers. Although it is expected that the process of reconcentration would start soon, the interim period would be one of weaker performance than under traditional capitalist control with clearly identifiable owners of the controlling block of shares. To lower these unavoidable costs somewhat, the privatization should envisage a mix of methods. A combination of free distribution of assets to citizens could be combined, for example, with a small scale (10-20 percent) free distribution of shares to employees. This combination would create the clearly identifiable group of owners right from the start. Of course, there are disadvantages to even temporary employee control: shares would not be concentrated in the hands of a group willing to effect radical change in the organization.

3   On Not Putting All Eggs in One Basket

The last issue to be considered is the choice of the one and only versus that of many methods of privatization. Given the fact that the road to success is unknown, a simultaneous application of a broad array of privatization approaches is another insurance against failure. Sale of small and middle-sized enterprises to individuals, sale of some larger firms to foreigners, free distribution of shares in most larger firms to citizens — all these are complementary rather than competing solutions. Those countries employing simultaneously a variety of approaches stand a better chance of success. Hungary appears to be in the lead in this respect, with Poland ahead of Czechoslovakia (perhaps due to the head start of the transition in Poland).

While considering a broad array of privatization approaches as an insurance against failure under high uncertainty, yet another issue should be noted. The analysis here has focused on what Gruszecki (1990) and Gruszecki and Winiecki (1991) call "privatization from above," or the reassignment of property rights of the formerly state-owned enterprises. On the other hand, the success of the change in the ownership structure of post-communist economies depends also on the "privatization from below," that is, on the unfettered establishment and expansion of private firms.

These considerations of not putting all eggs in one basket would be incomplete without mentioning the demand for the creation of a network of market institutions attuned to the needs of the expanding private sector (at this stage, composed almost exclusively of small businesses). Small business development banks, agricultural development banks, small business-oriented insurance companies, innovation centers, and venture capital institutions are urgently needed as ingredients for success.

There is a bias in governments' efforts in favor of the more glamorous aspects of institution-building: establishment of the two-tier banking system, privatization of large state enterprises, and the establishment of a stock market. But small businesses, whether privatized or built by their owners from scratch, all critically depend for their expansion on a network of institutions that in no post-communist economy are yet in place, even in a rudimentary state. The deficiencies of these institutions are so great in all of the countries in question that no ranking of nations is even possible.

But regardless of ranking, difficulties are enormous everywhere, and many things may happen in East-Central Europe on the way to the future. We do not know all the answers and paths leading from here to there. And let us not forget that "there," meaning the West, is a moving — not a static — target.

16 Political Economy of Privatization: Poland, Hungary and Czechoslovakia

Scott Thomas

In 1990 the world witnessed sweeping systemic changes in the political and economic landscape of Central and Eastern Europe. The impetus was Soviet withdrawal, politically and then militarily, from its coercive rôle in the region. The speed of the subsequent transition and the alacrity with which the peoples of former Soviet-bloc satellites embraced the precepts of democracy and capitalism were striking. But the next phase for the new democracies would be the harsh task of making the transition to market economies. They faced much higher oil import costs, mainly because the Soviets began requiring payment in hard currencies. The progressive unravelling of their principal export market — the Soviet economy — was particularly worrisome. Some countries faced very high debt burdens inherited from previous regimes that had borrowed in part to avoid having to make systemic economic reforms. Others were in the throes of convulsive economic and financial crises.

The transition from central planning to market economies would mean having to shut down a great deal of unsuitable productive capacity, leading to declining output and loss of privileges, jobs, and income. The remaining capacity would have to be subjected to market prices and weaned from government subsidies. Privatization of the vast holdings of state enterprises, seen as the best means to enforce market discipline and promote efficiency and productivity,

Dr. Thomas is Principal Economist for Eastern Europe, Europe and Near East Bureau, Agency for International Development. The views and analysis presented here are entirely his own, and do not necessarily reflect those of AID. The author wishes to thank Chris Clague and Gordon Rausser for their comments and editing suggestions on an earlier draft.

became the principal objective of the economic programs in Poland, Hungary and Czechoslovakia. It was a daunting task, both because of the sheer scale of the state sectors in those countries and because it would require the complete departure from one set of economic institutions — central planning and command control — to another set, those of free markets.

This chapter reviews the recent economic performance of Poland, Hungary and Czechoslovakia, highlighting macroeconomic developments, economic stabilization and reform programs, and each country's plans for privatization of state-owned enterprises. Subsequently, some of the principal constraints to rapid privatization are examined in light of the privatization program that each country plans to pursue.

1   Poland

The economic situation inherited by Poland's new Solidarity government in 1989 was extreme: hyperinflation caused by a complete collapse of budgetary discipline under the old Rakowski government and rapidly falling production. In many respects, this situation meant that there was no real alternative but to pursue a "shock therapy" economic stabilization program. The crux of the program introduced in January 1990 was a strict monetary and fiscal policy, as well as the imposition of a confiscatory tax on inflationary wage increases. Interest rates were raised, and the currency devalued. To its credit, the new government under Prime Minister Mazoweicki also promised and delivered rapid and comprehensive systemic economic reforms to facilitate the movement to competitive market mechanisms. Most prices were freed, private business activity was legalized, and the trade and foreign exchange systems were liberalized. The government committed itself to privatize most state-owned assets and began to strengthen competition especially in local markets and sectors without foreign competition. Substantial progress was made in the reform of the banking and tax systems.

Results were quick and dramatic: monthly inflation reduced to 3.5 percent[1] by June 1990 (from 80 percent per month in January 1990); a hard currency trade surplus of $3.2 billion for the year through September 30; worker absenteeism down by over 40 percent. Shortages of consumer goods were all but ended, and the exchange rate stabilized. With a Paris Club rescheduling and a debt payment moratorium in effect, net foreign exchange reserves increased by over $3 billion in the first half of the year. But these achievements were accompanied by deep recession; GDP fell by 12 percent and investment by 9 percent in

---

[1]This paper relies upon data derived from a variety of sources including the International Monetary Fund.

1990. The decline was sharpest in the socialized industrial sector and was only partially offset by strong growth in the nascent private sector. Unemployment rose to 6-7 percent of the labor force.

Problems with inflation returned in the third quarter of 1990 as the government began to relax its credit policies in an effort to stimulate the economy. Preferential credit to agriculture and housing rose particularly sharply. The actual increase in net domestic assets of the banking system exceeded the increase agreed to under the IMF Standby by 62 percent. Average wage increases also exceeded IMF Standby limits, rising by nearly 10 percent on the average monthly in the fourth quarter. By that time, although real wages had fallen by 30 percent from their peak in the third quarter of 1989, they still exceeded their January 1988 level. The acceleration of wage awards in the second half of 1990 was apparently facilitated by rapid expansion of bank credit. The final two tranches of the IMF Standby were not disbursed when it became clear that the government would not meet its stabilization targets.

With monetary growth faster than planned, inflation began to accelerate to monthly rates of 5-6 percent in the final quarter of 1990 reflecting, in part, the rapid wage increases. Consumer prices rose by over 250 percent for the year as a whole. The very solid trade performance of the first half began to wane as imports, which had fallen abruptly early in 1990, more than doubled in the final two quarters. Much higher oil costs, due to the Soviet requirement for payment in hard currencies, and a dramatic drop in exports to the Soviet Union contributed to the increase. These problems were compounded by a steadily appreciating real effective exchange rate. The surge in imports brought the hard currency trade surplus for 1990 down to about $2.2 billion; the trend worsened in the first quarter of 1991. Poland's foreign exchange reserves began rapidly to erode.

In spite of these setbacks, based on a record of very substantive progress made in economic transformation in 1990, discussions were initiated by President Walesa's incoming government concerning a comprehensive 3-year economic reform program supported by an IMF extended funding facility. Agreement was reached in March 1991. The government renewed its commitment to economic stabilization, backed by credit ceilings and wage limits. Inflation was to be reduced to an annual rate of 36 percent by the end of 1991. The new stabilization program was accompanied by an ambitious structural adjustment effort that aimed to privatize some 50 percent of state-owned assets by the end of 1993. The exchange rate was devalued against the dollar and then pegged to a basket of currencies. In support of the program, President Bush proposed that Western nations reduce Poland's debt outstanding to official bilateral creditors, and agreement was reached in the Paris Club to write down such loans by at least 50 percent.

By mid-1991 the government's fiscal position had again become precarious. Part of the sharp swing into surplus during 1990 had arisen from windfall income tax receipts. These receipts resulted from large profits in enterprises that were selling from inventory goods that had entered their books at much lower costs when prices were controlled. In contrast, government revenues were projected to fall by 2 percent of GDP in 1991, notwithstanding the estimated proceeds from privatization and the imposition of additional petroleum taxes. Accordingly, budgeted expenditures were reduced sharply, particularly for subsidies, which were cut by an amount equivalent to 2.5 percent of GDP. Some spending decisions were delayed until revenues from privatization began to materialize.

The fiscal surplus in 1990 had allowed sufficient cushion for dramatic credit increases to be extended to the non-socialized sector. At the same time, credit to the socialized sector continued to expand. But these trends reversed in 1991, with fiscal balances turning sharply into deficit. This deficit, in turn, raised serious concerns about the prospect of private enterprises being crowded out of credit markets. Moreover, since the fiscal program anticipated that proceeds in 1991 from the sale of state-owned enterprises would yield revenues to the government of 1 percent of GDP, it was clear that if the sale of state-owned enterprises stalled, something would have to give. Yet, with the fiscal situation, virtually no government funding could be made available for the restructuring of those enterprises.

Privatization Program   The Polish program to privatize small-scale retail and service outlets proceeded very rapidly, with an estimated 70 percent of those activities already having been divested by early 1991. This divestiture was accompanied by an explosion in registration of new enterprises in the small business sector. In contrast, the program to privatize medium and large-scale enterprises got off to a slow start. Public reaction was strongly against alleged sweetheart deals in which managers would agree with workers to sell their own firms directly (or "spontaneously") to foreign investors. The perception was that only former *nomenklatura,* black marketeers, and foreigners would benefit from such deals. Debate over the privatization law, which in effect re-asserted state ownership over enterprises whose operational authority had been devolved to enterprise management and workers' councils, was prolonged.

There are nearly 9,000 state-owned enterprises in Poland, of which some 500 are large scale. By the first quarter of 1991, only eight privatizations of large-scale enterprises had been successfully completed; five were accomplished through public offerings, two through direct sales to foreign buyers and one through a worker buy-out. Total proceeds were about $40 million. Some 60 companies had been transformed into Treasury-owned joint-stock companies, the step preliminary to privatization.

Medium-scale privatization was more successful. By the end of the first quarter about 150 enterprises of medium size had been privatized, mainly through leveraged buy-outs by workers. In such buy-outs, although no direct loans from the government are extended *per se,* enterprise lease agreements specify that workers initially must put up the equivalent of 5 percent of equity followed by another 15 percent over two years. The remaining 80 percent of the lease is paid with an option to purchase so that if the option is invoked, the effect is very similar to a direct loan from the government.

The government set for itself the goal of privatizing 50 percent of state-owned assets by the end of 1993. The privatization program included four basic elements:

Small-scale shops   Continuation of the sale of small-scale retail and service outlets.

Small and medium-scale firms   A wide variety of privatization mechanisms was to be allowed, including outright sale, protected "liquidation" and formation of a new company. For small-scale enterprises, leasing of assets to large corporations was also permitted. Most "liquidations" through mid-1991 were leveraged buy-outs by workers.

Case-by-case privatization of large state-owned enterprises   These individualized cases have occurred through direct sales or auctions. In 1991, 40 to 50 large enterprises, after having been valued by specialist consulting firms, were to be sold through public offerings, private placements and joint ventures. The government intended to nullify legislation requiring approval of foreign equity stakes of more than 10 percent.

Mass privatization   This method was the principal means by which the government intended to accomplish its goal of privatizing 50 percent of state-owned assets by the end of 1993. Groups of large enterprises were to be packaged for allocation in phased intervals. In 1991, shares in at least 100 of the largest enterprises were to be allocated approximately as follows:

Free distribution (60 percent) of shares to between five and twenty investment funds which would, in turn, hold those shares in trust for each adult citizen. Shares in the investment funds would not be tradeable for a period of two years. The funds would exercise direct corporate control over the enterprises.

Workers (10 percent) in the enterprise to be privatized would automatically be allocated a fixed proportion of its shares.

Government (up to 30 percent): The government would retain a large proportion of the shares, which at a later time could be offered for direct sale or auction, distributed to the investment funds or to targeted recipients, or retained. In the interval, control of these shares might be entrusted to the investment funds to give them additional management control.

Under the program announced in June 1991, the Polish government made clear that it intended that the investment funds should take full responsibility for enterprise oversight and control, with fund management to be drawn at least partly from the ranks of foreign corporations. The plan also envisioned that owners and their heirs whose property had been confiscated by the communists would be offered compensation in the form of bonds rather than restitution of their former holdings. Still, many aspects of the privatization program remained under discussion, including the extent to which the option of direct sale, without resort to mass distribution of shares, would be employed. One of the most important unresolved issues was how to mobilize resources, both foreign and domestic, to be used in the restructuring of viable enterprises.

2   Hungary

The Hungarian economy inherited by President Antal's democratically elected government in 1990 differed significantly from those of other Central and East European countries. Reform communists, under the rubric of the New Economic Mechanism (NEM) begun in 1968, had gradually pulled the economy away from rigid central planning. That experiment, undertaken under conditions of adherence to strict communist political orthodoxy, was guided by the concept of decentralized economic management. Hungary joined and began technical and financial relationships with the IMF and the World Bank in 1982. In 1987, with *glasnost* and *perestroika* having loosened the reins even further, the regime planned a gradual transition to a market economy. But decentralized management without private ownership, continuing subsidies to state-owned enterprises in spite of efforts to enforce bankruptcy legislation, and pervasive "indirect" economic controls turned out to be a prescription for inefficiency and stagnation. In 1988-89, the economy slid into persistent recession compounded by large current account deficits.

In late 1989, an interim socialist government began to impose fiscal and monetary austerity. The Hungarian Democratic Forum, which came to power after the election in the spring of 1990, re-committed the nation to an IMF-backed program of economic stabilization. But it had won the elections promising gradual economic reform and at first made slow progress in removing direct and indirect price controls, liberalizing trade, and introducing other key reform measures. Hard budget constraints were not enforced against state-owned enterprises. By mid-year, budgetary slippage threatened to derail the program. Part of the problem derived from rising subsidy costs, particularly to housing, deteriorating trade with the Soviet Union, and higher oil import costs. But there were also unanticipated governmental expenditures such as special pension supplements.

In spite of this slow start, considerable progress was made in 1990. Cuts in agricultural subsidies and increased taxes helped bring the stabilization program back on track, under revised targets, while increases in domestic prices for petroleum and other energy products limited the potential for further budgetary slippages derived from subsidies. Foreign investment and profits repatriation were liberalized. Participation by foreign firms in joint ventures was significant. Although popular reaction against alleged sweetheart deals slowed the process, the government promulgated an oversight process to serve as a check on privatizations initiated outside of government channels and allowed such "spontaneous" privatizations to proceed.

The recession deepened in 1990: industrial production fell by an estimated 10 percent, and GDP by 5.6 percent. Employment and output in enterprises with more than 50 employees fell by 10 percent. This decrease was only partially offset by increased jobs in smaller firms. Inflation rose to 30 percent for the year, much of it attributable to one-time price adjustments, cuts in subsidies and tax increases. Average wage increases, on the other hand, remained well below price increases, an important indicator that underlying inflation was not allowed to get out of hand.

Trade performance was stronger than expected, as the economy reduced its dependence on Soviet-bloc-oriented trade. But this strength was achieved primarily through declining trade with Soviet-bloc countries rather than through an increase in trade with the West. Preliminary data indicate that convertible currency trade remained very nearly flat in 1990 as a whole while trade with socialist countries fell by about 30 percent. In the first three quarters of the year, the overall trade surplus reached $665 million with imports falling by more than 10 percent and exports falling by nearly 6 percent compared to the same period a year earlier. The trade surplus began to wane in the final quarter as increased oil import costs, falling exports to the Soviet Union, and drought combined to hold the trade surplus to an estimated $535 million for the entire year.

A $1.4 billion current account deficit in convertible currencies in 1989 turned into a small surplus in 1990. This improvement was due largely to positive unrequited transfers, which occurred apparently because residents began shifting savings from foreign currency accounts to domestic ones. But the balance-of-payments situation continued to be precarious because of high levels of hard currency debt (over $20 billion, the highest per capita debt level in Eastern Europe) and increased uncertainty on the part of foreign creditors. By the end of 1990, the stock of foreign currency reserves had fallen to the equivalent of only two months of imports. Although Hungarian officials sought to avoid a rescheduling, foreign debt payments due in 1991 rose to $4.6 billion, 14 percent higher than the previous year.

By December of 1990 the Hungarian government was ready for swifter and more comprehensive reform. A new finance minister began to centralize economic decision making under his control. Agreement was reached on a far-reaching, 3-year economic program backed by an IMF extended funding facility. In January, 1991, the forint was again devalued and the share of prices free of controls rose to 90 percent. Oil import cost increases were passed through to the consumer. The government removed trade and exchange restrictions on all but 10 percent of imports from hard currency countries, fully exposing to foreign competition an estimated 70 percent of industrial production. Authorities planned to continue restraining monetary growth and external debt accumulation.

Reinforcing the economic stabilization program were plans to restructure public finances radically. In particular, the plans included reducing the absorption or intermediation of resources through the state budget, intensifying economic competition, continuing the liberalization of prices, restructuring or allowing bankrupt loss-making state enterprises to fail, developing an efficient and competitive financial system, and reforming the social security system while providing an adequate social safety net.

Finally, the government aimed to reduce state-owned assets to less than 50 percent of total assets in the competitive sector by 1993. Given its precarious balance-of-payments position, the success on this front depended in no small part on its ability to attract foreign investment. Authorities were hoping that foreign direct investment in 1991 would total between $800 million and $1 billion — an amount two to three times greater than that achieved in 1990. Still, without a rescheduling, even that amount would cover only one-fifth to one-quarter of the foreign exchange required for debt-service payments.

Privatization Program Early efforts to sell off large state-owned enterprises were more successful in Hungary than in any other Central or East European country with some 10 having been accomplished through March 1991 for a total value of almost $100 million. There was also considerable success with "spontaneous" privatization of medium-sized enterprises, initiated by enterprise management and workers in tandem with outside investors and not central government officials. Early negative reaction against such deals was muted by the establishment of the State Property Agency (SPA), which was charged with their oversight and regulation. Through the first quarter of 1991, some 50 to 70 "spontaneous" privatization joint ventures had been approved by the SPA with a total estimated asset value of nearly $300 million. Outright sales of another 41 enterprises were approved with a total estimated asset value of nearly $200 million.

The Hungarian government set for itself the goal that state-owned assets should decline to less than 50 percent of total assets in the competitive sector by 1993 through an ambitious privatization program that would rely mainly on market means: direct auction or sale. The program itself comprised four basic approaches:

Small-scale privatization Transfer of some 10,000 retail shops and restaurants to private owners by the end of 1992. By mid-1991, this program had moved somewhat more slowly than expected.

Large-scale enterprises Groups of about 20 larger state enterprises would be divested several times a year through the SPA. Some of the enterprises would require restructuring prior to divestiture.

"Spontaneous" privatizations would be promoted, and indeed would be the flagship of the privatization effort. Spontaneous privatizations might be initiated by enterprise managers, as long as outside investors could be found that would increase the capital of the firm. They also could be initiated by outside investors. Oversight, including the power to require valuations and veto proposed deals, would be exercised by the SPA.

Free transfers of state property were contemplated only on a limited scale to local authorities and the social security fund. One quasi-exception to this rule occurred in the case of owners whose property was confiscated by the communists after 1949. The government planned to offer these persons and their heirs compensation bonds which could be exchanged for shares in privatized enterprises. The stated goal was that the compensation be partial, even symbolic.

Secession and privatization of internal units of state-owned enterprises also was envisioned. These divestitures could be accomplished either through public offerings or spontaneous privatizations. Several funds were established to offer preferential credits to potential entrepreneurs wishing to buy shares in privatized enterprises. Proceeds from the sale of state-owned enterprises were to be used to reduce state debt.

3 Czechoslovakia

After the Soviet invasion of 1968, Czechoslovakia's communist regime stood out among the Soviet satellite states for its rigid adherence to central planning and command control. Socialist decentralization, which had loosened the reins of state ownership and control in Hungary and to some extent in Poland, was almost unknown. More than 95 percent of the nation's output was produced directly by the state, the highest proportion in Central and Eastern Europe (see table 10 in Fischer, Ch. 13). Nearly all agricultural land remained in the hands of state farms and collectives, in contrast to Poland, where agricultural land ownership remained largely private. Virtually all housing was publicly owned, in contrast to Hungary's nascent but growing private housing market (see Telgarsky and Struyk 1990). Czechoslovakia supplied relatively heavy machinery and other industrial goods to the Soviet bloc, which in 1989 accounted for over 60 percent of its exports.

Elected in the spring of 1990, the new democratic government of President Havel inherited an economy that was relatively stable, mitigating the immediate pressure for economic reform. The debt burden of $8 billion was relatively modest. Inflation during the late 1980s was less than 2 percent per year; unemployment remained negligible. The new government's goal was to lead the country toward a market economy by means of carefully sequenced reform. The program was defined in three basic phases. The first was creation of the legislative and institutional framework required for a market system to function. Much was accomplished on that front in 1990. The second phase was comprehensive liberalization of the price system, which began with a bang on January 1, 1991. The third was opening the economy to competition by liberalizing trade, moving to make the currency freely convertible, and simultaneously beginning massive privatization of state-owned assets. That phase, also begun in January 1991, was to continue for the next several years.

Czechoslovakia was singular among the three Central European countries in 1990 in that it enjoyed relatively mild inflation, unemployment and recession. Its slower pace to implement economic reforms, a relatively stable economy, and its small foreign debt added to its relatively strong economic position. After a series of deficits over previous years, the government ran a small budget surplus. Wage growth was low (2.5 to 3 percent for the year), and unemployment was kept to less than 1 percent of the work force. But the effects of preliminary moves to liberalize prices and rising financial pressures began to make themselves felt by the end of the year. Removal of retail subsidies on food and the pass-through of the effects of two devaluations in the form of higher retail prices for petroleum products contributed to an increase of 20 percent in retail prices. GDP fell by 4.3 percent for the year as a whole.

Financial pressures began to mount. By the end of the year, the government again had become a net borrower from the national banking system. A convertible currency trade surplus of $419 million in 1989 turned to a deficit of $219 million in 1990, driven by higher imports. Imports from socialist countries fell by 33 percent, while exports fell by 37 percent. The balance of payments deteriorated sharply as authorities financed a rising hard currency trade deficit by drawing down foreign exchange reserves. By the end of 1990, gross hard currency reserves had fallen to the equivalent of just three weeks of imports.

The government's main accomplishments in 1990 were to maintain tight reins on fiscal and monetary policies and to pass some of the laws that would serve as the institutional framework for private enterprise. Among these were laws permitting virtually all types of private sector activities, providing for taxation of small enterprises, setting out procedures for establishment of joint-stock companies, and allowing 100 percent foreign ownership in Czechoslovak companies. In September, Czechoslovakia became a member of the IMF and the World Bank. With the help of those institutions, it formulated an ambitious economic reform and restructuring program that was launched at the beginning of 1991.

Initiation of the program was immediately preceded by exchange rate unification at a competitive level, which amounted to a substantial devaluation. Virtually all wholesale and retail prices were liberalized January 1; quantitative trade restrictions were largely eliminated and current account convertibility established. Energy prices were raised, and the effects of higher oil import costs and devaluation passed through, as Czechoslovakia moved to a hard currency basis in paying for oil imports. The government maintained restrictive fiscal and monetary policies and instituted taxes penalizing enterprises that increased wages faster than an index of prices. Implementing regulations for an economic competition law were to be approved by mid-year to reduce the scope for local cartels or monopolies. Financial sector and tax reform were to be completed by year-end as was complete liberalization of private sector wage determination.

A program of rapid small-scale privatization through auctions was initiated in January 1991. A law was passed in February providing the legal framework for privatization of large-scale enterprises. A bankruptcy law enabling orderly restructuring or liquidation of those state enterprises unable to operate efficiently in the new market environment was also to be adopted by mid-year.

Privatization Program It was not surprising that by mid-1991 Czechoslovakia had achieved the least progress among all three Central European countries in privatization of its enormous state sector. In spite of early successes in small-scale privatization in which bids quickly rose substantially above initial offering prices, there had been little progress in privatizing medium and large-scale enterprises. Moreover, the government appeared unsure of exactly how to proceed.

Although the program for privatization of larger state-owned enterprises was still in design, some of its outline was known. The preliminary step would be to encourage the restructuring of enterprises into smaller, more competitive units and to register them as corporations (joint-stock companies). The resulting enterprises probably then would be grouped roughly as follows:

Public enterprises (25 percent): It was thought that approximately one-quarter of the current portfolio of 4,000 state-owned enterprises either could not or should not be privatized, because they were natural monopolies, because the state had decided to retain control for "strategic" reasons, or because they were bankrupt. It was estimated that the weakest 10 percent of state-owned enterprises probably could not be made viable under the market system and would be liquidated.

Public sale or auction (25 percent): The strongest of the state-owned enterprises would be offered for sale using market means of direct sale or auction. Virtually no limitations would be placed on foreign participation. Enterprises themselves would be encouraged to submit their own privatization plans, especially when they could find a foreign partner.

Voucher distribution (50 percent): The remaining state-owned assets would be auctioned via a "voucher" distribution procedure, as yet to be determined. The government appeared to prefer the concept of investment or mutual funds in which citizens would be allowed to invest in exchange for their vouchers. Several such funds would be set up by the government although they also could incorporate privately. Under consideration was a fee for registration of the vouchers and immediate trading of shares in the investment funds. Foreign investors would be allowed to buy in as majority shareholders in privatized enterprises and to set up wholly-owned subsidiaries.

The government's plans for mass privatization would appear to be at odds with the recent passage of laws providing for the return to former owners of smaller properties and small and medium-sized businesses expropriated by the communists after 1948. Former owners and their heirs were not supposed to receive the benefits of improvements made over the past 30 to 40 years, although how this rule would be applied in practice was problematic. The decision to reinstate property ownership rather than compensate for its loss at minimum could spell significant delay for implementation of the voucher scheme. Implementation was complicated further by the allocation of responsibility for the bulk of privatization to the two republics while retaining a smaller portfolio within the federal government.

4   Constraints to Privatization

The task of privatizing the Central European economies is monumental. The most basic constraint is resistance from workers and management concerned by the prospect of layoffs and plant closures. But even if the political will to proceed is sustained, privatization faces numerous financial, economic, and legal hurdles. Among them are the burden of large enterprise liabilities and contingent liabilities. The limited domestic savings of the economy narrows the range of choices considerably. Establishing effective ownership control over privatized enterprises is an essential prerequisite to the creation of functioning market economies. But there is little historical precedent for how to do so when starting from centrally planned economies with almost no private ownership or entrepreneurial class (Rausser and Simon, Ch. 14). These issues and the manner in which Central European governments are confronting them are examined here.

Liabilities and Contingent Liabilities   Enterprise liabilities and contingent liabilities, to the extent that they are known and can be associated directly with the enterprise, typically include debts, pension obligations, severance pay promises, the requirement to bring productive processes up to environmental code, prior ownership claims, etc. In theory, the stream of expected costs from such liabilities should be subtracted from the expected income stream from assets when the firm's present value is calculated. Indeed, in many cases, the offer prices might be zero or negative; that is, with existing liabilities intact, many enterprises are undoubtedly insolvent. The common practice in the West, however, has been for the state to absorb a good portion of liabilities during restructuring, prior to the enterprise's sale. Debts are absorbed by the state or written down by creditors. Pensions of past employees, too, often become the state's responsibility. Severance pay promises and other contingent liabilities are typically negotiated on a case-by-case basis.

Nonetheless, separation of liabilities and the cost streams that they entail from the income flows necessary to meet them can be risky. Consider the case of shell companies arising from "spontaneous" privatizations in Hungary. There, internal units of some enterprises have been hived off to be sold separately from the parent shell, taking most of the assets with them and leaving the liabilities behind. This situation is potentially dangerous for banks that have lent heavily to the parent company, many of which are alleged to be continuing to record income from non-performing loans.[2]   Likewise, governments cannot afford to strip themselves of the income-generating assets of the state-owned enterprises and retain their liabilities without substituting some other form of revenue (McKinnon, Ch. 7). And if enterprises are to be privatized through free distribution of shares, no revenue will accrue from their sale.

Still, the state might be in a better position than individual investors or the enterprises themselves to renegotiate the terms of such liabilities and contingent liabilities as pensions of former employees, promises of large severance payments, or prior ownership claims. In Hungary, for example, the state has attempted to assert the principle that prior ownership claims will be settled by partial compensation in the form of state bonds that can be exchanged for enterprise shares. The state may also have a general interest in limiting the financial damage from bankruptcies if the banking system is characterized by portfolios with a high proportion of bad loans. Revenue from the sale of restructured enterprises can help defray increased costs to the state of absorbing their financial liabilities. It is noteworthy in this regard that the Hungarians plan to apply revenue from the sale of state-owned enterprises to reducing the state debt.

One reason to disencumber state-owned enterprises of their liabilities prior to offering them for sale is that following price liberalization and other economic reforms to create market economies, many very likely could be profitable, if past liabilities could be written down or off. Firms are likely to be in this category in cases where the type of activity, like production for the retail consumer market, was not favored ideologically under the old regime or where the enterprises were loaded down with debt as a means to balance central government fiscal accounts. Without financial cleanup and restructuring including new investment there will be no buyers. These enterprises will have to be liquidated for their cash value. But this argument rests on the presumption that potentially viable firms can be distinguished from those that cannot survive, prior to subjecting them to the discipline of free and competitive markets.

The Polish privatization plan states that enterprise restructuring (including new investment) is only to take place after privatization by the private investor. In those cases where private investors cannot be found, restructuring can occur once it has been determined that the enterprise's activities can be made profitable in the market environment. Czech and Slovak authorities also explicitly recognize that many enterprises will simply have to be closed, but that others may be made profitable with financial cleanup and new investment. Still, under the best of circumstances, the determination of enterprise "viability" in the context of mass privatization — when private owners "cannot be found" — will be difficult. Experts in enterprise valuation report that tiny differences in assumptions can lead to enormous variation in results. The lack of capital markets that

---

[2] The Hungarian State Property Agency is actively reviewing this problem.

can be used to place a value on similar assets presents a distinct difficulty. But valuation cannot be avoided in the culling of those enterprises which should be liquidated from those in which new investment is to be contemplated.

Scarcity of Capital   Domestic demand for state-owned enterprises, if they are sold through public offerings, will be constrained by the availability of domestic savings with which to buy them (Lipton and Sachs 1990b). All three governments are exploring innovative financial mechanisms to mobilize foreign and domestic savings that can be applied to the purchase of equity in state-owned enterprises as a means to compensate for scarce domestic capital. Hungary, in particular, has had success with its program to encourage investments by foreign firms, reportedly netting some $350 million in foreign exchange inflows in 1990 alone. This foreign investment was facilitated by the government's encouragement of privatization joint ventures initiated by workers and management or by outside foreign investors, subject to the oversight and veto power of the State Property Agency. But for a variety of reasons relating to uncertainty during the transition period and questions of ultimate corporate control, foreign participation in the privatization of state-owned enterprises has not fulfilled expectations in Central Europe.

One means to mobilize domestic capital is for governments to exchange income from state-owned enterprises for income from loans extended to citizens to buy shares in those enterprises. In direct loan schemes, governments themselves extend credit to citizens for the purchase of shares in privatized companies. Domestic investors finance down payments on the loans, representing, say, 10 percent of the value of the shares to be purchased. The interesting aspect of direct loans is that they should allow fuller divestiture through sale rather than free distribution of shares. Since such loans are extended by the state to purchase enterprises already owned by the state, they have no direct monetary impact. The down payments and income from the loans may be used to help recapitalize restructured activities in the enterprise or to cover government expenditures; the apportionment should probably depend on whether and to what degree government absorbs the extant liabilities of the enterprise. By requiring down payments, and debt payments, in exchange for shares in state-owned enterprises, greater reliance on direct loan schemes would insure that investors acquired a vested interest in the performance of the enterprises. The worker buy-out leasing agreements in Poland are one context in which direct loan schemes have been utilized in Central Europe.

The alternative is free distribution of shares in large state-owned enterprises, a privatization method contemplated by all three governments although to a much lesser extent in Hungary than in the other two. The two principal methods are to target allocations of shares to specific recipients and to distribute them equally to all adult citizens. One targeted allocation scheme is to grant a fixed proportion of shares to workers in the enterprise to be privatized, as in Poland. This scheme is attractive mainly for political reasons, since it presumably would reduce worker opposition to privatization. Allocation of enterprise shares for the capitalization of social security or pension funds is another means to distribute shares to targeted recipients. This allocation is planned in Hungary and has been under serious discussion in Poland. The attractiveness of the idea is that, as they became sufficiently capitalized, the funds could reduce the liability of the state for direct entitlement payments. This allocation might be a *quid pro quo* for state absorption of enterprise pension liabilities.

Enterprise shares may also be given away directly to the population. In mass distribution schemes, vouchers would be distributed free to all adult citizens and could be exchanged either for shares in state-owned enterprises or for shares in investment trusts which, in turn, would own shares in those enterprises. With some variations, it is this alternative that both Poland and Czechoslovakia plan to use to achieve rapid and egalitarian privatization of large-scale enterprises. In Poland, the government plans to distribute 60 percent of the equity in 400 large-scale enterprises to between five and twenty investment funds. Shares in the investment funds will be distributed equally among all adult citizens who will not be allowed to trade them for at least two years. Share ownership will be concentrated by insuring that at least one third of the shares in each company will be held by one or another of the investment funds.

Finally, both Poland and Czechoslovakia plan to retain a substantial proportion of productive assets within the state sector, at least for the foreseeable future. In Poland, ownership of 30 percent of shares in mass-privatized enterprises will be retained by the state. The Czechs and Slovaks apparently intend to retain about a quarter of productive enterprises within the public sector. In Hungary, by way of contrast, of 2,200 companies under the State Property Agency's wing, authorities plan to retain only about 100 within the public sector.

Ownership Oversight and Control All three countries plan to "commercialize" their state-owned enterprises, meaning that they will be constituted as corporate entities under the control of independent boards of directors. In practice, although commercialization is only the first step in the privatization process, implementation has been slow, because so far it has moved forward mainly on a voluntary basis. In both Poland and Hungary, commercialization also involves the re-assertion of property ownership by the state at the expense of claims by workers and management.[3] Proponents of mass commercialization argue that it is necessary to avoid lengthy and protracted negotiations, firm-by-firm, with workers and management over the terms of privatization. But the political resistance is strong, from workers and management concerned about layoffs and enterprise closure. This concern was underscored in August 1991, when the Polish government began to reassess its entire privatization strategy

---

[3]In Czechoslovakia, where management control was never really decentralized to the enterprise level, the issue is less salient.

following the closure of a single tractor factory that had employed over 12,000 workers.

Once commercialization is achieved, if the enterprise is then sold, corporate control is established quite quickly. It is more difficult to do so when shares are to be distributed *en masse* to the public at large. The problem is that by dispersing ownership widely among citizens, voucher privatizations would not establish the kind of concentrated ownership and control usually associated with improved management. Several ideas were put forward to the Polish government to circumvent this problem (Lipton and Sachs 1990b). Among these were allocation of shares to social security funds, to banks, or to "core" groups of investors. Each of the proposals was intended to resolve the same dilemma: that under voucher distributions, dominant shareholders would be unlikely to emerge.

The only proposal which survived the negotiation process, at least for immediate implementation, was the recommendation to form several closed-end mutual funds (or "investment funds") to take over effective corporate control of the large enterprises. Enterprise shares would be allocated directly to the funds by government. As the plan ultimately evolved, the funds came to resemble *Treuhandanstalt,* the holding company charged with privatization of state-owned enterprises in eastern Germany. Professionals would be drawn from the ranks of successful entrepreneurs in Western countries (western Germany in the case of Treuhand) to manage the funds. Differences arose in that the Polish investment funds would hold 60 percent of the equity in large Polish enterprises in trust for the population at large, and 30 percent for the government itself rather than 100 percent for the government, as in Germany. The other difference was that while the *Treuhand* was specifically charged with responsibility for eventual sale of its portfolio of firms, just when and how the Polish investment funds would be expected to remove themselves from the role of dominant shareholder was unclear.

What is ultimately to be done with the government's 30 percent share in mass-privatized enterprises was also unknown. But the dispersion of 60 percent of enterprise shares among several investment funds would probably make the purchase by outside investors of a controlling stake in individual enterprises a difficult proposition unless the government sold its 30 percent stake to the investors at the same time. Although presumably domestic investors would be more willing than foreigners to attempt to control an enterprise through buying into a minority shareholder position, with 30 percent of the shares in each mass-privatized enterprise held by the government itself and another 10 percent by workers in the enterprise, it would be difficult for outside investors to be assured of ultimate corporate control without a majority stake. In any event, sale of an investment fund's stake in any enterprise apparently would have to be approved by the government on a case-by-case basis, according to officials intimate with the negotiations over procedures.

The question of how corporate control is to be established over the investment funds themselves, especially given the two-year prohibition on trading by fund shareholders, has also arisen; presumably, in the interval, capital would have to be raised by issuing new shares. The hope is that foreign industrial concerns and investment banks can be induced to buy into and take over management of at least some of the investment funds. The formation of "core" groups of domestic investors that would combine with foreign investors is also a possibility. But, again, investors might be reticent to commit new money to an attempt to gain corporate control of an investment fund as long as government and workers combined continued to control 40 percent of the shares of each enterprise within that fund's portfolio. This reticence, in turn, could severely limit the capacity of the funds to raise the capital necessary for restructuring of otherwise "viable" enterprises.

One means to increase the attractiveness of that proportion of enterprise shares (or investment fund shares) that is to be offered for sale, as opposed to being given away, would be to develop the practice of preferential shares. In the past, non-voting shares were issued on the New York Stock Exchange to raise capital while retaining concentrated corporate control by allocating reduced voting rights to shareholders not expected to influence enterprise management. In Central European countries, it should be possible to adapt this concept to enhance the voting rights of investors who purchase shares rather than receiving them through mass distribution or targeted allocation schemes. The simplest would be to distribute non-voting shares to non-paying recipients. If this distribution were not feasible, it should still be possible to offer enhanced voting rights to both foreign and domestic investors who purchased new issues of shares in mass-privatized enterprises or in investment funds which controlled those enterprises. This idea apparently is implicit in the structure of the intended Executive Boards of the Polish investment funds, which would give a controlling number of seats to core fund management groups.

17 Strategies for the Transition

Arnold C. Harberger

Reaching back into our accumulated economic knowledge may shed light on some of the issues involved in Eastern European economic reform. One of the crucial issues in the transformation of the Eastern European economies is the speed of reform and restructuring. How fast or how slow should the process be? On that issue quite a lot of work has been accomplished in the area of trade liberalization. The results of studies to date of trade liberalization processes are quite easy to summarize: ten years is too long and one year is too short. Something in between is needed; perhaps something like five years. A second lesson from trade liberalization processes is that it is important to move ahead decisively. To be tentative or pusillanimous is disastrous. As long as reform proceeds steadily in a decisive and credible manner, five years is not a bad time frame to think of. Ten years is too long, because credibility is lost, and the opposition has time to organize.

There is also a more technical lesson that we learn from the theory of trade liberalization, concerning the benefits of what is called a "radial reduction of distortions," by which an economy that is highly distorted (in terms of its links to the rest of the world) can be transformed into one that is much less distorted. For the purposes of this chapter, one can think of free trade, or something close to it, as being the goal. Consider an example in which there are four importable sectors of the economy, each with a different level of restrictions, that are to be liberalized. The first step in the liberalization process — and this point is again well-documented — is to get the water out of the tariffs while simultaneously converting the non-tariff barriers into something like equivalent tariffs. Once the decks are thus cleared, the next step is to reduce the levels of the separate restrictions. What happens if the process moves sector by sector, first liberalizing sector 1, then sector 2, etc.? When each sector is liberalized, the demand for foreign currency increases, and the real exchange rate rises. This rising real exchange rate is an essential part of the process, because that is what attracts resources into high comparative advantage industries. If the real exchange rate did not respond, the process would not be working properly. So as the restrictions are eliminated in sector 1, resources are called into all of the tradeable sectors including 2, 3, and 4. Next, the restrictions in sector 2 are eliminated, calling resources into sectors 1, 3, and 4 plus other tradeable sectors, and so on down the line. If these four sectors are addressed sequentially, resources in each of the four sectors receive one big signal to go elsewhere (through the sharp reduction of that sector's import barriers), plus three small signals to come back into the sector (through the real-exchange-rate effects that ensue when barriers are reduced in the other three sectors). Obviously, these signals are contradictory. What is necessary is to reduce the restrictions *pari passu* in all the sectors, thus giving signals in a single direction all the time.

This model of radial reduction of distortions is an excellent model for the Eastern European countries to follow in trying to move from a completely distorted price vector to a new set of prices that derives from the world market (i.e., world market prices for tradeable goods, and for non-tradeables, equilibrium prices that are compatible with the world price vector). There are useful analogies to be drawn between the Eastern European economies and highly trade-restrictive economies in the Western world. Therein lies the relevance of the above lessons, derived from the study of how to liberalize highly restricted economies. These lessons include those that refer to timing as well as those that indicate the advisability of a radial reduction of distortions. One of the reasons why instantaneous adoption of the world price vector probably would not be wise in these countries is that it is very likely that one-third to one-half (or even more) of the industries of any of these economies would not be currently viable if exposed to world prices at one fell swoop. It is far better to "program" an adjustment through something simulating a radial reduction of existing distortions. If properly operated it could also have beneficial results for the public treasury, for an early step in the process would entail converting into tariffs (which **do** raise revenue) the whole list of existing prohibitions and other explicit or implicit quantitative restrictions that do not raise any revenue.

On the issue of public versus private operation of industries, there seem to be a few tremors suggesting that perhaps the public sector can be just as efficient as the private sector. While occasionally one really does find efficient public sector enterprises, experience suggests that one only finds them in places where the government encourages the enterprises to behave independently. Many governments fail to resist the temptation to use public sector enterprises as instruments aimed at other policy objectives. Typically, public sector enterprises are asked to take the government off the hook by not firing their workers, by not dropping bad product lines, by paying higher wages to their low-skilled workers, and by keeping executive salaries in the public enterprises low (i.e., in line with those of bureaucrats and elected public sector officials). In short, it should be recognized that public sector enterprises suffer from serious endemic disadvantages that are very hard to overcome; hence overall, the pressure in favor of privatization is undoubtedly wise.

The methods by which privatization is implemented, however, are of critical importance. The whole program can be thrown into jeopardy by taking a few steps in the wrong direction. One very serious risk, for example, is that of "giving away the store". If a perception arises that a government is not only selling the country to "those damned foreigners" but is virtually **giving** it away (i.e., receiving far too low a price), that government is probably not long for this world. Perpetuating monopoly might not be as incandescent a subject, but certainly it is one of the risks about which economists should be worried. Yet another problem is that of letting the wolves eat the sheep: the poor little stockholders, to whom a lot of shares may be distributed at the beginning, do not quite know what to do with them and could easily fall prey to people who can exploit their lack of knowledge and experience in financial matters. Perpetuating inefficiency through inadequate corporate control is still another problem.

It is difficult to foresee which risks are the greatest in any particular case. Any one of the risks discussed above could prove to be the nemesis of any given privatization scheme. Experts can each invent ten or fifteen different scenarios, all of which can be made to sound plausible, but which scenario will be right? The objective situation calls for a mixed strategy. As Fischer (Ch. 13) argues, no single strategy can be justified given the level of uncertainty and the high cost of failure if any one strategy goes wrong.

The idea of giving enterprises to the people may be a good idea, but it surely is not wise to give each individual shares of each and every enterprise. It is preferable to give the people shares in mutual funds rather than in individual firms. The idea of setting aside some blocks of shares in certain privatized enterprises to fund a long-term pension scheme makes a tremendous amount of sense. Indeed, there is a wonderful example of this idea actually in operation in Chile, where it has worked extremely well to the benefit of all the participants. Mutual funds can also help in solving the management problems of enterprises, although mutual funds are certainly not good hands-on managers. Holding companies would be of benefit in this regard. Perhaps these holding companies could have a self-destruct component built into them, so that there exists from the very beginning some safeguard against their perpetuating themselves.

Another idea, that of the government holding back shares for later sale, makes a great deal of sense. The market valuation of all the land, buildings, stocks (all the marketable assets that together make up the economy) of the Chilean economy in late 1973 equalled only about one year's national income. Yet, by 1979, the corresponding value was at least five years' national income, in spite of the fact that the national income in the meantime had gone up quite dramatically. Between 1973 and 1979, therefore, the capital gains perceived by entities within the Chilean economy amounted to about one initial (1973-level) national income **per year** over that entire period.

In the Eastern European countries, the first assets are going to be sold at low prices — and for good reason. If the governments behave as representatives of all the people (as they should), then it seems to be the course of wisdom to save important shares of these assets to be sold later in this process. In addition to recognizing that some of the firms that are sold are going to go bust, one should realize that others are going to bloom and multiply in value by 10, 15, or 100. All of these considerations give a sound basis for a gradual rather than an instantaneous divestment of public sector assets.

To sum up, economic analysis strongly supports the idea of a mixed strategy of reform. The programs of several of the Eastern European governments, Poland and Czechoslovakia in particular, have in fact followed such a mixed strategy to some degree.

18 Institutions and the Transition to a Market Economy

András Nagy

The institutional aspects of the transition to a market economy in Central and Eastern Europe have been largely neglected in economic theory and in the practice of economic policy. How and why are institutions created? Why are they very adaptive but, at the same time, very conservative? Why are they so evidently resilient in changing circumstances? Answers to these and similar questions are obviously very important for the success of the transition, but thus far they have been inadequate. Western economic theories are instructive in this respect, especially social or collective choice theory and institutional economics. As Eastern Europe's situation as well as its history are so different from the West's, however, adaptation and application of these theories will have to take into account these differences.

Recently, observers have been surprised at how quickly mass demonstrations, revolts and revolutions caused the collapse of communist one-party rule and of noncompetitive, planned economic systems in much of Central and Eastern Europe. The expectation was that this wave could not be resisted for long in Romania, Bulgaria, Serbia and then in the Soviet Union, Cuba, and China. There was a widespread feeling of liberation, happiness, and euphoria linked to great expectations of political democracy, pluralism, and the results of social and economic changes.

The mood equally unexpectedly is so different today: one cannot find much happiness (even if the joy of changes, of freedom, of hope lingers on) but rather a general disillusionment, because many of the expectations have not been realized.

The author acknowledges financial support from the Center for Institutional Reform and the Informal Sector.

301

There is much stronger resistance to change than expected, and economic conditions have deteriorated considerably while disgust with political quarrelling has spread rapidly among the people. In both cases, the unforeseen nature of the developments was closely related to the lack of understanding of the resilience of institutions, which have resisted fundamental change and adapted only superficially in response to attempts at systemic change.

While the collapse of the communist regimes has been sudden, there was a long period of preparation leading to the widespread and deep social and economic crisis. All the Kremlinologists, East European experts and comparative systems economists without exception made a great error of judgement: they confused stability with immobility. The immobility of the Soviet-type societies, stubbornly resisting reform, was regarded by many as stability, while it became a source of destructive instability. The more immobile these societies were the more unstable they became. Symptoms of the growing crisis included misallocation and misuse of resources, lack of competitiveness, slow adaptability, stagnation, deterioration of living conditions (especially with regard to the environment), shortages of all kinds in parallel with wastefulness and squandering, and a deterioration of worker morale. These symptoms were well recognized not only by outside observers but within these countries as well. Still, most reform efforts failed, leading to the conspicuous failure of the system.

The resistance to radical, fundamental change is closely related to the institutional structure of the communist parties and states. This structure has evolved and changed considerably over the last forty years, but much of this change — in many cases against the wishes of both reformers and state planners — went in the wrong direction: instead of curing the sicknesses of the system, it aggravated them.

One can find a striking contrast between the first and last decade of the postwar East European economies. The first period was characterized by sudden and extreme nationalizations, rapid industrialization, the expropriation of peasant farmers, and the creation of great estates (the so-called cooperatives), followed by relatively fast adaptation to the new conditions. In the last decade, however, rigidity, conservatism, and stubborn resistance to change and adaptation were prevalent. The best example of this resistance is the failure of the implementation of economic reforms, recognized as necessary already twenty years ago.

Following the works of Mancur Olson (1965, 1982), this pattern can be explained in terms of the theory of interest groups (Nagy 1989, 1991). The double destruction of the Nazi political structure and the short-lived democratic system of the postwar period eliminated most existing special-interest organizations and other "distributional coalitions," clearing the way for the radical structural changes introduced by the communists. This destruction made possible the coalition of liberal, peasant, social democratic and communist parties in the semi-democratic conditions of the time. As a consequence, the new organizations and institutions had a strongly encompassing character, representing not a narrow but a large segment of the society.

As the communist parties gained complete control of the East European countries, a gradual transition could be observed. Economic and political organizations, state and local bureaucracies, and the communist parties evolved into special-interest organizations and collusions, losing their encompassing character. Monopolies were created in an historically unprecedented dimension in industry and in services. Through mergers of agricultural cooperatives, large estates came into existence with the intent to eliminate competition. A strongly protectionist, autarkic trade policy subsidized import substitution. Elimination of competition was of course consistent with the interests of industrial and service enterprises as evidenced by the absence of effective resistance to these measures. One of the most influential lobbies emerging in the cold-war period was the military. By creating war hysteria, it succeeded in receiving an enormous share of the national product and created a large sector of the economy in which economic efficiency could be completely neglected.

These special-interest organizations became powerful lobbies, which did not simply obey central plan directives, but increasingly came to influence and shape them. As the various industrial, agricultural, and regional lobbies became more and more numerous and powerful, all of the negative effects so well described by Olson occurred. As the distributional struggle among the lobbies increased, attention was focused more on grabbing a larger slice of society's pie than on making the pie larger. By fighting for funds for unprofitable investments and unjustified military expenditures and by lobbying for subsidies, favorable prices, high wages, large bonuses for managers and big Soviet contracts for outdated, low-quality products, they not only obtained a larger slice but in fact reduced the pie, i.e. the GDP, itself.

As the original hierarchical structure of the socialist economies evolved into this complex network of interest groups, the task of the central authorities became more and more to reach compromises among squabbling "feudal lords". In this distributional struggle, the well-organized military lobby usually received first priority on resources, while education, health care, and environmental concerns suffered.

Some of the basic features of the institutional system inherited by the Central and East European societies merit review:

A nearly perfect monopolization of the market and total protectionism in foreign trade   Competition was excluded not only in such natural monopolies as oil or aluminum production, but in potentially competitive markets as well. Even butcher shops and candy stores belonged to trusts that monopolized these markets. Foreign trade was completely under state monopoly, and quantitative restrictions limited most imports. The aim of monopolization and protectionism was to eliminate competition, as it was regarded not only harmful for planning, but also inefficient. Practice proved the opposite of Marxist theory: the elimination of competition served only the interests of inefficient producers and made them inefficient if they had not been so before.

A neglect of consumer interests In the absence of competition, the producer may completely disregard the demands of the consumer. Under the conditions of an economy of shortage, described in great detail by Kornai (1980), a seller's market prevails which further strengthens the position of the producer. The symptoms are well known: queues, poor quality, little variety in goods, and empty shelves. Consumers had no influential organizations to defend their interests against producers and other groups. When free markets are eliminated, the conflict between consumers' and producers' interests is resolved by politics in which the more easily organized producers have the upper hand, as recognized by collective choice theory.

One-party rule, state ownership, over-politicization, and supremacy of military consideration in decision making An overwhelming majority of all property belonged to the state: natural resources, financial capital, land, schools, theaters, hospitals — everything! There is much discussion in the literature of what state ownership actually has meant: was the state a real owner? Was it a good or bad owner? If we follow Cooter's (Ch. 5) definition of what ownership means: a right to use, develop, transform, destroy, sell, etc., one can say the state exercised an unlimited right to do all these things, with certain limitations on selling its property. It could sell plots of land or houses to private persons, but it could not sell a factory or a mine, because private or foreign ownership of these organizations was prohibited. It could not sell, not because its rights were limited, but because no buyers were allowed.

The state was a "bad" and a "good" owner of capital at the same time. It was a bad owner because most of its possessions were misallocated, misused, and insufficiently safeguarded. But it was a "good" owner, because it protected the interests of its enterprises in a very effective way: by the elimination of both domestic and international competition. This feature of state ownership was obviously harmful for consumers and for growth, but it served well the short-term interests of the lobbies mentioned above. The consequence of one-party rule, Soviet dominance, over-politicization and over-militarization was that political and security considerations dominated all decisions. Politicians, the military, and the secret police were above the law. Arbitrariness ruled, and criticism was silenced.

A reform movement With the growing discontent of the population and with the growing influence of the special-interest organizations, reform activity developed with cyclical hopes and failures. It was in a sense a liberation movement of the enterprises from the tutelage of the central authorities. However, their demands were rather ambiguous: they wanted to have as much independence as possible, but at the same time they did not want to lose their monopolistic position and their protection from foreign competition. As a result, the half-hearted reform measures that were enacted did not increase efficiency and, hence, did not strengthen the political position of those who favored them. One should not forget that a certain kind of efficiency pressure existed in the hierarchical planning system: the central authorities demanded larger outputs and offered lower inputs than the enterprises offered and demanded. If this pressure is eliminated, as the large enterprises desire, the result can be even lower efficiency, unless the stronger pressures of competitive markets are introduced. The optimal solution for monopolies can be the worst solution for consumers and for economic growth.

The remarkable slowness and inadequacy of structural changes in Central and Eastern Europe are not only the consequences of the failures and inexperience of the new governments' economic policies, but they are in great part due to the rigidity of institutions and to their characteristics mentioned above.

The main areas of this resistance to change are important to address:

Resistance to demonopolization and to opening It is easy to create monopolies but extremely difficult to break them up and to "create" competition. Even if they are broken up administratively, the firms previously comprising the monopoly can still engage in collusion, which is difficult to stop. Foreign direct investment may not be of much help, as investment in these monopolies is often considered more profitable than establishing new competing firms. It is luckily difficult for the new governments formally to resist formal trade liberalization, but — under the influence of the big lobbies behind them — they learn quickly how to build non-tariff barriers. The desire for increased inflows of foreign capital through the so-called "selling out" of national property conflicts with the aim of creating a new national middle class through distributing shares of state-owned enterprises to the public.

Resistance to diminished state intervention It was widely expected that with the introduction of a pluralistic democratic system, intervention by governments in economic matters would be reduced and a rapid decentralization and privatization would ensue. No such development can be observed: there is no decrease in the budget share of the GNP; neither has the extremely heavy tax burden diminished. Even though there is general agreement that bureaucratization in the socialist system reached incredible proportions, state offices have not closed but have merely changed names, and there is no unemployment among civil servants. Contrary to expectations, privatization has increased the power and prestige of the state authorities: they decide what assets to sell, at what prices, and to whom. They "create" the new bourgeoisie, which provides great opportunities for political discrimination and for corruption. The structural change in production, the reorientation of trade (especially because of the collapse of East Bloc trade), the unbalanced budget, the enormous debt burden, inflation — all call for central regulation and intervention, which instead of diminishing has increased.

There is a strong resistance to demilitarization and to the abolition of the secret police and "covert activities". An unexpectedly strong nationalistic hostility broke out in nearly all these countries after the collapse of the old regime. Chauvinistic jingoism seems to be the last refuge of the extreme left, joining the extreme right. In the power vacuum created by the collapse of the previous security system, they have succeeded in influencing government policies with the support of the military lobby. Secret services were not dissolved, and their archives were neither disclosed nor abolished. On whose behalf the secret services will use their resources remains an open question.

Resistance to efficiency pressures Those with an interest in improving efficiency are weak and unorganized while forces with vested interests in resisting any efficiency improvements are relatively strong and well organized. It is a hard task both for the managers and for the workers to change the production structure, technological processes, product quality, or orientation toward markets. It is especially hard to raise productivity, to decrease featherbedding, to create unemployment, and to re-educate the personnel. The reduction or abolition of subsidies and of protection from foreign competition is very uncomfortable, especially if a firm benefitted from them for decades. All these hardships could be overcome if the interests for an improvement of efficiency and for adaptation were sufficiently strong and organized. Consumers, like citizens in general, are unorganized, however. Privatization, which is proceeding very slowly, has not yet created enough capitalists with a stake in reducing inefficiencies within firms. The moral, rational, or theoretical arguments for efficiency-enhancing measures are not sufficient to prevail against the political power of the strong interests opposing them.

Political weakness The fourth factor hindering change is not a resistance to it, but a political weakness which prevents the introduction of radical measures, even when they are recognized as necessary. The political situation in all of these countries is unstable, and the power struggle is undecided. The political institutions are new, and there are no generally accepted "rules of the game". While the politicians squabble and jockey for power, the fundamental problems of economic transformation are being neglected. Popular support for the new political parties is weak and volatile, hence election results are misleading. The growing disappointment leads to discontent, alienation, and disgust with politics. These feelings are exacerbated by the lack of economic improvement, further reducing the feasibility of radical measures.

The Central and East European countries are paying a high price for the nonviolent democratic character of the transition process. As there has been little change in the economic organizations and in their network, their systems can be changed only gradually and with great difficulty, because they preserved a strong capacity to resist fundamental changes. If Olson (1982, p. 75) is correct in explaining the "economic miracles" of Japan and West Germany by the argument that "countries whose distributional coalitions have been emasculated or abolished by totalitarian government or foreign occupation should grow relatively quickly after a free and stable legal order is established," it is no wonder that rapid growth is not occurring in Central and Eastern Europe.

It is evident, as argued above, that more radical changes are needed to abolish the old institutional structure and to restrict the influence of lobbies and other special-interest groups, but it is not evident where and how to find the necessary social and political forces to implement such changes. Experience while to date lacking seems to suggest that neither political pluralism and conflicting parties (as in Hungary) nor a dominating party (as in Poland or Romania) can solve this problem. Nor is it evident either that "great coalitions," advised by some experts, can do this job.

As the opportunity to emasculate many special-interest organizations and their coalitions was missed, there is likely to be a relatively long period of coexistence with the old institutions and with only guarded change. It can be expected that liberalization of trade and capital movements, deregulation, privatization, and the establishment of new small and medium-scale enterprises will, step-by-step, change the economic environment, and the institutions will have to adapt to it. A crucial factor in this development is how far state intervention in economic life can be limited, or in other words, to what extent and how quickly the authorities will understand that allocative efficiency is not their business. Instead of supporting inefficient monopolies and conserving privileges, they have a lot to do to defend the consumers, prohibit limitations on competition, and facilitate entry of new firms into the market.

It is too early for social scientists to analyze and evaluate the results of the different approaches economic policy makers have chosen in Poland, Hungary, and Czechoslovakia. Future development will depend, to a great extent, on how their privatization processes will be linked to the destruction of monopolistic organizations, to the establishment of competitive markets, and to the emergence of new efficient business organizations. This development cannot be judged by the ambitions and declarations of decision makers, but only by the results of their decisions, which remain to be seen.

PART V
Conclusions

19 Lessons for Emerging Market Economies in Eastern Europe

Gordon C. Rausser

1 Introduction

The transition task facing the countries of Central and Eastern Europe is monumental in economic, political, and socio-economic terms. The risks posed by unanticipated developments will be exacerbated if potentially important details of the transition process are ignored. The advice and counsel offered by economists to policy makers will inevitably fail to take into account certain important aspects of both the design and implementation processes. Moreover, these lacunae can be expected to be more serious when the advice is formulated in the absence of any vision of the transition process as a whole.

Little direct evidence is available on the transition from a central planning communist regime to a pluralistic, democratic market-oriented regime. The clarity that does exist relates to the end points of the transitional process. At one end, the evidence is overwhelming that communism throughout Eastern Europe and the Soviet Union has failed miserably. The extraordinary events of the last two years have left the ideological appeal of the communist political system irrevocably damaged.

At the other end of the transition process, much evidence has accumulated on the prerequisites for achieving sustainable economic growth comparable to that of the western industrialized world. These distinctions have led to a vision for Eastern European countries — of where each country wants to arrive. Unfortunately,

Robert Gordon Sproul Distinguished Professor, Department of Agricultural and Resource Economics, University of California at Berkeley. The author thanks Richard Ball, Chris Clague, Chas Cadwell, Chris Calvin, Stan Johnson, and Leo Simon for helpful comments and suggestions on an earlier draft of this manuscript.

the ideal path from "here" to "there" is less obvious. All the conference participants agreed that a most important task is the development of a market-oriented
and anti-monopolization economic structure. However, some individual policies
that have been the basis for successful market economies, if introduced with the
wrong timing in isolation from other reforms, can make an inefficient economy
perform even less efficiently.

The clues that do exist for designing and implementing a transition path
emerge from empirical evidence in both the developed and developing world.
This evidence is drawn from countries which differ, not only in the details of
their economic policies, but also in their underlying constitutions and institutional frameworks, the extent of freedom and liberty, and their entire approach to
growth and development. Serious analysis of this evidence reveals a number of
lessons that must be kept in mind:

1. the design of the underlying constitution that establishes the guidelines and
mechanisms for the "rules by which rules are made" must be credible;

2. the legal and regulatory infrastructure (LRI) that emerges from the underlying constitution must provide an environment that is conducive to a vibrant
market economy;

3. the political-economic configuration must admit a public sector and political
agents that are able, for crucial matters, to rise above immediate self-interest; and

4. the policies that encourage anti-monopolization forces (privatization,
antitrust policy, trade policy, and foreign investment policy) must be jointly
designed to attain sustainable economic growth.

2 Constitutional Design

For the first lesson, prescription in the case of Eastern Europe should focus on
the underlying constitution that establishes the guidelines and mechanisms for
economic, political, and civil freedoms. Not simply the rule of law, but also the
choice of law and the extent of liberty must be primary concerns. This choice
includes selection from among the legal traditions that rule mankind: civil law,
common law, oriental law, Hindu law, Moslem law, and socialist law. In this
choice, as with all constitutional economic selections, the political-economic
landscape, the culture, and the customs of the country in question must play a
dominant role. Constitutional selections result not only in documents, which in
some countries collect dust on the shelves of legal scholars, but also in whether
the rules by which rules are made are accepted by the majority of the country's
citizens. If citizens expect the selections to be followed, then there may be "a
large range of things they will accept without opting out of the system, and will
vent their approval or disapproval in some sort of orderly political process"
(Steiner 1969, p. 39).

Empirical evidence, not the tunnel vision of some theoretical constructs, has been the foundation for an emerging consensus on economic, political, and civil freedoms. This emerging consensus means more than simply adjusting public policies, achieving stability, and selling government-owned enterprises to set countries off on a path toward broad-based economic growth. Rather, it means creating a vision of an open economy underpinned by an open political system; identifying and removing the obstacles to economic participation (obstacles that have often placed citizens in straitjackets); enhancing the availability of information resources; encouraging more efficient organization of economic activity in ways that lead to fundamental restructuring of an economy; and fostering institutional frameworks that expand the role of human choice and promote entrepreneurial energies.

For analysis of constitutional alternatives, the basic questions that arise are: is the constitutional order of the country conducive to free inquiry and social experimentation, or is it fundamentally repressive? Does the constitutional order provide ease of entry into the economic system and the political system, an ease with which legal foundations of new institutions can be established? Does the constitutional order provide sufficient self-correcting mechanisms to limit excessive predatory governmental behavior? Does the constitutional order motivate agreement on basic values and processes for conflict resolution and a sense of civil order that effectively reduces the cost or risk of innovation? Does the constitutional order encourage and facilitate self-governance, as well as entrepreneurial and political leadership?

The potential impact of constitutional rules can be quantified in terms of the expected transaction costs that arise in pursuing the public or collective interest (Rausser and Zusman 1992). The selection of a particular constitutional design must address setting the rules by which rules themselves are established: voting rules, law and order, property law and property rights, and laws governing exchange. The transactions costs that arise in pursuing the public interest, by construction, include the wasteful rent seeking of special interests. At its core, any constitutional prescription must essentially define the degree of centralization, the balance of power, those interests that have access to the policy-making process, the space of issues over which those interests can negotiate, the degree of consensus that is sufficient to conclude negotiations, and the appropriate course if the negotiations break down. To be sure, "constitution-makers" cannot predict with pinpoint accuracy the response to their choices; rather, they must consider future responses and understand the crucial relationships between the initial design and these consequences.

The issues of access and authority or admissible coalitions continue to dominate the landscape in Eastern Europe and the Soviet Union. Regional disputes over power sharing threaten cohesion and impede the economic reform process. In the Czech and Slovak Federal Republic, the division of authority between the federation and the two republics over policy making and budgetary control remains opaque. This problem is magnified in Yugoslavia and the Soviet Union, where reaching consensus on political relations and the distribution of power between the center and the republics will continue to be a prerequisite for macroeconomic stability and large-scale reforms. In Poland, the 1989 round-table agreements that gave the communists 65 percent of the seats in the Parliament's lower house may have more to say about trade, macroeconomic reforms and privatization than any well-designed prescription that is offered for these particular areas of public-sector policy.

The constitutional design of access, the space of issues, admissible coalitions, and default options must have the capacity to identify policies that are robust and important not only economically but, in a fundamental sense, politically. As the Czechoslovakian Minister of Finance, Vaclav Klaus, noted in his presentation at the conference,

> When I first became involved in the reform process in Czechoslovakia, I believed that the design and sequencing of reform could be controlled. Having been a part of the process for some time, I am now convinced that I was wrong.

Clarifying these remarks in a subsequent private discussion, Klaus explained that the process of negotiating a privatization program involves so many diverse political forces — each with a different private agenda — that even if analysts and a political leadership were in basic agreement on how to proceed in theory, the ultimate outlook of the political process may well bear little resemblance to the leadership's original intentions. The implications of Klaus' remarks seem obvious. It is not sufficient for political reformers to perceive correctly what should be done; they must also be able to influence — or at least understand — the process by which the reforms they initiate are transmuted as they navigate the turbulent waters of the political process. This navigation cannot be controlled, but it certainly can be guided by the design of the constitutional framework.

In recent studies, Scully (1988) and McMillan, Rausser, and Johnson (1991) (MRJ) have quantified the links between various levels of freedoms set by constitutional rules and economic growth. Both studies employ the annual ratings available from the Freedom House on various countries' political rights and civil liberties.[1] Only the MRJ study examines the directions of causality: namely, it

---

[1]The Freedom House annually rates two features of a country's institutional structure: its political rights and its civil liberties. Freedom House ratings are compiled by averaging ratings on a 20-point check list (7 for political rights and 13 for civil liberties). Each point on the check list is awarded a 0, 1, or 2, reflecting the degree of freedoms; and these raw scores are then averaged and compared against a 7-point scale (1 being the most free, and 7 the least free). Freedom House has established weights to transfer the average raw scores to the primary scale. Countries with civil liberties of 3 include Brazil, Botswana, Colombia, and the Dominican Republic, while countries with civil liberties of 6 include Iran, Madagascar, Malaysia, Rwanda, and Tanzania.

distinguishes whether political and civil liberties are the result of or the cause of economic growth. The MRJ study specifies a dynamic empirical model which can be used to investigate the link between changes in freedoms and growth. Their research finds that constitutional reforms that enhance freedoms lead to significantly higher economic growth, but only after an initial period of decreased economic growth. Thus, while there is a payoff to constitutional reforms, it is a reward that accrues to those countries which are patient enough to persevere through the early, costly years of reform.

The MRJ study used annual data from 56 countries (both developing and developed) over the time period 1973 through 1985. As revealed in Figure 5, the effects of civil liberties reforms on economic growth are quite dramatic after a period of 5 years. This linkage has a far larger impact than changes in a number of conventional economic variables. In particular, to achieve the same impact on economic growth that a reform of civil liberties from a rating of a 6 to a rating of 3 would motivate, an annual increase in the capital-labor ratio of $1,276 (US) would be required.[2] Moreover, although political liberties have little direct impact on economic growth, probit estimates of the duration of reforms in civil liberties reveal that political rights are important in sustaining civil liberty reforms. Accordingly, the indirect effect of reforms in political rights on economic growth, through the effect of sustained reforms in civil liberties, is quite positive.[3]

It must be acknowledged, as argued by Sir Alan Walters (Ch. 6), that the best examples of successful economic developments in the 1980s were not nascent democracies, but, rather, holdover authoritarian regimes. Chile, Thailand, and Korea are the most often cited; examples from earlier decades might include Hong Kong, Taiwan, or Singapore. Yet, the overwhelming weight of empirical evidence in modern times suggests that the most open and democratic societies are the most successful economically. Moreover, free and decentralized markets are the most successful in producing sustained economic growth, a condition conducive to political liberty. Sustaining economic success in the long run, in fact, may require democracy. Certainly, there are no examples of modern industrial countries that have continued to achieve success in economic growth and development under authoritarian or totalitarian governments. Even over a horizon of five or so years, the civil, legal, and political institutions of democracy, in

---

[2]An increase of $1,276 in capital-labor ratio is indeed dramatic; for the sample of countries included in the analysis, the mean increase in this ratio is $425 and the median increase is $188.

[3]Unfortunately, Freedom House does not publish measures of economic freedoms over the same list of countries and the same annual time series from 1973 through 1985. To be sure, extending the empirical analysis to examine how reforms in economic rights interact with civil liberties and political rights is crucial in enhancing understanding of how constitutional rules affect economic growth.

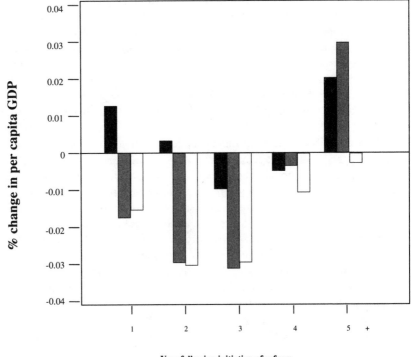

Year following initiation of reform

 Reform Size > 1

Reform Size > 2

Reform Size > 3

FIGURE 5

Effects of Civil Liberties Reform

many cases, seem to be an important ingredient of success in the economic sphere.

Democratic systems sometimes produce extremely disappointing economic policies, hence the lure of authoritarianism. Likewise, there sometimes are significant instances of market failure that can be improved through nonmarket organizational structures, including governmental intervention and regulation. Moreover, in many developing countries, the pain of adjustment in attempts to move from "here" to "there" is often blamed on the new policies rather than on the failed policies of the past, as was the case most recently in Poland. If the distribution of political power leads to an unwinding of currently designed reforms, market expectations of failure will induce inflation, capital flight, and hoarding. This painful adjustment has often led to reversals of economic policy reforms. The experience in Poland is particularly instructive in this regard.

The irony is that dictatorship, far from being necessary for economic growth, may be its antithesis. In this instance, corrupt and inept regimes cannot be changed by the will of the citizenry. There is no better confirmation of this statement than the postwar experience of Eastern Europe under communist dictatorship, or the post-revolutionary experience of Stalinist Russia. And it is also true that for every example of economic success among the authoritarian regimes of the third world, there are several examples of failure. The distinctive feature of dictatorship is that, by its very nature, it is unaccountable to most citizens and their representatives. Although this lack of accountability may seem like an advantage when unpopular decisions must be taken that would be in the public interest, it also means that economic policies which hurt society generally but benefit a "crony elite" are immutable, at least through constitutional means.

In contrast, democratic pluralism can and does provide an important discipline in the performance of governments and officials. Democratic pluralism means a political and legal system that allows citizens to assemble and to speak out against and remove from office governments that do not serve their interests. Moreover, it means protecting their human and civil rights so that they can perform these responsibilities. Unless one is willing to believe that politicians and bureaucrats are inherently benevolent and wise, democracy is ultimately necessary for successful economic performance. In the final analysis, elections allow citizens (who may on occasion be confused about cause and effect) to replace inept and corrupt officials and governments that have pursued failed economic policies. An open polity may be the single most important underpinning for an open economy in the sense that diffusion of political power, ease of entry and representation in the political arena by alternative economic factions, the fair rule of law, and clear limitations on the powers of and access to governmental officials all facilitate the growth of decentralized and private markets. Productive economic reforms and capitalism flourish best in a climate of freedom and diffuse political power. In turn, diffuse political power is alive and well in a world of ample mobility and widely diversified asset portfolios (Rausser *et al.*

1992). Operational freedoms, of course, depend on whether or not the general population respects the constitutional rules. Rules, or for that matter rules by which rules are made, only influence expectations and constrain behavior to some degree. It has even been argued that, "No constitution can be effective without the support of at least a majority of the electorate" (Bennett and DiLorenzo 1984, p. 226).

3   Legal and Regulatory Infrastructure (LRI)

Constitutional reform is a necessary, but not a sufficient condition for protecting and enhancing political, civil, and economic rights. Accordingly, a judiciary must be designed that reinforces the constitution in a reliable, responsible manner to secure basic rights. Clearly, legislation alone cannot create a favorable environment for enhancing resource allocation and entrepreneurial initiative; there must also be mechanisms and designs for infusing confidence in the underlying constitution and the rules by which rules are made. The three pillars of the legal system underlying every market economy lie at the core of any viable LRI: security of private property, enforcement of contracts, and assignment of liability for wrongful damage.

One of the striking features of many developing countries is that LRI mechanisms enhance monopoly, inefficiency, and corruption. Mechanisms required to foster credibility, confidence, and market efficiency are ineffective or absent. Citizens without political power have little confidence that their property is secure, that their legitimate interests will be upheld if another party violates a contract, that they will be able to collect damages from another party responsible for a tort, that they will be treated equally under the regulations, or that they will have equal access to concessions offered by the public sector to encourage economic activity.

Throughout much of the world, an inadequate LRI has proven to be a major barrier to broad-based economic growth. Such barriers are many and are often subtle in their design. A thriving market economy requires, *inter alia,* institutions or the rules themselves that secure individual rights. Enforcement, security, and protection of these rights through LRIs often distinguish one country's market economy and economic growth from another's. Without the security of basic rights, compatible incentives will be impossible to achieve. Individuals can thus advance their interests only if they and the organizations they may create can secure rights that are undeniably enforceable. Incentives to save and invest do not exist without private property rights.

Unfortunately, there is no private property without sufficiently strong government. Neither are there contracts or torts or patents. But just as governments through their underlying constitutions and implementable LRIs are essential for freedoms and liberties, so governments are also the greatest threat to these rights

(Olson, Ch. 4). Throughout history, it is governments that have expropriated property on a grand scale, systematically restructured advantageous trade among private citizens, as well as unilaterally changed the covenants of private contracts. Hence, to achieve sustained economic development, governments must be sufficiently powerful to implement LRIs but must also be limited and restrained by the judiciary so that individual rights are not abrogated.

Constitutional guarantees for property and contract — as well as basic political, civil, and economic freedoms — can only be secured by an effective judiciary. An effective judiciary is measured by the confidence it instills throughout the citizenry. Confidence is enhanced by creating a judiciary as a separate branch of government; assigning ultimate appeal for disputes over property and contract to the courts; increasing the impartiality of judges by assigning long tenure; making judicial decisions transparent to the scrutiny of their peers and the press; compensating judges well and placing them in positions of honor within their respective societies; and subjecting judges to stringent conflict-of-interest laws, screening them for their integrity, and requiring them to make their wealth and sources of income transparent to the general public. Any legal reform that does not include these basic features is not likely to achieve sufficient credibility. A violation of any one or more of these features may lead to laws being ignored, masked, or simply suppressed. Without credibility, LRIs will fail to take on substance and improve the underlying conditions for sustainable and effective public policy implementation. In the final analysis, the performance of the judiciary will turn on three categories of implementation: dispute settlement, executive enforcement, and institutions promoting transparency.

The fundamental element of the LRI package is the system of property rights. The economics of property rights play a crucial role in the new institutional economics literature. In essence, a system of property rights is economically efficient if the rights are universal, exclusive, and transferable (Cooter, Ch. 5). As countries have learned throughout the world, including those in Eastern Europe, a resource that has no legal owner is likely to be abused. However, the experience of some countries strongly suggests that ownership rights may need to be qualified where concentration of land holdings, for example, passes certain limits. Empirical evidence in Japan, Korea, and Taiwan shows that state-imposed land redistribution, apart from its merits on grounds of equity, can lead to more efficient use of factor resources.

In contrast to the theoretical and empirical work that has emerged on property rights, the economics of contract law has received much less attention. Nevertheless, contract law plays a crucial role in promoting market economies by spelling out the terms of implicit contracts, establishing procedures for implementing the terms of both implicit and written contracts, settling disputes about implementation, determining remedies for breach of contract, and responding to contingencies that naturally arise from incomplete contracts. Effective contract law maximizes predictability and enhances credibility, reducing significantly *ex post* opportunism. As Leonid Hurwicz (1973) demonstrated some time ago, efficient exchange can be realized if one of the parties to the exchange behaves in a rule-bound way that is reliably free of opportunism. If the judiciary reliably enforces contract law, opportunism will be significantly lessened, as will be strategic threats.

Another component of the LRI that has proven to be a significant barrier to broad-based economic growth is tort law. Tort law covers the space of individual relationships that is not addressed by contract law. It identifies wrongful damages caused by action or inaction and sets procedures for assessing their value. To the extent that tort law leads to predictable consequences, the basis for efficient insurance contracts to spread risk is established. The most important test for tort law is its predictability; the second is the expectations it generates with respect to fairness; and the third is the incentives it provides for agents to undertake efficient precautions to avoid causing damages. These three tests cannot be met if basic economic and civil freedoms are not maintained; otherwise, the court can be easily bent in favor of powerful operators.

After the three cornerstones of the LRI come the remaining components for the private sector: a commercial code; company laws; bankruptcy law; various business regulations; and in the case of the public sector: conflict-of-interest laws, safety-net institutions, and, in some countries, significant civil service reforms. The need for a sound commercial code is self-explanatory, while the essential function of company law is to limit the liability of shareholders to their equity position. Bankruptcy laws are crucial in automatically triggering conditions under which a firm will be liquidated or will undergo a significant reorganization, while contract law provides incentives for owners and management to self-enforce efficiency.[4] Finally, secured transactions are needed to facilitate the availability of credit and liquidity. Investments will not be financed in part by credit if lenders are unsure of their ability to secure whatever collateral might be available in the event a borrower defaults.

As part of the LRI, regulations of the private sector cover the gamut: licensing and concessions, labor regulations, financial market regulations, environmental regulations, anti-monopoly or antitrust regulations.[5] In structuring each

---

[4]One of the distinguishing features of developing countries is their unwillingness to close down inefficient firms. In many of these countries, bankruptcy laws are actively debated and passed, but implementation is grossly inadequate (Mitchell 1990). Many developing countries are unable to achieve a sustainable path of economic growth, simply because the link between actions and consequences is broken by various governmental interventions. The risk of failure does not exist in many of these countries and, as a result, irrational investments are undertaken (Woods 1989).

[5]The bureaucracy and centralized planning that continues to be pervasive throughout Eastern Europe suggests that excessive regulation may well be a serious problem over much of the transition process.

of these regulations, the trade-off between serving powerful special interests versus the public or collective interest must be explicitly recognized (Rausser and Zusman 1992). In many instances, these regulations can also serve to establish safety-net institutions. In effect, if major transformations and new regulations harm some individuals, the issue of compensation naturally arises. If the costs experienced by disadvantaged individuals and interested observers are slight, compensation is indeed unnecessary. However, if the costs are great and if losses can be easily ascertained, then compensation may be warranted. From a political-economic perspective, compensation may be required to maintain political support and stability. Otherwise, the transition may well reach a point where public dissatisfaction over unemployment and the cost of living forces the current political leaders to be removed from office.

As argued in section 5, anti-monopoly and competitive policies should be jointly designed with privatization policy. These regulations are also critically related to official conflict-of-interest laws. As witnessed in one country after another, the participation by public officials in business activities on their own account is a serious obstacle to the development of competitive markets. With such conflicts often come the establishment of monopoly rights in well-protected industries. The LRI must create and support the authority and means to ferret out such activities and impose stiff penalties.

Civil service reform is another component of the LRI, necessary for promoting the transparency that, in turn, enhances the integrity, timeliness and predictability of economic regulations. To support the effectiveness of the LRI in this respect, the public sector must provide accurate and timely data on the performance and current health of the economy. The accuracy and quality of these data must be seriously investigated by external institutions such as the free press. Economic journalists should be rewarded for exposing corrupt and self-interested actions of government officials. The free press should also be actively engaged in assessing the investment in and production of useful statistical data on various sectors of the economy. Perhaps more importantly, the free press has a role to play in the maintenance of civil, political, and economic freedoms. As Thomas Jefferson observed in his 1801 inaugural address as President of the United States, "If there be any among us who wish to dissolve this union, or to change its republican form, let them stand undisturbed as monuments of the safety with which error of opinion may be tolerated where reason is left free to combat it."

4   The Political Economy of Public Policy

Unfortunately, much of the economic advice and counsel that has been offered to Eastern European countries takes the constitutional economic landscape and the LRI as given. Accordingly, much of the economic intelligence has been devoted to the question of the design of economic policies rather than to the question of the appropriate institutional framework for establishing credibility, enforcing commitments, and enhancing confidence in the public sector's and judiciary's pursuit of the public interest. A few examples illustrate the overemphasis on policy prescription.

The "Balcerowicz Plan" in Poland consisted principally of macroeconomic measures such as credit restrictions, wage restraints, and reductions of subsidies designed to arrest inflationary pressures in the economy. These measures, undertaken in January 1990, and similar measures undertaken in January 1991 in Czechoslovakia, were expected to create much of the necessary conditions for a market economy. As suggested by the discussion in various parts of this book and the actual experience of Poland over the last 16 months, this expectation has not been realized. Without a well-structured constitutional and LRI set of prerequisites, it cannot be expected that more accurate measures of costs and revenues will place state enterprises at the threshold of sound, anti-monopolization norms. Moreover, the open-trade regime established in 1990 was reversed during the summer of 1991. Tariffs were raised on many imports, and the government has expressed real concern about companies that may need to be rescued.

Second, Western observers are virtually unanimous in advising that governments institute policies that promote free entry and use foreign competition as a device to discipline the domestic marketplace. Meanwhile, many of these advisors pay little attention to the process by which anti-competitive provisions may be introduced into the privatization plans that are negotiated for each enterprise. Yet, these enterprise-level negotiations, conducted behind closed doors and subjected to very little public scrutiny, may effectively derail the implementation of policies that have been legislated by the central authority. The recent agreement between Volkswagen and the Czechoslovakian automobile company Skoda, suggests what can happen.[6] If agreements like this one proliferate, the prospects for a successful transition toward competitive, efficient, market-oriented economies will be severely compromised. Such dangers are not avoided by the policy prescriptions of economic advisors. The probability of such events can, however, be minimized by an implementation process that emphasizes the public interest through the design of access; the space of issues over which those interests that have access can negotiate; the degree of consensus that is sufficient to conclude negotiations; or, more generally, the constitutional selection that enhances the quality of collective decision making.

---

[6]The agreement specifies that unless Skoda makes a profit within a certain time period, restrictive import quotas for automobiles will be imposed. That is, in its enthusiasm for accomplishing the privatization of Skoda, the Czechoslovakian government has been willing effectively to cede its sovereignty over foreign trade policy to a foreign corporation.

Third, given the pervasive bureaucratic structures that remain throughout Eastern Europe, there is a natural propensity to "over-manage" all economic and social policies, especially the privatization process. The bureaucratic conditions throughout Eastern Europe suggest quite simply that bureaucratic interest groups will remain a major feature of the political-economic landscape. The only effective means of overcoming the obstructionist behavior of bureaucratic interests is to move rapidly along the transition path. Only a successfully reformed economy will provide the incentives and conditions for breaking bureaucratic coalitions and reducing their effective power. Unless various interest groups secure a stake in the success of reform, the bureaucracy can be expected to position itself strategically to delay and obfuscate policy reforms. Over-managing is a powerful and insidious way to defeat reform.

Throughout Eastern Europe and the Soviet Union, centralized executive authority has been thoroughly discredited. As a result, the pendulum has swung toward greater decentralization and autonomy for provincial and local governments. Although a generic constitutional design must emerge from the center of the public sector's organization, the LRI and specific policies may be designed and implemented at the provincial or local governmental levels. At a minimum, it can be expected that the policy-making process, policy selection, and policy effects will be more transparent at local governmental levels. If powerful special interests cannot be effectively opposed at the centralized level, it is possible that they may be countered at the provincial or local government level. In any case, the battle lines should be drawn wherever the political-economic landscape admits the possible implementation of significant reforms. If one provincial or local government is able through its implementation of an LRI and specific policies to lead to a more sustainable path for economic growth than that experienced in some other province or locality, the demonstration effects may create beneficial spillovers that will lead to enhanced LRIs and growth-promoting economic policies in other provinces.

While traditional factions throughout Eastern Europe may have a stake in opposing change, there often fails to emerge viable alternative factions within the political system that benefit from major reforms. Peruvian Hernando de Soto (1989) has detailed the enormous political and institutional hurdles that must be overcome by individuals and businesses when they are not a part of the dominant political-economic faction. His prescription is to mobilize alternative factions so they can represent their own interests. However, this mobilization may not be feasible without political and institutional reforms to remove the barriers to such advocacy. Even in a democracy, alternative constituencies must be enlightened as to what various policy options would imply. They must also be given the means to voice their concerns and interests within the constitutional process. Finally, there must be checks and balances that limit the ability of any single faction to gain and retain unchallenged political and economic control.

Available evidence suggests that when domestic constituencies have emerged that favor and benefit from new policies, reforms have been sustained and credible. Occasionally, special inducements (e.g., export subsidies and export-processing zones) have succeeded in creating those new constituencies. Often the objective is not to achieve a trade-neutral regime but, instead, to bias the system in favor of exports, at least temporarily, in what might rightfully be called redistributive governmental policy making. This policy in isolation, however, has not generally been successful. Once again, it is crucial that comprehensive economic reforms be designed covering the mix of policies across all sectors as well as fiscal, monetary, and exchange-rate policies. When accompanied by appropriate exchange-rate and macroeconomic policies, special inducements can assist in sustaining export-oriented policies in the initial stages introducing structural reform. Successful examples of this tactic in the 1980s include Costa Rica, the Dominican Republic, and Mexico.

Economic developments can shift the balance of political power, creating new institutions and strengthening the power of interest groups that want to defend these institutions. It is important to foresee these secondary developments and to anticipate their economic consequences. For example, in Czechoslovakia, relatively little attention is being paid to the problem of industrial concentration. The expectation is that foreign competition will discipline the domestic monopolies and that, to compete, the monopolies will have to restructure themselves into smaller, more efficient units. Indeed, from private interviews, the perspective seems to be privatize, then evaluate and restructure; waiting until after restructuring before beginning the privatization process may prevent the latter process from getting off the ground.

The problem may be that the political power of the managers of the newly created monopolies will be enhanced as the economy develops, and they will be able to defend their position by political means, i.e. they will apply pressure for legislation that protects their privileges. If their industries are threatened by import competition, they will apply pressure for protectionism. If foreign companies try to set up competitors within the countries, they will apply pressure for capital prohibitions. If competitors do become viable, they will attempt either to beat them by predatory pricing or collude with them, and they will resist attempts to regulate this activity through antitrust laws. The point here is that these political forces based on economic privilege are not currently in position, but they will be later and this development should be anticipated.

In Poland, the planners are relying on minimal barriers to entry to ensure market discipline. But the economic situation will change, and with it, the political configuration. The cultural ethic of free entry will have to withstand the threat of new forces. The forces will include not only the management and shareholders of new industries, who will fight to preserve their interests, but also the workers, who will fight to preserve their jobs. It should not simply be assumed that these forces will be resisted. Another example of the failure to consider fully the danger of feedback problems concerns the formation of holding companies in Poland. Several authors have suggested that the charters of these companies should include instructions to self-destruct after a certain time period (Blanchard and Layard 1990, for example, suggest 10 years). Nevertheless, it is most likely that even in the presence of such clauses, once the holding companies are established, they will develop into a new political constituency that will surely resist its own destruction.

Formally, political-economic feedback effects during the transition should be modelled within a dynamic, closed-loop framework. In static, political-economic models of transition, the current configuration of political power is an "input" of the model and the "outputs" of the model include the set of economic policy decisions that determine the entire process of transition. In a closed-loop, dynamic model, the transition is viewed as a multi-phase process in which the outputs of earlier phases are the inputs of later phases. In particular, the early phases of transition will change the configuration of political power, as the beneficiaries of these early phases apply political leverage based on their newly acquired economic power and as the prime movers of the original privatization program gain or lose political support depending on initial assessments of the success or failure of the program. To the extent that the private objectives of these early-stage beneficiaries conflict with the public interest, these changes in the political configuration will tend to detract from the success viewed from the perspective of the public interest of the transition process. Whenever these "feedback effects" are neglected, it can be expected that the prospects for a successful transition will be overestimated.

In the final analysis, the constitutional design and the LRI set the initial governance structure for the public sector. However, in any organizational structure that might be dictated by the underlying constitutional design and LRI, the public sector is naturally exposed to attempts by various interest groups to exert their influence. In this setting, since not all power resides with policy makers pursuing only the collective interest, some degree of organizational failure will naturally arise. Economic policies can thus be viewed as the outcome of a political-economic process conditional on the underlying constitutional design and LRI. This process is at work, regardless of how sound any particular policy proposals might be from a pure economic efficiency perspective. And while each governmental decision has impact on the evolutionary process, only if the underlying constitution and LRI are well designed can one reasonably expect policies serving the collective interest to dominate policies serving the interests of powerful groups.

5   Privatization and Anti-monopolization Policies

The countries of Eastern Europe have not been unique in their re-examination of the state role in promoting economic development. Throughout the 1980s much of the developing world came to the conclusion that rapid economic growth requires vigorous private-sector development. This shift is apparent in the reforms and privatizations that have put Chile and Mexico on an economic path that seemed impossible even a few years ago, in the reduction of government economic controls in Indonesia during the 1980s that spurred the country's economic growth, and in the impressive response of Chinese farmers when economic reform provided them with powerful incentives to produce. These are only a few examples where governments reduced their control over aspects of economic activity. This change in focus has allowed some governments to turn their attention and resources to critical functions of the state in the economic sphere, including the provision of an enabling environment. The enabling environment relates directly to the underlying constitution and LRIs along with stable macroeconomic conditions, essential social and physical infrastructure, poverty reduction, and environmental protection.

Developing countries that have implemented policies which permit and encourage the private sector to be the principal engine of growth have found themselves to be more flexible in adjusting to uncertain economic environments and have had greater access to private external capital. As a result, these countries are experiencing a new dynamism, reflected in rising private investment, including foreign investment, and a diversification and rapid growth in output and exports. Partly because of this experience, the war cry throughout much of Eastern Europe has been to privatize, privatize, privatize. While some conference participants accepted this perspective, with most Eastern European attendees arguing that privatization should happen as quickly as possible, largely for political-economic reasons, many others offered serious reservations.

In the case of privatization schemes that require no restructuring prior to the transfer, numerous observers hold the view that this process without accompanying competitive policies will simply involve replacing a state monopoly with a private monopoly. For the case of the "classical" British approach to privatization, restructuring is accomplished prior to the transfer. Here, the great concern is that the process would take far too long; in fact, the estimates in the case of Poland suggest that the implementation of the classical privatization approach would take as long as one century to complete.

More subtle reservations have been expressed by Murrell (Ch. 3) and Krueger (Ch. 12). Murrell argues in support of gradualism in the transition process in large part because of organization and economic system inertia. This view is supported by Kornai (1990) and McKinnon (Ch. 7). The evolutionary approach advocated by Murrell focuses on the formation of new enterprises in the private sector, arguing that existing state enterprises are difficult, if not impossible, to reform. Krueger (Ch. 12) is also pessimistic about the privatization of state-owned enterprises, arguing that in Turkey and South Korea economic growth can be directly traced to the generation of new earnings streams in the formation of new organizations, not to the privatization of state-owned enterprises. In fact, in the case of Turkey during the 1980s, Krueger argues that reforms focusing solely on privatizing state economic enterprises would have failed miserably.

While the above reservations reveal worthwhile insights, it must be realized that they raise many other concerns. The concern should not be how long the privatization process might take but, instead, whether a credible, anti-monopolization norm for state-owned enterprises can be established. The concern should not be whether economic systems and organizations change slowly and that one must, as a result, be pessimistic about privatizing state-owned enterprises but, instead, what are the entry conditions facing the formation of new firms and organizations in the private sector and the exit conditions that face state-owned enterprises. The concern should not be whether Eastern European countries have a misplaced fixation on old assets, occupying too much time and other scarce resources of governmental officials (Krueger, Ch. 12) but, rather, what degree of privatization is necessary to lower barriers to the formation of new companies in the private sector. Entry of new firms requires that state enterprises release resources and allow new firms to purchase goods and services from state enterprises. Under the "right" LRI, state enterprises could be privatized quite slowly and yet the nascent private sector could flourish.

Privatization, in and of itself, cannot be expected to achieve efficiency. Only if a privatization policy is jointly determined with an anti-monopolization or antitrust policy, a trade policy, as well as a foreign investment policy, can one expect the proper environment for the emergence of a vibrant market economy. All of these policies must be designed and implemented hand in hand. Throughout Eastern Europe, given the overwhelming proportion of state-owned enterprises, a sound anti-monopolization policy cannot exist without an active and credible privatization policy. A credible privatization policy may be nothing more than the effective threat of "exit". In this setting, exit refers to transferring the state-owned enterprise to private ownership, thereby placing the current management at risk with respect to their current positions as well as future employment opportunities. Exit may, in fact, be triggered by anemic innovative activity, and there is no reason why, in principle, the same type of incentives cannot be offered to managers of state-owned enterprises that are available to their counterparts in the private sector.

If state-owned enterprises have established monopoly rights and the corresponding political influence to maintain those rights, the barriers to entry in the formation of new entities supplying the same goods or services will indeed be formidable. Given that each of the Eastern European countries is a price taker on world markets for most if not all sectors of their economies, a domestic anti-monopolization policy will be made more effective if it is joined by an open trade policy. Similarly, a policy for privatization will be far easier to implement and will be more effective if combined with an open foreign investment policy. Only by designing jointly all four of these policies will it be possible to achieve the right balance between the utilization of existing assets and the formation and investment in new assets. The effective integration of all four policies, if under-pinned by a freedom-enhancing constitutional design and a credible LRI, can be expected to reinforce a decentralized and pluralistic determination of the transi-tion to a market economy.

The joint design of privatization, anti-monopolization, trade, and foreign investment policy coupled with appropriate management incentives of state-owned enterprises may result in a set of conditions where the speed of imple-menting privatization is no longer crucial. In particular, even if the bulk of the state assets remain in the public sector and are not transferred for many decades, economic efficiency may still be achieved. By credibly designing and imple-menting these four policies, a country is able to buy time and enhance the quali-ty of its privatization process (Rausser and Simon, Ch. 14). The passage of time allows the population to accumulate savings, markets for corporate control to emerge, credit and capital markets to improve, prices and arbitrage opportunities to become more predictable, effective managers to be identified, and investors to develop confidence. Marketization as defined by Clague (Ch. 1) can be expect-ed under an appropriate design of these four policies to emerge naturally. Accordingly, the key to success is not to change enterprise ownership but instead, to provide incentives for entry and exit that are credible. To be sure, if a government has little integrity or competence, this process will be ineffective and state-owned enterprises will not be at risk; soft budget constraints will once again prevail. Under these circumstances, the speed of the privatization becomes crucial (Lipton and Sachs 1990b), but the quality of the process will be difficult, if not impossible to control.

All four policies must be effectively combined to set regulations that replicate those that would be enforced by the market pressures of entry and exit. These regulations must be designed for those economic activities that enjoy substantial economies of scale and scope, for infant industries, as well as for those economic activities that meet the conditions of perfect competition. Regardless of whether a natural monopoly exists or whether a persuasive case can be made for an infant industry, all entities in the private sector must be disciplined by the threat of entry. Moreover, all commercial enterprises in the public sector not subject to natural monopoly must be disciplined by the threat of exit and entry. Ultimately, to reduce opportunities for cross subsidies and other anti-competitive preferences to state-owned commercial operations, the government should transfer all of these commercial activities to ownership control in the private sector. Obviously, however, economies of scale and oligopoly cannot be wished away or abolished by fiat. As a result, regulations emerging from privatization, anti-monopoliza-tion, trade, and foreign investment policy must effectively deny market power to both private and state-owned enterprises without, of course, hampering their abil-ity to compete, their efficiency, or their growth in productivity.

The risks of entry and exit for both private and state-owned enterprises may, in fact, be the most effective incentives for entrepreneurs and firms to innovate, grow, and take advantage of economies of scale and scope. For state-owned enterprises that are subject to diseconomies of scale, the threat of exit will provide incentives to restructure these enterprises, eliminate unnecessary or unutilized factor resources and attempt to meet an anti-monopolization norm. For natural monopolies, or those enterprises that can naturally take advantage of economies of scale and scope, some fairly straightforward rules reflecting the market pressures of entry and exit must be designed. Conceptually, as argued by Baumol and Lee (1991), these regulatory rules set upper and lower price bounds that are calculated to ensure that the market pressures of entry and exit are represented. Simply, the price floor would protect the legitimate interest of competitors while the ceiling could protect the interest of buyers or consumers. Moreover, as noted by Baumol and Lee (p. 15), "A sensible way of ending the inertia that permits continued X-inefficiency in the public sector is to encourage private-sector participation in various infrastructural functions and activities, ranging from production of services to distribution, operation and maintenance, and billing and revenue collection."[7]

As argued by Willig (Ch. 10), anti-monopolization policy dictates the formation of an antitrust agency to prevent collusion, predatory pricing, and other abusive business practices. Such an agency may well have to have powers that extend beyond those necessary in a mature market economy. Specifically, they may be concerned not only with the emergence of private monopolies but public monopolies as well. In particular, any public monopoly abusing the public interest must be at risk for privatization or entry of other organizations that supply substitutable services or products.[8] Legal protections that are afforded to public monopolies must be at risk if these monopolies violate the anti-monopolization norms set by the antitrust agency.

The holding companies that are advocated by some of the privatization schemes (Rausser and Simon, Ch. 14; Tirole 1991) must also be subjected to antitrust regulations. As Tirole notes, "Holding companies restructure firms; they make sure that labor hoarding is eliminated and that insolvent firms are shut down. They reallocate capital and eliminate inefficient vertical integration. They monitor the firms' managers in their attempt to organize production efficiently." This description is one spin on the possible activities of holding companies. However, holding companies may have incentives for concentrating ownership and assets and attempting to establish monopoly rights. As a result, an antitrust agency must also have the power to regulate these holding

---

[7]X-inefficiencies encompass all forms of inefficiency aside from allocative inefficiencies.

[8]While privatization is not a punishment, it is most likely viewed as an unfavorable consequence by managers currently administering these monopolies, assuming, of course, that competitive and trade liberalization policies are credibly pursued.

companies.[9]   Another antitrust problem that could naturally arise in the context of holding companies is posed by interlocking directorates. Possible collusion arising from such arrangements must be prohibited by antitrust or anti-monopolization laws. In the final analysis, if state-owned enterprises face hard budget constraints as well as an active antitrust policy, there will be significant incentives to trim their administration, reduce their wage bills, rid themselves of unprofitable activities, and pursue profitable activities.

Throughout the Western world, antitrust efforts to control monopoly through structural means (dissolution, divorce, divestiture) have sometimes been effective and other times, ineffective. Accordingly, a more effective way of promoting competition is to rely not only on an antitrust bureaucracy but on an open trade regime as well. In fact, in the case of Eastern Europe, the extraordinarily high degree of industrial concentration (Clague, Ch. 1) calls for an opening of the economy to foreign trade. An open trade regime means that even a domestic industry whose activities require new domestic entrants to incur substantial costs may be threatened by a good many firms for which entry and exit are easy. In effect, these firms are located elsewhere in the world and have already laid out the sunk expenditures needed for entry. At the appropriate opportunity they will supply the domestic market — provided, of course, that protectionist trade policies are avoided.

An open trade policy, of course, stands in sharp contrast to the desire to protect infant industries. Among governmental officials in Hungary, Poland, and Czechoslovakia, as with managers of state-owned enterprises who believe their enterprises qualify as infant industries, there is much support for gradualism in moving toward the free trade regime. In fact, some have argued that free trade for the industrial sector may lead to wholesale collapse (McKinnon, Ch. 7). Many infant firms, however, grow up to be huge protected monopolies. Accordingly, a competitive and open-trade-policy transition path must provide clear signals that any qualifying infant industries will one day be exposed to foreign competition with probability one. Once again, the various Eastern European countries that are unprepared to expose their industries to the unrestrained rivalry of established firms from other countries must design policies that reflect the market pressures of entry and exit. Without the virtue of such pressures, both economic and political power will be accumulated and an open trade regime for the activity in question will not likely be implemented.

---

[9]Similarly, some privatization schemes call for the creation of mutual funds. Initially, such funds might well be subjected to diversified portfolio requirements as part of any anti-monopolization policy. As argued by Rausser *et al.* (1992), the more diversified the asset holdings within a particular economy the less incentive will exist for rent seeking, including the seeking of rents to establish monopoly or oligopolistic rights.

Turning to the fourth policy, the quality of the privatization process may well suffer immensely if restrictions are imposed on foreign investment. A new-found fear seems to have emerged in some quarters that windfall gains may accrue to foreign investors during the privatization process. As Frydman and Rapaczynski (1990a, p. 24) have emphasized, politicians do not wish to face the threat of being accused of "having given away the national wealth to foreigners". Another force underlying the desire to impose formidable restrictions on foreign investment lies with those interests that will benefit from less active competition in the acquisition of selected state-owned enterprises. Both of these forces must be countered by the view that privatization is not a one-shot event, but a continuing process of which the original disposition of state-owned enterprises is merely the first step.

Complex voucher and auction schemes are designed in part to preserve domestic ownership of enterprises in both Poland and Czechoslovakia. The exact formula for stock distribution has been the subject of prolonged political debates in both countries. It is hoped that all the Eastern European governments will recognize the hazard that such formulaic approaches to privatization (such as 20 percent of the shares to workers; 20 percent to pension funds; and 10 percent to commercial banks) have on the speed and quality of reform. To be sure, the elimination of foreign investor restrictions can be expected to hasten the privatization process and counter the disincentive effects of formulaic allocations. Unfortunately, the active discouragement of foreign capital during the early stages of large-scale privatization eliminates one of the major sources for the infusion of capital so badly needed by many state-owned enterprises.

One of the other major benefits of active foreign participation in the privatization process is that technical assistance with real incentives will be available to assist in setting up the governance structure of the newly privatized enterprises. The incentives for providing wise counsel and advice can be expected to include the design of low-powered incentives and the appropriate transition to their high-powered counterparts. The structure of voting or control shares versus ownership shares can also be designed more effectively with active foreign investors. For the culture that exists in Eastern Europe and specific enterprises, it can be expected that foreign investors will prove to be a positive influence on designing the appropriate separation of ownership and control (Fama and Jensen 1983).

6   Concluding Remarks

The orthodox prescription for the public sector focuses on the policy space: macroeconomic instruments to control inflation, the removal of price controls, trade liberalization, currency convertibility, financial discipline, privatization, and de-monopolization. Few would argue with these prescriptions. However, can they be effectively implemented and sustained without an underlying constitution and LRI? Available evidence suggests with few qualifications that the answer is no. In fact, the trade-off between the speed of privatization and its quality can be significantly altered by the design of the underlying constitution and the implemented LRI.

A well-designed constitution and associated LRI instill confidence and policy credibility. In a world of perfectly rational expectations and confidence in the underlying constitution and LRI, the sequence of reforms matters little. In such a perfect world, reforms that will occur well into the future are perfectly anticipated today; actions are taken by agents as though the reforms will occur with certainty. Accordingly, given macroeconomic stabilization, whether price reform comes before or after enterprise reform, whether large-scale privatization is immediate or slow and more careful, whether trade liberalization comes early and fast or later and slower, whether full-scale financial sector reform goes hand in hand with enterprise reform or it comes earlier makes little if any significant difference.

In a world of total credibility of public-sector announcements, the sequencing of reforms is largely irrelevant. Short of such credibility or the formation of rational expectations, reforms need to be simultaneously pursued on many fronts. The first and most important activity is to redefine the role of the state, setting a constitution that clearly defines and secures basic political, civil, and economic freedoms and designing an LRI that creates a fertile environment for a vibrant market economy.

Only if a constitution is designed that defines basic rights and an associated LRI secures those rights can economic policy reform be sustained on a number of fronts. This reform includes macroeconomic stabilization, price and market reform, restructuring and privatization, and so on. Privatization, anti-monopolization, trade, and foreign investment policy must be jointly designed to allow market pressures of free entry and exit and entrepreneurial innovation to be pervasive.

References

Abernathy, W. J. and Clark, K. B. (1985). "Innovation: Mapping the Winds of Creative Destruction." *Research Policy*, 14, 3-22.

Ackerman, B. A. (1977). *Private Property and the Constitution*. New Haven, Conn.: Yale University Press.

Arnott, R. and Stiglitz, J. E. (1991). "Moral Hazard and Nonmarket Institutions: Dysfunctional Crowding Out or Peer Monitoring." *American Economic Review*, 81, 179-90.

Arrow, K. J. (1974). *The Limits of Organization*. New York: Norton.

Arrow, K. J. and Fisher, A. C. (1974). "Environmental Preservation, Uncertainty, and Irreversibility." *Quarterly Journal of Economics*, 88, 312-9.

Atkinson, A. B. and Hills, J. (1991). "Social Security in Developed Countries: Are there Lessons for Developing Countries?" in E. Ahmad, J. Drèze, J. Hills and A. Sen, eds., *Social Security in Developing Countries*. Oxford: Clarendon Press.

Atkinson, A. B. and Stiglitz, J. E. (1980). *Lectures on Public Economics*. New York: McGraw-Hill.

Austin-Smith, R. (1966). *Corporations in Crisis*. New York: Anchor.

Baechler, J. (1980). "Liberty, Property, and Equality." in J. R. Pennock and J. W. Chapman, eds., *Property: Nomos XXII*. New York: New York University Press.

Banco Central de Chile (1984). *Boletin Mensual*.

Bardón, A. (1973). "Situacion Monetaria e Inflacion." Universidad de Chile, mimeo.

Barro, R. and Sala-i-Martin, X. (1991). "Convergence Across States and Regions." Harvard University, mimeo.

Bator, F. (1958). "The Anatomy of Market Failure." *Quarterly Journal of Economics*, 72, 351-79.

Baumol, W. and Lee, K. S. (1991). "Contestable Markets, Trade, and Development." *World Bank Research Observer*, 6 (1), 1-17.

Baumol, W., Panzar, J. and Willig, R. (1982). *Contestable Markets and the Theory of Industry Structure*. San Diego, Cal.: Harcourt, Brace, Jovanovich.

Baums, T. (1990). "Hochststimmrechte," *Die Aktiengesellschaft*, 35, 221-42.

Becker, G. (1968). "Crime and Punishment: An Economic Approach." *Journal of Political Economy*, 76, 169-217.

Beksiak, J., Gruszecki, T., Jedraszczyk, A. and Winiecki, J. (1990). *The Polish Transformation: Programme and Progress*. London: Centre for Research into Communist Economies.

Bennathan, E., Gutman, J. and Thompson, L. (1991). *Hungary: Reforming the Road Transport Industry*. Washington, D.C.: World Bank, mimeo.

Bennett, J. T. and DiLorenzo, T. J. (1984). "Political Entrepreneurship and Reform of the Rent-Seeking Society," in D. C. Colander, ed., *Neoclassical Political Economy: The Analysis of Rent-Seeking and DUP Activities*. Cambridge, Mass.: Ballinger.

Beristain, J. and Trigueros, I. (1990). "Mexico's Stabilization Program," in J. Williamson, ed., *Latin American Economic Adjustment*. Washington, D.C.: Institute for International Economics.

Berle, A. and Means, G. (1933). *The Modern Corporation and Private Capital*. New York: Macmillan.

Bitar, S. (1979). *La Politica Economica de la Unidad Popular*. Santiago, Chile: Siglo XXI.

Blanchard, O. (1990). "Elements of a Reform Program." Massachusetts Institute of Technology, mimeo.

Blanchard, O. and Layard, R. (1990). "Economic Change in Poland," in *The Polish Transformation: Programme and Progress*. London: Centre for Research into Communist Economies.

Blanchard, O., Dornbusch, R., Krugman, P., Layard, R. and Summers, L. (1990). "Reform in Eastern Europe." Report of the WIDER World Economy Group.

Blejer, M. and Szapary, G. (1989). "The Evolving Role of Fiscal Policy in Centrally Planned Economies Under Reform: The Case Of China." IMF Working Paper 0407. Washington, D.C.: International Monetary Fund.

Bokros, L. (1990). "Privatization in Hungary." National Bank of Hungary, mimeo.

Borensztein, E. and Kumar, M. S. (1990). "Proposals for Privatization in Eastern Europe." Washington, D.C.: International Monetary Fund, mimeo.

Bornstein, M. (1978). "The Administration of the Soviet Price System." *Soviet Studies*, 30, 466-90.

Brainard, L. J. (1990a). "Reform in Eastern Europe: Creating a Capital Market." *AMEX Bank Review Special Papers*, Number 18.

Brainard, L. J. (1990b). "Strategies for Economic Transformation in Eastern Europe: The Role of Financial Reform." Bankers Trust Company, mimeo.

Calvo, G. and Frankel, J. (1991). "Credit Markets, Credibility, and Economic Transformation." *Journal of Economic Perspectives* (forthcoming).

Calvo, G. and Vegh, C. (1990). "Credibility and the Dynamics of Stabilization Policy: A Basic Framework." Washington, D.C.: International Monetary Fund, mimeo.

Collins, S. M. and Rodrik, D. (1991). "Eastern Europe and the Soviet Union in the World Economy." Washington D.C.: Institute for International Economics.

Cooter, R. (1989). "Inventing Property: Economic Theories of Market Property Applied to Papua New Guinea." Olin Foundation Working Paper #88-5, University of Virginia.

Cooter, R. (1990). "The Structural Approach to Adjudicating Social Norms: Evolution of the Common Law Reconsidered." John M. Olin Working Papers in Law and Economics, School of Law, University of California at Berkeley, #905.

Cooter, R. and Freedman, B. J. (1991). "The Fiduciary Relationship: Its Economic Character and Legal Consequences." *New York University Law Review* (forthcoming).

Cooter, R. and Gordley, J., eds. (1991). "Symposium: Economic Analysis in Civil Law Countries — Past, Present, Future." *International Review of Law and Economics* (forthcoming).

Cooter, R. and Landa, J. (1984). "Personal Versus Impersonal Trade and the Optimal Size of Clubs." *International Review of Law and Economics*, 4, 15-22.

Corbo, V. and Sanchez, R. (1985). "How Firms Adjusted to the Reforms in Chile." Washington, D.C.: World Bank, mimeo.

Corbo, V. and Solimano, A. (1990). "Chile's Experience With Stabilization Revisited." Washington, D.C.: World Bank, mimeo.

Coricelli, F. and Calvo, G. (1990). "Stagflationary Effects of Stabilization Programs in Reforming Socialist Countries: Supply Side vs. Demand Side Factors." Washington, D.C.: World Bank, mimeo.

Coricelli, F. and Rocha, R. (1991). "Stabilization Programs in Eastern Europe: A Comparative Analysis of the Polish and Yugoslav Programs of 1990." Washington, D.C.: World Bank, mimeo.

Cremer, J. (1987). "Corporate Culture: Cognitive Aspects." Virginia Polytechnic Institute, mimeo.

Czech and Slovak Federal Republic (1990). "Small Privatization Law."

Czechoslovaka, Federal Republic of (1990). "Law Governing Privatization." Prague: Ministry of Finance.

de Jasay, A. (1990). "Market Socialism: A Scrutiny." London: Institute of Economic Affairs Occasional Paper 84.

de Soto, Hernando (1989). *The Other Path: The Invisible Revolution in the Third World.* New York: Harper and Row.

Dewatripont, M. and Roland, G. (1990). "Economic Reform and Dynamic Political Constraints." Universite Libre de Bruxelles, mimeo.

Dornbusch, R. and Edwards, S. (1991). "Macroeconomic Populism in Latin America," in Dornbusch and Edwards, eds., *The Macroeconomics of Populism in Latin America.* Chicago, Ill.: University of Chicago Press.

Dornbusch, R. and Wolf, H. (1990). "Monetary Overhang and Reforms in the 1940s." NBER Working Paper 3456.

Dunne, T., Roberts, M. and Samuelson, L. (1989). "The Growth and Failure of U.S. Manufacturing Plants." *Quarterly Journal of Economics,* 104, 671-98.

Eaton, J. (1986). "Lending with Costly Enforcement of Repayment and Potential Fraud." *Journal of Banking and Finance,* 10, 281-93.

Edwards, S. (1985). "Stabilization with Liberalization: An Evaluation of Ten Years of Chile's Experiment With Free-Market Policies, 1973-83." *Economic Development and Cultural Change,* 33, 223-54.

Edwards, S. (1988). "Terms of Trade, Tariffs, and Labor Market Adjustment in Developing Countries." Washington, D.C.: World Bank, mimeo.

Edwards, S. (1989a). *Real Exchange Rates, Devaluation and Adjustment.* Cambridge, Mass.: MIT Press.

Edwards, S. (1989b). "The International Monetary Fund and the Developing Countries: A Critical Evaluation," in *Carnegie-Rochester Public Policy Series.* Amsterdam: North-Holland.

Edwards, S. (1990). "Mexico and Argentina: Comments," in J. Williamson, ed., *Latin American Economic Adjustment.* Washington, D.C.: Institute for International Economics.

Edwards, S. and Edwards, A. C. (1991). *Monetarism and Liberalization: The Chilean Experiment.* Chicago, Ill.: University of Chicago Press (revised edition).

Eisenberg, M. A. (1988). *The Nature of the Common Law.* Cambridge, Mass.: Harvard University Press.

Ericson, R. E. (1991). "The Classical Soviet-Type Economy: Nature of the System and Implications for Reform." *Journal of Economic Perspectives* (forthcoming).

Fama, E. (1980). "Banking in the Theory of Finance." *Journal of Monetary Economics,* 6, 38-58.

Fama, E. and Jensen, M. (1983). "Separation of Ownership and Control." *Journal of Law and Economics,* 26, 301-26.

Feige, E. (1990). "A Message to Gorbachev: Redistribute the Wealth." *Challenge* (May-June), 46-53.

Ferejohn, J. and Weingast, B. (1992). "Limitation of Statutes: A Strategic Theory of Interpretation." *International Review of Law and Economics* (forthcoming).

Fiorina, M. and Plott, C. (1978). "Committee Decisions under Majority Rule: An Experimental Study." *American Political Science Review*, 72, 575-98.

Fischer, S. (1986). "Issues in Medium-Term Macroeconomic Adjustment." *World Bank Research Observer*, 1, 163-82.

Fischer, S. and Gelb, A. (1990). "Issues in Socialist Economic Reform." Washington, D.C.: World Bank, mimeo.

Foreign Broadcast Information Service (1991). FBIS-EEU-90-093 (May 14), 29.

Freedom House (1973 through 1985). *Freedom in the World*. Westport, Conn.: Greenwood.

Frydman, R. and Rapaczynski, A. (1990a). "Markets and Institutions in Large Scale Privatizations." Paper presented at the Conference on Adjustment and Growth: Lessons for Eastern Europe, Pultusk, Poland.

Frydman, R. and Rapaczynski, A. (1990b). "Privatizing Privatization: Markets and Politics in Eastern Europe." Department of Economics, New York University, mimeo.

Frydman, R. and Wellisz, S. (1990). "The Ownership-Control Structure and the Behavior of Polish Enterprises During the 1990 Reforms: Macroeconomic Measures and Microeconomic Response." C. V. Starr Center Economic Research Report 90-50, New York University.

Fudenberg, D. and Maskin, E. (1986). "The Folk Theorem in Repeated Games with Discounting or With Incomplete Information." *Econometrica*, 54, 533-54.

Gely, R. and Spiller, P. (1990). "A Rational Choice Theory of the Supreme Court." *Journal of Law, Economics and Organization*, 6, 263-300.

Giavazzi, F. and Giovanini, A. (1989). *Limiting Exchange Rate Flexibility: The European Monetary System*. Cambridge, Mass.: MIT Press.

Gomulka, S. (1989). "How to Create a Capital Market in a Socialist Country, and How to Use it for the Purpose of Changing the System of Ownership." Prepared for the LSE Financial Markets Group Conference on New Financial Markets: Economic Reform in Eastern Europe.

Greenwald, B., and Stiglitz, J. E. (1986). "Externalities in Economies with Imperfect Information and Incomplete Markets." *Quarterly Journal of Economics*, 101, 229-64.

Greenwald, B. and Stiglitz, J. E. (1988). "Pareto Inefficiency of Market Economies: Search and Efficiency Wage Models." *American Economic Review*, 78, 351-5.

Greenwald, B. and Stiglitz, J. E. (1990). "Macroeconomic Models with Equity and Credit Rationing," in R. G. Hubbard, ed., *Information, Capital Markets and Investments*. Chicago, Ill.: University of Chicago Press.

Greenwald, B. and Stiglitz, J. E. (1991). "Information, Finance and Markets: The Architecture of Allocative Mechanisms," in *Journal of Industrial and Corporate Change.* Oxford: Oxford University Press (forthcoming).

Greenwald, B., Stiglitz, J. E. and Weiss, A. (1984). "Informational Imperfections in the Capital Markets and Macroeconomic Fluctuations." *American Economic Review,* 74, 194-9.

Grierson, P. J. H. (1903). *The Silent Trade.* Edinburgh: William Greene and Sons.

Grosfeld, I. (1990). "Prospects for Privatization in Poland." *European Economy,* 43, 139-50.

Grossman, S. (1981). "The Informational Role of Warranties and Private Disclosure about Product Quality." *Journal of Law and Economics,* 24, 461-84.

Grossman, S. and Hart, O. (1980). "Takeover Bids, the Free Rider Problem and the Theory of the Corporation." *Bell Journal of Economics,* 11, 42-64.

Gruszecki, T. (1990). "Privatization in Poland in 1990." Paper for the Conference on "Implementation of the Polish Economic Programme," Warsaw (forthcoming in *Communist Economies and Economic Transformation,* 1991).

Gruszecki, T. and Winiecki, J. (1991). "Privatization in East-Central Europe: A Comparative Perspective." *Aussenwirtschaft,* 46, (forthcoming).

Hadfield, G. K. (1990). "Problematic Relations: Franchising and the Law of Incomplete Contracts." *Stanford Law Review,* 42, 927-92.

Hayek, F. (1945). "The Use of Knowledge in Society." *American Economic Review,* 35, 519-30.

Hess, J. (1982). "Risk and the Gain from Information." *Journal of Economic Theory,* 27, 231-8.

Hinds, M. E. (1990a). "A Note on the Privatization of Socialized Enterprises in Poland." Washington, D.C.: World Bank, mimeo.

Hinds, M. E. (1990b). *Issues in the Introduction of Market Forces in Eastern European Socialist Economies.* Report No. IDP-0057, Internal Discussion Paper, Europe, Middle East, and North Africa Region. Washington, D.C.: World Bank.

Hirschleifer, J. (1971). "The Private and Social Value of Information and the Reward to Incentive Activity." *American Economic Review,* 67, 561-74.

Holmstrom, B. and Milgrom, P. (1990). "Multi-Task Principal-Agent Analyses: Incentive Contracts, Asset Ownership and Job Design." Yale University, mimeo.

Holmstrom, B. and Tirole, J. (1989). "Theory of the Firm," in R. Schmalensee and R. Willig, eds., *Handbook of Industrial Organization.* Amsterdam: North-Holland.

Hungary, Central Statistical Office (1987). *Statistical Yearbook 1985,* Budapest.

Hurwicz, L. (1973). "The Design of Mechanisms for Resource Allocation." *American Economic Review,* 63, 1-30.

International Monetary Fund (1990). *The Economy of the USSR: Summary and Recommendations.* Washington, D.C..

Iwanek, M. and Swiecicki, M. (1987). "Handlowac Kapitalem W. Socjalizmie (How to Trade With Capital Under Socialism), *Polityka*, June 16 (in Polish).

Jackson, M. (1990). "The Privatization Score Card for Eastern Europe." Leuven Institute for Central and East European Studies, Catholic University, Leuven, mimeo.

Jedrzejczak, G. (1990). "Privatization in Poland." Warsaw: Ministry of Ownership Changes, mimeo.

Jedrzejczak, G. and Majcherczac, W. (1989). "Privatization of the Polish Economy in View of the Creation of Capital Market." Warsaw, mimeo.

Jensen, M. and Murphy, K. (1990). "Performance Pay and Top-Management Incentives." *Journal of Political Economy*, 98, 225-64.

Jensen, M. and Ruback, R. (1983). "The Market for Corporate Control: The Scientific Evidence." *Journal of Financial Economics*, 11, 5-50.

Jorgenson, E., Gelb, A. and Singh, I. (1990). "The Behavior of Polish Firms after the 'Big Bang': Findings from a Field Trip." Washington, D.C.: World Bank, mimeo.

Kiguel, M. and Liviatan, N. (1990). "The Business Cycle Associated With Exchange-Rate-Based Stabilizations." Washington, D.C.: World Bank, mimeo.

Kim, K. S. and Roemer, M. (1979). *Growth and Structural Transformation: Studies in the Modernization of the Republic of Korea, 1945-1975.* Cambridge, Mass.: Harvard University Press.

Kopits, G. (1991). "Fiscal Reform in European Economies in Transition." IMF Working Paper 91/43. Washington, D.C.: International Monetary Fund.

Kornai, J. (1980). *Economics of Shortage.* Amsterdam: North-Holland.

Kornai, J. (1986a). "The Hungarian Reform Process: Visions, Hopes, and Reality." *Journal of Economic Literature*, 24, 1687-1737.

Kornai, J. (1986b). *Contradictions and Dilemmas: Studies on the Socialist Economy and Society.* Cambridge, Mass.: MIT Press.

Kornai, J. (1990). *The Road to a Free Economy.* New York: Norton.

Kupa, M. and Fajth, G. (1990). *The Hungarian Social-Policy Systems and Distribution of Incomes of Households.* Budapest: Ministry of Finance.

Laffont, J., and Tirole, J. (1990). "Privatization and Incentives." Mimeo.

Larrain, F. and Meller, P. (1991). "Populism in Chile, 1970-1973," in R. Dornbusch and S. Edwards, eds., *The Macroeconomics of Populism in Latin America.* Chicago, Ill.: University of Chicago Press.

Le Grand, J. and Estrin, S., eds. (1989). *Market Socialism.* Oxford: Clarendon Press.

Lewandowsky, J. and Szomburg, J. (1989). "Property Reform as a Basis for Social and Economic Reform." *Communist Economies*, 1 (3), 257-68.

Lipton, D. and Sachs, J. (1990a). "Creating a Market Economy in Eastern Europe: The Case of Poland," *Brookings Papers on Economic Activity*, 1, 75-147.

Lipton, D. and Sachs, J. (1990b). "Privatization in Eastern Europe: The Case of Poland," *Brookings Papers on Economic Activity*, 2, 293-334.

Litwack, J. (1991). "Discretionary Behavior and Soviet Economic Reform." *Soviet Studies*, 43, 255-79.

Luders, R. (1990). "The Privatization of the Chilean Economy." UCLA, mimeo.

Mansfield, E., Rapoport, J., Romero, J., Villani, E., Wagner, S. and Husic, F. (1977). *The Production and Application of New Industrial Technologies.* New York: Norton.

Mayer, C. (1989). "Financial Systems, Corporate Finance and Economic Development." Center for Economic Policy Research, mimeo.

McKinnon, R. I. (1973). *Money and Capital in Economic Development.* Washington, D.C.: Brookings.

McKinnon, R. I. (1979). *Money in International Exchange: The Convertible Currency System.* New York: Oxford University Press.

McKinnon, R. I. (1991). *The Order of Economic Liberalization: Financial Control in the Transition to Market Economy.* Baltimore, Md.: Johns Hopkins University Press.

McMillan, J., Rausser, G. C. and Johnson, S. R. (1991). "Liberties and Economic Growth." Washington, D.C.: Institute for Policy Reform, Working Paper.

Mejstrzik, M. (1990). "The Transformation of Czechoslovakia to a Market Economy: The Possibilities and Problems." Mimeo.

Milanovic, B. (1990). "Privatization in Post-Communist Societies." Washington, D.C.: World Bank, mimeo.

Mitchell, J. (1990). "Managerial Discipline, Productivity, and Bankruptcy in Capitalist and Socialist Economies." *Comparative Economic Studies*, 23, 93-157.

Monsen, R. J. and Walters, K. D. (1983). "Managing the Nationalized Company." *California Management Review*, 25 (4), 16-26.

Montias, J. M. (1982). "Poland: Roots of the Economic Crisis." *The ACES Bulletin*, 24 (3), 1-20.

Murrell, P. (1990a). *The Nature of Socialist Economies: Lessons from Eastern Europe Foreign Trade.* Princeton, N.J.: Princeton University Press.

Murrell, P. (1990b). "Big Bang Versus Evolution: Eastern European Reforms in the Light of Recent Economic History." *PlanEcon Report*, June 29, 1990.

Murrell, P. (1991). "Can Neoclassical Economics Underpin the Economic Reform of the Centrally-Planned Economies?" *Journal of Economic Perspectives* (forthcoming).

Murrell, P. and Olson, M. (1991). "The Devolution of Centrally Planned Economies." *Journal of Comparative Economics*, 15, 239-65.

Myers, S. C. and Majluf, N. S. (1984). "Corporate Financing and Investment Decisions When Firms Have Information and Investors Do Not." *Journal of Financial Economics*, 13, 187-221.

Nagy, A. (1989). "Why Doesn't the Hungarian Economy Work?" *Business in the Contemporary World*, 1 (2), 71-83.

Nagy, A. (1991). "'Social Choice'" in Eastern Europe." *Journal of Comparative Economics*, 15, 266-83.

National Bank of Hungary (1990). *Market Letter*, 8-9. Budapest: National Bank of Hungary Information Department.

Naughton, B. (1991). "Why Has Economic Reform Led to Inflation?" *American Economic Review*, 81, 207-11.

Nelson, R. and Winter, S. (1982). *An Evolutionary Theory of Economic Change*. Cambridge, Mass: Harvard University Press.

Nelson, R. (1981). "Research on Productivity Growth and Differences." *Journal of Economic Literature*, 19, 1029-64.

Nelson, P. B. (1981). *Corporations in Crisis: Behavioral Observations for Bankruptcy Policy*. New York: Praeger.

Nelson, R. (1990). "Capitalism as an Engine of Progress." *Research Policy*, 19, 193-214.

Newbery, D. M. (1991). "Reform in Hungary: Sequencing and Privatisation." *European Economic Review*, 35, 571-80.

Newbery, D. M. and Stern, N. H., eds. (1987). *The Theory of Taxation for Developing Countries*. Oxford: Clarendon Press.

Nordhaus, W. D. (1990). "Soviet Economic Reform: The Longest Road." *Brookings Papers on Economic Activity*, 1, 287-308.

Nuti, D. M. (1988). "Competitive Evaluation and Efficiency of Capital Investment in the Socialist Economy." *European Economic Review*, 32, 459-64.

Nuti, D. M. (1989). "Remonetization and Capital Markets in the Reform of Centrally Planned Economies." Prepared for the LSE Financial Markets Group Conference on New Financial Markets: Economic Reform in Eastern Europe.

Olson, M. (1965). *The Logic of Collective Action*. Cambridge, Mass.: Harvard University Press.

Olson, M. (1982). *The Rise and Decline of Nations*. New Haven and London: Yale University Press.

Olson, M. (1984). "Beyond Keynesianism and Monetarism." *Economic Inquiry*, 22, 297-321.

Olson, M. (1986). "Why Some Welfare-State Redistribution to the Poor is a Great Idea," in C. K. Rowley, ed., *Public Choice and Liberty: Essays in Honor of Gordon Tullock*. Oxford: Basil Blackwell.

Olson, M. (1990a). "The Logic of Collective Action in Soviet-Type Economies," in *The Journal of Soviet Nationalities*, 1 (2), 8-33.

Olson, M. (1990b). *How Bright are the Northern Lights?* Lund: Lund University Press.

Perkins, D. (1991). "China's Industrial and Foreign Trade Reforms," in A. Koves and P. Marer, eds., *Foreign Economic Liberalization*. Boulder, Co.: Westview Press.

Poland, Government of the Republic of (1990a). "Program for the Privatization of the Polish Economy."

Poland, Government of the Republic of (1990b). "The State Enterprise Privatization Act of July 13, 1990." Economic Review: Special Issue, Polish News Bulletin of the British and American Embassies, Issue No. 6-90.

Priest, G. L. (1985). "The Invention of Enterprise Liability: A Critical History of the Intellectual Foundations of Modern Tort Law." *Journal of Legal Studies*, 14, 461-533.

Ramos, J. (1977). "La Economia de la Hiperestaflacion en Chile," *Cuadernos de economia*, vol. 14.

Rausser, G. C., Foster, W. E. and Gray, R. (1992). "Mobility, Diversification, and Sustainability of Trade Reform," in G. C. Rausser, ed., *GATT Negotiations and the Public Economy of Policy Reform*. Berlin, Heidelberg, and New York: Springer-Verlag (forthcoming).

Rausser, G. C. and Simon, L. (1991a). "A Noncooperative Model of Multilateral Bargaining." Department of Agricultural and Resource Economics, University of California at Berkeley, mimeo.

Rausser, G. C., and Simon, L. (1991b). "Burden Sharing and Public Good Investments in Policy Reform." Department of Agricultural and Resource Economics, University of California at Berkeley, mimeo.

Rausser, G. C., and Simon, L. (1991c). "Burden Sharing and Public Good Provision: A Numerical Sensitivity Analysis." Department of Agricultural and Resource Economics, University of California at Berkeley, mimeo.

Rausser, G. C., and Thomas, S. (1990). "Market Politics and Foreign Assistance." *Development Policy Review*, 8, 365-81.

Rausser, G. C., and Zusman, P. (1992). "Public Policy: Explanation and Constitutional Prescription." *American Journal of Agricultural Economics* (forthcoming, February).

Rocha, R. (1990). "Stabilization Programs in Yugoslavia." Washington, D.C.: World Bank, mimeo.

Roland, G. (1990). "From Plan to Market: The Political Economy of the Transition Period." Universite Libre de Bruxelles, mimeo.

Rubinstein, Ariel (1982). "Perfect Equilibrium in a Bargaining Model." *Econometrica*, 50, 97-109.

Sajo, A. (1990). "Diffuse Rights in Search of an Agent: A Property Rights Analysis of the Firm in the Socialist Market Economy." *International Review of Law and Economics*, 10, 41-60.

Salop, S. (1979). "Strategic Entry Deterrence." *American Economic Review*, 69, 335-8.

Schmalensee, R. (1982). "Product Differentiation Advantages of Pioneering Brands." *American Economic Review*, 72, 349-65.

Schotter, A. (1981). *The Economic Theory of Social Institutions*. New York: Cambridge University Press.

Schumpeter, J. A. (1934). *The Theory of Economic Development*. Cambridge, Mass.: Harvard University Press.

Schumpeter, J. A. (1950). *Capitalism, Socialism, and Democracy*. New York: Harper.

Scully, G. (1988). "The Institutional Framework and Economic Development." *Journal of Political Economy*, 96, 652-62.

Shapiro, C. (1983). "Premiums for High Quality Products as Returns to Reputations." *Quarterly Journal of Economics*, 98, 659-79.

Shavell, S. (1979). "Risk Sharing and Incentives in the Principal and Agent Relationship." *Bell Journal of Economics*, 10, 55-73.

Sheshido, Z. (1991). "Comparative Business Systems: US-Japan" (two lectures, Berkeley Law School).

Shiller, R. J. (1989). *Market Volatility*. Cambridge, Mass.: MIT Press.

Smith, Adam (1910). *The Wealth of Nations*. New York: E. P. Dutton.

Stahl, I. (1972). *Bargaining Theory*. Stockholm: Stockholm School of Economics.

Stahl, I. (1977). "An N-Person Bargaining Game in the Extensive Form," in R. Henn and O. Moeschlin, eds., *Mathematical Economics and Game Theory*. Berlin: Springer-Verlag.

Steiner, P. O. (1969). "The Public Sector and the Public Interest," in *An Analysis and Evaluation of Public Expenditures: The PPB System*. Compendium of papers submitted to the Subcommittee on Economy and Government of the Joint Economic Committee, Congress of the United States, Vol. 1, 14-65.

Stiglitz, J. E. (1972). "Some Aspects of the Pure Theory of Corporate Finance: Bankruptcies and Take-Overs." *Bell Journal of Economics*, 3, 458-82.

Stiglitz, J. E. (1975). "Incentives, Risk and Information: Notes Towards a Theory of Hierarchy." *Bell Journal of Economics*, 6, 552-79.

Stiglitz, J. E. (1982). "The Inefficiency of the Stock Market Equilibrium." *Review of Economic Studies*, 49, 241-61.

Stiglitz, J. E. (1985). "Credit Markets and the Control of Capital." *Journal of Money, Credit and Banking*, 17, 133-52.

Stiglitz, J. E. (1988a). "Why Financial Structure Matters." *Journal of Economic Perspectives*, 2, 121-6.

Stiglitz, J. E. (1988b). "Money, Credit and Business Fluctuations." *The Economic Record*, 64, 307-22.

Stiglitz, J. E. (1989a). "Incentives, Efficiency, and Organizational Design." NBER Working Paper No. 2979.

Stiglitz, J. E. (1989b). "Using Tax Policy to Curb Speculative Short-Term Trading." *Journal of Financial Services Research*, 3, 101-15.

Stiglitz, J. E. (1989c). "Imperfect Information in the Product Market." in R. Schmalensee and R. Willig, eds., *Handbook of Industrial Organization, Vol. 1*. Amsterdam: North Holland.

Stiglitz, J. E. and Weiss, A. (1981). "Credit Rationing in Markets with Imperfect Information." *American Economic Review*, 71, 393-410.

Stiglitz, J. E. and Weiss, A. (1983). "Incentive Effects of Termination: Applications to the Credit and Labor Markets." *American Economic Review*, 72, 912-27.

Stiglitz, J. E. and Weiss, A. (1991). "Banks as Social Accountants and Screening Devices and the General Theory of Credit Rationing," in A. Courakis and C. Goodhart, eds., *Essays in Monetary Economic in Honor of Sir John Hicks* (forthcoming).

Sugden, R. (1986). *The Economics of Rights, Cooperation, and Welfare*. New York: Basil Blackwell.

Summers, L. H. and Summers, V. P. (1989). "When Financial Markets Work Too Well: A Cautious Case for the Securities Transaction Tax." Harvard University, mimeo.

Summers, R. and Heston, A. (1991). "The Penn World Table (Mark 5): An Expanded Set of International Comparisons, 1950-1988." *Quarterly Journal of Economics*, 106, 327-68.

Svejnar, J. (1990). "A Framework for the Economic Transformation of Czechoslovakia." *PlanEcon Report*, January, 1990.

Swiecicki, M. (1988). "Reforma Wlasnosciowa" (Ownership Reform). A paper for the seminar on "Transformation Proposals for the Polish Economy," Warsaw: Main School of Planning and Statistics.

Telgarsky, J. and Struyk, R. (1990). *Toward a Market-Oriented Housing Sector in Eastern Europe*. Washington, D.C.: Urban Institute Press, Report 90-10.

Tirole, J. (1988). *The Theory of Industrial Organization*. Cambridge, Mass.: MIT Press.

Tirole, J. (1991). "Privatization in Eastern Europe: Incentives and the Economics of Transition." *NBER Macroeconomics Annual* (forthcoming).

Triska, D. and Jelinek-Francis, C. (1990). "A Study of Privatization in the Czech and Slovak Federal Republic." Prague, mimeo.

UK, Central Statistical Office (1990a). *Economic Trends*, No. 439, London, HMSO.

UK, Central Statistical Office (1990b). *Annual Abstract 1990*, London, HMSO.

UK, Central Statistical Office (1991). *Social Trends 21*, London, HMSO.

Underkuffler, L. S. (1990). "On Property: An Essay." *Yale Law Journal*, 100, 127-48.

van Wijnbergen, S. (1990). "Intertemporal Speculation, Shortages, and the Political Economy of Price Reform: A Case against Gradualism." Washington, D.C.: World Bank, mimeo.

Varady, T. (1991). "Transformation via Privatization," in *Socialist Law in a Period of Change, Law 2652*, School of Law, University of California at Berkeley.

Vickers, J. and Yarrow, G. (1988). *Privatization: An Economic Analysis*. Cambridge, Mass: MIT Press.

von Furstenberg, G. (1990). "Pareto-Optimal Privatization for Gaining Political Support." Indiana University Working Papers in Economics, #90-050.

Weitzman, M. (1974). "Prices vs. Quantities." *Review of Economic Studies,* 41, 477-91.

Williamson, J. (1985). *Indexation and Inflation*. Washington, D.C.: Institute for International Economics.

Williamson, J. (1991). *The Economic Opening of Eastern Europe*. Institute for International Economics, Policy Analysis 31.

Williamson, O. (1985). *The Economic Institutions of Capitalism*. New York: Free Press.

Williamson, O. (1991). "Economic Institutions: Hands-On and Hands-Off Governance." Haas School of Business Administration, University of California at Berkeley, mimeo.

Winiecki, J. (1990a). "No Capitalism Minus Capitalists." *Financial Times*, June 20.

Winiecki, J. (1990b). "Post-Soviet-Type Economies in Transition: What Have We Learned From the Polish Transition Programme in its First Year?" *Weltwirtschaftliches Archiv*, 126, 765-90.

Winiecki, J. (1990c). "Why Economic Reforms Fail in the Soviet System." *Economic Inquiry*, 28, 195-221.

Wong, Christine (1990). "Central-Local Relations in an Era of Fiscal Decline: The Paradox of Fiscal Decentralization in Post-Mao China." Working Paper #210, University of California, Santa Cruz.

Woods, A. (1989). *Development and the National Interest: U.S. Economic Assistance into the 21st Century*. Washington, D.C.: Report by the Administrator, U.S. Agency for International Development.

World Bank (1990). *World Development Report 1990*. New York: Oxford University Press.

Index

347